The Journey
to Wisdom

PAUL A. OLSON

The Journey to Wisdom

Self-Education in Patristic and Medieval Literature

University of Nebraska Press
Lincoln and London

Publication of
this volume was assisted by
The Virginia
Faulkner Fund, established in memory
of Virginia Faulkner,
editor-in-chief of the University of Nebraska
Press.
Library
of Congress Cataloging-in-Publication Data
Olson, Paul A.
The journey to wisdom : self-education in
patristic and
medieval literature / Paul A. Olson.   p.   cm.
Includes bibliographical
references and index. ISBN 0-8032-3562-3
(cl. : alk. paper)
1. Education, Medieval. 2. Self-culture.
3. Education –
Social aspects 4. Literature, Medieval –
History and criticism.
5. Comparative education. I. Title.
LA93.O47   1995
370'.94'0902 – dc20
95-3042 CIP

Contents

Preface

This book grows out of three long-term interests of mine: education, the environment, and the historical criticism of medieval works. From the 1960s through the 1980s, I headed a number of federally funded education projects in curriculum reform and multicultural education. In these, I observed a lifelessness in wholly structured education and a chaos in more open forms. While I was influenced by Jean Piaget and Noam Chomsky and favored more open forms in the experiments I led, I asked myself what education might do to give itself both shape and freedom. At the same time I was involved in the community-control movement in education in many American minority communities; from my Native American friends, especially Leonard Springer and Reuben Snake, I learned a sense of the sacredness of the creation (I have more recently pursued the implications of that sense in work with sustainable agriculture groups and various Native American communities as well).

Yet as a medievalist, I was troubled by the common characterization of the medieval period as both technologically primitive and responsible for the foundations for a radical subduing of nature. I did not see how it could be both. As a teacher I advocated a respect for cultures other than "our own." At the same time I encountered a troubling tendency to display disrespect for many aspects of medieval culture in the criticism of medieval literature and to make the literature play at modern language games manifestly unrecognizable to medieval readers. To clarify my thinking concerning these three subjects – education, nature, and medieval culture – I began to look at patristic and medieval pictures of education, particularly at the Wisdom tradition. I found there answers, or possible answers, to the questions that arose in the educational reform that I had pursued.

My focus in this book is on the shape of medieval education, its sense of humankind's capacity for self-direction, its interest in the physical universe, and its view of how language works. For reasons that will become obvious, I do not pursue the feminist implications of the femaleness of the Wisdom figure. The mathematical and natural investigations that are my subject are not heavily developed even in excellent female medieval Wisdom writers such as Hildegard of Bingen (the deficiencies of medieval culture in offering advanced studies to women are significant). Furthermore, I pay only cursory attention to the Jewish Wisdom tradition, although I recognize that patristic and medieval Wisdom writing owes almost everything to Judaism. I had hoped to do more with Judaism and received help from my colleague, Bruce Erlich, but I found the pursuit of Jewish themes beyond the secondary sources to be both beyond my powers and beyond the scope of this work. Finally, my project does not pretend to be exhaustive even in the areas that it covers; I focus on a few great writers and a few significant instances of interpretation. I cite other scholars only when their work permits a shortcut, or when I disagree strongly with their findings and they seem central to standard assumptions about the field.

In my original draft, I included most foreign language quotations with translations, but in order to shorten the book I eliminated most quotations and substituted my translations. Readers who wish to see the original language quotations may write me. In other cases when I use a foreign language quote, I paraphrase it in the text immediately surrounding it. I have consulted many other translations in making mine, and though I have tried to keep the translations my own, I suspect that echoes of other voices will be heard in them. I cite Dante commentaries primarily from the Dartmouth Dante Project because the commentaries are easily accessible there. I capitalize " logos" in the "Logos within" phrase.

I owe much to others, especially to my lifelong friends – Professors Robert Haller and Leslie Whipp of the University of Nebraska, Professor Doris Myers of the University of Northern Colorado, Professor David Brumble of the University of Pittsburgh, and Professor Lewis Soens of Notre Dame University. All have read the whole book at various stages, and their mark appears in both the style and substance of every page. Professor John Turner of the University of Nebraska gave me the benefit of his magnificent knowledge of Wisdom in the ancient world, as did Dan Conradt. I received help with the Augustine chapter from Professors Robert McMahon of Louisiana State University and Karl Morrison of Rutgers University. Professor Robert Lamberton of Princeton read my epic chapter and saved me from many foolish errors, and Professor John Moorhead of the University of Queensland helped with the Boethius chapter, as did John Turner. Professor Thomas Roche of Princeton made excellent suggestions concerning the medieval and Renaissance chapters in his reading of the book. Finally, Professors Stephen Buhler and Raymond Haggh, both interested in Renaissance music, assisted me with chapter 8. To my research assistants – Karma Larsen, Roma Rector, John Holberg, Chris Oehrmann, Stacy Magedanz, Nicolle French, Rebecca Busker, and Sarah Croft – I owe more than I want to let on. To my wife, Elizabeth, I owe whatever clarity and straightforwardness the book has. Its mistakes are my own.

Three institutions helped me – the U.S. Office of Education by funding my numerous educational projects in the 1960s and 1970s, the University of Nebraska by paying my salary and supporting some research leaves, and the Institute for Advanced Studies in the Humanities in Edinburgh by giving me research support. I am grateful to all three.

This book is dedicated to my teachers, to those listed on the dedicatory page and those not named who may have done as much for me. The book emphasizes the power of informal education. What I remember of these teachers almost invariably comes from outside the classroom – a letter, a discussion, a loving action, a cup of coffee or a glass of wine, a pointed observation. Though they are all dead, I hope that the book in some measure repays their efforts by calling some of us back to the vocation of imagining what education can be.

Introduction:
The Journey through
the Natural World

Dante reflects the educational journey undertaken in the patristic and medieval literature described in this book when he takes his bachelor's level orals from Peter, James, and John.[1] The apostles ask him three basic questions: what is faith? what is hope? and what is love? Ever true to his scholastic commitments, Dante defines faith to St. Peter by describing the Old and New Testaments as the propositions of a syllogism pointing to one Christocentric conclusion supported by evidences physical and metaphysical. He responds to St. James concerning hope by citing Psalm 9.11, Isaiah, and the Apocalypse as pictures of the hope for a beatified afterlife. Finally, when John, representing love, asks him to describe the goal of his soul, Dante affirms that his goal is the good of the celestial court that by definition kindles love. The essence of this goodness (i.e., God) manifests itself in Aristotle's *Metaphysics*, in the Mosaic books, and in 1 John (presumably in its description of the Logos creating the world and coming into it) – through philosophic arguments, heavenly authority, and the creation.

This goodness also fires Dante's human love. When the discourse turns to talk about love for the creation, Dante asserts that the whole creation inspires in him a measured love:

> Le fronde onde s'infronda tutto l'orto
> dell'ortolano etterno, am'io cotano
> quanto da lui a lor di bene è porto.
>
> (*Paradiso* 26.64–66)

[I love the leaves wherewith all of the garden of the Eternal Gardener is enleaved to the degree that He has placed good within them.]

Behind this passage lies a picture of the cosmos as God's garden that has within it degrees of good reflective of God-the-Creator. The poet loves this garden to the degree that each part reflects the divine goodness. To love with such precision, the poet must understand the universe through which he journeys. Hence the references to the scriptures and to the scholarly disciplines, physics and metaphysics.

Dante assumes a referential theory of meaning (see chapter 3). He places his remark about the world's garden and its proper love at a point that sums up his learning of the quadrivium's world of things and permits him to graduate to the final part of his journey, the empyrean trip to a vision of God in relation to the universe. The remark also leads into the *Commedia*'s summative statement on language, the subject of the trivium, given by Adam, the first speaker of language. Here Adam clarifies how language can reflect a diverse reality through conventional forms. As he explains, human names for God change as linguistic convention changes. Yet the entity, God-the-Word, remains the same since language, however conventional in form, takes its meaning from a reality external to it. For Dante the sciences from physics to metaphysics reveal the creation as the garden of God, and the verbal arts reflect its reality. In the remaining cantos of the *Paradiso* the poet goes forward to a metaphoric and then an increasingly direct cognition of God as the author of creation.

In placing a baccalaureate examination near the end of the journey to God, Dante invites his reader to understand the *Commedia* as an educational excursus that has a fixed meaning and shape culminating in a vision of God and the creation as a unified entity. The apostles' test ends the *Commedia*'s intellectual quest. Thereafter the work presents visionary encounters with supracelestial metaphors – the circle of the cosmos, the river and bees, the white rose, and knotted volume of light – relating the garden and God in ways that go beyond the disciplines.

Dante's view of education as a journey with a fixed meaning that leads to right love of the garden and its Creator sets this book's theme. His picture of that journey was preceded by similar pictures created by Origen, Augustine, Boethius, and writers of ancient and medieval epic commentary. It is a picture that leads into early Renaissance science and offers a useful model for contemporary education. The purpose of this book is to examine why Dante's journey proposes a structure for education that leads to the love of the garden and to an understanding of language as referential. It examines what that journey may say about some problems troubling contemporary education.

This book rests on a definition of the universe current in classical and medieval times. The definition says that the universe is essentially an aesthetic artefact, a creation made by an Architect (the standard metaphorical equivalent of Dante's Gardener)[2] who remains as hidden as Pascal's God. However, He reveals Himself through His agent, the Logos, and through an architectural plan imposed on material reality. (Medieval language about God is insistently masculinist save for references to the Sophia figure to be treated in chapter 2 and following.) If God manifests or reveals Himself through the good with which he endows every leaf of the universe, then the student must strive to understand each leaf. Generally the study is self-initiated or evoked by dialogues such as those promoted by Socrates or, alternatively, by dialogue with a book or the corpus of books represented by such figures as Boethius's Philosophy or Dante's Virgil. Such study can be self-initiated because the universe is beautiful and invites the student to see its glory, and because human beings have within them a faculty – a Logos or rational faculty or "Philosophy" – that urges them to understand beauty in increasingly systematic and abstract terms. Hence, in the *Commedia* prior to his examination, Dante, as interpreted by Pietro Alighieri, works his way from rational philosophy, which inspects earthly material reality, to ethics and the mathematical disciplines, which inspect heavenly reality, to theology and metaphysics, which lead to the above-the-heavens where the Gardener creates the garden.

The antecedents of Dante's philosophy of education and the artistic tradition that celebrates it develop gradually; this book will picture their development. The works studied depend on the notion that education can encourage social reform, that social reform requires that individuals first reform themselves, and that to reform themselves they must know how they fit in the universe through which they journey. Reform is modeled on art forms that tell of the journey of the self through the seas of learning, forms that woo the reader to follow an exemplar, to learn from that exemplar, and to act on what the exemplar teaches so that the reformative energy so generated will ultimately have historical consequences.[3]

In looking at how Dante and his forebears apply directly or indirectly to our contemporary educational scene, this book endeavors to escape three beasts or problems that haunt modern education and that have been thought to be imbedded – perhaps to originate – in medieval education.

The first beast is formless education. The shapelessness of medieval education bothers most people. Philippe Ariès tells us that hardly any systematic progress toward anything was possible in the medieval curriculum, burdened as it was by little sense of sequence or of the difficulty of this or that text (see chapter 1). Medieval education appears to be essentially without structure and, implicitly, without ideology. A similar kind of structurelessness terrifies contemporary conservative critics who argue that modern education has no goal or too many goals. Paradoxically, these critics sometimes appeal to the tradition of the liberal arts formulated in ancient times and continued in the middle ages as an alternative to what we have now.[4]

A far different fear haunts radical critics who say that contemporary education has goals, but that these are projections of the institutional power structures that control modern education.[5] Other critics on the left, such as Ivan Illich, wishing to escape from the hegemony of modern education, have argued for an education without goals: an abolition of school bureaucracies, compulsory education, and fixed curricula, all to be replaced by networks of learning resources among which the student can pick and choose without institutional coercion. These critics apparently want to return us to the medieval condition, but they do not identify the actual shaping force in medieval education that made it possible outside of elaborate bureaucracies. That force was, as this book will show, the imagination of an ideal shape for an education, whatever the available institutional support.

The second beast or problem is education that leads us to despoil the environment. A familiar argument is that medieval education (and civilization) had no sense of the sanctity of the creation. The millions of dollars that we are currently spending on environmental education attest to our fear that we may have equally little sense of this sacredness. Beginning with Lynn White's famous essays on Christianity and the environment (see chapter 2), this critique asserts that the despoiler tradition in our culture begins with patristic and medieval culture, and that medieval intellectuals were obsessed with the Genesis command to subdue the earth. White argues that the Judeo-Christian doctrine of the creation places humankind above nature so that people can control it in almost any way they wish; the business of education then becomes the promotion of this imperial sense through the teaching of responsibility and stewardship. Similarly, the landscape architect Ian McHarg claims that the Genesis text gives license to those who seek increases in radioactivity, the creation of canals and harbors using nuclear weapons, the increment of poisons, and the spread of the bulldozer mentality.[6] Although the excesses of industrialism primarily appeared after the middle ages, environmental scholars commonly assert that medieval culture provided the West with a world view and an education that encourages polluting.

The third beast is chameleon education that constructs endless linguistic and moral ambiguities that lay no mandate on the student and provide no precise knowledge. Chameleon education changes colors to match its cultural surroundings, changing patristic and medieval meanings in contemporary criticism to make the ancient modern. In this way the force of the work's critique is either eliminated or made into a contemporary critique unaccompanied by the necessary recognition of differences between our time and earlier ones, our language and that of earlier cultures. Education that aims to find only the chameleon possibilities in ancient and medieval uses of language foists on that language an avoidance of reference to "real" objects and situations; to put the matter more complexly, it avoids situating language in what Wittgenstein calls the "forms of life" that gave rise to it (see chapter 3).

Modern education's interest in explaining the polysemous possibilities of both medieval and modern language (rather than language's capacity to create structures of authoritative statement) has deprived some forms of language of their power and utility. Nonetheless, the postmodernist view possesses an element of plausibility. There is a tradition in medieval education of reading works against each other and for complex levels of intertextual meaning. But that tradition does not exclusively concern intertextuality or the relationship of writers to previous writers; nor does it deny reference to words ipso facto. It argues that words and numbers can make statements about the nature of reality outside the text and assist one to comprehend the cosmos.

This book argues that medieval education was not so heavily influenced by the three beasts ascribed to it as its critics have assumed. It argues that modern education – insofar as it has problems with formlessness, arrogant attitudes toward the environment, and an incapacity for precise statement – could learn from some forms of medieval education. The book begins with the classical and patristic culture that underlies medieval culture. Chapter 1, starting with the quarrel in ancient Greece between the Sophists and philosophers over the nature of proper art and education (a quarrel out of which the tradition centering education in reality, as opposed to social convention, develops), describes early efforts to limit formlessness in education by defining a journey for education that does not depend on institutional forms alone but on an imagination of the objective order to which learning leads and a conception of the development of human cognition. Chapter 2 continues with the spread of this philosophic tradition to Israel in Hellenistic times, and its modification there by Old and New Testament Wisdom thinkers and by the Alexandrians, especially Origen and Gregory Thaumaturgos, the latter of whom creates a very early autobiography to celebrate his own self-initiated education in Origen's circle and his learning to love the creation. This chapter also deals with early efforts to turn aside the despoiling beast – the proclivity to feel contempt for the environment sometimes ascribed to monotheistic cultures.

Chapters 3 and 4 move to the Roman Christian world. Chapter 3 deals with the high point of the autobiographical tradition in ancient Christian times – Augustine's *Confessions* – as an effort to set words in a fixed historical and cosmic context where their significance may be complex but not chameleon. It shows how the *Confessions* take us through a rehearsal of the informal but carefully staged educational ascent and self-emptying in the late Roman empire. In order to set aside the ambiguities of the verbal disciplines, of law and of the empathic readings of Virgil, Augustine rejects the seductions of rhetoric and turns to "scientific" philosophy, seeking sufficient scientific learning to read the cosmos "objectively" while listening to the inner voices that also move him toward the God that created the cosmos. Chapter 4 speaks of writers who read Augustine to shape their own lives toward divine ends and who sometimes mastered the more objective forms of learning that he advocated.

The one instance where poetic creation is radically wrenched from its original context and meaning receives treatment in chapter 5, which analyzes the ancient epic commentators, their medieval counterparts, and the medieval poets who used the epic form to give shape to their educational journeys. Since the journey metaphor is so prominent in the account of education studied in this book, the epic form tossed aside by Augustine does not long remain exiled from the new educational theory (though the rhetorician's mode of reading it does). As the ideology of self-initiated Logos-based education infiltrates more significant Greek and Christian philosophic circles in the fourth through sixth centuries A.D., Neoplatonic commentators of both the pagan and Christian variety transform Homer and Virgil to make them the heralds of the educational journey. These figures transform the epic from an account of a fantastic journey that culminates in a military victory to a pseudo-autobiographical account of the heroic journey to the One, the Logos, or Wisdom.

Chapter 6 examines how the Neoplatonic centering of education in an imagined structure rather than in a schooling bureaucracy, the patristic employment of autobiography to represent education, and the Neoplatonic/Christian allegorizations making epics into metaphors for education come together in Boethius's *Consolation of Philosophy* and medieval works derived from it. For those who believe in periodization, the decline of Roman hegemony and the rise, in Italy, of the state governed by Theoderic and Boethius seems to mark at least one beginning for the medieval period. Boethius, more than any other figure, establishes for the new age the significance of the battle with the three beasts or problems just outlined. He uses epic conventions to model his own struggle, he advocates the disciplines that study the creation and Creator in relation to the self, and he cares about mathematics and precise, unambiguous language as he endeavors to set down a structure for education that does not depend on the hegemony of Ostrogothic institutions. Thus he prepares his world for a time when its educational institutions are not stable, and when education, if it is to exist at all, has to base itself in the individual search for knowledge.

Looking from the other end of the medieval period, chapter 7 studies how Dante relates to Boethius's old vision and yet advances the Aristotelian revolution promoted by new universities. Finally, chapter 8 shows how the visions found in Dante, in the medieval Plato and Virgil, and in the Platonic and Virgilian commentators in the Florentine Platonic Academy, come together to form part of the framework necessary for the creation of the forms of Renaissance deductive science practiced by Copernicus, Kepler, and Galileo. The tradition described in this book begins with the claim that the discovery of truth is possible, even in the face of tyranny. It ends with the conviction, on the part of scientists, that truth has been grasped and can be defended both from tyranny and subjectivity.

One could include other works in this discussion. I have tried to confine it to works in which a student, an apprehending mind, is included, and in which the student journeys to Wisdom, or its equivalent, through the mathematical disciplines, theology, and metaphysics. I do not, for example, include Martianus Capella's *Marriage of Mercury and Philology* because it represents only a list of the disciplines and their relationships without including the student who apprehends them. I do not include Abelard's *Historia Calamitatum* and letters because, though they are autobiographical, they do not show much interest in the creation and Wisdom. I do little with John of Salisbury because his interest extends almost exclusively to language disciplines and not to those that study the creation. I do not include Guibert of Nogent because he seems to me to be almost wholly frivolous and self-centered.

Anyone could add to or subtract from the works that I treat. I have tried to respect the medieval sense of how the works and genres in the mainstream of the tradition I describe are related to each other. My interest in doing this is to point to resources in a previous culture that were useful to it and may be useful to ours as we struggle with issues of formlessness and bureaucracy in education, with the problems of offering good environmental and scientific education in a polluting age, and with the discovery of a literary and philosophic tradition that is more than intertextual – one that fosters a serious exploration of the cosmos in which we live and what that cosmos means for our effort to construct meaning for our individual lives.

The Journey
to Wisdom

The Journey to Sophia: Plato's Sophists and Forms of Education

One beast sometimes discovered in the medieval mists is the beast of formless education, a beast that fosters an education without concept of childhood or development or clear steps to success. Though all of us probably come to be educated in more chaotic ways than we are willing to admit, medieval education, as described by Philippe Ariès, would be the bane of contemporary theoreticians of education, gabbling as they often are about the goals of education. Critics of education on the Right assert that it now has too many goals and generally trivial ones.[1] Those on the Left argue that the goals of education promoted by capitalistic institutions are simply power and hegemony posing as reason, that the child or adult in conventional capitalistic institutions must be envisaged as a bank to be filled up with skills useful to the economic order.[2] Both Left and Right make the quality of institutional life the criterion of what makes an education.

However, institutional life was not always what made an education. In his brilliant *Centuries of Childhood*, Ariès shows that medieval education was, regarded from an institutional perspective, without sequence or order. Ariès argues that this was because medieval people had no sense of childhood and no sense of childhood's developmental stages. As Ariès puts it, "medieval art until about the twelfth century did not know childhood or did not attempt to portray it," and "nobody thought about having a graduated system of education."[3] As a statement about how the institutions of education were arranged, *Centuries of Childhood* makes some sense; there is remarkable variation in the method and canon of medieval education for children and adults from school to school, monastery to monastery, and intellectual center to center.[4] However, Ariès does not speak to the sense of development or the imagination of education that did exist in the patristic and medieval periods – how education happens, what its purposes are, to what goal it tends. He does not write of the notion that study implies a ladder of ascent through a sacred nature to nature's God. The patristic and medieval writers treated here do have a sense of a developmental staging in the ascent through the faculties from the senses to the imagination to reason to the intellect (though the development is not seen to be inevitable or attached to specific ages, as it is by modern developmentalists).[5] This faculty ascent implies an order for studying the disciplines: not an invariant order, not a bureaucratic schooling structure, but still an order. Most of all, the writers depend on an imagination of education, not a bureaucracy, to provide the sense of order, something sorely missing from contemporary discussions of the educational process.

The developmental pattern assumed by patristic and medieval writers was widely understood in their time. Patristic and medieval thinkers about education did not buy into the notions of human development promoted in Charles Radding's *A World Made by Men: Cognition and Society, 400–1200*.[6] Radding endeavors to show that late classical and early medieval people adopted thought modes that exist on a primitive level, essentially on Piaget's preoperational and concrete operational level. Thus, according to Radding, the late classical and early medieval periods were largely incapable of formal operational thought in the Piagetian sense. However, though the writers studied in this book sometimes approached events as preoperational expressions of a personality in nature, a God – though they believed in miracles and a providential deity – this does not mean that they were incapable of understanding formal systems or organizing events and objects in terms of formal categories. They understood complex logical inference and complex systems such as the Ptolemaic one. Though the central text that patristic and medieval people read, the Bible, was full of miracles (as were some of the central pagan texts, such as Virgil's *Aeneid* and Ovid's *Metamorphoses*), medieval intellectuals also mastered texts in geometry and astronomy and developed complex systems (e.g., systems for engineering cathedrals).[7]

What was the order of learning conceptualized on the basis of the ancient and medieval understanding of the hierarchy of the faculties? The ascent through nature to nature's God (under the metaphors of autobiography, Platonic dialogue, and epic poetry) begins with ordinary experience and goes finally to a reality that transcends metaphor (i.e., to the unmediated perception of God, the unitive experience). However, between ordinary experience and the unitive one comes, in medieval faculty psychology, an abstractive process that requires an examination of nature and nature's laws. Yeats asserts, in "Meru," that "Civilization is hooped together, brought / Under a rule, under the semblance of peace / By manifold illusion," but that humankind also goes ravening through the centuries to come into "the desolation of reality."[8] In Yeats's vision, understanding is made of two parts: the socially constructed illusion that hoops a civilization together, and the transcendent reality that goes beyond social mythos. The patristic and medieval thinkers studied here would probably have agreed, given their distinction between fable, which is untrue, and history or theology, which is true. However, in the late ancient and Christian worlds, a third element appears between the manifold illusion and the unitive reality. That element involves the concept of nature's laws, an interest that mediates between the hoops of social myth and the "desolation" of knowing God as the One. Though scholars of the Renaissance commonly patronize medieval science, Greco-Roman and early Christian philosophy assume with Plato that the higher disciplines seek to find a reality in the natural world that can be measured and that reflects divine Wisdom, on the one hand, and that can form a paradigm for human societies on the other. Renaissance science would not have been possible without the epistemological assumptions of late classical and medieval Platonism (see chapter 8).[9]

THE WISDOM TRADITION BEFORE PLATO AND
THE SOPHISTS: HERODOTUS ON SOLON

The evolution of a patristic/medieval imagination of education begins with Herodotus's account of Solon and continues with Plato. Herodotus introduces some of the vocabulary crucial to understanding the journey to Wisdom and the battle between the Sophists and philosophers. As he puts it in section 1.29 of his history, "There came to Sardis all the sophists (or teachers: σοφισταί) from Hellas who then lived in this or that manner, and among them came Solon the Athenian man." Having finished

making the laws for the Athenians at their request, Solon leaves his home
for ten years, setting out on a voyage, as he said, "for the sake of *theoria*
(θεωρίης)." Later in the journey, Croisos of Lydia addresses him, speaking to him as one who has become famous "by reason of his *sophia*
(σοφίης) and his wandering around the world for the sake of *theoria* (θεωρίης)." He is known as "one who philosophizes (φιλοσοφέων)" ([1.30],
perhaps the first use of the conception of "philosophy").[10] Solon's journey becomes, in later philosophers' writings, a curricular journey to
sophia or its equivalents, but here it is both a physical journey and an
intellectual one. Indeed, throughout this book the metaphor of a journey – with all of its unpredictability and wonder – is crucial to the understanding of the imagination of patristic and medieval deinstitutionalized
education. Jürgen Gebhardt says that Herodotus assumes that Solon wan-
dered to observe purely disinterestedly, that *theoria* here means a god-like
clarity and detachment about the nature of things, and that *sophia*, for all
of the early *sophoi*, embodies the idea of an orderly society fitted to "the
comprehensive order of the cosmos."[11] Solon is not simply a wandering
scholar; he leaves Athens for both serious philosophic purposes and for a
long-range pragmatic reason – so that the Athenians cannot force him to
change the laws that he has made and which they have sworn to accept
unless he changes them. The travel and travail of "philosophy" at its very
outset combines the theoretical and practical social aspects central to the
patristic and medieval writers studied throughout this book.

By Plato's time, the journey's more detailed structure and its implications for the social order begin to take shape. Prior to Plato, the pre-
Socratic Eleatic and Ionian philosophers, who have a more impersonal
view of nature than do Homer or Hesiod, do not refer to philosophy,
wisdom, or theory.[12] One cannot know what developments occurred in
the Pythagorean movement prior to Philolaus and Plato. Indeed, after
Herodotus the idea of relating *philosophia, sophia,* and *theoria* with learning lies fallow for about fifty years. Herodotus's approximate contemporaries, Parmenides and the other Eleatics of the sixth to mid-fifth century
B.C., study the notion of an orderly cosmos embracing everything and
transcending the chaos offered by mere sense perception, but they draw
from their study little that has implications for the human order. Among
the Ionian philosophers, Heraclitus (540–470 B.C.) develops a cosmic
theory of a coherent underlying principle or Logos that governs the

cosmos and of an inner Logos or reason that knows the cosmos. Yet even Heraclitus does not speak of *sophia, philosophia,* and *theoria* as related concepts (though his universal Logos anticipates the Platonic intermediary source of order called the Nous and the Jewish and Christian *Sophia* or Logos figure).[13] Furthermore, Heraclitus's cosmic speculations do not relate to his ethical ones or imply an education. What Herodotus envisages and attributes to Solon – the idea of a human order based on the cosmic order and of philosophic study "traveling" to find more of both – is left largely unexplored for nearly half a century until Socrates and Plato appear.

Plato does imagine how to journey out of the cave of material appearances to Wisdom and truth by imagining a structure for education that remains the center of disputes for nearly two thousand years. It is an educational journey that rejects verbal learning as the source of truth and argues that the study of dialectic, mathematics, and theology or metaphysics will lead the student to know the light of the cosmos and announce civic wisdom. Plato is the original proponent of the notion of an essentialist education that will lead human beings on what William Spanos calls the "recuperative circuitous education journey back to the origin," whatever that origin is.[14] Though this journey and the search that goes with it are seen as repressive by Spanos and other critics of Western education, these same critics do not propose serious substitutes for the physical science that emerges from Plato's search or for the critique of tyranny implicit in it.[15] In developing his sense of the journey to origins, Plato begins with a consideration, in the *Gorgias* (388–370 B.C.) and *Protagoras* (399–388 B.C.), of the Sophists' claims to teach how to construct social reality through their communication of the techniques of conventional persuasion and civic virtue.[16] But later, in the *Republic* (388–367 B.C.), he looks at the effects on civic government of the literature that the Sophists use and finds that the study of literary lies damages the state. His alternatives to literature and rhetoric as the centers of education are the cosmic and mathematical investigations that can undergird rulership by giving the rulers a sense of the truth to which human society must conform.[17] Later, in the *Timaeus* and *Parmenides,* he describes the kind of universe and the kind of deity that the student might expect to discover on the journey.

In his attacks in the *Gorgias* on the Sophists, Plato represents Gorgias,

Socrates's chief antagonist, as a rhetorician who claims to teach virtue before he teaches rhetoric (449b–497c),[18] but who actually speaks for the academic needs of the powers that be. Plato says that Gorgias claims to teach the arts of persuading in matters of justice and injustice, the arts an orator might display before a law court (454b). Under questioning, though, Gorgias admits that an unjust student of rhetoric could use his skill for evil ends. In such a case, Gorgias argues, the teacher deserves no blame for his student's actions: the teacher taught the tools and not the evil. In replying to this travesty of academic responsibility, Socrates demonstrates that Gorgias's rhetoric is only a technique, that it can be separated from the pursuit of virtue, and that it can make the worse appear the better cause in civic deliberations. Thus it can "corrupt youth." Socrates makes clear that a relativistic discipline cannot be the consummate or absolute form of human knowledge. As if to confirm Socrates's analysis, Polus, the next Sophist to speak, praises the tyrant's power to make or break laws (466c–471c), implicitly sanctioning physical force's power to create the forms of human culture. Thus, through a juxtaposition of Gorgias's and Polus's speeches, Plato implies that a Thucydidean kind of force can create laws and that an Isocratic kind of orator can be used to achieve the self-interested goals that may collaborate to create tyranny. One may be reminded of the hermeneutics of Heidegger and de Man.

Socrates does not win the day through besting Plato's rhetorical straw man, Polus. He does so by advancing dialectic as a substitute for rhetoric: the dialectic of a detached, orderly form of discussion opposed to the overpowering forms of the Sophists. Such conversation seeks truth rather than persuasion.[19] It requires participants who never endeavor just to score points, who ask clear questions and offer straightforward answers, and who base their arguments on clear definitions illustrated by transparent examples. The premises of a dialectician must be lucid and explicit (448d–489e),[20] stating a truth that puts poetry and rhetoric to flight.

"Can the Sophists really teach true virtue; can they teach something that goes beyond bureaucratic competence?" Plato's Socrates asks. To answer this question, Plato has to show that the Sophists – persons without principle, like Auden's unknown citizen who was "for peace when there was peace" and went when there was war – do not so much comprehend virtue as conventional behavior. In the *Protagoras*, Protagoras, claiming to teach excellence in speaking and to make his students a little more virtuous every day, represents the Sophists' assertion that virtue can be taught. Each day his students achieve more and more of the competence necessary to civic (perhaps bureaucratic) life because they know what they need to know to function as conventional citizens. Socrates, however, will not recognize such bureaucratized truth and conventional behavior as goodness. He wants to act on full truth. He wants his leaders to have the excellence of a Pericles, a civic genius whose greatness comes from a divine source. Socrates implies that one can partially teach some virtue based on a knowledge of the final good, but he also recognizes that the full realization of that good is not a narrow pragmatic skill but comes only from comprehending the cosmos and its origins. Herein lies the basis for his imagining a dialectic curriculum that will arrest the tendencies to formlessness in education and yet allow it to be divorced from the routines of conventional institutional power as it exists in Athens or the other Greek states.

The *Republic,* advancing new disciplines that will lay hold on absolute truth, argues that one can know Socrates's good and achieve virtue by studying dialectic, mathematics, music, and theology (while throwing out the Sophists' favorite study, poetry). Plato imagines institutions invented by his utopian state for the purposes of educating the young. He outlines how the state should carry out a compulsory childhood education of rulers: nurses will teach the basic elementary subjects to the state's children in common classes and not tell them idle stories (*Republic* 5.460a–d). At a higher level, the rulers must study the disciplines of music and mathematics, through which one perceives the ultimate truth and learns to frame laws that fit the human species to the cosmos.[21] Finally, rulers must study theology or metaphysics late in life, when they are ready.

This imagination of education remains central to the two-thousand-year tradition described in this book. In its later forms it is detached from state intervention in the process of education, partly because rhetorical and linguistic education dominates the Greek and Roman schools and, perhaps, partly because of another strain in Plato. While the *Republic* praises an institutionalized compulsory education that will lead to a return to the original reality, the *Symposium* assumes in Diotima's speech that the inner daemon of love will move one to the world of the eternal Ideas without external constraints. Plato's successors, believing in this daemon, empower later versions of Platonic education that are altogether divorced from the Academy or long-term bureaucratic institutions.

The Plato of the *Republic,* like Herodotus's Solon, seeks principles on which to construct the human order by looking at the cosmic one. While he carries on Parmenides's cosmology, he bases his educational proposals on a remodeled version of the Spartan schools (Xenophon, *Lac.* 2; Plutarch, *Lyc.* 16–17; Plato, *Laws* 1.633).[22] These proposals would assign nurses to teach ethical principles to all of the guardians' children in compulsory schools or pens (*Republic* 5.460–61). After a period of learning through play, the educational process would require dialectics, mathematics, music, and the scientific subjects – disciplines that would enable one to rule properly – for an elite group selected from the guardians (*Republic* 7.514a–541b; 6.511a–e). Again and again, the *Republic* attacks the tragic and epic poets admired by Gorgias for their knowledge of that "truth-in-contradiction" that makes civility possible. The tragic works themselves, whether by Homer or the stage tragedians, encourage the Dionysian ecstasy that Gorgias commends, an emotion that leads human beings away from quiet contemplation of the good, the mathematical, and the reasonable (10.603–7). The *Republic* condones only straightforward, didactic poetry that helps one to climb the ladder to the good, a restriction related to Plato's attack on the Sophists' "empty rhetoric and misguided criticism."[23]

Plato offers us a theory of learning as well as a theory of what ought to be learned. For example, the *Republic* attacks the Sophists' notion of what conventional Greek education should be because it is based on a "filling up" concept of learning that enforces trivial memorization and regurgitation rather than true reasoning (*Republic* 1.331d–335e). Such an education, by emphasizing the memory bank of conventional literary studies, paradoxically destroys the nonrational insights praised at other times by Gorgias.

EDUCATION TO CREATE THE SOCIAL ORDER VERSUS EDUCATION TO KNOW THE COSMIC ORDER

The differences between the philosophers and the Sophists are not trivial, for they concern both the form and content of education and the basis of the social unit. The Sophists and rhetoricians assume that education seeks to create the social order, and they order education through verbal drill directed by an authority figure, a teacher hired by the state who putatively embodies the virtues and skills that the state seeks. In contrast, the philosophers following in Plato's footsteps argue that education quests to know the cosmic order and to critique local social conditions on the basis of such knowledge.[24] Education for them requires a self-directed inquiry that is independent of or opposed to the state (Plato's proposal that the state mandate compulsory elementary education and philosophic education for the rulers never amounts to much in the writings of his followers).

The Sophists of the generation before and contemporaneous with Plato (mid-fifth century B.C. to the end of the century) – Protagoras, Gorgias, Prodicus, Hippias, and Thrasymachus – turn Greek intellectuals away from the Eleatic and Ionian scientific speculations to a preeminent concern with language. Language is the tool by which, in their thought, human beings form states or societies, language and statecraft coming together for them in the teaching of the arts of "virtue" to the citizen and of rhetoric to the would-be leader.[25] Hence, the Sophists commonly divide the human world into *physis* (the physical forces in nature, including human instincts and impulses such as "greed, power hunger, lust, and cruelty")[26] and *nomos* (custom, law, conventional agreements developed to control the *physis* of human beings).[27] Some Sophists (especially Thucydides, who derives his theories from Gorgias)[28] make the physical force of *physis* the source of *nomos,* or human culture and law, especially in times when groups fight for political power.[29] Thus the Sophists' early taxonomies of the disciplines sometimes place ethics and physics on the same level because both deal with the direction of mundane drives and forces. To them, law is a mere convention or social contract that derives from physical force. When might makes right, persuasive oratorical power, the effective use of the human logos, offers society a means to channel force to create law and civic order.[30]

Plato, given his belief in a state that derives its authority from the structure of the cosmos, objects to the Sophists' favorite subjects, poetry and rhetoric, because the Sophists' relativism requires them to base human society on force and the creative use of language.[31] Plato may represent the Sophists correctly if one concedes a bit to satire. That is, Gorgias's writings do appear to advocate an epistemological skepticism and to regard tragedy as coming as close to human truth as is possible. Trag-

edy does so by holding contradictory, terrible perspectives in tension
while appealing to the irrational in its spectators. For Gorgias, tragedy
gives its spectators a sense of empathy with its heroes while accepting the
unresolved contradictions of their lives. The tragedian creates social solidarity by generating the logos, the verbiage that creates the *nomos* of
social custom.[32] Oratory's logos generates the same social solidarity by
uniting speaker and audience. Instead of deriving the human from the
cosmic order, Gorgias derives it from the verbal arts, especially tragedy – a
position that Plato, Augustine, and Boethius attack.

The relativism of the Sophists was, to Plato, related to the commercial-
ization of their teaching. One of the greatest of the Sophist educators was
Isocrates, who wrote *Against the Sophists* to attack his purported antag-
onists for charging a fee for their teaching and for creating oratorical
how-to-do-it books that vulgarized the teaching profession. However, he
himself charged for his instruction. He became a rich man after 390
B.C. when he founded his own school of rhetoric based on an analogy
between the rhetorical and military arts. According to Isocrates, rhetoric can be learned through drills that imitate commonplace model
speeches – whether these be juridical, eulogistic, or political speeches.
These speeches have a commonplace organization: an opening, a narrative of the circumstances of the matter discussed, a proof of the speaker's
position, and a summary statement.[33] Isocrates's rhetoric teaches one
how to persuade others so as to gain an advantage for oneself. As Plato
and the philosophers saw it, Isocrates urged his students to use any means
to gain such advantage. One may, for example, depend on the ignorance
and irrationality of the masses, and one may tell them what they want to
hear (Isocrates, *De Permut.* 275; *De Pace* 28; *Ad Nic.* 40–49).[34] The teacher
teaches through drill and the expectation of absolute obedience:

[W]hen [the teachers] have made [the students] familiar and thoroughly conversant with these lessons, they set them at exercises, habituate them to work, and
require them to combine in practice the particular things they have learned, in
order that they may grasp them more firmly and bring their theories into closer
touch with the occasions for applying them. . . . [T]he master must painstakingly
direct his pupil, and the latter must rigidly follow the master's instructions.[35]

Here we have the empty vessel or banking picture of education later
promoted by Quintilian and most institutionally based educators up

through the Protestant educators of the sixteenth century. Such an approach is praised today by the advocates of programmed learning and teacher-proof curricula; it has been attacked by all sorts of philosophic educators from the Platonists through Friere and Freud. Thus, by the end of the fourth century B.C., as Hellenistic civilization was about to spread throughout the ancient Near East, Greece had two proposed shapes for the curriculum, the cookbook and the journey to the good: one practical and without ideals, the other ideal without practical institutionalization.

At the outset, Isocrates triumphs over Plato. The Hellenistic and Roman common school descending from Isocrates uses "workbook" exercises and standardized ideology. It dominates Hellenistic "compulsory," municipal education precisely because it assumes a formulaic body of knowledge, a fixed procedure for teaching it, and a predictable civic realm governed by force and verbal superstructures through which the individual freeman can seek advancement.[36]

In the Hellenistic and even in the Roman periods, Platonist methods of education become countercultural, using Plato's imagining of education, but separating it from fixed institutions. In reply to Sophistic relativism and cynicism, Platonism produces a religious response to Gorgias and the Sophists that is not a fundamentalist affirmation of traditional religion-based ethical codes or literal belief in the gods. Rather, it formulates a scientific (or pseudoscientific) religion that affirms a remote absolute good (or God) in some measure revealed through the *Demiurge* and the *Nous*.

The *Demiurge* expresses itself in the creation by studying the eternal designs or molds for the making of things, the Forms, and preparing a plan for the creation based on these Forms. The Forms can be understood through mathematics, which measures the seen and gets at the design behind the seen world, for the Forms' designs have been transmitted to the material world by a middle figure or figures, the world's *Nous* (or Mind) and its Spirit. The Forms are the foundation for the good society, which is based on a knowledge of universal principle, or what is later called natural law.

Whereas the Sophist makes the human words that channel physical power create the civic world, the Platonist makes the divine structure, understood by mathematics, serve as a model for what the civic world ought to be – the "word" or Logos that tells human beings what is required of them.[37] The ruler must then interpret for citizens how they must act to conform to the divine model. To act properly, human beings must understand the material world as a construct guided by the same transcendent patterns or rules that also govern humankind when it acts justly. Philosophic and mathematical education, based in dialectics and numbers – not in poetry – provides the way to know these patterns. This requires the imagination of a formed curriculum or life dedicated to learning the truth.

SOPHIST AND PHILOSOPHER IN THE NON-CHRISTIAN WORLD AFTER PLATO

The Middle Platonists and Neoplatonists make the curriculum issues raised by Plato and the Sophists come to focus for medieval culture. These issues concern both the subject and structure of education. As the philosophers tell the story, the dispute concerned whether human society is properly the product of human language, especially oratory and tragedy, or whether it is properly determined in its form by the design of the cosmos. Ancient educators split over whether one ought to consult Gorgias's Logos or Plato's Logos, whether the sequences of childhood and adolescent education ought to concern primarily language or scientific studies.

The professional Sophist worked in the same Hellenistic world as the professional philosopher. But while the Sophists and rhetoricians ran most of the Hellenistic and Roman municipal schools that formed the first systems of compulsory (or nearly compulsory) education in the Western world, the philosophers were outsiders, for the most part without stable institutional support. The Hellenistic and Roman schools in the Greek world used Isocrates's handbook or descendants of it,[38] remained Sophistic in spirit, and deemphasized mathematics. They emphasized the external and externally measured oratorical performances that created civic leadership, especially in the municipal *ephebia* (or *gymnasia*) teaching rhetoric. All schools taught the arts of grammar and persuasion on the basis of a conventional civic morality.[39] Teachers were to be highly 'moral' citizens in the Protagorean mode, and the magistrates controlled public schooling through educational foundations that got their support from general fund drives directed by voluntary organizations and appealing to private individuals.[40] Such a system served civic solidarity, but it created no fresh vision of good conduct based on what mathematics, music, astronomy, the other sciences, or philosophy might tell us about humankind's place in the cosmos.

The Sophistic view and rhetoric still found proponents in the late Roman empire, when Christianity came to power. Even during the Second Sophistic in the second century A.D., the Sophists' and philosophers' visions continued as powerful alternatives to each other.[41] For example, the issues posed in the *Gorgias* were treated in exactly opposite fashions by two non-Christian writers of the late republican and early Christian eras: Aelius Aristides (A.D. 118–80), a defender of the Sophists and oratory, and Cicero (106–43 B.C.), also a rhetorician but a philosopher and opponent of Sophistic rhetoric.

On the Sophistic side, Aristides assumes that language can, and should, create *nomos* (though he cannot be called a relativist in a strict sense since he believes in some kind of system of transcendent gods and conventional ethical rules).[42] His system of morality simply rehearses the conventional four cardinal virtues as discovered and preserved by oratory ("To Plato: In Defense of Oratory," 1.235; "To Plato: In Defense of the Four," 600–609).[43] Aristides never creates in his writings a sense of cosmology or cosmology-derived ethics.[44] Much of his answer to Plato's charges in the *Gorgias* asserts, probably correctly, that Plato only characterizes the bad orator: the flatterer, the technician, the panderer to the masses, the corrupter of youth, the sycophant who bows to tyrants. One part of Aristides's argument, however, reflects what Socrates claims that the Sophists say: that oratory creates the state or society, the polis. In Aristides's view, human beings naturally fall into two categories – the strong and the weak, the exploiters and the exploited – a condition that would persist in society if oratory did not create civic life and laws, legislation, or the grounds for legislation in the body social. Oratory thus converts brute force as the basis of life into law ("To Plato: In Defense of Oratory," 1.205–17), and law is merely the written formulation of speeches used to persuade the legislative assembly or the body politic to come to consensus. Aristides thereby brings us back to the fifth century B.C. Sophists' assertion that *physis* through oratory is converted into *nomos*.

In his literary defenses of Miltiades, Cimon, Themistocles, and Pericles (*In Defense of the Four*), Aristides answers Plato's attacks against the tragedians and orators. Plato, he asserts, banished from his world all who make up the canon of Greek culture; and would, if followed, allow no Greek cultural pattern to remain (600–609). Aristides understands that, when Plato attacks tragedy, he attacks the Sophists' description of it as formative of truth and human culture; therefore, Aristides appeals to conventional Greek culture as the grounds for rejecting Plato.

Cicero, also a rhetorician, has enough of the philosopher in him to present the contrary "Platonic" notion that the knowledge of cosmic law and a transparent dialectical or mathematical representation of truth are necessary to decent human social order. Cicero is careful not to be confrontational in his treatment of the ancient Sophistic arguments, but he relates philosophy to the formation of virtue and to the good society as the Socratics and Platonists do. In his *Brutus,* he summarizes the *Gorgias* by saying that, after a good clear style of Greek prose had been invented, Gorgias, Thrasymachus, Protagoras, and Hippias began to teach that clear style but also taught the Sophist's immoral art of making the worse appear the better cause. Socrates opposed these four individuals and, in the process, created philosophy, especially that part that treats of human beings, namely ethics (*Brutus* 8; cf. *De Oratore* 3.32). In his own writings, Cicero clearly believes that a good orator must be more than a Sophist, more than a mere rhetorician or master of the handbook (*De Oratore* 3.31); he must be a philosopher, one who unites philosophic understanding, comprehensive knowledge, civic understanding, and eloquence (3.31–55). Cicero's orator does not create the state but founds it on a transcendent vision, as he makes clear in his *Republic* (modeled after Plato's work carrying the same name and much beloved by writers to be treated later in this book, especially Dante and Petrarch).

Cicero's *Republic,* like Plato's vision of Er, demonstrates how the just government is formed on a cosmological rather than an institutional vision. In its dream of Scipio, modeled on the vision of Er, Scipio the Elder states that the creation of associations and commonwealths seeking justice is the human activity most pleasing to God and is rewarded in the afterlife. He then shows the just apotheosized after death in the Milky Way, living amid the cosmic music.[45] To put Cicero's point another way, human beings, in their uncorrupted form, take from nature a common sense of law and justice (*De Legibus* 1.12); if nature and God do not mandate the law, it dwindles to a mere search for utility and ultimately ceases to be significant (*De Legibus* 1.15). Presumably the sight represented by Scipio in the *Republic* mediates what nature and law at the cosmic level demand of corrupted human beings and shows that society (and the social contract) is the product of something beyond legislative rhetoric.

Cicero and Aristides do not say much about childhood, education, or the basic sequences essential to the formation of social order. Other late Roman figures such as Quintilian, Jerome, and Augustine do: all describe sequences for education that mean an escape from formlessness. They do so through different and opposing strategies for accomplishing the escape. Whereas Quintilian and Jerome as rhetoricians propose something like grade levels, grades, and performance examinations, Augustine as a would-be philosopher proposes something like a sequence based on cognitive growth – a sequence separated from the institutional support of the Roman rhetorical schools.

Cicero stands on the edge of the Christian era. As the Roman empire begins to lose its power and Christianity begins its rise, the battle continues with the ascending Christian party placing itself increasingly in Plato's camp. At least one part of Christendom models its understanding of education on Plato (and does so initially independent of hegemonic institutions). As the equivalents of philosophy and rhetoric develop in the Hebrew and early Christian world, related forms of education develop in Hebrew and Christian Alexandria in the early Christian period. The philosophers are exiled from most of the institutions of formal education in the next few centuries after Plato, but they live to fight another day. They change the Platonic view of the nature of education, society, and the mathematically based cosmos to make it more religious. They do not forget Plato's belief that the objective study of scientific reality and natural law undergirds any decent society – a view denied by most modern legal theorists (who have repudiated natural law arguments), by most social constructivists, and, implicitly, by modern educational leaders in both literature and the sciences.[46]

Philosophy, the Creation, and Learning: Gregory Thaumaturgos and Origen

Hellenistic Jews and Christians continue the philosopher's educational project with its repudiation of the acquisition of mere verbal skills. They, like the philosophers, imagine a form of education that has no state support and that leads through the mathematical disciplines to theology and metaphysics. Worshipping a God who, through the woman Wisdom (Sophia), creates the world in beauty,[1] they add, to the philosophers' perspective, an emphasis on the sanctity of the creation. Insofar as they oppose the human inclination to ravage the natural world, they do so by worshipping the Maker of a garden of the world – a garden that requires stewardship of the place in which His steps can be traced.

Much of the spoiler-beast's power for critics of medieval education comes from Lynn White's claim that the whole source of the Western environmental problem lies in the legitimization given to a radical manipulation of the environment by the Genesis picture of the creation as planned "for man's benefit and rule."[2] White insinuates that Christian civilization took the command to subdue as requiring a technological mastery and conquest of nature. He argues that medieval humankind took the injunction seriously by inventing new varieties of technology for keeping time, plowing, using wind power, and the like.[3] Finally he implies, as do other scholars, that medieval society believed the world was made to serve humankind's purposes. According to White, the very idea of ecology (which implies respect for the whole system and not just for human appropriations from it) first appeared in the English language in 1873, after Christianity had lost its hold on Western attitudes toward the environment.[4] John Macquarrie, following White's position, argues that the Judeo-Christian tradition allows four perspectives on humankind and the natural world: (1) humankind has a "unique power and dignity" that permits it to "bring the phenomena of nature more and more under [its] control and more and more into [its] service," which is part of the task of education; (2) the Judeo-Christian God separates Himself from the world into the realm of transcendence and therefore leaves the material world "open to exploitation for the sake of man"; (3) the world as God's creation is worthy of research and study; and (4) the idea of a Logos in the world and a Logos in humankind, both of them ordered, allows for the idea that the inner Logos can discover the order in creation. Though these four positions are not compatible, they are all, according to Macquarrie, derived from the biblical doctrine of creation, and they require, "in the further education of the human race," a self-conscious teaching of doctrines about stewardship and responsibility in relationship to the natural world – about the obligations that go with the right to study and alter the world.[5]

The first of these positions is closely related to White's indictment. However, Jeremy Cohen has shown that White's reading of the Genesis injunction to subdue the earth as a command to violate the environment is itself an "illiterate reading," uninformed by knowledge of how Jews and Christians in the classical and medieval periods actually understood the verses.[6] Yet Cohen's findings and those of others like him have not much influenced the Western environmental movement's sense that environmental education cannot turn to Western sources for inspiration.

Of course, there are demons other than the Genesis passage that can be blamed for our making a pigsty of so much of the world. David Ehrenfeld, for example, has blamed the "arrogance of humanism" for our problems: its assumption, beginning with Bacon and the Enlightenment, that all "problems are soluble by people" (by technology or politics or economic planning), and its belief that our resources are either infinite or replaceable with human ingenuity. Ehrenfeld shows how these assumptions have led to radical and irreversible changes in many fragile environments and for many fragile species.[7] Though this book is sympathetic with Ehrenfeld's argument, ultimately we must do more than blame past intellectual traditions for our problems; we should rather recuperate past assumptions about how the world was taught in times when it was not so despoiled. These assumptions can be the basis of some reconstruction of Western environmental and scientific education, an exploration that would supplement the present tendency to go to Native American and other indigenous and Asian cultures to find a new environmental ethic.[8]

In his remarks about Lynn White, Cohen does not deal extensively with the positive side of ancient or medieval environmentalism, and there is no reason why he should, since his locus of concern is Genesis and commentary on it. However, for the first fifteen hundred years of the Judeo-Christian tradition, the central biblical texts about how the creation is to be seen come not only from Genesis but from the Wisdom books of the Old Testament, from Wisdom-derived concepts in the New, and from related patristic and medieval commentaries, including Wisdom-related literature. These works often dictate how Genesis is read by the fathers and medieval writers who loved the glory of the garden and the Gardener. Dante is not unusual when he writes, "The glory of Him that moves all things / Penetrates and shines out throughout the universe / In one part more and in another less."[9] This glory can extend to very small events. For example, following White's line of argument, Augustine's regret, in the *Confessions,* at sighting a lizard and losing himself in interest at its catching flies seems to support the idea that Augustine saw the very creation as filthy.[10] However, if one looks carefully at the passage, Augustine only regrets his interest in the lizard because he does not refer the creature to the whole created system and to God. Augustine does not express contempt for the lizard but for the scope of his own perception:

Yet in how many little and insignificant minutiae is our curiosity entangled each day and how often do we slip. . . . I no longer attend the circus to see a dog running after a hare, but if I should, in going through a field, happen to see such a sight, it might easily distract me from some serious thought and attract me to itself, not that it pushes my horse from its path but that it draws my heart from its. If you had not turned me aside from my weakness, and instructed me to ignore such a sight, to pass beyond it, or at least to make it help me to raise my thoughts to you, I would, vain as I am, remain immersed in it. What shall I say for myself when, even when I do not leave my house, a lizard catching flies or a spider that holds in its net those flies that fall into it often captures my attention? Because these are small animals, should I say that my curiosity is not of the same order? I do go on to praise you, wonderful Creator and Ordainer of all things; but it is not for this purpose that I first became attentive. It is one thing to rise quickly; it is another never to fall. (*Confessions* 10.35)[11]

Augustine clearly finds his problem not in his seeing of the lizard, but in his seeing it isolated from its place in the whole system. Hence, he despises his own visual possessiveness at the level of elementary sight and imagination, a possessiveness that is, surely, in modern society a source of our abuse of the world about us.[12]

The idea that the creation is structured and beautiful and offers itself as a path for those who wish to make the journey to the origins appears in the works of philosophical Jews and early Christians. These persons also keep alive the debate with Rome and its rhetorical forms of education. Caught up in the controversies over Sophistic and philosophic education, they separate themselves by their unwillingness, in the first through third centuries, to subscribe fully to the premises of Roman society or the rhetorically based Roman schools. They adopt the biographical and autobiographical mode of the Platonic dialogues to present their imagination of a somewhat deinstitutionalized structure for education and a Platonized religious aesthetic for responding to the creation.

Like the Platonists, Jewish intellectuals after Philo and Christians after Origen vault from earthly studies, such as ancient versions of physics and ethics, to the Logos or Wisdom – generally by way of mathematics. The Wisdom figure in the Old Testament is the Hebrew version of the Nous or middle figure that mediates between God and the creation.[13] In the New Testament, the same figure is called either Wisdom or the Logos and is identified with the historical Jesus. In the Platonic Jewish version of the creation, Jewish Wisdom, like the later Platonic Nous, takes the rules governing the creation from the highest God and forms the creation according to these rules. Both Jews and Greeks in the Hellenistic world argue the transcendent origin of the creation provides it with luminance and intelligibility. However, the Jewish Wisdom figure is, at least on the surface, a more personal force than any Greek middle figure, appearing, as she does, as a beautiful woman who woos her followers, marries them, mothers them, and calls them to an intellectual journey to know and construct the good society. In the Christian world, she comes to be identified with Christ-as-Logos, an even more personal figure who calls for a journey. In the Jewish and Christian worlds, the beauty of Wisdom becomes a metaphor for the beauty of the world's structure, and the search for her includes the higher reaches of education and study as defined by Plato, especially mathematics and theology. The book of Wisdom tells us that Wisdom "is indeed more splendid than the sun, she outshines all of the constellations; compared with light, she takes first place"; deploying "her strength from one end of the earth to the other," she orders "all things for good" (Wisdom 7.29–8.1).[14]

The cosmopolitanism of the Hellenistic world's middle figure should not surprise us, for Alexandria produces the central Wisdom theologies of the late ancient Jewish and early Christian world. As a cosmopolitan city, it contains both Jewish and Greek centers for learning at the beginning of the Christian period. Though it allows numerous Greco-Roman persecutions of the Jews, culminating in Trajan's fierce suppression of the Alexandrian Jews after A.D. 115, it also forms the setting for Philo Judaeus's formulation of his crucial syntheses of Jewish and Greek thought and for Origen's appropriation of Philo. As the Christians rise in political importance, they also produce increasingly harsh laws directed against the Jews. But before that happens, the Christians learn from their Jewish neighbors the essential syntheses of Jewish and Greek philosophic and scientific thought that the Wisdom of Solomon, Philo, and the Jewish centers of learning in Alexandria make possible.

Perhaps Alexandrian Greco-Roman Jews and Christians create a learned tradition there in the first and second centuries to legitimize their beliefs in a skeptical world. In any case, Alexandrian Jews and Christians are a kind of rejected underground, and to defend themselves they forge tools for resisting the appeal of the conventional pagan rhetorical schools and for inviting others to travel their religious road. The Jewish and Christian road often includes some sort of invitation to identify with the middle figure, whether it be called the Nous, Logos, or Wisdom, and to make an aesthetic-religious exploration of this figure's beautiful creation. Jews and Christians connected to Alexandria also tell the stories of their own lives as an enfleshment of the middle figure and an exemplar of their growth in moral and aesthetic perception.

Georg Misch's view that Augustine is the first real autobiographer is, at best, a partial truth.[15] For example, Ben Sira's account of Jewish life in *Ecclesiasticus* and Gregory Thaumaturgos's account in the early third century A.D. of his experience of Origen (185?–254?) as a teacher are autobiographical works that anticipate Augustine's in almost all essentials.

Ben Sira and Gregory are related as educators also: Ben Sira anticipates Origen, and Gregory reflects him. Ben Sira and Gregory, together with the other Wisdom writers in the Old and New Testaments (and some of the other Alexandrian Wisdom writers), formulate the basic principles of the early Judeo-Christian educational theory related to Hellenistic philosophy.

The Wisdom figure implies for education in Hellenistic Jewish culture what the middle figure implies for Platonists. Jewish and Christian Alexandrian culture, as exemplified in the theories of education elaborated by Ben Sira, Origen, and Gregory, makes this clear. To make sense of Ben Sira or Gregory Thaumaturgos, one must know what Plato's theories of the role of the disciplines and the middle figure come to mean for Hellenistic Jews and Christians.

THE MIDDLE FIGURE IN HELLENISTIC JEWISH CULTURE AND BEN SIRA'S THEORY OF EDUCATION

Plato's Nous, together with his World-Soul, allows the creative first force to structure the creation; the figure of Wisdom or the Logos, in the period 200 B.C.–A.D. 200, essentially allows a Jewish or Christian hidden God to do the same thing: to "speak," to transfer His plans for the creation to a second figure so that she (or he) can execute His plans for the creation's architecture. Wisdom raises up God's creation out of chaos and builds it according to God's plans. Reflecting the interest of Hellenistic Jewish intellectuals in an intermediary person or hypostasis like the Nous, Wisdom first appears to be central in Hebrew theology in the Hellenistic period.[16] The Hellenistic Nous or Logos, discussed in the last chapter, and the Hebrew Wisdom figure function analogously; some scriptures even appear to sanction the identification of the two. An Alexandrian biblical book, the Wisdom of Solomon, speaks of Wisdom and the Word of God in parallel. In "Solomon's" prayer in Wisdom 9.1–4, Solomon addresses God as follows:

> God of our ancestors, Lord of mercy,
> who by your *word* have made all things,
> and in your *wisdom* have fitted man
> to rule the creatures that have come from you,
> to govern the world in holiness and justice
> and in honesty of soul to wield authority . . .
>
> (italics mine)[17]

Wisdom and the Logos eventually become one figure in Hellenistic philosophic Judaism and Christianity. This chapter will not fully trace the web of relations that develops between the Nous, the Logos, Sophia, and other middle figures in the ancient world. In Hellenistic thought and in Jewish philosophy influenced by Hellenism, the Logos developing from Heraclitus's thought is the idea of ideas, the form of forms, and the source of natural law. He (it) initially stands for the unity and interrelationships among all things. Among the Stoics, He (or it) creates all that unifies and orders the material world. Like a combination of Plato's Nous and World-Soul, He produces the first order in visible things. By the time of Antiochus (first century B.C.),[18] He further defines the patterns or mathematical relations behind the creation.[19] By Origen's time, He is the Word that transmits to the creation the intelligible principles that govern it.[20] Through the study of physics, mathematics, astronomy, and other cosmological sciences,[21] an aspect of Him reflected in human beings examines the connections among the parts of the cosmos and its ultimate unity.

Perhaps through the influence of Gnosticism, the Logos or Nous in Hellenistic thought fuses with the somewhat comparable Wisdom figure in Hebrew religion.[22] As Jerusalem and Athens meet, they create a Hebrew and Christian educational tradition opposed to the rhetorical tradition – as opposed to that tradition as the Platonic philosophers had been, but embodied in the forms of biographies and autobiographies concerning the search for the origins of things.

One Hebrew Wisdom thinker, Ben Sira (200–175 B.C.), may help us to see the basis on which Gregory Thaumaturgos and Origen develop their theories of creation and education. Ben Sira describes the study of Wisdom as the contemplation of a theophany that combines the characteristics of the divine Nous and the World-Soul in Greek thought. Wisdom is both the preexistent architect of creation and its sustainer:[23]

> Wisdom speaks in her own praises,
>   in the midst of her people she glories in herself.
> She opens her mouth in the assembly of the Most High,
>   she glories in herself in the presence of the Mighty One;
> "I came forth from the mouth of the Most High,
>   and I covered the earth like mist.
> I had my tent in the heights,
>   and my throne in a pillar of cloud.

Alone I encircled the vault of the sky,
  and I walked on the bottom of the deeps.
Over the waves of the sea and over the whole earth
  and over every people and nation I have held sway.
Among all these I searched for rest,
  and looked to see in whose territory I might pitch camp.
Then the creator of all things instructed me,
  and he who created me fixed a place for my tent.
He said, 'Pitch your tent in Jacob,
  make Israel your inheritance.'
From eternity, in the beginning, he created me,
  and for eternity I shall remain."

(Ecclus. 24.1–9)

Clearly this middle person manifests the holiness of the pristine world to Israel.

Though Ben Sira resides in Israel, his grandson, who translates his work into Greek, appears to live in Alexandria and specifically directs the translation to Egyptian Jews living abroad, thus making Wisdom a cosmopolitan figure appropriate to their culture. Like the Greek Logos in Antiochus, this Wisdom is the source of natural law, movement toward her is a journey "at first through winding ways," and in the end the journey to her goes on "the straight road" where she, both mother and bride, reveals her secrets to her sons and lovers (4.11–22; 15.2).[24]

Ben Sira's *Ecclesiasticus* illustrates how Wisdom teachers conveyed the journey to origins in pre-Christian Hebrew culture through the use of biography or autobiography. When Ben Sira describes education as a journey to the beautiful woman, Hokmah, and a quest for right living in conformity with her order,[25] his grandson uses the word *Sophia* as the Greek equivalent of the Hebrew *Hokmah*. *Sophia* is obviously closely allied with *philosophia*. Indeed, the grandson domesticates, in the Greek world, the Hebrew thought of Wisdom as the intermediary force described in Proverbs 8, a domestication prepared for by some Greek thought that conceives of the intermediary figures as women: for example, in Plato's *Timaeus* the receptacle of the Forms is female, and in the philosophic allegorists Athena emblemizes the creative intermediary.[26]

Ben Sira and his grandson make clear that the beauty of the woman is what woos one to learn. The grandfather discusses Wisdom informally with his followers in his home or outdoors and has no such tool as the compulsory school that Plato assigns to the nurses of the guardians to make his students learn. He is obliged to make Wisdom's pursuit attractive, for he has little else to bring the student to learn.[27] To initiate a child in the quest for Wisdom, the father in Ben Sira's world places the child under Wisdom's discipline in the "liberal arts" – not in a "school in the pedagogical meaning of the word," but in a conversation.[28] The goad that the teacher uses to inspire the young student is the fear of offending the middle figure and, by doing so, of missing out on the end of a climb to the divine (Ecclus. 1.11–25). Ben Sira's teacher must be quick, must snare the student – offer a call, an intellectual seduction, a proverb to answer the world's wiles. Because compulsion is not available, Ben Sira's Wisdom, like that in most of the Wisdom books, presents herself in literary forms designed to make a quick effect in the open marketplace or in a home discussion outside the routine of the scholastic institution and its captive audience. In the other Wisdom books, Wisdom uses proverbs and numerical sayings (Prov. 16–19), riddles and conventionalized autobiographical lessons (Prov. 24.30–34), didactic poems and personal dialogues (e.g., Job's dialogue with his friends), fables and allegories, and wisdom psalms (Ps. 49, 73, 139).[29] Ben Sira also uses most of these forms. The use of dialogue is common both in the Hebrew Wisdom literature and in Greek philosophic works, and Ben Sira gives us a simulation of dialogue when "the sage" speaks to his "son." His Hebrew dialogue, however, does not pretend to assign plausibility to anyone aside from the normative speaker (a characteristic of much later patristic and medieval dialogue). Thus the Hebrew Wisdom teacher adapts to the exigencies of Hebrew culture a version of the biographically based pedagogy of Socrates and Plato while continuing a whole range of techniques that seem to rise specifically out of Hebrew or adjacent Middle Eastern cultures.

The Greek analogies in the Hebrew Wisdom tradition are extensive. Plato, in the *Republic* and elsewhere, argues that mathematical study constitutes a road to objective truth and to the sources of authority in the cosmos. Ben Sira also assumes a certain amount of scientific study moving toward objectivity, an effort to see the light that God has put in the hearts of human beings to show them the greatness of his creation (17.1–12), an attempt to discover the order that God has imposed on his creation, which human beings are to contemplate (42.17–26). This interest in something like scientific study also appears in other Wisdom books, particularly in the Wisdom of Solomon and Ecclesiastes. Ecclesiastes's talk, in some translations, of Wisdom and number (7.26) was thought to imply that Wisdom, like the Nous, is reached through number. Wisdom 7.15–21 has God, through Wisdom, teaching Solomon "the structure of the world," "the properties of the elements," astronomy, zoology, botany, and other disciplines so that he may speak as God would have him speak. Other Wisdom philosophers follow the same course. For example, Philo makes Moses, one of his Wisdom orators, learned in "arithmetic, geometry, poetry and music, theology and astronomy" from his study under the Egyptians, Greeks, and Chaldeans (*De Vita Mosis* 1.23).[30]

The "scientific" study of Sophia attracted the Hellenistic and Roman Jew because she was thought to sponsor the creation's aesthetic beauty based on the proper "Pythagorean" proportions uncovered through mathematical natural studies. Using these studies and gifts to understand the creation's beauty, human beings could learn to practice the cardinal virtues and attain an inward Eden where beauty reigns (Ecclus. 24.23–34; Philo, *Leg. Al.* 1.53–87).[31] By knowing the architectural harmonies of the natural world, the Hebrew Wisdom teacher knew how the structure of the cosmos carried implications for the meaning of life and the order of society.

CHRISTIAN PEDAGOGY PRIOR TO ORIGEN AND GREGORY

The first Christians seeking an audience outside Judea and traditional Jewish culture seize on techniques similar to Ben Sira's. In the Hellenistic Roman world, these Christians claim to be successors to the Greek "philosophers" and the Hebrew Wisdom teachers. As teachers, they become vagabond philosophers, resembling modern Buddhist sages more than contemporary university or secondary school teachers. They go about "preach(ing) a popular moral and religious ideal" about the "concrete realities of everyday life" and offer people the ideal of a different, more noble life through teaching forms designed to engage the student speedily.[32] The apostles in Matthew 10 leave behind the synagogues and go on the road to teach in people's houses and the city streets. Paul hits the road after he and Barnabas receive the call at Antioch (Acts 13.2–3), sometimes teaching in rivalry with the Epicureans and Stoics (Acts

17.18). In 1 Corinthians 1–4, he warns against rival Wisdom teachers who do not understand the role of suffering and self-crucifixion in Christian Wisdom teaching. Typically, early Christian teaching begins with a paradoxical challenge. In the gospel account, Christ plays with paradoxical meanings of water with the Samaritan woman; in Acts, Paul manipulates the definition of the unknown god on the Areopagus to gain a hearing.[33]

Eventually, as early Christians attempt to win converts in the Greco-Roman world, the paradoxical challenge and somewhat formal sermon have to make space for the addition of "Platonic" dialogue and advanced work in the disciplines. Christianity, after all, competes with the philosophers who, by this time, have become semireligious figures. Very early in the history of Christianity, Justin Martyr (A.D. 100–165) writes dialogues and clothes himself in philosopher's garments to enter into discussion with others not of his persuasion.[34] Robert L. Wilken argues that "sometime in the 150s or 160s a few Christians began to claim that Christianity offered men a philosophical way of life," a novel claim since earlier "Christians had only criticism for philosophy."[35] But the claim is not surprising.[36] Though apostolic Christians have few kind words for the Jewish or Gnostic thinkers or "pagan" philosophers, when they compete with them for students in the second-century world, they naturally adopt their rival's deinstitutionalized pedagogy (Acts 17.16–32; 1 Cor. 2.1–8; Col. 2.8).[37] To succeed at all against these rivals, Christians have to develop teaching methods that combine the Wisdom teacher's quick thrust with the philosopher's dialectic.[38]

On the other hand, to compete against the pagan rhetorical schools, they have to represent their learning as countercultural, as reaching beyond official municipal or imperial culture. Yet to remain Christian, the early fathers who know philosophy have to supplement philosophy's dialectic and scientific discourse with Christianity's understanding of crucifixion and suffering and late Judaism's understanding of Wisdom and the creation.

GREGORY THAUMATURGOS'S PRAISE OF ORIGEN AND WISDOM AUTOBIOGRAPHY

Gregory Thaumaturgos's oratorical autobiography in praise of Origen's teaching at Caesarea, written some time after A.D. 231, displays what

Christian Wisdom education was like in the Alexandrian world. About to leave Origen's school, Gregory summarizes his experience prior to his encounter with Origen and then describes Origen's methods of instruction.[39] Pretentious in its rhetoric and perhaps self-serving, the work is no great shakes as a piece of literature. Yet it is important for what it reveals about philosophic Wisdom pedagogy in the early Christian world. It also comes as close as anything written prior to Augustine to being a genuine autobiography – a work in which the life of an authorial self struggling against itself is described.

The structure of the work is simple enough. After a highly rhetorical disavowal of rhetoric, Gregory establishes who his teachers are by asserting that he cannot accurately praise Origen the teacher because Origen as temporal being is not really his teacher. Rather his teacher is Origen the philosopher, the lover of Wisdom, an inner or divine Origen in the process of achieving apotheosis, the revealer of the Logos within the limitations of mortality (section 2).[40] In praising this Origen, Gregory can give proper praise to Christ-the-Logos: the middle figure ("τῷ πρωτογενεῖ αὐτοῦ Λόγῳ"), the Word of the First Mind itself ("Καὶ αὐτοῦ τοῦ πρῶτον Νοῦ Λόγος ῎Εμφυχος ὤν"). As creator and ruler of creation, this Christ is the Wisdom ("σοφία") of the universe, both in God-the-Father and also in the creation in the form of the providence that watches over created things. He is both Wisdom (or Sophia) and Logos, both the Greek and the Hebrew intermediary figure, and He mediates between the Father or the One and the created universe (as does the Nous in Plato and, especially, in later Platonists). This mediator-teacher acts as Origen's and Gregory's teacher in all essentials; as Gregory's teacher, He manifests Himself as both an inner and an outer force (section 4). A secondary teacher, an angel-tutor, also guides Gregory's intellectual activity and organizes his life, presumably as the angels shaped things for Isaiah or for the shepherds at the time of the nativity (section 4).

Having established the teaching roles of Origen and the Wisdom-Logos figure, Gregory uses section 5 of the oration to describe how the two, working together, caught him. He starts with his pain at losing his pagan father at fourteen. But when he is orphaned and his individual Logos or higher human reason begins to develop, he finds the divine Logos dwelling in him (a pattern also typical in later autobiographers).[41] The father is replaced by a spiritual father, and the mother remains a powerful force because of her passive hopes for her son. Orphanhood initiates Gregory into knowledge, as the Logos that has existed at large in the creation (not mere human reason) comes into him and substitutes for his human father. The higher Logos, his own individual Logos, and his human reason work together to direct his education (section 5). Gregory assumes that the Logos is both the pattern of natural law and the human mental capacity to grasp that pattern: education begins with the collaboration between pain (i.e., his father's death, which empties him) and the providence of the Logos that puts something else in its place.

Later, when Gregory's widowed mother wishes him to become an orator, he encounters the rhetorical or Sophistic alternative, receiving instruction in public oratory (section 5). One of his instructors in rhetoric, led by Gregory's guardian angel ("θεῖος παιδαγωγός"), encourages Gregory to study the Roman tongue and law as a vocational application of rhetorical training. Thereafter, two *logoi* – that of the Sophistic rhetoricians' words and that of the philosophers' divine reason – compete for Gregory's life until, contrary to his conscious will, he is guided to escort his sister to Berytus near Caesarea (where Origen had moved from Alexandria) instead of going to Rome to study law. In the school of law at Berytus, Gregory studies rhetoric and law. But instead of emphasizing these studies, a sort of "accident," cooked up by the "guardian angel," turns him over to Origen to study philosophy and journey above the stars.

Origen woos Gregory to study with him by praising philosophy as a life in the company of the intelligences (angels or semidivine beings who oppose the beasts). He apparently means not only that Gregory will know the angels through study with him, but that he will know how the intelligences move the heavens through a study of mathematics and astronomy. Sophia replaces sophistry. The teacher urges Gregory to "know himself" in a context where "know thyself" means a knowledge of the higher self in relation to the pattern of the universe and the Logos.[42] Gregory's Origen heads no formal educational institution and promises his students no institutionalized reward (he does not even seem to have to support himself). Clearly Origen does not depend on institutional or financial pressures to get his students to learn; instead, he relies on a "fiction" or picture of the world of *theoria* that he places in his students' imaginations. If Gregory learns what Origen has to teach, he can live with the angels and know himself – surely a more extravagant promise than the Sophists' promise that one will become a better person each day. Origen appeals to Gregory to know himself and to know the cosmos (i.e., life among the angels); the two knowledges meet insofar as the inner Logos reflects the outer.

James Olney argues that the understanding essential to comprehending autobiography comes from Heraclitus, who implies that we all embody the principles of the whole: "In every individual, to the degree that he is individual, the whole principle and essence of the Logos is wholly present, so that in his integrity the whole harmony of the universe is entirely and, as it were, uniquely present or existent."[43] Origen knew Heraclitus well,[44] and his appeal to Gregory to achieve integrity in relation to the "whole harmony of the universe" and life among the angels becomes the inspiration for learning when no school exists. Similar fictions inspired the educational journey later when Rome's compulsory rhetorical schools had declined in social utility at the time of Augustine and Boethius.

Through his fiction and teaching style, Origen rouses in Gregory a fire of love for the Logos principle and its unutterable beauty. Whereas the educational mode of the rhetorical classroom distances the teacher from the student, Origenian dialogue, according to Gregory, emphasizes warmth, love, and common experience. Gregory abandons his oratorical career, his homeland, and his friends to attach himself to Origen and philosophy. Though the change would normally be painful, Gregory makes little of the pain, saying only that the sole objects now worthy of his love are philosophy (or the love of Wisdom) and Origen as philosopher. Thereafter, Gregory is knit to Origen by the Logos as Jonathan was knit to David in a spiritual attachment transcending the pederastic friendship of Socrates for his loves (section 6).[45] As a friend, the teacher evokes the individual Logos in the student and moves it toward the divine Logos by employing a Socratic dialectic fused with the Wisdom teacher's challenge to the individual's moral life and the gospel teacher's sowing of seed.

Origen's method apparently seems to recall, for Gregory, Christ's georgic parables that a religious guide should "teach" others by cultivating soil, pruning vines, or tending trees. Gregory says that Origen digs into the person and waters and prunes (section 7). Origen's Socratic discussion is not the rhetoricians' filling of an empty vessel but a painful tending of the Logos's seeds (section 7): "At times, [he] attacked us in the manner typically used by Socrates and tripped us up with his arguments when he saw us becoming restless with him, like unbroken horses that ran away from the road and galloped crazily about randomly until with a bridle he persuaded us. And this process was at first unpleasant and painful to us, when he drove and cleansed us with his own learned discourse, we who were certainly inexperienced and unprepared for reason." The method, as the account has it, is like preparing soil for seeding, awakening people from sleep, separating truth from sophistry or reasoning from rhetoric (section 7). Origen wishes the thinker who studies under him to test truth in the inner person: to search to see if propositions are true there, to test things there one by one, and, only after such an exploration, to give outward assent. Furthermore, Gregory describes such education as necessary not to elites but to all persons wishing to avoid self-deception and find truth (section 7).

This painful education also has a cosmic dimension. Beginning with ordinary problems and events and bringing what can be known to bear on them, Origen asks his student ultimately to learn about everything: especially about the beautiful and wise architecture of the world taught by the sciences. Origen offers his student no world to be subdued and polluted. He offers a world that is a divine work of art. Hence, he teaches physics, the nature of the universe's elements and their mutations, and the related studies of geometry and astronomy, hoping that reason will gradually replace unreason in the student's understanding of the cosmic process:

He dealt not only with that part of our mind that dialectics controls but sensibly with the humble part of us who marvel at the great and marvelous structure, the varied and wise workmanship of the world, and we marveled struck dumb with astonishment and did not know how to think about such things, being more like wild than reasonable creatures. And he stimulated us and lifted us up with other natural disciplines, clarifying each thing of those things that exist, even with regard to the foremost simple component until he filled our minds with his reason and teachings – partly his own and partly teachings derived from others – with a rational admiration, substituting for an irrational awe, of the sacred ordering of the entire universe and of unconditional nature. This study was doubtless the lofty and divine discipline that he taught, i.e., natural philosophy, a study most attractive to all. What need is there now [also] to recall holy mathematics? Or geometry precious and definitive to all or astronomy ranging through the heavens? (section 8)

In Origen's teaching, students cannot know themselves if they do not know the cosmos. The word that Origen uses for natural philosophy is synonymous with physics, the study of physical phenomena on the earth. Physics then leads into the typical middle Platonic ascent to the mathematical and astronomical studies and beyond to theology.[46]

To know oneself is also to know oneself as an ethical being; Origen teaches ethics in connection with this ascent (sections 10–11) because ethics usually, in ancient culture, derives from natural studies. Plato's *Republic*, which treats the study of the mathematical ideas in relation to the ideal society, summarizes what is to be found in the study of ethics. Origen teaches ethics in the context of his study of physics and the natural sciences because he believes that natural study leads to self-knowledge: to an observation of the movement of the instincts and passions in relation to the pattern of the divine mind within oneself (sections 10–11).

From the study of physics, the mathematical sciences, and ethics, Origen ascends to the study of theology. He covers not just the Christian system but all the known religious and philosophical systems save the atheistic (i.e., Epicurean), and he ventures widely to prevent hasty judgement and to avoid sophistry or ego-attachment to one's own set of beliefs ("σοφίσμασι"; section 13). In the context of theological discourse, he gives his students hermeneutic tools for understanding the prophetic and enigmatical in the scriptures, since the same divine gift that empowers the composition of enigmatic scriptural works also facilitates their understanding (section 15).

Gregory, in ending his autobiography on the eve of his return home to Pontus, describes his return from Origen to his home as a type of exile. He anticipates further suffering, since he knows the agony of exilic return while bearing philosophy's insights. In a far deeper sense than Thomas Wolfe meant, he knows that he cannot go home again. He says that he is Adam leaving Eden to work among thistles and thorns, the prodigal son leaving his father, the Israelite who goes from Jerusalem to a Babylon without song (section 16).

For Gregory and Origen, only by stepping outside the circle of conventional culture and its educational processes, thereby descending deep into oneself to recognize the culturally constructed self, can one step beyond this self to recognize what the deeper self is and what the cosmos and the Creator are. Origen's education of Gregory displays six salient points in this process of discovery of the self and the cosmos that find confirmation in Origen's own writing and that relate the teacher, the Logos, the cosmos, pain, and pedagogy to one another. These six points are crucial to a later Christian ideology of education.

First, Gregory's education centers in the redemptive appropriation of pain, the kind of pain that does not affect the Olympian Plato or Socrates, his master, even in death. In contrast, Gregory tells us that the pain of the "death" of the father, the pain of Origen's pummeling dialectic, and the pain of departure from Origen shaped his formation. Origen's recognition of the educative function of pain clearly aligns him more with St. Paul than with Plato. St. Paul's Christ figure in 1 Corinthians 1–4 connects the Wisdom of the first creation with the recreation implicit in "crucifixion" and "resurrection": a connection also requisite in Origenian education.[47] In 1 Corinthians, Paul asserts that he is beyond the divisions in educational theory that infect his day, that he did not come to Corinth with "any show of oratory or philosophy" (1 Cor. 2.1). Rather, he came with a Christ who is the Wisdom and power of God (1 Cor. 1.24), in contrast to Gnostic Hellenistic or Hebraic human wisdom, the wisdom of the world. Paul's Christ here appears as a crucified and potent figure who anticipates the eschatological restoration through crucifixion and resurrection:[48] "While the Jews demand miracles and the Greeks look for wisdom, here are we preaching a crucified Christ; to the Jews an obstacle that they cannot get over, to the pagans madness, but to them who have been called, whether they are Jews or Greeks, a Christ who is the power and the wisdom of God" (1 Cor. 1.22–24).

In his weakness, "fear," and "trembling" (2.3), Paul focuses on the crucifixion's implications for the present sufferer who knows that he lives in the end-time. He is especially offended by the pride of those who follow Gnostic or rhetorical "human wisdom" teachers (1.20). Hence, appealing to the Corinthians, who might become self-important from following such teachers, he asks that they understand that they are nothing. The apostles are countercultural – "at the end of (God's) parade, with men sentenced to death" (4.9). They are "spiritual m[e]n" (2.15), men required to destroy in themselves an old physical man (or Adam) who must be daily crucified in order for the "new" man to rise. This new man, far from being self-important, lives in anticipation of martyrdom and of the *parousia* that will unify him with Christ, who is the Wisdom of God. This Christ then, in Paul's vision of things, is the model of *gnosis* or knowing for those who undergo the death of the self or who empty themselves to become part of the cosmic pattern (cf. Rom. 6.6; 2 Cor. 5.1–20; 1 Cor. 15.20–34). Origen merely transforms Pauline emptying as death and preparation for resurrection into the basis for an educational theory.

Paul and Origen teach Gregory that suffering recreates the self, opening a new self to learning.[49] Based on 1 Corinthians 1–2, Origen assumes that academic learning may be either selfless or selfish, founded in the wisdom of the crucifixion or on human wisdom. The same disciplines may work for human pride or for the community of nature and humanity. The basic academic disciplines – later to become the medieval trivium and quadrivium[50] – may do service either to the Wisdom of God, which promotes the foolishness of the Cross, or to the egoistic wisdom of the world. The former Wisdom does not come piecemeal but is born of study and suffering that comprehends the whole order and beauty of creation. As Origen asserts, "If the soul, gazing on the splendor of the world, sees from the beauty of creatures that God is the maker of all and praises him and his works, to this soul life enters in through the windows of the eyes."[51] No promise of subduing the earth there.

Second, pain leads the student away from the rhetorical, legal studies and mechanical pedagogy to a struggle with real life problems. The interpretation of these problems comes from the inner Logos and from a providentially provided teacher. After Gregory studies law, Origen tells him to know himself and study philosophy to achieve life among the angels; thereafter Gregory simply changes directions (section 5). Origen's first thrust in Gregory's direction is his challenge that he know himself. He continues from that with the painful, troubling dialectic that the student describes.

Third, after an experience of emptiness and after a first invitation to learn in beginning dialectic engagements, the student encounters the conventional scientific academic disciplines. These fill him with a knowledge of the plan of the Creator in the creation, a study that permits the seed of fire within the student to apprehend the ultimate Logos. In Origen's pedagogy, the Platonic doctrine of recollection as the basis of learning does not govern.[52] Rather, Wisdom (the Logos) acts on the human mind partly through the human teacher to guarantee the accuracy and objectivity of conclusions drawn from the senses as the mind moves from the sensory to the mathematical to union with the divine.[53] One can hardly overestimate the importance for later scientific development of Origen's moving of the locus of learning from Plato's "memory" to the mathematical analysis of sensory experience: a movement reflected in Boethius and in later medieval science. As the student studies, a Logos within, answering to the external Logos, promotes rational thought and action and diminishes the need for the external teacher. Though Origen depreciates the verbal arts, he requires some of them – logic or dialectic – to give discipline to the study of scripture and to move one beyond the physical creation through the process of mathematical inference.[54]

Gregory asserts that Origen moved his students on to the higher scientific disciplines and theology. Origen, like Clement, makes the disciplines stages on the road to transcendence or grace.[55] He says that the Greeks speak of three disciplines aside from the verbal discipline of logic: ethics, physics, and contemplation (i.e., metaphysics or theology).[56] Of these disciplines, physics corresponds to what Gregory calls natural philosophy, and the mathematical subjects and contemplation correspond to the theology that ascends above the creation to the Logos. Origen locates these "philosophic" disciplines in the Solomonic books as well as in Greek works. He asserts that ethics is found in Proverbs; physics in Ecclesiastes (which teaches of the cycles, vanities, and uses of natural things); and "contemplation" in the Canticle of Canticles.[57] The allegorical progress which Origen finds in the three Solomonic books is analogous to that which he says are also to be found in the "works of the Greeks" (i.e., in Plato) by certain Platonists. The *Republic* proposed a study, for its philosophic rulers, that climbed from good conduct under the nurses to mathematics to the contemplation of the One (533E–540B).[58] Later Platonists proposed a sequential study of Plato's three major works which parallel the *Republic*'s sequence. Chalcidius (sixth century A.D.) and Proclus (A.D. 410–85) propose that the educational ascent mounts from the *Republic*'s examination of ethics to the *Timaeus*'s study of physics (including physics proper, mathematics, and the heavenly phenomena studied with the aid of mathematics) to the *Parmenides*'s study of theology or metaphysics (cf. chapter 6).[59] One suspects that this sequence had been noticed before Origen, and that he only appropriates it to Solomon's books. In any case, the disciplines and order of disciplines mentioned in Origen's introduction to his Canticle commentary parallel those that Gregory attributes to him.

Fourth, "scientific education" culminates for Gregory and Origen in knowing how Wisdom undergirds the creation and how it imposes on it the mathematical rules governing it (section 8). Origen fuses the Logos figure from Greek philosophic mythology with the Wisdom figure from the Hebrew tradition to make Wisdom the name for the middle person when she relates to God and the Logos when she relates to the creation.[60] If one looks at the subjects leading to the Logos that Origen discussed with Gregory, they include those that apprehend the scientific structure of the cosmos (physics, geometry, and astronomy), and they do so because the middle figure contains the mathematical designs for the creation. In Gregory's life of Origen, the latter promises Gregory that Logos-education will be a life among the intelligences that leads to an understanding of the movement of the stars and of the celestial bodies which are governed by the "intelligences." This study is not simply analytic but generates a sense of the beauty and sublimity of the creation (section 8).

Fifth, Origenian-Gregorian education makes the student see the human teacher as a vehicle mediating between the Logos within and the divine Logos. Gregory, for example, says that he does not praise the human Origen but the Origen who is in the process of being apotheosized by the divine Logos. In much of the Wisdom literature, the seeker not only seeks Wisdom, but Wisdom seeks, even assaults, him.[61] She comes down from above even as her seeker ascends to discover her, and this element in the Wisdom conception of education appears in Gregory's portrayal of the Logos as having invaded him shortly before Origen hunted him down to make him know himself. Learning thus becomes the result of a collaboration between the teacher, the Logos that structures the universe, and a Logos that comes to dwell within the individual to drive him to learn. In the patristic and medieval form of this understanding, Wisdom may come in the form of a mother or lover or friend-teacher. It may have a human name and face – as Origen does in Gregory's account.[62]

The mediating human teacher does not work out of the formulaic texts of the Sophists or rhetoricians but appeals to a "teacher" within that presses the student to learn, an idea that Origen borrows from the slightly earlier Clement of Alexandria.[63] In the "Pedagogue" 1.1–1.4 and 1.7, Clement presents the Word as an inner pedagogue who teaches male and female human beings through a certain style of apprehension of the natural world.[64] Though Clement uses phrases for childlikeness or help-lessness to describe the Christian initiate whom the pedagogue teaches (Paed. 1.5),[65] he explicitly denies that these metaphors apply to an in-fant's or young adult's educational development (Paed. 1.6).[66] Though he asserts that some inward, divine direction acts didactically on the adult Christian to affect him as Phoenix did Achilles (Paed. 1.7),[67] he confines his theory to adults.[68] Yet by a slight change in emphasis, Origen and Gregory can make Clement's pedagogue or Logos within the educator apply to those receiving their first education. In Gregory's version, this Logos acts through the help of a friend, Origen, in whom the same force is particularly active. Origen is here the ancestor of such later Logos/friendship figures as Augustine's Monica, Boethius's Philosophy, or Dante's Beatrice. The teaching he mediates does not fill an empty mind or mark a tabula rasa; it wrestles with and pains the whole person until a new self emerges.

Sixth, Christ himself is the ultimate Wisdom/Logos taught by Origen and studied by Gregory: Christ is the first new self and source of the natural law, not the modern Christ who undergoes his last temptation as part of a wholly human drama. Indeed, Origen's Christ is almost wholly "other" – Christ-the-geometer of medieval illuminations, the end of the scientific study that climbs through mathematics to Ideas in the mind of God transmitted to creation through Christ-as-Logos.[69] John 1 says that the world was made through the antemundane Christ, that without Him nothing was made, and that the Logos is the light and life coming into the world, a passage that could easily be attached to the middle Platonic conception of light as the reality outside the cave of empirical experi-ence. This conception of Christ is central to the assumptions of Origen's teaching.

Gregory's Origen identifies the Wisdom and the Word of God as the same entity. In doing so, he anticipates modern Biblical scholarship. Following in the steps of Philo Judaeus, he helps to lay the groundwork for an education attached to the scientific search for the Logos/Wisdom figure.[70] As a philosopher both in the technical sense and in the sense of a lover of Sophia, Origen attacks "Greek rhetoric as taught in the West or practiced in the sophistic schools of Alexandria and Antioch."[71] In his commentary on the gospel of John, he presents Christ as the definitive Wisdom/Word that makes creation possible.[72] Fusing the Philonic second and third figures, Wisdom and Logos, into the one Wisdom/Logos/Christ, he asserts that that one figure is the beginning and end of knowledge.[73] This figure employs mathematical ideas not as a pure mathematician does – or not only so – but as a Vitruvian classical architect does: to lay out the rules for a realization in matter of the beauty of divine design.[74] As an architect uses a plan and rules of work to build a building, God creates by rules transmitted by his Wisdom-Word, who communicates the forms of things to creatures (1.114):

We have available so many meanings for the word "arche" (beginning) that we must ask in what sense it is meant in the phrase, "In the beginning was the Word." . . . It is as the beginning that Christ is the demiurge – insofar as He is the beginning – because it is because He is Wisdom that He is called beginning. Wisdom says in Solomon, "The Lord formed me in the beginning of his Ways for his Works," so that the Word was the archetype [that existed] in Wisdom: because Wisdom functioned in the vision that founded the universe and in the thought that constituted things, and the Word in the communication of that thought to creatures (or spiritual beings). . . . As a house or a ship is fashioned by an architect and that house or ship begins with a general plan and plans for implementation of the builder's designs, so all things were created according to rules laid out ahead of time by God in his Wisdom for his creation because he created all in Wisdom. One should add a "vital" Wisdom because God assigned to her the job of giving the shape, the form, and even existence to beings and to matter according to the models that she carries in herself.[75]

Origen always assumes that the world is beautiful and intelligible. It is so because the earth, the sun, the moon, the things before us existed in design in Christ-as-Wisdom before they existed in our eyes.

Origen's journey to Wisdom is a journey to a Christ that is the author of what science studies. The central metaphor in post-Origenian stories of the life-journey often becomes a journey to restore a building or to discover it in its original grandeur. It is a journey to the architectural structure in God's mind or to the building now ruined whose designs still exist in the mind of divinity (Augustine's and Dante's metaphor). Origen's metaphor also makes the journey go the other way: it represents Christ as the light coming to the seer (cf. John 1.1–10), a Wisdom-Word who is the Platonic "light" of the creative Forms or seeds of things that fosters them as light appears and sustains the form of visible objects.[76] As the truth, the Logos includes all of the knowledge of the universe (1.186), all of the Ideas that bind the creation together in a unified system.

As the journeyer upward begins to know the One through His effects, he finds himself on a journey through metaphors of light and design, an ontological journey into knowledge and beauty. To discover Origen's Word is to discover the cause of nature. As Berchman puts it, "(i)n the philosophical theologies of Nichomachus, Moderatus, Philo and Clement a hierarchy of first principles is postulated . . . not . . . of (an) energetic" but of "paradigmatic" cause and effect. In Origen, God is "Mind," the active first "principle" and "the cause of all creation."[77] He is, therefore, in some sense scientifically knowable. Though He is what the believer believes, He is also what the learner learns. Origen's conception of God makes possible the curriculum that he provides to Gregory in a systematic deductive physical science related to theology and metaphysics.

If one follows John 1 as Gregory and Origen do, the Logos principle operates both in the cosmos and in history and individual lives (the autobiographer's simultaneous apprehension of the Logos's cosmic and individual operation is crucial to many of the works included in this study). The Word is made flesh historically and in individual lives so that what appears to the modern reader as "subjectivity" is often an effort on the part of the autobiographer to show how part of his learning was really an encounter with the Logos or a reenactment of aspects of the life of Christ. Life stories become a way of appropriating the gospel. Like most of the earlier Wisdom writers, Gregory assumes that a special providence operates in his life to bring him to learning and to the Logos.

In the Wisdom writers from Ben Sira to Origen, Wisdom or the Word is a person who inspires an intense contemplative quest based on experience and science, which is, after all, a formalized version of experience. Hence arises the significance of history, biography, and autobiography in the Wisdom writers. Ben Sira differs from his Greek contemporaries in presenting a picture of a God/Wisdom who is not an unmoved Mover but a force that works in history to produce emotion and learning in the seeker. In inspiring fear, his Wisdom uses the individual's and the na-tion's suffering to instruct. She can do so because her source is the con-troller of history, because through her, history, like the cosmos, is provi-dentially governed, because her understandable providence and design can be found in the text of the Bible. In contrast, the text of the cosmos can only be fully read through scientific investigations. Bickerman sug-gests that Ben Sira and the sages of his generation make Israel the people of the Torah as the Greeks had made themselves Homer's people, and that the historical revelation of God's law contained in the Torah in Jewish culture occupies the place for Ben Sira that the text of Homer occupies for the Greeks. It is the source of *paideia,* the empowering edu-cation.[78] However, there is a difference between Homeric story as pattern and Ben Sira's version of Biblical narrative. Because Ben Sira regards the Torah as straight history and not as a half-fabulous Homeric style of history, he makes the knowledge of history in the Torah confirm the scientific knowledge of "reality" possessed by Wisdom from the creation. In contrast, Plato sets the false knowledge of Homer and other "lying" poets who write about history against the true mathematical and musical knowledge of the philosophers. Ben Sira's Wisdom has taken root in Zion, and Zion's history under the law of Moses appears in the sacred book of a passion-filled deity as well as in the foundations of the universe (24.1–47).

Early Christianity, arguing that its Logos announced a new Torah for which the center of history is not the history of a nation but of the Christ person, turns Israel's emphasis on history toward the history of individ-uals. Christianity initially claims to be a religion somewhat outside cul-ture – neither Jewish nor Greek, bond nor free. For Origen and Gregory, the incarnate Wisdom that gives structure to nature also appears in the literary text of a Bible that is to be understood in terms of the contempla-tive disciplinary ascent, a Bible that is to be read as history but also as a Platonic philosophic fable (section 15). The semiotic system of the Bible itself, like the shadows on Plato's cave, can be fully understood only after the disciplinary ascent to contemplation. Later autobiography formed on the Biblical and Origenian model describes the ascent and shows how one imitates Christ-as-Logos both in one's suffering toward empti-ness and in one's rapt contemplation of the beauty of the creation and Creator.

These six points define Gregory's and Origen's sense of a Wisdom education that is separated from conventional political institutions and not devoted to the institutional subduing of the natural world. Origen's and Gregory's concept of a community of learners, studying the community of nature and Wisdom, is a far cry from the Valentinian Gnostic solitary climb to the ultimate that Harold Bloom sees as the basis for modern writing. One finds, at the root of the Origenian and Gregorian conception of education, no struggle to surpass a previous writer in achieving direct contact with the divine. The past and the cosmos are both there to give instruction in the ultimate. One finds a sense that education possesses a structure (though its structure may become apparent for differing people at different times in their lives). The universe is beautiful in its organization and proportions and does not require radical subduing or alteration to become a fit home for humankind. Contrariwise, human beings must alter themselves to fit the universe through self-emptying and seeking diligently to learn the ways of the cosmos. Origen does not (in those times unsafe for Christians) offer much of a civic critique save for rejecting the pagan gods, pagan rhetoric, and service in the Roman army. He does not need to do so since he is at work creating a society outside Roman society.

Perhaps the chief communicator of the educational theory invented by the Wisdom thinkers (Ben Sira, Philo, Origen, and Gregory) is Augustine. As Henri de Lubac points out, Augustine knows the life story of Origen in the version recorded by Eusebius and translated by Rufinus. He also reads Origen's homilies on Genesis – homilies that contain many of the same conceptions as the Greek father's commentary on John 1. Augustine develops specific exegeses that recall Origenian explanations of the relationship between Wisdom and the cosmos in his own comments on Genesis and John, and he practices the same hermeneutic as Origen, probably drawing his image of using pagan learning as stealing Egyptian gold from Origen's letter to Gregory Thaumaturgos.[79] If Augustine is the first autobiographer, Gregory is his prophet. Both are historians of a particular form of the soul's journey to the origin of things – a form that becomes central in Western civilization's sense of the inwardness of human beings. What Augustine does with education in the *Confessions* is best understood as a continuation of the project to be found in Gregory and Origen.[80]

3

Augustine's *Confessions:*
Naming, Education, and Empire

Augustine's *Confessions* assume that language may have clear and determinate meaning both in its description of the natural world and in its commands to the individual.[1] Augustine recognizes that language sometimes is indeterminate, ambiguous, polysemous, multiple; his *De Doctrina* sent exegetes in quest of multiple meanings for a thousand years. In the *Confessions* it is important for him to establish that, at some points, language has multiple meanings (for example in his interpretation of the creation sections of Genesis) and that, at other points, it says one authoritative thing (for example in the "Tolle, lege" garden or in the prediction of the movement of heavenly bodies). Augustine points to the determinate character of language by emphasizing the specific context of his life and of the natural world. For him, language has reference as well as meaning, and education that reaches beyond Roman cultural assumptions to the world of the creation may depend on a referential accuracy in both natural and mathematical language. Education, based in the study of truth, can change the students' "reality" to make them no longer subject to Roman myth but capable of exploring the cosmos for themselves. The *Confessions* follow on the work of Origen and Gregory and contextualize what the early Augustine says in his other works on education. They form a model for later medieval works of autobiography that pattern out a deschooled education and indicate the importance to patristic educational theory of *some* language referenced to a historical world or a mathematically understood natural cosmos.

The *Confessions* are in spirit, if not in letter, a child of Gregory Thaumaturgos's oration, even as Augustine (however much he conceals his lineage) is Origen's child. They indicate how important to late Roman Christianity was the creation of a structure for education outside the conventional Roman rhetorical schools. But the *Confessions* cannot function as a model for the kind of education they propose if they can be made to mean just anything. Augustine presents them as a model for living, having a specific set of meanings that can be discovered through a mimetic reliving of his life as he relived St. Antony's life.

Poststructuralist criticism and educational theory commonly argues for a polysemous (as opposed to univocal) reading of texts and a multiple or subversive reading of cultural institutions, especially educational institutions. In some ways, this seems to resemble Augustine's approach to texts and institutions. In *De Doctrina*, he endeavors to establish a unitary meaning for the text of the Bible that can be wrenched from all biblical contexts whatever their immediate meaning. At the same time, he allows for a plurality of meanings in individual biblical passages. As a Christian, he "deconstructs," in the *City of God* and in the *Confessions*, the major civic and educational institutions of Roman society to show that they are either hindrances to what they were established to accomplish or irrelevant to the good life.

At the same time, Augustine is about as far from anticipating poststructuralism as anyone can be. At the core of his life, he assumes that he can read and hear definitive messages on which he must act. His skepticism with regard to the common language and institutional life of the rest of his world rests on the notion that verification is possible and that definitive messages exist that run counter to what Roman culture has told him. In asserting the possibility of verification and the existence of definitive messages, Augustine struggles with the chameleon-like in language in a way that deserves our attention.[2]

At the beginning of the *Philosophical Investigations*, Ludwig Wittgenstein quotes a passage from the *Confessions* that he intends to dispute:

When they (my elders) named some object, and accordingly moved towards something, I saw this and I grasped that the thing was called by the sound they uttered when they meant to point it out. Their intention was shewn by their bodily movements, as it were the natural language of all peoples: the expression of the face, the play of the eyes, the movement of other parts of the body, and the tone of voice which expresses our state of mind in seeking, having, rejecting or avoiding something. Thus, as I heard words repeatedly used in their proper places in various sentences, I gradually learnt to understand what objects they signified; and after I had trained my mouth to form these signs, I used them to express my own desires.[3]

Wittgenstein uses this passage to illustrate what he often criticizes in Augustine, in other philosophers, and in his own *Tractatus* – a picture or naming theory of meaning. Of course, Augustine also expressed more complex understandings of how we learn to use language in *De Magistro* and in *De Doctrina Christiana*.[4] But Wittgenstein is correct. Augustine never entirely lets go of the notion that many properly used sentences have referents in the world of objects and situations, and that questions may properly be asked about the truth of such sentences (indeed, the same notion, much modified, appears in Wittgenstein in both the *Tractatus* and the *Investigations*).[5] Since Augustine holds to a naming or picture theory of meaning, he does not subscribe to the Sophistic position that we live in a world made by language and power. Like Wittgenstein when he speaks of learning a series of language games that are imbedded in what he calls forms of life, Augustine in the passage above emphasizes that a child who has learned the language of the elders speaks the names of objects in a tongue held in common with the elders, the "mother" tongue. But Augustine does not specify how the child learns what the language refers to.[6] What Wittgenstein criticizes about Augustine's view in the *Investigations* is not the idea that words may have naming functions but Augustine's overly simple sense of how we learn their naming functions, of how we learn how they name.[7] For our purposes, what is important about Augustine's view of language is his denial that language is referenced only to other language, as poststructuralist theoreticians would have it. He writes his autobiography to get away from the world of lying texts and myths and into the world of history and the cosmos.

However, Augustine also writes to place himself under the authority of previous writers – St. Paul, Cicero, St. Antony, and the like. To do this he has to believe that, in certain crucial passages, they have determinate things to say. Augustine's strategies as a reader and agent in his own life contrast with those posited in post-structuralist theories that emphasize the significance of the strong self in making meaning. Harold Bloom argues that the post-Enlightenment poet creates an "intertext" through a series of standard moves: the strong poet, in creating a new poem, accidentally or deliberately misreads a previous strong poet. The new poet creates, on the basis of this misreading, a crisis poem that aspires to transcend the meaninglessness or emptiness the poet finds in the work of predecessors and to create a personal absolute. The (strong) critic repeats the process when reading the strong poet's text. He too makes his own personal meaning. The process of substituting one's own quest for that of one's predecessor involves a series of echoic, ironic, or substitutionary moves that allow one to replace the language of one's predecessor with language that expresses one's own vision and undercuts that of the predecessor.[8] Meaning rises out of intertextuality, but the relationship of the strong self to previous strong selves is more crucial than the specific historical context. Though Bloom generally restricts his theory to post-Enlightenment poets, the theory has been extended back into earlier periods.[9]

Augustine, in contrast, argues that his education depends on his accepting in a specific context a definitive determinate meaning of texts by Paul or Cicero or about Antony. He searches for an accurate representation of experience as it can be codified in historical discourse, regularities, laws, and mathematical formulations; he looks for meaning in his understanding of his experience of the authoritative texts. In Augustinian education, the self is not so much the creator of truth as its servant, a truth that includes both scientific truth and the source of truth, what Augustine calls Truth, Wisdom, or the Logos.

Karl Morrison has documented (in *The Mimetic Tradition of Reform in the West*) how this servanthood is created, how patristic and medieval authors represent mimesis as a tool of reform. In Augustine, the essential mimesis is not a mimesis of poetic myths but of a real life rendered in words that have reference to objects and situations outside the work. The fathers and medieval thinkers whom Morrison discusses treated mimesis as a "strategy of reproduction that motivated such asymmetries as those between parent and child, between action and potential states of existence (e.g., between an acorn and an oak tree), and between the archetypal world in God's mind and its image, the actual world of human experience."[10] In such a world, Augustine's education takes him from a quotidian sensory experience that changes constantly to a knowledge of the world of the archetypes, regularities, or natural laws created by Wisdom, and then to Wisdom herself. The crucial turns in the ascent come with

encounters with pain that outline the limitations of the self, with definitive though not necessarily canonical texts, with definitive science, and
with an absolute Logos or Wisdom.

Consistent with his theory of meaning and reference, Augustine im-
beds his ascent in what purports to be his actual life insofar as it is imita-
ble. Although the creation of metaphors for the ascent begins with the
story of the cave in the *Republic* and the account of the creation in the
Timaeus, these stories are dialogues covering a brief span of time in a
continuing philosophic conversation. Augustine claims to write of his life
until mid-career, not just of an evening,[11] and he develops Gregory's
tactic of naming oneself to model how an education that goes beyond the
formal processes can take place (a self-naming continued in Boethius,
Aelred of Rievaulx, Dante, and Petrarch).[12] But when the *Confessions*
name the self, they do so, paradoxically, as part of the process of sur-
mounting egotistical selfhood. Thus they constantly raise and reverse
Bloom's issue of the role of the self in the self-generated work of literature. Rousseau, when he wishes to demolish the conservative edifice of
the ancien regime that begins with Augustine and to assert the power of
the ego in creating a meaningful world, names his work *Confessions* in a
backhanded tribute to Augustine.[13]

SOPHISTS AND PHILOSOPHERS IN THE PATRISTIC WORLD

After Origen, the decline of literal belief in the Roman gods does not
much affect the conventional education that examines oratory and literary texts. Roman education, still primarily rhetorical in Augustine's time,
remains Sophistic in content and externally measured in method; Roman official education resembles the earlier Hellenistic municipal rhetorical education discussed in chapter 1.[14] Obviously, by the fourth century this old style of education serves a largely defunct pagan Roman
culture and a Roman empire in which Christians continue to be ill at ease
despite the Empire's recent Christianization. The retention of pagan
content is no surprise in a conservative civic system that protects the
schools from the ceaseless flow of intellectual life. Fourth-century Roman
education is state education, controlled by a magistrate and funded by
public foundations or general appeals to prominent government figures.[15] The state's domination of education is firmly entrenched by Augustine's time: after Vespasian (A.D. 70–79) teachers pay no municipal

taxes, and the state supports professorships;[16] after Trajan (A.D. 98–117) Roman foundations fund impoverished freeborn children in school, and, in the provinces, the authorities take aristocratic hostages to force them into "melting-pot" schools.[17] Finally, after Antoninus (second century A.D.) the imperial power requires teacher examinations for credentialing municipal teachers and regulates school openings and the wages of teachers.[18] Throughout the imperial period, the municipalities and wealthy benefactors support education;[19] but in the late imperial period, the emperor becomes the first among equals in developing school benefactions.[20] The Roman empire's *physis,* or physical power, does in fact create its *nomos,* or educational culture, and its *nomos* returns the favor by preparing bureaucrats and lawyers for the writing-centered imperial system. That the texts used to create that proficiency in writing are "outmoded" canonical pagan texts is neither here nor there to school authorities. Thus Roman education remains the centerpiece of the Roman imperial culture with which the early church struggled.

Roman education's picture of education as an operation that fills the empty vessel of the youth's mind with proper knowledge allows little space for learning from the world outside the schools. The school protects the student from the knocks of the forum, prepares him for its rhetorical demands, and indoctrinates him in the *mythoi* of Roman culture before he can have any serious encounters with experience. This is not unusual in any state-run system, but it does separate what Roman rhetorical educators, Christian and non-Christian alike, do from what philosophers, Christian and non-Christian, say education ought to do.[21] Quintilian's Roman school (only for boys), so protects the child that it precludes student questioning of contradictions in the public world.[22] His responsible Roman parents act in an equally one-dimensional fashion by keeping the child under nine or ten at home under the watchful eye of a moral pedagogue (1.1.8–10; 1.2.10); then they send the child to grammar school under a highly moral master who forces him to compete, evaluates him rigorously, and uses praise or blame to win good performance (1.2.1–15; 1.3.1–7). Finally, if the child is able, the parents send him to a rhetorical school for adolescents – ages 14 to 15 – where a teacher without vices and without toleration for them will command (2.2.4–8). Quintilian's education trains only the public person by filling an empty student-vessel with civic subject matter (1.2.25–29).[23]

Quintilian's system encourages social emulation through prizes given monthly to the best student competitors and classroom recitations in which each boy speaks in the order of his "ability." According to Quintilian, the Roman boy goes to the schools rather than to the tutor because he needs public competition and a foretaste of the forum (1.2.17–21). The boy's classroom environment and literary study are to include heroes who will prod him to achieve as a Roman citizen (1.2.17–31), while his history exercises present fixed civic exemplars to be fitted to the formulaic outlines of the themes he is to write (2.6.1–3). Here we have a perfect instance of the banking form of education so often and rightly condemned by modern radical educators.

Quintilian's nonlinguistic sciences also exist only for their civic uses. Although he mentions Plato on music, he ignores the latter's attribution to it of mystical or transcendent functions (1.10.15), and his ideal student discovers in music only an incitement to war (1.10.14–16), a stimulus to work (1.10.16), or a banquet entertainment (1.10.20). His ideal mathematics student discovers, in geometry and the mathematical disciplines, bases for arguing from premises to conclusions or for giving help in law cases requiring boundary surveys (1.10.34–37). If this student aims to become a general, he should learn astronomy to avoid fear in the presence of unpredictable astral or planetary events (1.10.46–48). Indeed, Quintilian's concessions to mathematical training, instead of implying either a criticism or a transcendence of imperial culture, imbed the student more deeply in it.[24]

Quintilian's spirit lives in the Christian Roman age among those powerful Roman Christian intellectuals who, unlike Origen, see rhetorical education as more than a necessary evil: for example, Jerome loves his early schooling under Donatus the grammarian,[25] attends a rhetorical school in Rome such as Quintilian might have directed, and, still later, employs the Quintilianesque methods encountered in the Donatan and the Roman schools to teach Christian males at Jerusalem and to advise others how females are to be educated.

Jerome's most complete educational statement, the letter to Laeta on the education of her daughter, Paula, is highly reminiscent of Quintilian (*Epistola* 107.4; cf. *Inst. Orat.* 1.1.24).[26] Laeta should teach her daughter the alphabet with Quintilian-style devices: letters of boxwood or ivory whose names are made part of a game or a song (cf. *De Inst. Orat.* 1.1.20

and 1.1.27–29). She should make certain that Paula begins to make the
letters of the alphabet while having her hand held by her teacher. Later
she should make certain that her teachers give her prizes for proper
spelling and stimulate her to compete with fellow students by praising
them. All of these tactics echo Quintilian. This education, like Quintilian's, is primarily mnemonic. Paula will learn pronunciation by mem-
orizing the names of the prophets, apostles, and patriarchs (*Epistola*
107.4), will memorize much Greek and Latin daily (*Epistola* 107.9), and
will learn vast quantities of the scripture by heart. Thus Paula will construct a world by rote and, in her protected world, will avoid encounters
with men, with public baths, with elaborate dress, with fine foods, with
others at her parents' table, and with women who mispronounce words!
So educated, she will become the perfect virgin. At last she will come to
the ascetic life, the substitute for Quintilian's forum as the end of learning. All that has happened to Quintilian's education in Jerome's hands is
that Christian protection and indoctrination have been substituted for
their Roman equivalents.

Jerome's advice concerning Paula reflects his understanding of what a
woman's education should be. Although it is probably more restrictive
than a comparable Jeromian plan for men would be, his advice to Laeta
fits both an earlier dream (A.D. 374), which portrays him as a Ciceronian
rather than a Christian (*Epistola* 22, 30), and an earlier precept that
pagan literature (like the pagan woman made captive by the Hebrews)
could be cleaned up and used for Christian purposes (*Epistola* 70).[27] In
his Jerusalem school for males, Jerome appears to have used techniques
similar to those he advocates for Laeta, though the range of literature
studied is broader. More than any other early Western father, he demonstrates that one could baptize the content of Roman rhetorical education
while keeping its traditional drill-based form (*Epistola* 107.4–13).[28]

In contrast to Jerome, Augustine (in the *Confessions* and elsewhere)
proposes a philosophic or "dialogic" education more resembling Plato's
and more in touch with the world outside the official Roman myth system – one that purports to have structure, goes beyond social convention
to the cosmic, and seeks to speak of real events through determinate and
determinative words (or a determinative Word) while opposing the fictions of poetry. Augustine apparently practiced such an educational
form at Cassiciacum and elsewhere early in his postconversion career

(the later Augustine, as a bishop, comes to be more interested in indoc-trination).

The Augustine of *De Magistro* (387?) and of the *Confessions* (397–98) detests the notion that learning comes from outside the person rather than being a development from within. He despises the rhetorical schools, has little truck with their teachers after his conversion, and agrees with the philosophers in that he uses dialogue about ordinary life problems and the mathematics that explores creation as his central learning tools. His practice of philosophic education is part of a conscious rejection of later Roman Sophism. For instance, in *Contra Cresconium Grammaticum* he crit-icizes Sophistic studies in rhetoric for their emptiness and their replace-ment of truth with ornament.[29] He also objects to Jerome's commentary on Galatians, implicitly from the same perspective, for its view that Paul, in his chastisement of Peter at Antioch, only pretends to reprimand Peter – a casuistry apparently condoning lying for a good cause (incidentally, also a charge made against the Sophists).[30] Augustine's letter 40 argues that any attribution of sophistry ("officiosa mendacia") to the apostles under-mines the authority of scripture,[31] and his letter 71 suggests his distrust of persons overly given to philological niceties: he objects to Jerome's trans-lation of the Vulgate directly from the Hebrew (as opposed to the Greek Septuagint) on the grounds that the differences may split the Greek and Latin branches of the church.[32] Finally, Augustine's *De Doctrina* expresses far less interest in philological exactitude than in allegorical "charitable" readings that treat the Bible as a philosophic fable for the univocal truths of Christianity. For him, in *De Doctrina* and elsewhere, words generally refer to real things, among which divine love is foremost. All of the scriptures speak of charity as all of nature speaks of Wisdom. Moreover, charity and Wisdom are related: in book 13.20 of the *Confessions,* Au-gustine argues that the working out of the stable truths of Wisdom and knowledge in the temporal order (in material operations) is varied in differing contexts even as "scripture speaks of the same things over and over in many ways."[33] Following Plato, Augustine pursues a "philosophy" directed toward Wisdom to get beyond the ephemeral in order to know the objective order of the cosmos and to understand its genesis in a middle figure such as Wisdom.[34] In contrast, as Kelly notes, Jerome enlists the philosophers in his prose primarily as persuasive decoration.[35]

The Augustine of the *Confessions,* in order to show others how to grow in the cognition of Wisdom, must present himself as a historically recognizable figure; but he need not precisely represent the historical Augustine *seen by others*, and the *Confessions* do not pretend to represent this latter Augustine because much of what they represent as central to him and to his education is interior.[36] When Augustine turns to the informal study of texts and disciplines that could interpret his life, he turns to the words about growth in Origen's and Gregory Thaumaturgos's theories of education: (1) the conception that authoritative words emerge from a cognition created by pain, especially the pain created by the life of St. Antony, told by Ponticianus's friends; and (2) the conception of a Word reached through the Wisdom texts and through mathematical study, without the help of a teacher. Pain is the push force in Augustine's education, and the pull force is the learning of accurate words or numbers.

AUGUSTINE AND ST. ANTONY: THE EMPTYING
THAT ENABLES LEARNING

Augustine begins his intellectual life by indulging in a Virgilian empathy for the sufferings of fictional people who act as he does (e.g. Dido); he feels empathy for them regardless of the evil they do. Later he learns to employ his own suffering as a way of learning existential truth when he hears an account of a biography of St. Antony that he believes to be both historically accurate and to define the meaning of his own life. Antony's life story is not, as William Bennett or Allan Bloom would have important books be, a canonical text.[37] In fact, Augustine has little use for canonicity where important life choices are involved, little sense that the great works of the past have a perdurable significance for anyone who reads them. He rejects a canonical Virgil for a relatively obscure saint's life that has little literary flair, little "greatness" as it is conventionally conceived. Augustine's earlier rhetorical and literary training in the canonical texts had taught him the Sophists' and rhetoricians' amoral empathic stance: to weep for Dido, real self for literary self, when he did not weep for his own sin. The lying poets of official Roman culture offer him perverse models of suffering and joy – Dido of suffering and Jove, descending to fornicate with Danae, of joy (1.16). In the literal and figurative fornication of his youth,[38] Augustine constructs himself in the perverse image of the literary gods and heroes whom he worships. He only realizes that his suffering signals the limitations of the self (of the body and of physical perception unaccompanied by scientific discipline) when he hears of the text of the life of St. Antony that Ponticianus has encountered through his friends.[39]

Ponticianus tells the double story of Antony and his friends when Augustine's official Roman sense of self has been weakened by his struggle with Roman rhetoric, with the Manichaean's fantasies, and with promiscuity (8.9). Having gradually come to follow a Christian Platonist, Victorinus, Augustine appears ready to abandon his rhetorician's occupation, partly because he knows that, rather than give up the Word, Victorinus gave up his rhetorician's position in a school of words supported by the emperor Julian (8.5).[40]

Before he tells the double story of St. Antony and his friends, Ponticianus (like Augustine, an African and holder of an imperially supported position) notices a Bible open on Augustine's gaming table. Surprised at Augustine's apparent interest in Christianity, he tells the story of St. Antony and his effect on his friends. What follows epitomizes Augustine's sense of how suffering empties one for education, giving words a definitive meaning in specific contexts, and how we are to read the determinate word of suffering elsewhere in the *Confessions*. When Ponticianus tells Augustine the life of St. Antony of Egypt, he probably reflects the passages in Athanasius's rendering of Antony's life where Antony receives power from the Logos to become a hermit, achieves emptying through resisting temptations in the form of the often-painted beasts and grotesques, and rejects an Arianism that seeks to deny his knowledge of Christ as the eternal Logos and Wisdom. After Antony has rejected the Arian's Christology, he receives the power to overthrow the Arian ruler, Balacius, and to reject Greek philosophy (philo-Sophia) because it concentrates on arguments rather than on healing acts. What Augustine learns from this story and from Ponticianus's acquaintances' appropriation of it reverses what he does with the Dido text and directs us to how we are to read biographical texts, including Augustine's own.[41]

The first model reading comes from Ponticianus's friends, who read Antony's life in a house near a garden at Treves (significantly, the emperor is in his circus nearby). As Ponticianus's friend hears the story, he agonizes over his own sins. His agony, in turn, moves Ponticianus's other friend to change his way of life by tearing himself from the emperor's service and palace to follow St. Antony's example and live in a hut (8.6). (The *Confessions* use the phrase "novae vitae" to describe the second friend's choice of a new vocation – the precise Latin equivalent of the phrase "vita nuova" later used by Dante to name the text describing his renewal.)[42] As a picture of the achievement of a vita nuova, Antony's monastic asceticism becomes a metaphorical rather than a literal exemplum for Ponticianus's friends, who do not go to the desert to become saints but learn quite different withdrawals: the denial of Roman imperial culture and the achievement of asceticism in the active life.[43]

The two friends' vita nuova, in turn, shapes Augustine's life.[44] As the friends recognize that they must abandon Roman imperial authority and rhetorical persuasion to search for cosmic truth (labor at the emperor's court can only win them the emperor's friendship, while labor for God can earn them the respect of God [8.6]), Augustine recognizes that he too must change. He (or grace) reconstructs the St. Antony plot in his own life in a tripartite sequence that gives the biblical words a reference in his own life, a determinate semantic value and a definitive meaning for the direction of his life.

First, after he hears Ponticianus's story, Augustine goes apart with Alypius in the *secretum*, or solitude, of his garden – to *his own* garden: the reverse of the alien neighbor's place from which he stole pears as a youth. (The "Tolle, lege" garden also recalls the garden where Ponticianus's friends walked and turned their lives round near the circus.)[45] In the *secretum* of the garden, bound by the metaphorical chains created by his previous habits, he twists around, unable to will what he wishes to will and tears his own body apart as if he were a woman in labor or a person dying (8.8). He then implicitly reimagines Ponticianus's friends wavering between the palace and the hut (or Antony's choices between the beasts and Christ)[46] in the form of his own hesitation between his pleading mistresses and a Continence who offers him her joys in the form of "children" given to her by Christ, the Spouse (8.11).[47] Augustine's mistresses imply sexual attachments but also his "carnal" or "temporal" service to the Roman state's traditions of rhetoric and law while he keeps his philosophic, Christian musings secret (8.6; 8.11).[48] When Continence chooses Augustine and he accepts her, he makes a sexual, a political, and a vocational choice.[49]

Second, Augustine leaves the company of Alypius and goes off by himself to achieve more solitude in the garden – to "read" the texts important to him by beginning to live them. For Augustine, genuine reading is always living. In going off alone, Augustine imitates St. Antony's going to the desert. By standing under a fig tree, the saint-in-process also imitates the Nathaniel of John 1.48 who is about to hear John's Logos. Under the fig tree, Augustine has an enigmatic sensory experience with words when he hears a sing-song voice chanting like a child and does not know whether he hears the voice of a boy or a girl or something else. He knows that the voice is not singing a song usual to a child in a game (8.12). Implicitly, it is as if Continence's children sing, perhaps in the house next door or perhaps as a transcendent voice, in the same way that the Logos speaks both outside and inside of Gregory.[50] Augustine now plays a child-like game with eternity. Something having authority over him seems to chant a command to do a *sortes Virgilianae* with the scripture: "Tolle, lege." And this childlike voice, pointing to the biblical Logos and singing in dialogue with Augustine's old self, celebrates a new life coming to birth in Augustine, a birth like that which came to Ponticianus's friend in the Treves garden earlier. The child sings – uses the discipline of numbered music – to draw forth the new Augustine and to suggest the importance of the number disciplines in the redemptive process both before and after the scene.

Third, in response to the voice, Augustine returns his imagination to St. Antony's appropriation of a passage from Matthew heard in a public gospel reading. Imitating Antony and seeking his own special biblical passage, he goes to the gaming place where Ponticianus had earlier noted a Bible, finds the Bible open to Romans 13.13–14, and reads the determining words: "not in rioting and drunkenness, not in lust and impureness, not in quarreling and jealousy; instead, make the Lord Jesus Christ your armor and do not seek to satiate your natural concupiscence." The passage has, for Augustine, no ambiguity, no deferred meaning, and he wills to surrender immediately to a reconstituted self both because of grace and experience, miracle and exemplum (8.12). At the moment when he begins to empty himself of his old fantasies (whether incontinence, Manichaeanism, or rhetoric) the scriptural words he reads become flesh in his flesh – in his subsequent conduct.[51]

The structures of two reimagined events spoken to him orally – Ponticianus's friends' encounters with St. Antony in the garden and St. Antony's with the scripture – lead Augustine to reenact the Antony story as his imagination captures it: to place his imagination, his reading of a written text, under a mandate that he has not heard definitively to this point. Nothing indeterminate appears in the reading. No strong misreading, no assertion of the ego. No turning from text to text. The crucial relationship is life to life. Hearing of Antony, Augustine has to go apart, to become a solitary, to read a definitive text. Responding to the "Tolle, lege," Augustine's will now allows him to choose the new life, the innocent aborning in him manifested in the written text from Romans and the child that sings inside or outside him. Augustine chooses the child rather than the tearful man who is the other part of his self, the codger that prepares a sacrifice of tears while wondering whether God will be forever angry with him. He sacrifices a self for another self. As he says later (repeating this kind of experience when he resigns his professorship of rhetoric): "There where I was angry within, in my own resting place where I was wounded, there I made sacrifice, slaying my old self, and there where upheld by my hope in you, I thought upon the renewing of my life, there it was that you began to sweeten in me and gave joy to my heart" (9.4).

Pain often acts as a Pauline or Origenian defining power to force Augustine to empty himself so that he can see the significance of a text or an event. It does so with increasing ferocity as the book proceeds. In the earlier sections of the *Confessions,* the narrator-Augustine, from the perspective of later experience, sees how an implicit providential "syntax" has governed his life: how undeserved school punishment that forced him to study what he hated justly punished him for worse faults (1.12), how the hateful compulsion in the grammatical and rhetorical schools that sprang from evil in the schoolmasters bore holy fruit in his preparation for his vocation (1.12), and how the death of his friend after his deathbed baptism and apparent recovery created in him a grief that became an intuitive prayer (4.4–13). As Karl Morrison has reminded me, Augustine, at every juncture where he receives enlightenment, first "falls ill or endures disabling pain."[52] Eventually the message of all this suffering comes home when Augustine has a toothache that makes him experience a trivial imitation of the Word's resurrection.[53] As the pain becomes harsher, its redemptive power becomes greater so that this toothache "emptying," coming after the "Tolle, lege," almost kills him and becomes the occasion of his baptism. Augustine's ruined flesh literally struggles with the Logos that grants health, and the sick man can accept baptism only after suffering pain so severe that he loses all use of the spoken word and has to depend on others' prayers inspired by his writing a message to them. Augustine by this time seems to prefer writing – texts – to speech, contrary to Derrida's sense of philosophy's general trend.[54] The toothache is a "word" that reminds Augustine that his nature is ruined, and this word, in turn, inspires other words that lead to his choosing a baptism, a second birth or resurrection that sets him on a definitive course ("renasci": 9.6).

At the same time, Augustine's fifteen-year-old son, Adeodatus, is baptized with him. Adeodatus enters into dialogue with Augustine almost immediately thereafter to form the conversations basic to the *De Magistro*. This dialogue is Augustine's first "Christian" dialogue, a fundamental treatment of the notion that all genuine education comes when Truth (the Logos) is allowed to work in the inward person.[55]

Pain teaches Augustine the limitations of the self and tells him of real teaching that immerses the self in the external world. Augustine has to experience pain to see the limitations of Roman culture and to understand that the Logos that created the universe sets rules beyond culture and speaks with words that are written in the heavens. On the intellectual level, Augustine begins to move from the phantasmata of the rhetoricians to the pursuit of a more objective wisdom when he reads the *Hortensius* by Cicero, a rhetorician but also a philosopher (3.4). There he finds a paean to the pursuit of Wisdom and of the eternal rather than the culturally determined.[56] He returns to this pursuit of the Logos later when he seriously studies the Neoplatonists (7.9) and learns that the Word was in the beginning, that He was with God and was God, that He made all things through the light shining in the darkness, and so forth. Unfortunately, the Neoplatonist power and Wisdom of God has not known pain, has not emptied Himself. The Neoplatonists could not teach Augustine the meaning of pain or the message of Antony's life, the meaning of 1 Corinthians 1.24. They could not communicate what Augustine learns in the "Tolle, lege" garden (7.9).[57] But after pain has opened Augustine to the world beyond myth and outside himself, he is ready to seek a more objective knowledge.

AUGUSTINE AND WISDOM: THE JOURNEY TO OSTIA

If the Antony-Ponticianus material and like episodes tell how pain empties one of an old sensory, imaginative, and self-willed self, the more explicitly philosophic "Wisdom and number" texts in the *Confessions* tell how Wisdom fills a self destroyed by pain with a new life, a new rationality, a word that has meaning. The early sections of the *Confessions* show Augustine falling away from Wisdom and number, and the middle sections see him recovering them as he reaches through pain, study, and grace for a selfhood that conforms to Wisdom's design. The final sections, through an exegesis of Genesis, celebrate Wisdom's design as a model for human conduct.

Augustine often mentions the basic Wisdom texts in the *Confessions* and his other work. What he means by the concept of Wisdom gives much of the *Confessions* its structure. Augustine's Wisdom represents the law of the universe that created all things,[58] and human reason or human wisdom contains the seeds of the same knowledge.[59] The *Confessions* apostrophize Wisdom and the Logos from the beginning to the end. For instance, their first address to God calls him the God of power and of Wisdom beyond number in 1.1. In 1.10, Augustine calls on God as the creator of natural things (Wisdom is his Creator), and in book 3.4, he tells how philosophy as the love of Wisdom attracted him and exclaims that Wisdom is God's (cf. Job 12.13). In 3.6, Augustine describes himself as following that meretricious rival of Lady Wisdom from Proverbs 9.17, who merchandises the "stolen waters" that are sweetest and the "breads" good to eat because no one sees. Under the parallel Logos terminology, he says in 4.11 that the Logos appeals to his soul to return to it, and in 5.3, he notes how the inscrutable Wisdom of God (Ps. 146.5), the Logos, appears as a foil for the foolishness of the misguided mathematicians or astrologers. In 7.9, he tells how the Logos became apparent to him when he read in the Platonist books of the Wisdom that visits other souls and of the power of the Logos independent of Christ's suffering.

In some cases the imagery of light associated with the Logos in John 1 dominates. In 5.4 Augustine sees the intellectual light of the Logos (John 1.9–12), and in 9.10 he experiences the culminating Ostia vision that images the life of Wisdom. Finally, in books 12 and 13, he meditates on the creation to examine the nature of Wisdom, number, and proportion and their implications for human conduct in the active life.[60] These references, however, do not operate, as Bloom's theory would have it, only in intertextual structures, but become part of the tissue of Augustine's life.

Though Augustine was no great mathematician,[61] he knew the mathematical disciplines and the Neoplatonic ideas that went with them well enough to believe that they gave one access to the Logos, enabling one to see the vision of true reality that the soul "enjoyed in its preexistent state."[62] Augustine's search for mathematical regularities constitutes part of his search for a certitude that extends beyond the flux of experience emphasized by contemporary poststructuralism. Hence, for Plato's memory of preexistence, Augustine substitutes a remembrance of past divine actions in Wisdom's creation of things and of experienced providential actions that call people back to their divine origins.[63] When the hero of the *Confessions* falls, he does not plunge into the evil matter of Platonic or Manichaean belief but attaches himself to specific temporal things and self-indulgent myths that substitute for ultimate goods (e.g., the mistresses or the position of rhetorician achieve a godlike power in Augustine's life). In falling, the hero submits to the language of myth and phantasy; he abandons his sense of the sacredness of the creation's general design and measured love in order to hoard a few of its fragments.[64] Consequently, the hero's rise requires a study of Wisdom's texts and of Wisdom's designs in the world of number, measure, and weight – a study that replaces his study of Roman poetry's imaginary or rhetorical phantasms. These Wisdom texts and experiences make his confessed life move through grace from phantasy to reality, from unmeasured to measured, from private pleasure to joy in cosmic measure.[65]

Augustine gives to Wisdom's manifestations a local habitation and a name when he attaches features to Monica that he or the scriptures also attach to Sophia, the mother of creation.[66] In describing his infancy, Augustine mentions the milk provided to him by God through the breasts of Monica and his nurse (1.5). He then asserts that the Word became flesh so that Wisdom might provide milk for his spiritual infancy (7.18). Monica's quotidian activities make her function for Augustine as the Lady Wisdom functions for Israel: her piety and prudence permit her to escape the pagan captivity of her marriage; her willingness to call out when no one hears makes her Wisdom to Augustine as does her opposition to the folly-like women of Babylon-Carthage (cf. Prov. 7–9; *Confessions* 3.1–11; 6.11–16). When Monica sees her dream of Augustine's conversion – a vision of herself standing on a wooden ruler and weeping until she learns from a luminous youth that Augustine will stand where she is (3.11) – the dream measuring stick suggests the measures which God and Wisdom use in forming the world (Prov. 8.23–35): the rule of number with which Wisdom surveys and orders the universe (Eccles. 7.26; Wisdom 7.25ff.).[67] Monica possesses a learning that permits her to participate in the Wisdom discussions at Cassiciacum and in the meditation at Ostia, where she and Augustine see the law-bound, symmetrical, and mathematical order in the heavens that is otherwise described in Wisdom 7.18–20 (cf. Wisdom 7.22ff.; *Confessions* 9.10). It is not accidental that, after Augustine leaves Monica in book 5, he falls into deep intellectual difficulties at Rome, or that, when he is reunited with her at Milan (6.1), he begins to achieve clarity. It is through Monica as metaphor that Augustine has a glimpse of how a definitive Wisdom or Word functions and directs him.

As part of Augustine's growth toward Monica and Wisdom, the *Confessions* present Augustine's deepening suffering at the hands of his own desire, at the hands of his rhetorical students, in the presence of ideas that he can neither accept nor reject, and, most importantly, at the hands of his own body. At the outset of the *Confessions,* Augustine speaks to God as a power and a Wisdom beyond number ("You are great, O God, and to be praised greatly; your power is great and your Wisdom beyond number"),[68] reminding the reader of the crucifixion implied in knowing Wisdom and recalling the Pauline passage about the Wisdom and power of God from 1 Corinthians 1.24: "[Y]our power is great and your wisdom goes beyond number." As Augustine makes clear in *De Genesi ad Litteram,* his God extends beyond number in the creation – perhaps in the same way that the One, in Neoplatonic thought, surmounts efforts to know it. But Augustine's God is also the author of number and can be approached through it in some measure.[69] The God/Wisdom of this beginning passage creates the seeds of things, Augustine's equivalent of the Platonic archetypes, filling all things as if they were His vessels ("vasa": 1.3). He overflows and stabilizes things in the cosmos. Hence, He is approached through number, "is Number."[70] (*De Genesi ad Litteram* argues that in Him are to be found the number that gives number to all created things, the measure that gives measure to them, and the weight that gives them weight.)[71] When at the beginning of the *Confessions* (1.1–5) Augustine apostrophizes Christ as power and Wisdom, he fuses the invulnerable cosmic Wisdom with the suffering Pauline Wisdom that produces "fear and trembling," like that to be found in the "Tolle, lege" garden, and he appropriates to himself, as a model, a God who is both absolute and vulnerable. Through these allusions, he prepares us to see the Wisdom that is both the cosmic perfective force found at Ostia and the exemplar of the crucifixion-emptying that occurs in the "Tolle, lege" garden.

In seeing Wisdom as that which fills all things if allowed, Augustine is the obverse of Quintilian's student as empty vessel.[72] Augustine is full of real experiences, words, and numbers that can lead him to the ultimate, so long as he allows himself to be led. He requires emptying by pain only when he fills himself with a self-determined ego. A variant of this empty-ing-filling metaphor is the ruin-restoration architectural metaphor that relates to Augustine's conception of Wisdom-as-design. He employs, in his references to John 1, the same architectural metaphor for the struc-ture of the creation that Origen had used earlier in explaining John 1, and that he was later to use in his treatise on John. In using this metaphor in the *Confessions*, Augustine describes himself – his fallen self – as a ruin: "ruinosa" (1.5). Since his gloss on John 1 and Origen's similar gloss both assume that the Logos's designs for the universe resemble an architect's drawing for a building,[73] a person who departed from the divine plan would obviously collapse into a ruin that shows only obscure traces of its original design. In reforming the ruin, education and Wisdom restore a dilapidated temple according to its first scale drawings.

Augustine falls from comeliness to ruin in his relation to the Forms by the process of suggestion, delight, and consent that, in his other writings, he uses to describe the Fall.[74] The fall that he experiences begins with trivial suggestions, perhaps an unconscious envy at the pleasure in feed-ing of other infants (1.7). It continues in the delight stage that Augustine centers in his fantasies, not only in his sexual fantasies but in his indul-gence in fantasies derived from texts: false rhetoric and false literary fictions. It ends in malicious actions directed against a sacred creation, such as his destruction of the pears in another man's garden, interpreted as a defiling with unchaste love (2.6). In describing the second stage of this process, Augustine defines the limiting functions of the rhetoric and poetry that separated him from the world of objects or reference by cataloguing his childish attraction to the phantasmata provided by con-ventional Roman society – his indulgence in false stories ("falsis fabellis": 1.10), in epic or tragic tales such as those of Dido ("poetica figmenta":

1.13),[75] in theatrical shows reflecting his own internal disorder ("spectacula theatrica plena imaginibus miseriarum mearum": 3.2), and, later, in the theological fictions of the Manichee ("phantasmata splendida": 3.6).[76] Such fantasies, like the fictions of the poets in Plato, have no real-world reference.

At this stage, Augustine's imagination holds surrogate goods in view because the Roman grammatical and rhetorical schools have subjected him to texts that mediate pagan fantasies and bad morals, inspiring a self-centered materialism.[77] The temple-like curtains of the Roman rhetorical schools, by covering the idols of literary education, conceal the truth. The teachers in these rhetorical schools gag-feed him with what he has no wish to learn while starving him with rhetorical and poetic chaff (1.13), saccharine fictions (e.g., Terence's story of Jove showering himself into the lap of Danae [1.16]) that incite students to a perverse mimesis that recreates God in the human image.[78] These schools make even mathematics dwindle to a disgusting chanting of memorized numbers (1.13), ignoring the astronomical and cosmic realities that Augustine learns when he studies mathematics on his own. The texts taught in the schools of the Roman *grammaticus* and *rhetor,* ostensibly protecting the student from real evils, seduce him both to love fictions and lies and to make fictions and lies in the form of law court fictions (3.3; 4.1; 4.16; 9.2). If Augustine's early school life justifies Plato's loathing of the rhetoricians and poets, his mature encounters with such rhetoricians as Faustus and Hierus confirm this loathing; he discovers that they too are liars.[79] Essentially, Augustine's intellectual redemption requires that pain break through the fantasies of his myth-filled imagination and that he discover an accurate knowledge supplanting the schoolboy fictions that have governed his early life.

Augustine's alternative is an education that flows out of real experience and is controlled by no bureaucracy, an education leading to the apprehension of real objects, number, and the power of beauty. Such an education cannot depend on the human pedagogue, as Augustine makes clear in *De Magistro.* While Gregory Thaumaturgos sees Origen as the vehicle of the Logos, Augustine rarely assumes that one learns through a human teacher. In the process of education, a Logos (or truth) speaks within one while the external Logos speaks to one through the beauty and number of the universe. The psychology is developmental and dependent on experience. As Augustine asserts in his "De Octo Dulcitii Quæstionibus," his universe woos one away from sensory infatuation and false imaginings, so that one loves the "sweetness of a truth" that resides in the discovery of order, beauty, design, and system in the creation.[80] As something in us loves design, so also something in the external world responds as we seek the trace that can reshape our ruined self and bring it back to beauty.[81] James McEvoy has demonstrated that Augustine generally interprets Wisdom's "measure, number, and weight" to mean "measure, number, and order," or "being, species, and order," or "quiddity, species, and order," the syllables that speak of the definitive Logos. Augustine understands each entity to have its own unique wholeness and limits, relation to its own species and to the other species, and weight or place in the general order.[82] Each entity, therefore, deserves a love modulated to its reflection of the highest love created by the God who assigns a specific measure, number, and weight to created beings (Augustine could well have written the script for Dante's song of love for the leaves of the garden and the proportioned love that God has shed on them).[83] In the *Confessions* as elsewhere in Augustine (and echoing a concept going back to Plato's notion that mathematical "measure" in love constitutes an objective alternative to the subjectivist's and rhetorician's limitless love of pleasure and power), each thing fits in as part of an ordered syntax of things analogous to the syntax of language. Understanding each thing requires discipline-based learning.[84] Thus, while Augustine rejects the schools, he does not reject the academic disciplines or the liberal arts.

But Augustine's disciplinary ascent always requires both grace and learning for experience to be productive.[85] *De Ordine,* somewhat in the manner of Origen, speaks of a perfective disciplinary ascent that climbs from (1) language (grammar, rhetoric, and dialectic); to (2) music, poetics, geometry, and astronomy; to (3) the thought and contemplation of the Author of things, the soul, and unity itself.[86] The later *De Civitate Dei* (A.D. 426) sets forth a similar perfective scheme. There Augustine says that Plato converted the Socratic active life disciplines and the Pythagorean contemplative or scientific ones into three basic disciplines relating to God. The Socratic discipline is ethics, which studies the nature of the good or beatitude. The Pythagorean discipline is natural philosophy, which regards God as the cause of the cosmos. The third discipline, rational philosophy or logic, distinguishes truth from falsehood, things discerned by the mind from things discerned by the senses.[87] Rhetoric has no place in the later scheme. Both *De Ordine* and *De Civitate Dei* accept an ascent that includes (1) a correct study of language and ethics;[88] (2) a continuation in the mathematical disciplines and natural philosophy; and (3) a culmination in theology and metaphysics.[89] This three-stage scheme moving toward the Logos also constitutes the ascent that counters Augustine's fall into ruin in the *Confessions*.[90] Pushed by his own problems and without a human teacher, he ascends from misdirected or "ruined" verbal learning and action in the early books to study of the Logos and ethics (i.e., reading the *Hortensius*); he goes on to the study of dialectic, the mathematical disciplines (4.16), and a natural philosophy that leads to Wisdom or Christ-the-Logos in the middle books (5.3). Finally, he moves upward to theology and to the full enjoyment of God at Ostia and after.

Though Cicero and the Neoplatonists direct Augustine beyond language and rhetoric to natural philosophy and number studies, he does not at first understand how to use them. He reads and believes the astrologers or false mathematicians (4.3). At about the same time, he writes his first treatise, the Manichaean *On Beauty and Proportion* (ironically, to attract the attention of an orator). Though we know nothing about this work, it was probably Augustine's first excursus into mathematical or number-based aesthetic theory (4.13–14).[91] Later without a teacher he studies geometry, music, and arithmetic and some of the verbal disciplines (4.16),[92] and he investigates the philosophers' accuracy in predicting eclipses:

They have discovered much and forecast eclipses of the sun and the moon years in advance of their happening – the day, the hour, whether complete or partial. And their calculations were found to be correct because things happened as they had anticipated. They wrote down the rules discovered in their researches, and their books are still read today and used to predict the year, the month, the day and the hour of the day of eclipses of the sun and the moon. (5.3)

The study of the philosophic astronomers becomes the basis of Augustine's rejection of the Manichee. He does not reject Manichaeism because he expects Faustus, as a Manichaean, to assign a "meaning" to the natural regularities, as Radding suggests in *A World Made by Men*.[93] He finally rejects the religion because Faustus's explanation of heavenly phe-

nomena is a prescientific series of fictions and not a rule-governed, pre-
dictive set of mathematical calculations concerning the movement of the
heavens (5.7). He is looking for a definitive, accurate word that will
define the Word that constructed things and that can provide a model for
his life. For Augustine, truth must satisfy the whole self. As Augustine's
experience of suffering leads him to reject the Platonists on the affective
grounds that they lack humility and love, his mathematical learning leads
him to reject Faustus on the intellectual grounds that he is ignorant of
the liberal arts, scientific astronomy, and Wisdom (5.3; 5.5).

Contrary to Radding, Augustine has a high appreciation for the discovery of natural law and the formal operational thinking that goes into a
discipline like astronomy. However, like Origen, he also cares about one's
attitude toward the sacredness of the creation. A person who has a tree
and thanks God for it is better off than a person who knows the tree's
measurements and does not give thanks; a person who does not know the
measurement of the sky and honors the Creator is better off than one who
measures the sky and does not acknowledge that God gave to all things
their "measure, number and weight" (5.4). To both know and give thanks
is best. In Augustine, the whole person – reason, will, imagination, and
senses – turns toward the new life. In consequence, as Augustine-the-
pilgrim moves toward the apprehension of number, Augustine-the-narra-
tor's prose moves toward a more ordered feel; the pear tree scene, with its
jerky prosody (2.4), bears little comparison to the hymn to creation, with
its metrical order (7.13). In beautifully ordered Latin, Augustine calls in
that hymn on all the forces mentioned in Psalm 148 – fire, hail, snow, mist,
flora, fauna, and all conditions and cultures of people – to praise God:

> For you there is no evil, and not only for you but for the entire creation, because
> beyond you there is nothing that could break in and spoil the order that you have
> imposed on it. . . . And all of those things that are not mutually fitted to each other
> are fitted to the lower part of the creation that we call earth, which has its own sky,
> cloudy and windy, fitted to it. For the things of the earth give praise to you – sea
> reptiles and all of the deeps, fire, hail, snow, ice, and the spirit of the storm that acts
> on your word, the mountains and all of the hills, the fruit trees and all of the cedars,
> wild beasts and all of the cattle, creeping things and feathered flying things.[94]

When Augustine rejects the phantasies of the Manichaean world that
regard material reality as evil, his use of words and Biblical references

becomes insistent. The Augustine who is a student of nature and Wisdom reaches an inner utopia; he "no longer desire[s] a better world" because he thinks of the whole of this one (7.13). In passage after passage in the later books of the *Confessions,* the symmetry and clausal balance of the syntax of praise enact this sense of mathematical form apprehended in a better world, of natural relationships perceived and systems understood. This perception of Wisdom in the mathematical and musical – the prosodic – order of nature permits Augustine to prepare for the order of the Ostia vision.

If the "Tolle, lege" is the central episode in Augustine's emptying, the Ostia episode, which O'Donnell links to 7.13,[95] is the center of his filling with a determinate and determinative Word. While his emptying comes in his own garden as he hears the metrically ordered song, "Tolle, lege," his filling, his brief experience of enlightenment, comes beside a garden at Ostia with Monica. Five days after the quasi-hypothetical beatific ascent at Ostia, Monica dies. At her death, Augustine praises the Creator with Ambrose's "Deus Creator Omnium"; he is now able to praise the Creator in his own right. Monica's presence in the Ostia scene as a kind of lower Sophia makes her function as Augustine's companion on the ascent to Wisdom, a guide and friend who has many successors – Lady Philosophy, Beatrice, and Petrarch's Truth, among others. The visionary flight to Wisdom in book 9, section 10 culminates the ascent that Augustine experiences in books 5 through 9, after he has moved from Cicero to the Neoplatonists to the Johannine Christ, from rhetoric to mathematics, from Carthage to Milan.[96]

At the beginning of the Ostia ascent, Monica and Augustine stand alone at a window, looking out over yet another garden, which is neither the pear-tree garden nor the "Tolle, lege" one. They converse about physical light – physics – and the bodily pleasures it illumines; they talk of the transcendent equivalent of this pleasure, the joy of the life of the saints, and speak together of their corporeal pleasure in the sun, moon, and stars – a kind of astronomical excursus. Then, passing from material to spiritual in their talk, they come to their own souls. Having come to themselves, "to know themselves" in Gregory Thaumaturgos's terms, they are empowered to pass, panting with intellectual thirst, to touch momentarily that uncreated Wisdom through whom all past, present, and future things are made in an eternal present. Monica and Augustine

speak finite words about the infinite Word or Wisdom that they momentarily touch. As they do so, they are able to imagine how the phantasmata
that have disturbed Augustine from his childhood in the Roman schools
could fall permanently silent:[97]

If for anyone the tumult of the flesh should be silent, silent the phantasies of
earth and water and air, silent the poles and silent the soul itself to itself, no
longer thinking of itself, if all dreams and imagined revealings should fall silent,
silent every tongue and every sign and every transient thing (since should any
persons hear them, they would hear them say "We did not create ourselves but He
made us who abides forever"), if having uttered this, they too should fall silent (as
if directing our ears to hear Him), and if He should speak directly to us, not
through them but speak Himself, not by a fleshly tongue or an angelic voice or
thunder from a cloud or through enigmas and similitudes, if He should speak so
that we might hear Him whom we love in his creatures (as he just did when we
strained ourselves up to such a Word and came, in quick thought, up to that eternal Wisdom which is over all), and if hearing as we have just heard, we could have
continued this vision so that all other far inferior visions were removed, and this
one alone ravished, swallowed and enwrapped us in its inward joys, so that our life
might everlastingly be like that which we have just had and now sigh for: would not
that be to us the call, "Enter thou into the joy of thy Lord?" (*Confessions* 9.10)[98]

This would-be ascent undoes the stages of suggestion, delight, and
consent in Augustine's youthful fall. It undoes the mistaken suggestions
of the senses and makes them fall silent; it stops the delightful imagining of temporal goods as gods, the phantasmata of natural things posing as autonomous "deities" and of subjectively created dreams and visions. The flight renders even the books of nature and supernature silent
("every tongue and every sign and every transient thing" and "angelic
voice[s] or thunder from a cloud or . . . enigmas and similitudes"). As
grace and pain have undone Augustine's old self with all of its culturally
controlled imagining of things, he can now see himself potentially rap-
tured upward with Monica, until he hears the Logos speak in Himself:
"And He should speak alone not through these things but by Himself
so that we would hear His word" (9.10). For Augustine at his center
no indeterminate words speak but the Word that is the very structure
of creation. This may define the difference between Augustine's will to
create new and determinate institutions of education as the Roman ones

crumble, and the poststructuralist's desire to create an emptiness beyond the forces of hegemony. Augustine is a thinker for whom the meaning of life appears in a surrender to the creation and Creator. Modern post-structuralism finds its meaning in the dissipation of other meanings, in the very indeterminacy of words: it makes this indeterminacy the center of its educational project.

THE LAST BOOKS OF THE *CONFESSIONS*

After Ostia, Augustine presents what he has learned as an example of how the human species learns. He looks not just at his own memory, as Proust does, but at memory-in-general, where events speak as words.[99] He looks at how events are remembered, how the liberal arts enter into memory (10.9–12), how mathematics is recalled, and how sensory life relates to the structured, remembered life of Wisdom and number (10.30–39). God becomes for him the beauty at the beginning and end of his memory (10.27), a kind of cosmic memory bank.[100]

In the last three books of the *Confessions,* as Augustine almost disappears as the subject of his own narration, the Creator and creation – Wisdom and her works – replace him as the central subjects. Book 11 describes the theology of the relationship between God the Father and the Logos-Wisdom through whom things were created in discourse comparable to that found in Augustine's *Treatise on John.* Book 12 deals with the relationship between uncreated Wisdom or the Word and the created wisdom that is embodied in the visible world. Book 13 represents a summation of praise, returning, as does the *Republic,* to the work of the active life. It also illustrates, as Karl Morrison has reminded me, "the multiplicity of possible interpretations in normal verbal discourse and the inexhaustibility of scripture."[101] It does not do so by displaying the indeterminacy of the scriptural text but by showing that all interpretations point to one grand interpretation that must be imbedded in action, by showing how God's acts of creation continue in human acts of love (i.e., allegorically, the actions of the Logos continue in merciful acts by human beings). Earth's fullness in bringing forth seed becomes mercy to the needy. The lights of the firmament become enlightened provision for the naked and hungry. The greening of the earth itself becomes an act of complete generosity like that urged on the rich young ruler. And, to return to the spoiler beast, mankind's dominion over the creatures implies a requisite stewardship of them and of fellow human beings. The choir of great creating nature provides a logic for charity – Wisdom emptying itself. The end is a recapitulation of the themes of rest (1.13–37) and the holiness of the creation (13.37–38). Here Augustine writes as a bishop and social critic, implicitly calling attention to how human beings fail to care for each other and the world around them. This book tells us that learning the order of the cosmos, losing the self in the other, and the contemplation of Wisdom should lead to a more loving and civilized society.

4

Reading the *Confessions:*
Boethius, Aelred, Dante, and Petrarch

The *Confessions* were not the most popular of Augustine's works in the middle ages. However, some medieval authors read them and attributed to them their capacity to find a definitive "word" or direction for themselves and a respect for the natural world. The most important of these authors are Boethius, Aelred of Rievaulx, Dante, and Petrarch. Their responses to Augustine are one test of this book's understanding of how patristic and medieval people read a text to find self-definition and meaning. It is as if they shaped their lives to conform to the model (or text) of an earlier life that claimed to have touched Wisdom as the model of models.

Though some readers see Augustine as anticipating the repressive tendencies that, in their opinion, have unsettled our culture for fifteen hundred years,[1] his first readers did not see him so. The more ascetic and materially unstable climate of the years that followed the demise of Rome encouraged intellectuals to seek for themselves the detachment from material circumstances, the intellectual freedom, and the authenticity that they found in Augustine's life. Boethius in *De Consolatione*, Aelred of Rievaulx in *De Spirituali Amicitia*, Dante in the *Vita Nuova, Convito*, and *Commedia*, and Petrarch in the *Secretum*[2] see Augustine as a representation of what they should become. They do not interest themselves in Augustine the bishop, Augustine the heresy-hunter, or Augustine the predestinarian. The Augustine of the *Confessions* allows each to work out his individuality in a pattern that facilitates his traveling a part or all of the journey to Wisdom. Each, like Augustine, first experiences one or more destructive loves. Then each begins to turn in a new direction with a reading of

Cicero, Augustine, or philosophy; after that turning, each begins an ascent through the natural system to God.[3] Like Augustine, none of the four receives his primary intellectual impetus from a school but from the pain of his frustration with a love gone wrong; each avoids any assertion of superiority to Augustine while *reading* him by living a life given over to his ascent.[4] Augustine's life works on each as a literary paradigm and representation of transformation, as St. Anthony's life worked on Augustine. That is, Augustine-as-pattern works for them in a fashion different from the putative working of modern intertextuality. In contemporary critical theory that speaks to issues of literature and education, the flow of language goes from text to text.[5] In the medieval emulators of Augustine, on the other hand, the flow goes from Augustine's life to his autobiographical text to the lives of readers touched by him and then to their new autobiographical texts. Medieval lives are an embodied Logos. To put the matter another way: if, as Harold Bloom argues, romantic and postromantic subcreation claims a transcendent vision that reaches higher than that of a previous writer who has been misread and partially subverted, medieval subcreation imitating Augustine stresses the humility of the writer imitating him and claims only the hem of the garment of the *Confessions*.

Augustine acts as a pattern in different ways for each of the writers mentioned, even as Antony acts in one way on Ponticianus's friends and another way on Augustine. Augustine's early imitators, Boethius and Aelred of Rievaulx, seem to use the *Confessions* as a pattern for their whole lives, while the later ones, Dante and Petrarch, focus on crucial turnings that make their lives like Augustine's. But all these writers' circumstances are quite different from Augustine's in the *Confessions:* Boethius writes after his imprisonment by Theoderic and in expectation of a fate similar to that of Socrates; Aelred of Rievaulx begins with the troubles of false friendship and the monastic life; Dante begins with the death of Beatrice and his exile; Petrarch, in the *Secretum,* takes one emptying episode from the *Confessions* – the "Tolle, lege" garden events – and displays what he must do if he, while working out his relationship with Laura and with his poetic vocation, is to achieve the discipline and fulfillment that Augustine achieved.

BOETHIUS'S IMITATION OF THE AUGUSTINIAN PATTERN

The first apparent effort to recreate the patterned life of Augustine's *Confessions* is *The Consolation of Philosophy,* written in a prison away from the schools of Theoderic's state, even away from libraries (A.D. 522–24?). The *Consolation* may not imitate the *Confessions* alone; it may also articulate the early and middle Augustine's general assumptions about education. Boethius appears to take the internal dialogue and the ascent through the disciplines from the works of the Cassiciacum Augustine and the *Confessions* and apply them to his troubles with Theoderic. Whether Boethius knew Augustine's *Confessions* directly or imitated them precisely does not really matter (though authoritative opinion is increasingly turning to the notions that he did both know and imitate them).[6] If Boethius knew the outlines of Augustine's early thought, knew his early dialogues, knew the Neoplatonic life-story of the fall into "matter" and the rebirth through learning and climbing the *gradus* of the disciplines, he knew enough.[7]

In the *Consolation,* the search is for a life-determining word. The *Consolation* alters Augustine's formula by reducing the autobiographical element, but it presents Boethius as (like Augustine) an intellectual too much in love with tragedy, as a *rhetor* late converted to *philosophia.*[8] The Boethius that appears in the work has lapsed from the high Platonic purpose that, before his political fall, led him to model his ministrations at the "emperor's court" on Theoderic's behalf after those of the philosopher-king in Plato's *Republic* (1.pr.4; *Republic* 6.497A–502C).[9] His forced removal from the Mastership of the Offices in Theoderic's Ravenna after he tried to support the liberties of the Senate is similar to Augustine's resignation from his rhetorical position in Milan. His "emptying" during his imprisonment by Theoderic turns him toward the conventional subjects of rhetorical study, the muses, even to an apparent effort to write a tragedy (1.m.1.). On the basis of this fall into "literature," Philosophy, as both the bearer of the Logos and as a disciplined, determinate use of language (cf. chapter 6), comes to drive out the muses in the same way that Cicero's *Hortensius,* with its love of Philo-sophia, comes to Augustine to drive him to reach beyond rhetoric through the higher disciplines (cf. chapter 3). The Epicureans, Stoics, and Platonists distort Philosophy's words as do the Manichaeans and Platonists in Augustine's work (1.pr.3), and the protagonist must surmount philosophic error by climbing to the truth that the cosmos announces through the Neoplatonic ladder of the disciplines (cf. chapter 6). When the autobiographical kernel found in books 1 and 2 metamorphoses into the Boethian Neoplatonic/Christian ascent of the later books (books 3–5; cf. chapter

6), Boethius recovers the ascent of the Platonic *Republic, Timaeus,* and *Parmenides* climb in a structure whose analysis is best left for later chapters. What is important here is that Boethius begins with Augustinian autobiography when he offers his life and possible martyrdom as a pattern for those seeking to learn, as Eliot writes in *Ash Wednesday,* "to care and not to care" about political power.

AUGUSTINE AND AELRED'S LIFE: HUMAN AND COSMIC FRIENDSHIP

In the autobiography placed at its beginning, Aelred of Rievaulx's *De Spirituali Amicitia* also modestly gestures toward an Augustinian definition of how education patterns itself. More than Boethius's autobiography, it tells how love may play a role in one's achieving a correct reading of things human and divine. Early in the work, Aelred desires nothing more than to love.[10] As a school lad torn between conflicting emotional attachments, he reads Cicero's *De Amicitia* as he sets out to find a friendship that will restrain him from misdirected loves. Like Augustine, he finds renewal in Cicero. His personal text is Cicero's *De Amicitia;* this Cicero leads to his discovery of natural beauty, which in turn leads to his absorption in Wisdom: all themes from the *Confessions.*[11] He then enters a monastery, where he discovers a spiritual friendship that surpasses Cicero's conventional amity. Thereafter, his life story becomes a part of a Cassiciacum-style dialogue, culminating in dialogue 1 with its hymn to cosmic Wisdom as the basis of friendship: "Let us begin with the world of things that cannot feel – what soil or river bears stones only of one kind? Or what forest bears only a single tree from a single genus? Thus, even in the insensible world a love of the social manifests itself, since none of these things exists by itself but everything comes into being and grows in company with its own variety."[12] The Word speaks to Aelred as the Word at Ostia speaks to Augustine. While the animals play with one another and show their mutual love by their sounds and motions, Divine Wisdom cherishes the angels by providing many of them to increase their mutual charity. Human friendship also reflects a measure in love directed to the choir of being: an avoidance of infinite commitment to finite being. At the end, Aelred's friendship with his second friend, like Augustine's with Monica, carries him on his ascent until he knows a full love of human differentiation, of the natural system, and of its Author.[13] *De Spirituali Amicitia* does not pretend to give a full account of Aelred's education; it turns away from school to the monastery for the purpose of recognizing the message of the objective natural order and differentiating its demands from those of the erotic self. *De Spirituali Amicitia*'s monastic education also somewhat institutionalizes Augustine's path by providing a teacher: one who is more friend than pedagogue, though its "curriculum" still goes at its own pace, and its journeyer deliberately undertakes suffering to find a world ordered by love (chapter 6 below gives a brief account of why the personalistic patristic pedagogical style may have carried over into the monasteries). In Aelred's world, the initiate studies and praises the Creator and the community of creation as the end of his quest.

No other great *Confessions*-like work aside from Aelred's emerges from the twelfth-century monasteries. Rather, such works come from thirteenth- and fourteenth-century laity, Dante and Petrarch, who do not try to reflect the total Augustinian pattern but individual *Confessions* episodes where the mode of Augustine turned the writers in a new direction.

THE FRAGMENTS OF THE *CONFESSIONS* IN DANTE'S JOURNEY

Dante sketches out the form of his reenactment of the *Confessions* in the *Convito* passage, where he cites Augustine's *Confessions* as a model for using his own name in his work and offers the observation that the *Confessions* tell of Augustine's progress from bad to good, better, and best. John Freccero cites this passage as the basis for his argument that the *Commedia* Dante lives in Augustine's image.[14] Freccero's Dante makes the *Commedia* into a fictive autobiography and puts his own name on Beatrice's lips (*Purgatorio* 30.55–65) because "Dante" must ascend – like Augustine. He is not some generic Everyman, and Freccero makes *Paradiso* 10.37–39, where Beatrice appears as the force that must conduct this Dante from good to better, reflect the technical vocabulary that the *Convito* uses to describe Augustine's progress.[15] To expand Freccero's argument: if the purgatorial to paradisal ascent, by following Augustine, goes from good to better, the end of the ascent, when Dante addresses the source of his pure vision as the "Somma Luce" – "Supreme Light" or "highest good" (33.67) – is Augustine's best. Shortly after, the best appears again in the beatific light:

> ... ['L] ben, ch'è del volere obietto,
> tutto s'accoglie in lei, e fuor di quella
> è defettivo ciò ch'è lì perfetto.
>
> (33.103–5)[16]

[. . . All the good that is the object of the will Gathers itself in it (i.e. supernatural light), and away from this All is defective that is perfected in it.]

Freccero's argument could be extended to suggest that Dante goes from bad to good in following Virgil and recognizing sin in the *Inferno* and purging it in the *Purgatorio;* that he goes from good to better in purging himself and following Beatrice in the *Purgatorio* and much of the *Paradiso;* and that he goes from better to best through much of the *Paradiso* journey, but especially when he follows Bernard to the beatific vision.[17] However, Dante follows Augustine's journey toward a definitive meaning in a spezzato fashion.

Dante tells the tale of his fall and return repeatedly – in *La Vita Nuova*, in the *Convito,* and in various ways in the *Commedia.* Augustine's three-stage picture of the perfective process implies, for Dante, a three-stage movement out of evil through three forms of reading the pre-Christian and Christian versions of the Logos: the first stage reads Cicero and Boethius in the *Convito* and Virgil in the *Commedia* and imitates Augustine's *Confessions* reading of Cicero's *Hortensius* and the Neoplatonists on the Logos; the second stage reads what Beatrice has to say and follows in the footsteps of Augustine's number studies inspired by Monica and Wisdom, studies leading to his gradual acknowledgement of the Christian Logos; and the third ends in the *Paradiso's* beatific vision and addresses Augustine's direct apprehension, at Ostia, of Wisdom (and, perhaps, his analytic examination of Wisdom's work in the creation in the last books of the *Confessions*).[18] Dante's scattered autobiography in *La Vita Nuova, Convito,* and *Commedia* bears the imprint of these three *Confessions* ascents, and Dante references parts of all three of his major works to Augustine (but in no linear way).

La Vita Nuova moves from bad to good by presenting us with an emptying through suffering that extends to a birth of hope. Its name may derive from the "novae vitae" that awakens in Ponticianus's friend at the time of his conversion (*Confessions* 8.6):[19] " 'And when shall this be? If, however, I wish to be the friend of God, behold I can be so now.' And trembling with the birthing of a *new life,* he returned his eyes to the pages . . . and he drew his mind away from the world" (italics mine).[20] Further counterparts to Dante's *vita nuova* story appear in Augustine's responses to the death of a friend, his hearing the child singing "Tolle, lege" as his old self dies, his reading of Romans 13.13, and the emptying that leads to his standing on

Monica's rule of faith (8.12). Beatrice's death becomes a turning point for Dante, just as the death of the friend in *Confessions* 4.4 becomes pivotal for Augustine.

> [E] quale è stata la mia vita, poscia
> che la mia donna andò nel secol novo,
> lingua non è che dicer lo sapesse.[21]

[And what is the situation of my life, since my lady has gone to the new world – There is no tongue that can speak an understanding of it.]

The newness that Dante experiences, coming after Beatrice's death, extends the salutation/salvation that she gave him in section 3 of the *Vita Nuova;* in the same way, Augustine's friend's conversion during his illness hints at Augustine's conversion during a similar illness.[22] Beatrice's greetings create the love that leads to the grand vision through which Dante's "intelligence" rises to her; Dante begins, through Beatrice's death and suffering, to understand the beatitude and newness ("intelligenza nova") of the eternal world.[23] But he also comes to understand a force comparable to what Augustine experiences in Monica, for both Augustine and Dante present us with women who minister to the sufferer and work at the center of things. The differences between these women come from autobiography but also from the varying biblical images for the Wisdom woman.[24] In Proverbs 8 and 9, Wisdom comes as a mother like Monica (Prov. 8.32ff.), but in Wisdom 7 and 8, she is the bride, resembling Beatrice in the lucidity and intelligence that reflects the divine. At the beginning of *La Vita Nuova*, Dante says that in his youth he often went in search of Beatrice,[25] as "Solomon" in Wisdom 8.2 says that he often in youth went in search of Wisdom and resolved to have her as his bride. Dante is to make this quester's Beatrice into the Beatrice of the *Commedia*, her radiant eyes and attractive mouth (*Purgatorio* 30) responding to the call, *Veni sponsa de libano*, "Come, O spouse, from Lebanon" (Canticle 4.8). Beatrice speaks a kind of Word, a kind of "Tolle, lege" to Dante in her reproach to him, and toward her the Old Testament figures turn as they circle away from the ever visible constellation in recognition of the truth of Wisdom 7.29's remark that Wisdom is above all the constellations of the stars (*Purgatorio* 30.1).[26] Beatrice's counterpart is explicitly called Wisdom in the *Convito* (cf. chapter 7).[27]

Dante makes the Beatrice of *La Vita Nuova*, as the image of Wisdom,

into an anamnesis – not just a person or a number but a re-calling of the
One that makes beatitude possible. She is the three times three that
reflects the ultimate source of the good; her death inspires Dante to call
on the folk who pass through Florence on a pilgrimage to the veronica to
weep over his loss of Beatrice as if she were another veronica on whom a
picture of the Logos/Christ emerges. As the sister to Wisdom and the
Logos, she, like Monica, comes to be associated with visionary geometric
forms. In describing Monica's vision, Augustine says:

She [Monica] saw that she was standing on a wooden ruler, and coming toward
her was a brightly clothed young man who smiled at her in joy although she
herself was sad. . . . When she replied that her tears were for the soul I [Augustine]
had lost, he told her that . . . if she looked carefully, she would see that where she
was, there also was I. And when she looked she saw me standing on the same
ruler.[28]

In what appears to be a parallel vision in *La Vita Nuova,* Dante says:

In the middle of my sleep, I seemed to behold in the room a youth, seated near
me, clothed in the whitest garments. . . . Looking at him, I beheld that he wept
bitterly and appeared to wait for me to speak. Whereupon taking courage, I
began thus: "Lord in your nobility, why do you weep?" And he replied with these
words: "I am the circle's center from which each part is equidistant. It is not so
with you." . . . Hereupon I began to question him in respect of the salutation
denied me.[29]

The wooden ruler in Monica's dream predicts that both Augustine and
Monica will know salvation in the same structure, perhaps the same structure of Wisdom and number. Similarly, the circle, the geometric form
outside whose center Dante is placed, reminds him that he is still denied
the *salus* of Beatrice's "salvation."[30] In Augustine's dream a geometric
form stills Monica's weeping, but in Dante's comparable dream a geometric figure prompts the angel's weeping because Dante is outside it.[31]

The *Convito* comes next. After paralleling Augustine's emptying and
suggesting his initial discovery of the good through a right use of language and number in *La Vita Nuova,* Dante reenacts the Augustinian
Hortensius experience in the *Convito* by progressing to a more explicit
understanding of the good or the creating Logos treated by Boethius in
the *Consolation* (see chapter 6). In the *Convito* (2.12), Dante says that

before he learned Latin and read Boethius and Cicero seriously, he had
used his mind ("ingegno") "come sognando" – as if dreaming (i.e.,
under the influence of the imaginative mode).[32] He now wishes to write
the *Convito* in the more "virile" mode appropriate to manhood as his
fourth treatise makes clear (though he still sees *La Vita Nuova* as a work
appropriate to youth). In the fourth treatise, youth (the age of growth,
beauty, sweetness, and a certain shyness) lasts until the age of twenty-five,
when manhood (the period when the reason expands and learns to
control the appetite) replaces it. Manhood lasts from twenty-five to forty-
five, and the apex and midpoint of life comes at thirty-five, when the
moral self hardens itself for such virile battles as Aeneas's descent into
Hades (Dante undertakes the same descent in the *Commedia*'s middle of
the journey of his life).[33] In this period, education and rationality reach
their zenith. It is, therefore, not surprising that the *Convito* is centrally a
work about education set in ratiocinative discourse. As the *Hortensius*
experience comes to Augustine after the death of his friend, so the *Convito* experience of Wisdom and the Logos comes to Dante after the suffering and death of Beatrice described in *La Vita Nuova,* and with a like
reading of Cicero.

The *Convito,* when asserting that Augustine presents his life as an educative example of the perfective progress, cites both Boethius and Augustine as precedents for its autobiographical mode. It further argues
that Dante presents himself as Augustine and Boethius do so that anyone
reading the *Convito*'s odes will see that they do not represent Dante's
amorous adventures but speak, through the devices of allegory, to make
the poet a model as the *Confessions* made Augustine a model.[34] When the
virile mode comes into play, the dreamy meanings change. In the *Convito,*
the negatively portrayed *Vita Nuova* lady-at-the-window is explained allegorically as Lady Philosophy, and she embodies both what Dante found in
reading Cicero's teachings on friendship (*philo*) and Boethius's teachings
on Wisdom (*Sophia*). She also reflects what he discovered during his brief
sojourn at the friar schools and at public philosophic disputations ("le
scuole de li religiosi e a le disputazioni de li filosofanti").

Window-lady Philosophy comes to comfort the poet after the death of
Beatrice,[35] and she does so by explaining the structure of the disciplines
that lead to an exploration of a stable creation (see chapter 6). In short,
through Cicero and Boethius, Dante achieves the encounter with the
Logos/Wisdom that Augustine achieves when he studies the *Hortensius*.[36]

The *Commedia* recapitulates Dante's version of the movement in the *Confessions* from bad to good, better, and best but with a more explicit theological and literary structure and with more emphasis on the incarnate Christ-as-Logos.[37] In developing its theological and literary structure, it turns to one of Augustine's primary structural metaphors, architectural imagery. Dante begins the *Inferno* "rovinava" (1.61) as Augustine begins the *Confessions* "ruinosa" (1.5).[38] He begins, as Freccero argues, in Augustine's "region of unlikeness," where vision has begun and humility not yet come. Following Augustine's iterative use of contrasting ruinous and orderly geometric figures to suggest the dichotomy between disease and health, Dante descends through a human and architectural ruin uninformed by any visible Logos architecture, going through the woods to the Inferno's frozen lake by way of a series of ruined structures (cf. cantos 9 and 14 and circles 8, 9, 21, 28, and 31). He then ascends through the disciplines (see chapter 7), through the more symmetrical, less ruined Gothic tower of Purgatory, half mountain and half built-structure, the place of the rebuilding of the soul, to the perfect cosmic architecture seen in the climb through the planets and spheres. In the final beatific vision,[39] Dante gains sight of a place where, like a geometer trying to square the circle, he gazes on the paradox of the human form divine in the second person of the Trinity ("Qual è 'l geomètra che tutto s'affige / Per misurar lo cerchio, e non ritrova / Pensando, quel principio ond' elli indige, / Tal era io a quella vista nova." *Paradiso* 33.133–35). Even as Augustine hears a final Wisdom at Ostia that announces the death of the old self, Dante sees a determinate Word in the final geometry of the cosmos that ends in the surrender of the self.

The Dante of the *Commedia*'s beatific vision is a geometer, a practitioner of the medieval mathematical discipline that creates architecture, a man who has transcended suffering through being filled with the higher disciplines and the cosmos they describe (see chapter 7). His journey, like Augustine's (though more explicitly), goes from ruin to orderly cosmic architecture.[40] The increasing architectural orderliness of the *Commedia*'s realms parallels the increasing spiritual order in the pilgrim, who learns to understand the perverted, defective, and excessive love of created things in the *Purgatorio*, recovers his "old flame" of love for Beatrice-Wisdom at its end, and sees Wisdom's creations in the *Paradiso*.[41] Augustine's experiences of death – his friend's death, Monica's death, and his own spiritual dying in the "Tolle, lege" garden – parallel Dante's experience of Beatrice's and his own dying and birth in the *Commedia*. At the end of the *Purgatorio*, prior to entering Lethe stream, Dante becomes a bearded ancient (31.68–74) and then suddenly a child responding to a mother when Beatrice reproaches him for his sins (31.64–66). He weeps like a child, receives a name for the first time (30.55–57), moves through cleansing waters in second baptism (31.94ff.), dances in play with the cardinal-virtue nymphs who join hands above him (31.103–5), and learns to see with the nymphs of the theological virtues (31.109–11) in an emptying of the self that prepares him for the encounter with the scientific disciplines and the cosmic filling brought about in the *Paradiso* when he witnesses to the glory of the leaves of the creation.

PETRARCH'S "CONFESSIONS": THE "SECRETUM" SEARCH FOR WILL AND TRUTH

If Dante focuses on the search for a salutation or defining word related to the *Confessions*'s themes of the new life, Petrarch focuses on the difficulty of getting rid of the old words so as to come to new consciousness. Petrarch's *Secretum* version of the *Confessions* leaves the autobiographical journeyer incomplete, paralyzed in his private will at the point before he hears any "Tolle, lege"; yet he seems to forecast something else. When the *Secretum*'s Franciscus (or Francis Petrarch) enters into a dialogue with Augustinus (the Augustine understood by Petrarch at a specific stage in his spiritual development), he has no center. Dialogue 1, imitating parts of Augustine's dialogue in the "Tolle, lege" garden, rehearses Franciscus's Augustinian incapacity to will the good but also his potential for fulfillment. Dialogue 2, a conventional confession, specifies Franciscus's seven deadly sins; dialogue 3 looks at the root of his sin, his misplaced love of Laura and the laurel, and at his potential for being filled with an understanding of the creation and Creator.[42]

The *secretum* place, in both Augustine and Petrarch, is the place of partial solitude on the edge of rebirth, not the place of rebirth. In the *Confessions* (8.8), Augustine goes to his *secretum* on the edge of the "Tolle, lege" garden, and he is not transformed there. Similarly, in his *Secretum*, Petrarch does not write about his transformation but about his desire for renewal. Alypius accompanies Augustine as he plunges into solitude, and Petrarch's text-based Augustinus goes with Franciscus.[43] Yet to be fully changed, the *Confessions*'s Augustine has to go it alone from the *secretum* to the deeper solitude under the fig tree, a place where he has no Alypius to comfort him as he experiences the numinous (8.12).[44] The *Secretum* Petrarch also knows that he must go deeper as his book becomes his metaphor for an imagined conversation with a literary friend, Augustine, and for a deeper search for an authentic self: "Therefore, little book, fleeing the assemblies of men, you must be content to remain with me, not unmindful of your name. For you are my solitude (*meum secretum*), and you shall so speak."[45]

The book can become Petrarch's garden place of partial solitude because, through most of it, Franciscus, the Petrarch who resembles the early Augustine as rhetorician and lover, must speak with – read or emulate – the older Augustine who has passed beyond the *secretum* to a new life.[46] The interlocutors are not equals, for one speaks the Logos that Petrarch must hear while the other speaks primarily of matters that are the proper domains of poetry and rhetoric. Hence, Augustinus speaks to Franciscus condescendingly, calls him "midget," "homuncio," something like "bird-brain" (Virgil similarly calls Fulgentius "homunculus" in Fulgentius's commentary [cf. chapter 5]). However, even Petrarch's Augustinus is not fully perfected, for at moments he is only the Augustine who feels a paralysis of the will and partially turns, the incomplete Augustine of the *secretum* just before the "Tolle, lege" (8.8–11).[47] Franciscus at the stage represented in the work can read the *secretum* Augustinus but not yet the Augustine that hears the determinate "Tolle, lege" or the "Enter into the joy of your Lord" at Ostia.

Determinate Truth, the whole truth, sponsors the incomplete Augustinus's effort to educate Franciscus. This Truth, a mirror of Boethius's Lady Philosophy, claims authority through her origin above the heavens, her shining with an unusual light, and her superradiant face. Petrarch's *Africa* makes her worshippers come to the temple in the Atlas mountains where the seven liberal arts are her associates (cf. chapter 5). Like Boethius's Lady Philosophy (cf. chapter 6), she encompasses the philosophic disciplines through which exact truth about the universe is obtained.

Since her thoughts fly too high for Franciscus, she chooses a fallible Augustinus to be his teacher because, for all of his fallibility, Franciscus loves him: "Dear to me above a thousand, Augustine. . . . This (Petrarch) was always most in love with your name, and it is characteristic of all teaching that it is transmitted more readily to the mind of the disciple when the teacher is beloved; and . . . you endured much that is like what this student has endured when you were enclosed in your bodily prison."[48] Reflecting a cardinal point of medieval Wisdom pedagogy, Augustine's life teaches Petrarch precisely where teacher and student come together in struggle. It does not teach as a perfectly literal mirror of the *Confessions*'s hero, for Petrarch scrambles the actual time sequences of Augustine's life. Augustinus talks like the hero of the *Confessions* (8.8–11), but he has also written the later *On True Religion* and *City of God*. He knows the concepts of a Boethius who comes after him (he echoes him when he speaks of fortune, fame, virtue, the good, and the known world). Yet this fictive Augustinus has not achieved full conversion, only the incomplete *secretum* experience. He is only the Augustine who endures a little beyond what his student endures at this point.

In fact the Augustine of the *secretum* scene in the *Confessions* prefigures the two sides of Petrarch engaged in the debate as to whether he can know definitive words and use definitive language.[49] The Augustine of the *Confessions*'s *secretum* scene knows that he must will to go to God and do so powerfully and wholly,[50] yet cannot – cannot, by will, successfully will to control his will as he can by will control his body. However, though habit controls him (8.8–11),[51] his effort to will the good is not entirely futile. While still in the *secretum*, as he says, he came so close to properly resolving on a direction that he did not fully relapse into his original state (8.11). Augustinus can teach Franciscus, as Antony taught Augustine, because he has known a stiffness in the will such as Franciscus knows.

The verbal act of the *Secretum* simulates how the *Confessions* are to act on real lives. Augustinus tells Franciscus that his joy and sorrow depend wholly on his will: "no one can be unhappy contrary to his own will."[52] Clearly Augustinus assumes some freedom, as does the Augustine of the *Confessions* (unlike the later Augustine). Augustinus only tells Franciscus that he must will harder, not that he must depend on the grace that Augustine, after the *secretum* scene in the *Confessions*, recognizes. Though Augustinus speaks in the voice and with the limited authority of the *Confessions*'s Augustine still in the *secretum*, he knows what will happen to this Augustine later in the story when he predicts that grace will come to Franciscus and touch him (as if he is passive through all of this). Augustinus was, he asserts, transformed ("transformatus sum") to a *vita nuova* as he contemplated a new way of life ("novam vite viam").[53] Preparing Franciscus for his transformation, he urges Franciscus to remember the fig-tree part of the "Tolle, lege" scene reflecting Nathanael's call (John 1.43–51), welcoming its memory as one would welcome a port in a storm.[54] The Franciscus who remains in the *secretum* with Augustinus cannot yet hear the full "Tolle, lege" and read Romans 13.13 – cannot do so because he is still in the *secretum*, because he has not yet gone off completely alone to hear the absolute voice and read the text – Augustinus's transformative high meditation ("alta meditatio"). Both Dante's "alta fantasia," in the *Paradiso* (33.142) and Augustinus's "alta meditatio" in the *Secretum* flow from transformative grace leading to self-education and self-knowledge.[55]

Cicero, or rather Augustine's Ciceronian *De Vera Religione*, again comes to the rescue. Based on Augustine's assumptions in *De Vera Religione*, the *Secretum*'s Augustinus implies that the soul must journey inward to truth where it will see the final Logos, the primal numbers, and the universe's beauty as a system. There it will sense the Creator (39.72ff.). Since the study of numbers conventionally leads to beauty and Wisdom, mathematical learning is important to the meditation leading to liberation. But as the *Secretum* does not tell the full story of the call beneath the fig tree, it also does not expatiate about what Augustine has said in the *Confessions* or *De Vera*.[56]

Dialogue 2, the least interesting section of the work, makes Augustine, who has confessed before, act as the special confessor to Franciscus's seven deadly sins. Then dialogue 3 evaluates his loves, his love of the Laura-laurel and of the creation. Franciscus sees his love of Laura as the *stilnovisti*'s love for Wisdom women: "But you should know that the woman concerning whom you have made mention has a mind that cares nothing for earthly things but burns with heavenly desire. In her face, as the truth is true, shines forth a portion of the divine beauty. Her morality is the exemplar of perfect integrity; whose voice and light of eye go beyond the mortal, and her walk is not that of any human being."[57] Augustinus, on the other hand, sees that Laura does not act as Beatrice or truth in Franciscus's soul:

AUG: She has drawn your love away from celestial things and has turned your desire to the creature and away from the Creator. That path, more certainly than any other, leads to death.

FR: Do not give, I pray you, a precipitous judgement. The love of her is truly responsible for the fact that I love God.

AUG: But it has inverted order.[58]

The inverted "ordo" placing creaturely love above the Creator destroys, in Franciscus, the order that Augustine's *De Ordine* would rectify through the study of the higher disciplines examining and giving an accurate rendering of the creation. Augustinus points to something like *De Ordine*'s path when he demythologizes Laura and invites Franciscus to recall that he chose the Pythagorean lefthanded road of vice when he fell for Laura as both the woman he loves and the poetic laurel wreath he desires.[59]

Augustinus's emptying of Franciscus ends here, and the time for some fulfillment, some new creation has come. Augustinus finally ends Franciscus's laurel-Laura maundering with a cutting Scipionic/Boethian reference to the discipline that led to his own progress in achieving order. He reminds Franciscus of geometry and the minuscule earth described in the *Africa*, Cicero's *Republic*, and Plato's *Timaeus* (the reference calls us back to the quadrivium disciplines).[60] Near the end, Augustinus says that his student will hear an undefined spirit ("spiritum") calling to him, "This is the way to your homeland" ("Hoc iter est in patriam"). The "spiritum" is not specified, but it speaks of death and the beyond, as does the voice in the "Tolle, lege" garden.[61] Here Petrarch's appropriation of Augustine is both subtle and ambiguous, for though it predicts the remainder of Augustinian pattern, it does not assure it but rather offers to Franciscus and to the reader the reaching for the rest of the discipline.

The appropriation of Augustine in the four medieval writers discussed here is neither wholly indeterminate nor wholly ideological. The four writers do not claim that Augustine's *Confessions* offered them a pattern of self-repression or made them miserable, for each asserts that he was miserable and enchained before he began the journey inward and upward. Each by his act of subcreation implicitly assigns to Augustine a fairly similar and determinate meaning that he could imitate in his own life and in his literary creation. The further implicit claim of each is that the flow of literary influence does not go from Augustine's text to their text but from his text to their reconstructed lives to the text that each creates based on his new life. None of the authors studied in this chapter tries to overreach Augustine by making a chameleon's "strong misreading" of him; none tries to represent what he does as simply a matter of texts but as the emptying of a life and a filling that goes beyond the consolation of texts. Each encounters Philosophy or Wisdom as offering a meaning for his life, a Philosophy that appears as Athena-like in Boethius's prison, as Aelred's special experience of the cosmos, as Beatrice's salutation, and as Petrarch's wait to go beyond the *secretum* to find meaning.

The fashion of modern educational theory has been to treat the kind of quest for meaning contained in these four works as a mystification that violates the conditions of secular education in the modern liberal state. Yet what students hunger for in education are books and mentors that will assist them, without coercion and without explicit statement, as they look to find a meaning or direction for their lives. That is why career education is so popular, why counsellors are everywhere. Students do not hunger to read what an instructor tells them are canonical texts. They look for teachers who care about them and books or guides that can help them to make sense of circumstances as particular as those Petrarch faced. As children of the twentieth century, they generally are not much interested in a formal theological or religious systems but in a sense of what they ought to be about, a sense provided neither by what we call counseling nor by the heroes of chauvinist conquest and culture war that we provide.

This sense of meaning is not often found in modern culture. Elie Wiesel and Viktor Frankl find it in a concentration camp, Thomas Merton in a great city, George Orwell in Catalonia, and David Ehrenfeld in listening to baroque music:

Last night I listened to one of my favorite pieces of early baroque music. It reminded me, as it always does, of the sea pounding relentlessly on a dark beach where I have spent many nights waiting to watch the giant sea turtles, last of their noble race, heave themselves out of the depths to lay their gleaming eggs on the black sand. The music saddened me beyond my power to express, because I know that it could not have been written in my time; there has been too much progress; there is not enough peace. It saddened me because it reminded me of the sea, the sea that gave birth to human beings, that we carry with us yet in our very cells. It saddened me because it reminded me that in my century nothing is totally free of the taint of our arrogance. We have defiled everything, much of it forever, even the farthest jungles of the Amazon and the air above the mountains, even the everlasting sea which gave us birth.[62]

No discovered meaning worthy of the name can be entirely arrogant or ignore the creation's limits; it must construct a mandate for students that carries authority for them and, perhaps, can be communicated to the social group in which they operate. Students give up to a third of their lives to a bureaucracy where the question of meaning is replaced with maundering about values and achievement. They deserve better.

The Heroic Educational Journey:
Virgil and Medieval Epic Subcreation

The ancient epic, misinterpreted, defines the structure of the education dominant in the Neoplatonic and Christian worlds. This definition derives from a major form of patristic and medieval interpretation that falls victim to the chameleon beast: a misreading of epic that makes a part of the canon serve noncanonical purposes and appropriates the epic form to conquer the threat of educational formlessness. But the medieval misreading of ancient epic hardly ever resembles Harold Bloom's act of individual overreaching. Rather, it is a general act of cultural appropriation based on changes that occur between Greco-Roman culture as it exists in the period from 300 B.C. to A.D. 100 and in medieval culture as it exists after A.D. 500. What Bloom calls "strong misreading," when applied to the ancient epic in the late patristic and early medieval period, does not have the individualistic purpose that Bloom identifies in his readings of modern literature.[1] In both the ancient and the patristic-medieval worlds, readers explain what meanings they see in Homer and Virgil (and why they see those meanings) in a form that does not suggest the individual's construction of a private language and a private metaphysics or his efforts to surpass the flights of a previous strong poet.[2] Patristic and medieval readers change the epic to find in it a "message" germane to their lives, an adumbration of a proper structure for education. They use a canonical Virgil against himself – the archetype of Roman rhetoric and the Roman *imperium* against the rhetorical bent of the Roman schools. It is one thing to do the kind of misreading that Bloom describes – to misread another person's work so that one may construct a "superior" work, claiming for oneself a fuller divinity and a more elevated transcendence. It is another thing to treat epic language as indeterminate and manipulable because the circumstances that created the original work are so distant as to be without utility for the interpreter's audience. Neither procedure is entirely defensible, but the latter is surely more understandable than the former.

Deconstructionists have suggested that there is no such thing as closure in the reading of literary works, that when closure is suggested the police are not far away. But one may distinguish between using the language as it was used in its own time and appropriating that language for present purposes – between Wittgenstein's "seeing" language and "seeing" it "as." One example sometimes given to illustrate the indeterminacy of literary works is that the Greek's Homer is not Virgil's Homer who, in turn, is not our Homer.[3] When Derrida asks, "What are the borderlines of a text? How do they come about?," when he seeks to smudge the line between text and extratext, text and context, text and reader, he opens the text up to a reading without closure.[4] The deconstructionist might argue that the evolution of Homer's meaning licenses the notion that literary meaning is polysemous and, properly, the product of individual appropriation. But the argument, in the form in which deconstruction offers it, suggests that individual readers altered Homer's meaning – that altering Homer is anyone's game.

This is not generally the case historically. It is not as if somebody played Humpty Dumpty to a Homer placed in the position of Lewis Carroll's Alice, changing meaning for no reason or to make someone else look stupid. It may be that Homer's words gradually changed their meaning over time, say between 750 B.C. and Plato's time, because readers did not understand how many of Homer's words were once used (this happened to Chaucer in later periods). More likely, the functions of a text in what appears to be a continuous social unit, a nation or tribe, have changed. Altering meaning on the basis of changing functions – the changing of the social unit – is something done by interpretive communities and for historical reasons. Altering the meanings of the Homer or Virgil, in the view of this chapter, is not something that an ancient individual did in one fell swoop, not a series of unpredictable individual actions of appropriation. Instead, it was the product of cultural change across generations. The same may be said for the changes in Virgil's meaning.

Chameleon forms of interpretation were applied to the epic primarily in the late ancient and early Christian periods, when social values changed drastically. Crucial to those changes were the influences of Christianity, Neoplatonism, and the mystery religions, and then the invasions of Rome by Germanic groups. After this period, new and somewhat stable meanings were assigned to the ancient epics and used by writers imitating this kind of epic. Efforts to see the ancient epics as something other than what they could have been in the semantic world of their original audiences worked because the Homeric context and much of the Virgilian context had been lost, and critics needed to give readers some sense of a relevant meaning for a canonical text and some map of the kind of later education that they ought to expect. Students needed this map whether they undertook their education in the private study, the monastery, the court, or in other educational institutions, and often they used several modes of education.

Just prior to and during the sixth century, the readings of Virgil and Homer change again. But they do not do so because individual readers find a latent ambiguity in Virgil's or Homer's text; rather it is because the culture in which they are reading has changed, so that the old readings no longer have a function. In fact, Virgil is generally read thereafter in one way, from the sixth century through the sixteenth. The interpreters create new allegorical or figurative readings that are a map to development and learning and that have a real use in the new culture (critical theory may, of course, serve a somewhat similar transitional purpose in contemporary culture).

The evolution of the epic from a military to an educational focus initially has a purpose suited to the needs of the late Roman empire as it turns, in its intellectual centers, from concern for battle strength to concern for spiritual health. While allegory and iconology may be ideological tools of ruling groups, that need not be the case.[5] Though Virgilian epic appears in literary history and criticism as one of the founding documents of imperialism,[6] it is turned by Neoplatonic and Christian comment from that purpose to nonhegemonic allegorical purposes at a crucial moment in the disintegration of the late Roman empire. Literature read figuratively may rehearse a future state of things rather than a present one (as was apparently the case with much slave narrative and song of the American South). In the case of the allegorized epic, literature both rehearses a future educated state for the individual scholar and a general educational direction for late classical and medieval students, not the central ruling group of their periods.

The Neoplatonist and Christian construction of a figurative reading for Homeric and Virgilian epic rescues both from Greek and Roman chauvinism, making them pertinent to the changed circumstances of Latin scholars in the late ancient and medieval Christian worlds. Instead of recreating Greece or Rome to reinforce the claims to power of some medieval nation or clan (as some vernacular imitators and continuators of Virgil did), the Latin scholarly allegorists use the Virgilian epic to defeat the formless beast, to rehearse an ideal structure for education, and to create from the flotsam of heroic poetry a model of how a life dedicated to learning can be lived. They used a metaphor that people who sought learning encountered fairly early in their careers in the trivium: the story of Aeneas's journey read by most middle level students of Latin. In contrast to the Augustine who repeats scenes (and inverts scenes) from the *Aeneid* to give point to his autobiography and to show what a lie a life modeled after Virgil's work would be, the Virgil created by the epic commentators marks out a generalized biography that is a poetic lie on the surface and, in its inwardness, a true map of the journey through the ages of humankind and through the disciplines. The allegorizations of the *Aeneid* make poetry "tell the truth," using methods that differ from Augustine's practices for reaching truth as a glossarist. Beneath Augustine's practice in glossing the scripture, nature, or his own life lies an assumption that a single divine command to practice charity governs all, whatever the individual variation in interpreting events or words. On the other hand, the less ambitious commentators on the epic begin only with a developmental or educational assumption about the text under consideration and labor, word by word, to wrench that meaning out of it.

They do so for a reason. The attempts by Plato and Augustine to discredit the poets and rhetoricians did not fully succeed, for the kinds of rhetorical schools created by the old Greco-Roman culture stood long after Plato and Augustine were gone. But the Christian philosophers who tried to replace the pagan schools with centers more focused on dialectic, philosophy, and mathematics transformed the journey epics into their own tool by making the journey of the military hero become the student's journey to Wisdom, placing the rhetoric of what were, for them, indeterminate texts at the service of a structured education.

History provided reasons for the Christian allegorists to assign new meaning to Virgil and his epic journey. The Neoplatonists had already reinterpreted Homer, making him the master of the ascent to the source of the creation. In the postimperial society found in Africa, Italy, France, and Spain, schooling came to be less certain (and less certainly structured) in many places, even for people of means. The invaders destroyed the municipal rhetorical schools in some regions, and in others the Christians replaced or supplemented them with monastic schools or tutoring at home.[7] In the late Roman and early Romanesque worlds, one finds an increasing assertion that one must be one's own teacher and find one's own way. Early medieval education was, if not "deschooled," at least more complex, confusing, problematical. Whatever form there was must have been a form that had its primary life in the student's imagination. One can imagine the young person of the period saying, "What shall I study next and where will all of this lead me?" As students contemplated their futures, the allegorical epic must have helped them visualize where their educational journey might lead. Both the medieval autobiography and the medieval allegorical epic mark the stages in the assumed pattern of educational development in the individual, just as the Piagetian stages, with their somewhat differing assumptions, mark an assumed path for the modern child and young adult.[8]

Augustine's *Confessions* could not help all students chart their educational journey, since they were not universally read. Virgil's *Aeneid*, widely read fairly early in the sequence of Latin studies, could be converted through the solvent of allegory into a fictional *Confessions*, modeling the process of growth through suffering and study of the higher nonlinguistic disciplines. The transformation of Virgil imitates a similar conversion of Homer by the Neoplatonists. From Fulgentius to Petrarch, epic commentary and subcreation related to the *Aeneid* point out the road down which education should lead the student and rehearse the "biography" or "autobiography" of the growth of mind and soul as the more direct but less popular *Confessions* could not.

The Virgilian commentaries see Virgil's books as symbolizing infancy, childhood, boyhood, adolescence, and manhood. This follows Augustine's similar division of the *Confessions*. It is not accidental that such

writers as Dante, Petrarch, and the authors who were members of the
Florentine Platonic academy fuse an interest in Augustine's picture of
education with an interest in Virgil's. In modeling educational growth,
the epic commentaries differ from Augustine and his imitators: they give
less place to the suffering that empties the student and to the explicitly
Christian part of the educational journey (though they emphasize the
noetic function of the mathematical disciplines through which nature is
studied). They often lack an Ostia or a "Tolle, lege." The evolution of
epic commentary does not follow the pattern of *Confessions* imitations in
"style" or method of presentation, though the first two writers whom I
shall treat in this chapter – Fulgentius and Bernard Silvestris – respectively appear at roughly the same times as the first two writers treated in
the previous chapter, Boethius and Aelred of Rievaulx. Even Dante and
Petrarch, whom this chapter will treat as Virgilian imitators, and who
both imitate Augustine and comment on Virgil, adopt differing tones
when they allude to Augustine and when they treat the epic. What Virgil
lacks, even in allegorical form or in the sixth book of the *Aeneid*, is the
vatic mandate of Augustine's garden or Dante's Eden or Petrarch's anticipated experience. What he possesses in his allegorical form is a more
systematic sense of how one progresses toward the goal of knowing the
disciplines and the cosmos.

NEOPLATONIC COMMENTARY, BOETHIUS, AND EDUCATION
IN FULGENTIUS'S VIRGIL

As the Middle Platonists and the Neoplatonists try to deal with Plato's
accusation that Homer lied and with his precept banning poets from the
Republic, they turn increasingly to the solvent of allegory to make the epic
poets again palatable and truthful. Even Augustine is a bit affected. His
Confessions see the rhetorician's Virgil as one who made him "weep for
Dido" and ignore "his own sins"; but his *City of God* envisages a more
philosophic Virgil who tells of the life of the soul and its journey, an
Aeneas who is a Christian hero *manqué* who might have conquered the
demons and powers of the air (Hera) had he persisted in his spiritual
battle (*De Civ. Dei* 10.21).[9] A century later, Boethius completely adopts
the "new" hermeneutic and straightforwardly uses the Greek epic figures – Ulysses, the *Iliad'*s heroes, and Hercules – to dramatize his educational ascent. He makes these heroes, recently turned into philosophic

emblems, symbolize his own path to learning and to God. Boethius had reason, from the Hellenistic Neoplatonic and Neopythagorean traditions, to treat the epic in this way. Similar approaches were applied to Virgil in Boethius's time by Fulgentius (late fifth to early sixth century), who also relies on the Neoplatonic commentators.

Long before Boethius, the *Odyssey,* in Pythagorean, Middle Platonic, and Neoplatonic hands, models the heroic educational return of the soul to the Nous rather than the heroic military ethos of ancient Mykenae. As the Roman empire declines and the imperial myth celebrated in the *Aeneid* ceases to have meaning, the interpreters reinvent Virgil to make him follow the Homer whom the Neoplatonists and others modeled after Mykenae had disappeared from meaningful history. An extended philosophic astronomical interpretation of Virgil appears to have been assigned to the Greek philosopher Eustathius in Macrobius's fifth-century *Saturnalia,* though unfortunately that part of the work is lost.[10] The first extant full personification of the new attitude toward Virgilian epic is Fulgentius, who both summarizes the Neoplatonic tradition of Greek commentary on Homer and builds on earlier interpretations of Virgil. In this he prepares the way for the medieval epic and medieval glosses of Virgil. The readings that Fulgentius and the interpreters who follow him make are "strong misreadings" in the sense that they are impossible within the system of language games available to the original author of the work or to his original audience.[11] But as "strong misreadings," they are also coherent exercises in cultural appropriation,[12] not assertions of a Faustian or Gnostic ego.

Virgil's interpreters prior to Christian dominance of the intellectual life of the empire do not read him as a systematic allegorist. They do interpret concepts behind the poems or sporadic passages in them allegorically or figuratively – passages assumed to be secondary to the civic exemplum central in the *Aeneid.* Virgil's earliest extant commentator, Jerome's teacher Donatus, discovers in the *Bucolics,* the *Georgics,* and the *Aeneid* patterns for the lives of shepherds, farmers, and warriors respectively.[13] Yet he makes no effort to identify a continued figurative dimension in the *Aeneid.* His follower, Servius, in his still influential fourth/ fifth-century analysis, expands Donatus's finding of larger implications in Virgil through glosses on specific lines that make the poem recount a hegemonic history but also, in spots, act as a metaphor containing historical, moral, and euhemeristic allegory.[14] Servius's Aeneas is a mirror of Augustus; the stages of Dido's death represent the stages of Carthage's death in the three Punic wars; the twelve dents on Mezentius's breastplate advert to the twelve Etruscan tribes, and so on. Even as the Old Testament anticipates the New in Alexandrian exegesis, events in Servius's version of Virgil's central story, considered historically true, also anticipate true later history. Going beyond historical allegory, Servius views parts of Virgil's account as oriented toward neither what happened in Aeneas's life nor what happened in Virgil's time. For example, Servius's Virgilian gods are atemporal natural forces or regions: Venus the sexual power, Juno the air, Minerva the upper air, Jupiter the aether, and Vulcan the air's fire. Acting on or in the earth, Cerberus, Cybele, and Ceres symbolize the earth itself; Vesta symbolizes the earth as container of fire. In the realms of water, the nymphs are fresh water, and Neptune is salt water.

Continuing this atemporal mode, Servius's account of the descent into Hades in book 6 treats it as a formal allegory of the education of the soul in the virtues and vices. This innovation begins the "new" educational Virgil. Servius makes Tartarus the clothing of philosophy in a fiction that permits one to contemplate physical and moral reality. Styx's nine circles become the earth surrounded by the spheres of the heavens. What is studied in the underworld is the present world with its moral faults: Tityos's spread across Hades represents lust for empire; the chained Cerberus embodies lust controlled by heroic virtue; and so forth. The various lusts and sins of the Hades grotesques imprison the soul until it reaches the Pythagorean Y, where it achieves the possibility of free choice and can go on the educational, purgative journey rather literally described in the fields of light.[15] Thus Servius establishes the fundamental modality of Virgilian interpretation for over a thousand years.

About a century after Servius, Fulgentius makes the entire *Aeneid* into a continuous allegory of the kind that Servius finds in its sixth book. He does so by taking Neoplatonic allegories of Homer (e.g., those by Proclus) and imposing them on Virgil's poem. These, in turn, rescue Homer from the attacks of their master, Plato.[16] Fulgentius removes Virgil from the civic realm entirely and makes his work in books 1 and 2 concern nature's (i.e., human nature's) acquisition of corporeal powers. His books 3, 5, and 6, like Servius's book 6, treat the acquisition of learning that controls these powers. Everything after book 6 shows how human beings work in the active world to ornament learning through action consistent with it. Since Plato's *Republic* and Cicero's *De Re Publica* both emphasize that the just conduct of the active life depends on contemplation, Fulgentius portrays the achievement of full learning – full contemplation – as basic to proper rule.[17]

When Fulgentius's Aeneas (like Augustine at Carthage) falls victim to his appetites at Dido's Carthage (book 4), he does not experience any development or education that Fulgentius describes as positive. Lust only inflames the adolescent to commit adultery until the intellect redirects him toward proper ends. Unlike Servius's Aeneas – essentially a good Roman ruler who must escape Carthage to mature and found its rival empire – Fulgentius's Aeneas is Everyman or Everychild growing up, a figure who must escape adultery to learn intellectual skills and a Christian direction of desire. To remake Aeneas from an image anticipating Augustus to an image of Everyman growing up, Fulgentius has to apply the standard Neoplatonic and Neopythagorean ideas about the Homeric episodes imitated in the *Aeneid* to Virgil. Fulgentius deduces that Aeneas's story tells of birth in book 1 (Juno represents childbirth) and of childhood's roaming and education in books 2 and 3, where Aeneas travels from Troy to Carthage. Adolescence's lust appears in book 4, where the hero seduces Dido,[18] and Maturity's love of exercising the body and mind comes out in the games of book 5. In book 6, where Servius had seen the moral education of the hero taking place, Fulgentius finds academic education in the warrior's descent into the lower world – a fiction for adulthood's study of eloquence and wisdom.[19]

Whatever the merits of the intentional fallacy, Fulgentius believes in committing it, and he legitimizes his reading and anticipates Dante by having Virgil appear from the dead to ratify his own meaning. With a species of humor pretty much foreign to Dante, Fulgentius tells the ghostly Virgil who visits him in the work that he wishes only to know the childish interpretations of his work, the simple stuff that grammarians offer, not the deep soundings (presumably what philosophers adept in the mathematical and transcendent sciences would tell one, not Porphyry's kind of thing). In reply, "Virgil" dismisses the Fulgentius-persona as a Lilliputian in wit ("homunculus") and launches into his own explanation of his poem, an explanation as recherché as anything put in Porphyry's or Proclus's Homeric interpretations.[20]

Fulgentius depends partly on the fact that Roman critics had been well aware that Virgil imitates Homer. The fictional Eustathius in the fifth book of Macrobius's *Saturnalia* makes a catalogue of the ways in which the Roman poet borrows from and falls short of (or surpasses) his Homeric model: Virgil's fall of Troy continues the Iliadic Trojan account, Aeneas's journey parallels Odysseus's, and his battles resemble Achilles's. Some parts of the narration (e.g., Virgil's account of the storm and the Cyclops, or his account of Aeneas's funeral games for Anchises and his descent into the underworld) contain relatively straightforward elaborations of Homer. Others (e.g., the Dido episode, which combines echoes from the Nausicaa, Calypso, and Circe passages in the *Odyssey*) involve more complex interweavings. The same kind of interweaving appears in Virgil's treatment of Aeneas's Telemachus-like relationship to Anchises through the first six books. When Aeneas in the early books journeys from Troy and concerns himself about the safety of his father, Anchises, he images both Odysseus-in-journey and Telemachus in his concern for the welfare of his father, Odysseus.[21] Hence, details taken from previous interpretations of both Telemachus and Odysseus could be applied to the Roman hero.

Fulgentius's similar understanding of Virgil's complex filiation to Homer underlies his appropriation of Homeric interpretation in episode after episode. The *Virgiliana Continentia* interpretation of Aeneas's life combines elements from the Homeric commentators' allegories of Telemachus's and Odysseus's overlapping careers.[22] On the one hand, it makes part of the *Aeneid*'s meaning imitate that found in Greek Neoplatonic and Neopythagorean commentators, who see Telemachus's story as telling of the soul's education in the skills of childhood and early manhood. On the other hand, it makes other parts of the work's meaning imitate Homeric commentary that sees Odysseus's journey as an ascent of the human spirit to the higher realms of philosophy and the noetic region.[23]

The commentators made the noetic interpretation of Odysseus apply especially to the last part of his journey. In Eustathius's anthology of ancient readings of the *Odyssey*, the Penelope to whom Odysseus returns represents true philosophy by her spinning and weaving (Boethius uses the same idea in his Lady Philosophy, with her garment of gossamer threads finely woven).[24] Porphyry makes the inland region, to which

Tiresias says that Odysseus must go on the final stage of his journey, into the realm of the metaphysical that is reached after mathematical study, a kingdom far from the material sea through which Odysseus has traveled (*Odyssey* 11.106–68; Porphyry, *De Ant.* 80.20–81.1).[25] If one combines the journeys of Telemachus and Odysseus, one finds the representation of a movement from childhood's simple cognitions to the highest philosophic knowing, exactly how Fulgentius interprets Aeneas's journey.

Once one sees Aeneas as resembling both Telemachus and Odysseus and regards their journeys as respectively the educational journeys of childhood and manhood, the derivation of Fulgentius's reading of the *Aeneid* becomes obvious. The often-mocked Fulgentian notion that segments of Aeneas's epic allegory can represent, episode for episode, the progress of the soul from birth to its contemplation of the highest realities through the paths of education and philosophy also appears in Porphyry's readings of Odysseus's later journey. For example, Porphyry says that the Circe episode in book 10 of the *Odyssey* speaks of the soul's birth in a body. The body is presided over by a woman, in Circe's case, a child of the sun who rules over birth and death. Circe's island, Aiaia, is the place of emergence from death and of reincarnation to life. Souls may be tempted there by Circe's brew to seek entry into a body and bodily pleasures again; whereupon they encounter in the succeeding episode the three Hades roads that come together at the place where the incarnate soul chooses among the concupiscible, irascible, and rational lives. The soul should choose the rational road represented by Hermes or reason, the inner Logos. In order to make that choice, however, it must educate itself in philosophy (Stobaeus, *Ecl.* 1.41.60).[26] This interpretive line continues in Porphyry's account of the *Odyssey* (book 13), where the two openings of the nymph's cave represent the spiritual and the material universe (*De Ant.* 29–31). The olive of Athena at the top of the cave's bay represents Athena or divine wisdom (*De Ant.* 33); Athena's requirement that Odysseus hide his goods and become a beggar means that the soul must cast aside all that is material and sensual (*De Ant.* 79.12–19) and transcend the life of the senses while achieving contemplation (*De Ant.* 80.11–13). The meaning parallels that in Proclus's commentary on Euclid, where he says that the soul must liberate itself from Calypso and proceed until it contemplates both the transcendent mathematical realities and the Nous, which is the soul's ultimate destiny (*In Euc.* 54–55; *In*

Parm. 1025a.29–37).²⁷ In short, for Porphyry and Proclus, the progress from Circe through Hades to the cave of the nymphs to Ithaca and inland represents the educational progress from birth in the material world to contemplation of the eternal world.

Boethius, Fulgentius's contemporary, seems to have based what he does with the epic on Porphyry and Proclus. At the beginning of the *Consolation,* when Boethius complains of his imprisonment, the meta-phoric answer that comes to him from Philosophy says that the would-be innocent person who suffers and then frets at his bad fortune is not really innocent. Such a voyager sails in a sea of temptation, like Odysseus among the sirens (or "nymphs"). He lives with Circe or Calypso, exiled from his true home with the One (1.pr.1; 1.pr.5).²⁸ Though he is not a prisoner of his body as evil matter (Boethius's Christianity keeps him from seeing the body as evil or birth as a misfortune), he is in bondage to bodily appetite since he is bound by desire for the goods of fortune. By learning to see the state's and his own decisions as set apart from the material flux of fortune, which is neither to be desired nor feared, he places these decisions in the context of a natural law that is fixed, mathematically, by the One. He must regulate his own desire according to such law and according to the divine will in order to know true happiness.

Boethius's initial picture of Lady Philosophy, as she points his way home from exile, derives from Neoplatonic interpretations of Homer (summarized above). As Robert Lamberton has argued, Lady Philoso-phy, Boethius's new muse (substituting for the tragic muses she drives out), represents a metamorphosis of Athena.²⁹ Her enjoinder to Bo-ethius, in book 1, prose 5, that he should return to his true home after wandering resembles the Neoplatonic Athena's indication to Odysseus that he should return from Calypso's embraces to his home in the no-etic realm (*Enn* 1.6.8.16–21).³⁰ Philosophy's actions make her both the Athena who tells the traveler to go home and the Penelope who is the end of his journey.³¹ Her garments contain the finely woven threads that med-ieval commentators made into Philosophy's subtle reasoning (1.pr.1), threads like those that Penelope, who also symbolized philosophy in Eu-stathius's comment, was said to weave (section 1437, 11.19ff.).³² Philoso-phy's face, darkened as from work in a smoky room, recalls Penelope's night work over her "weaving." As both the beginning and the end of Boethius-Odysseus's journey, she combines subthemes from commentaries and Homeric plot. When at the beginning of book 4 she says that she ascends with swift wings to the throne of the high lord, she implicitly tells us not only to recall Penelope but also Athena, whose wing-sandalled journeys to Zeus show how divine intelligence is an aspect of God.[33]

Boethius appears initially as an Odysseus who begins with the Circean desire for fortune, a Calypso-embraced exile bound to his own sophistry and kept by the tragic muses from his true country in eternity with the One, as Philosophy explains (1.pr.5). But he develops. In the fourth and fifth books of the *Consolation,* he reaches above the planets to the throne of Jove even as Porphyry's Odysseus – representing the educational progress from birth in the material world to contemplation of the immaterial and finally to Wisdom – leaves behind his captivity as he progresses from Circe through Hades to the cave of the nymphs to Ithaca and inland.[34]

While Boethius, in the *Consolation,* creates a new work using the Neoplatonic and Neopythagorean commentators to define the stages in a Christian education (see chapter 6), Fulgentius, his approximate contemporary, uses the tools of the commentators to recreate Virgil. Once one has identified the Greek Neoplatonic hermeneutic tradition with which Fulgentius is working, one can readily lay out the parallels between his Virgilian exegesis and the earlier Homeric allegories:

PATTERN I. Odysseus's shipwreck in Calypso's realm, according to Eustathius, means birth's imprisonment of the soul in a body.[35] Aeneas's book 1 shipwreck in Libya in Dido's realm means the perils of birth (i.e., the journey of the soul into the body).[36]

PATTERN II. Odysseus's conquering of the Cyclops means that the wild movements of the heart are calmed by the wise man.[37] The *Aeneid*'s Cyclops episode and *Aeneid,* books 2 and 3, mean that childhood, wandering beyond a proper respect for adults, meets irrationality's one eye, the eye that Ulysses blinded with the fire of intellect.[38]

PATTERN III. Odysseus's encounters with Nausicaa, Calypso, and Circe suggest the life of pleasure and physical passion: the Phaeacians, with their gardens, feasts, and pleasant life represent the Epicurean life of pleasure.[39] (Circe is the pleasure of the sensual life;[40] Calypso in Eustathius's view represents the body imprisoning the soul [1389.42–44];[41] Hermes's bringing of the *moly* is eloquence or the Logos within bringing reason.)[42] Aeneas's affair with Dido in book 4 means that adolescence, moving beyond paternal control, is inflamed by passion and confusion of mind and commits adultery until the god, intellect, removes the passion.

PATTERN IV. The Homeric commentaries make the games following Patroclus's funeral stand for the warrior training his body for combat.[43] Anchises's death and the funeral games in memory of him in book 5 represent prudent maturity's celebrating the memory of the father by exercising the body in games and the mind in disputation (boxing) until the impulses (the ships) are destroyed by the fire of intellect.[44]

PATTERN V. Eustathius's Odysseus, having received the *moly* of wisdom, journeys to the underworld, which represents matter, where he sees punished souls representing vices.[45] Having completed youth, the mature person represented by Aeneas in book 6 turns to Apollo, or studious learning, sets aside vanity, and seeks the golden bough of wisdom and eloquence to descend to the lower world, where he contemplates the world of vice and achieves liberation by encountering the One, God, in Elysium.[46]

After book 6, Fulgentius sees Aeneas returning to the activities of the active life where, having "buried" or outgrown his teachers, he reaches an Italy that stands for the good. Through Vulcan's arms, he seeks to protect Wisdom from rage (Turnus), to prevent the despising of the Good (Mezentius), and to conquer many other active evils.[47] The work contains no sophisticated civic critique such as that found in Boethius and later works in the tradition. However, at the very least, it argues that the achievements of study and contemplation should come home to work in the active life. Though no Neoplatonic allegory anticipates this aspect of Fulgentius's interpretation, sophisticated readers probably expected it, given common notions of what one does in the active life after one ascends above "the cave" in contemplation.

What is crucial about the ancient world's Servian-Boethian-Fulgentian interpretation of the epic is that its appropriation of the epic to model learning enhances the notion of a self-directed education that is only occasionally helped along by the pedagogue or teacher, a notion already imbedded in Origen's and Augustine's educational theories and in the "true" life stories about Augustine and Gregory that accompany these theories. The new interpretations by Fulgentius and Boethius direct education to a goal beyond grammar and rhetoric and the civic concern that Quintilian asks one to keep centrally in mind. It assumes that education is fundamentally designed to teach the student to understand physical, moral, and transcendent realities that are more important than the linguistic devices mastered in the old Roman school.

TWELFTH-CENTURY EPIC COMMENTARY AND CREATION: BERNARD SILVESTRIS

Once Fulgentius had interpreted Virgil on the analogy of the Neoplatonic Homer, his later interpreters could build upon this understanding of Virgil's meaning so as to keep the beast of formless education at bay, especially where a coherently organized institutionalized learning was not easily available. One could study by oneself; one could study the texts of the disciplines. Poets, without feeling any visible anxiety of influence, could create epics using the Fulgentian-Virgilian logic to celebrate how learning perfects nature and accomplishes its goals in the active world. Bernard Silvestris, in his gloss on Martianus Capella's *Marriage of Mercury and Philology* – the union of trivium eloquence and quadrivium wisdom – argues that Virgilian epic, the Boethian utopia, and Martianus's story of the seven liberal arts, all celebrate the same journey. As Bernard explains it, in the *Marriage of Mercury and Philology*, Martianus imitates Virgil. As Virgil's Aeneas, guided by the sibyl, goes through the underworld until he comes to Anchises, so Martianus's Mercury journeys through his world until joined to virtue. So also in the *Consolation*, Boethius, led by Philosophy, ascends through false goods to the highest good. The three works, according to Bernard, express nearly the same idea, Martianus modeling his work on Virgil and Boethius modeling his on Martianus.[48]

The perception of pattern in texts is central to medieval hermeneutics, and to Bernard's eye, Boethius's philosophic journey, Virgil's heroic journey, and the study of the liberal arts described by Martianus represent the same intellectual journey. Anchises (who tells of the highest good), Jove, and Boethius's *Summum Bonum* are the same; the guides – the Sibyl, Mercury, and Lady Philosophy – are the same. All represent a journey that no spectator can see and that has nothing to do with hegemony or ideology. Bernard's version of late antiquity's forms of subcreation underlies his own work in his commentary on the *Aeneid* and in his *Cosmographia*. It also underlies Dante's and Petrarch's works in the genres of epic commentary and creation in the fourteenth century.

Bernard Silvestris, to emphasize the structure of the educational path, writes both a Fulgentian commentary on the *Aeneid* and his own epic, the *Cosmographia*. He gives no place to the active life in that part of his commentary that we have, nor does his epic poem talk about it. His is the work of a purely contemplative dabbler in epic. Bernard's gloss on the *Aeneid* is more detailed than Fulgentius's, but following Fulgentius he says that Virgil's book, beneath its outer layer (*integumentum*), tells of what the human spirit does and endures when placed for a time in a human body.[49] Like Fulgentius, Bernard makes Virgil's account of the Libyan tempest treat of infancy, the soul's birth into the material world of desire, perception, and passion;[50] his second book, concerning the fall of Troy, tells of childhood's learning to speak – learning to utter words that mix truth and falsity;[51] and his third, concerning Aeneas's wandering in the Mediterranean, describes the adolescent's journey through the vices. Anlandros stands for the adolescent period's inconstancy, Thrace for its greed, the Strophades for its storms of sensual temptation, the Cyclops for its aimlessness, Circe for its irrational delight in the temporal, Aetna for its Polypheman pride, and Drepanum for its childish bitterness.[52] Contrary to such historians of medieval and Renaissance culture as Van den Berg and Ariès, who say that medieval people do not conceptualize adolescence as a separate stage, Bernard clearly understands the storms of growing up and thinks that they stop only briefly (i.e., at "Delos," when Wisdom is worshipped). Knowing these characteristics of youth, he says nothing about education in the period of adolescence, where modern Western people think of education as having its primary locus.

Like many medieval educational theorists, Bernard assumes that serious education cannot begin until after adolescence, after Aeneas's affair with Dido in book 4 has ended, when "young manhood" is nudged from its immersion in the cave of impurity by Mercury, who is the eloquence to be joined to Wisdom that Bernard later describes as the beginning study of the trivium.[53] Only in the fifth book's "manhood" stage does the need for serious cognitive development unfold. Though the sporting contests in honor of Anchises's funeral in book 5 picture the development of the four cardinal virtues, its later parts concern what Piagetians would call a movement from preoperational thought to concrete and formal operations.[54] Iris's appearance in the form of Beroe to urge the burning of the Trojan ships represents how the world of senses (Iris) can pretend to be that of reason (Beroe) that judges beneath sense perception and sees the real order of things. Iris's command to burn the ships is sense pretending to be reason. Only when "Anchises" appears to Aeneas does a real mental image come to him, requiring him to look at and beyond earthly things with an analytic understanding that allows him to ascend/descend rationally to the Creator, who is their source.[55]

Book 6, adulthood, represents this ascent/descent, the educational action that both Servius and Fulgentius had found in this book.[56] In Aeneas's adult descent to the underworld, serious formal education begins: learning that probes beneath the surface. The whole Virgilian afterlife becomes a rehearsal of the soul's (or mind's) journey through academic studies. The temple of Trivia at the beginning of the trip underground is the *trivium* creating eloquence,[57] but its golden roofs are the *quadrivium*.[58] Among Aeneas's guides, Achates is study, the sibyl is divine counsel, and Apollo is Wisdom; the region where Apollo presides, mentioned just prior to the mention of the sibyl's cave, represents the three theoretical sciences: physics, mathematics, and theology. Over these sciences, Apollo as theoretical knowledge presides, but theory discovered for the sake of the Wisdom is given to the sibyl.[59] By descending to the "lower world" of the transcendent, the soul actually ascends to the higher studies described in Plato's three major works – the *Republic, Timaeus,* and *Parmenides* – and, as we shall see later, in Boethius's Philosophy's three heights.[60] No one represents the school or monastic pedagogue or external teacher at this point, for the teacher is the literary metaphor as guide.

In the mysterious world of the higher studies shown through the sibylline tour of the underworld, the student represented by Aeneas encounters the trivium and quadrivium disciplines through studying the authors who represent them.[61] The Euboean rock whose opening leads into the other adjacent rocks of the underworld represents the practical and the theoretical arts – the latter including theology, mathematics, and physics – that are studied under the sibyl's instruction.[62] When the sibyl becomes possessed, her appearance changes, and she becomes taller, ascending beyond mere rhetorical coloration to the integrity and plainness of mathematics and the sublimity of theology that reaches toward the divine (compare Lady Philosophy when her stature expands, chapter 6).[63] The journey through Hades that Aeneas anticipates (1.109) is the journey from physics to the mathematical disciplines to metaphysics/theology, a journey from the inanimate to the animate to the human and angelic to the Creator. The golden bough is also philosophy with its theoretical and practical divisions.[64]

Bernard's version of Aeneas's journey underground models the subduing of the senses by reason, the study of the disciplines that leads to the joining of eloquence to Wisdom so that theoretical knowledge can be achieved, expressed, and used. Knowing the disciplines necessary to overcoming the Hades monsters that from Fulgentian times have stood for various quotidian vices, "Aeneas" enters the life of contemplation near the Elysian fields. At about the same time, he looks at the circling walls of the Cyclops – circling spirits holding fast to the invisible, unchanging Creator that anticipate Dante's similar circling spirits.[65] Book 6 rehearses how the soul, immersed in the physical, rises through the contemplative and academic disciplines to a comprehension of the universe and a union with the divine.[66] This is, of course, a far cry from Virgil's hegemonic hymn to Augustus, but it probably meant a good deal more than Augustus might have signified to a student wandering about among the twelfth-century schools in the region of Paris. It was, at the very least, a kind of map.

Bernard's own *Cosmographia* recounts a similar heroic journey to the divine, but it does so by giving airy abstractions habitation in a literary plot rather than by making a received plot signify these abstractions (the device of Bernard's *Aeneid* allegory). In representing the creation of the physical in the *Cosmographia*, Bernard shows the transcendent reaching toward the physical before the disciplines reaching toward the transcendent can be formulated. In the first book, the power that makes the external universe, nature, joins Nous, or divine Sophia, and her companion, Endelichia – the World-Soul – to Mundus, the world. The world is the child of the formless wood of Silva, or matter, and the realm of generation. Given Endelichia's power of form, an ordered cosmos then comes forth from Silva.[67] Nous (or Noys) is basically the equivalent of Origen's Sophia, Endelichia the equivalent of his Logos,[68] the former apparently taking ideas from the hidden depths of God and making them available and the latter stamping them on matter. After this Platonic/Christian version of the origin of the physical universe, the epic journey presents the universe reaching toward the human mind to make it achieve self-consciousness and disciplined thought. After the creation, nature, ordered by Nous to create humankind, finds Urania (or the forms described by mathematics), Physis (or physics), and Physis's two daughters, Theory and Practice.

The discovery of Physis and her daughters permits Nous, the subject of metaphysical/theological knowledge, to come and make assignments to the other major personifications as to what each of them shall study. To Urania, or the pure mathematical disciplines, Nous assigns the study of providence and the ideas in the mind of God. To the applied mathematical disciplines, or nature, she assigns the study of destiny in temporal happenings. To Physis, or physics, she allocates the study of earthly or bodily creatures. Under nature's guidance, Urania and Physis create a human being capable of intellectual ascent.[69] The *Cosmographia* simply reverses the "point of view" of Bernard's *Aeneid* commentary to show the intelligible universe reaching toward the human mind in the form of the disciplines rather than mind reaching toward intelligibility in the universe. Both works set forth their positions without returning to any metaphors for the active life such as one finds in Fulgentius, perhaps a corollary of Bernard's immersion in twelfth-century scholarly life.

In contrast to Bernard, Dante and Petrarch make the active life a more important part of the epic's allegorical ascent, though they still do not prefer it to the contemplative life, as do some later fifteenth-century scholars.

DANTE'S FOURTEENTH-CENTURY PRESENTATION OF THE EPIC EDUCATIONAL JOURNEY

A relationship between commentary and creation similar to that found in Bernard's work exists in Dante. His *Convito* comments on the *Aeneid* and also elucidates the *Commedia*'s mode of treating education; his recreation of the *Aeneid* in the *Commedia* comments on Virgil and, by implication, reflects back on the *Convito*'s theory of education. As mirrors of each other, the *Convito* and *Commedia* limit each other's possible ambiguities or indeterminacies. Similarly, the numerous medieval commentaries on the *Commedia* in its time also tell what its language games are.[70]

In his *Convito* reflections on the *Aeneid*, Dante follows Fulgentius and remarks that the *Aeneid* speaks of the "different movement of the ages" (4.24.67–108). He adds that Virgil speaks of youth in the fourth, fifth, and sixth books, where Aeneas learns the bridling of the delight offered by Dido by disciplining himself and develops the fortitude to seek Anchises with the help of the sibyl (4.26.70–111).[71] It is on this reading of the *Aeneid* that the *Commedia* builds, and it is not without reason that Fulgentius is used explicitly twenty-two times by Dante's fourteenth-century critics and, implicitly, many more times.[72]

In the *Commedia*, Dante undertakes the Fulgentian-Bernardine journey through the ages and education levels in a broken pattern. For instance, he begins his travels "in the middle of the journey of this life" – the middle of Aeneas's journey – book 6, young maturity, the time of education in the lower world. According to the *Convito*, Dante's own education literally began at that stage in his life, after the death of Beatrice.[73] When Aeneas receives the education that comes to him in Hades during maturity, he has (allegorically) passed the ills of adolescence and early youth. In the *Commedia*, a fiction analogous to the *Aeneid*'s passage through the earlier ages appears in the *Purgatorio* with the information that Dante in his youth, after Beatrice's death, pursued loves that resemble Dido in their representing a lesser good until Virgil as his sibyl came to him as mid-journey (*Inferno* 1; *Purgatorio* 31). Though only Holy Week weekend and a few additional days go by in the poem, by the time the poet reaches Beatrice, he is a bearded adult, approaching old age. He is also a child coming toward a new life. By the end of the *Paradiso*, he has united with God in a symbolic, if not a literal, death that empties his will and all of his powers.[74]

Aeneas's descent into the lower world as a mature person represented, to medieval readers, a descent to contemplate the world of the *silva* or *physis* of matter or material sensation and its limitations. Such readers would not have been surprised to find the pilgrim Dante journeying first into the contemplation of a thickly material world of the *Inferno* as he begins his education: mud, fire, and other heavy and unpleasant substances that can be studied by medieval physics. Some critics have suggested that Dante moves through an Augustinian-Boethian sequence: matter as perceived by the sensorium in the *Inferno*,[75] the more abstracted world of images perceived by the imagination in the *Purgatorio*, and the abstract and systemic forms perceived by the intelligence in the *Paradiso*.[76] These realms correlate loosely with physics (which explores matter), the mathematical disciplines (which depend on imagination and explore nonmaterial shapes), and theology and metaphysics (which, according to Boethius, depend on the intelligence).

In the sensual, desire-dominated world of the prisoners in the *Inferno*,

Dante simply moves around the Virgilian/Fulgentian emblems as if they were chess pieces, using the general philosophic schemata that he derives from Aristotle's *Ethics* to declare his interpretation of the medieval Virgil. The medieval readers who compose the commentaries on Dante allow the basic interpretations developed by Fulgentius to remain in force; but they modify such interpretations using the *Inferno*'s structuring in terms of Aristotle's *Ethics*. In Dante's version of Aristotle's *Ethics*, incontinence, violence, and fraud appear as successively more severe sins (cf. *Ethics* 7.1 [11.79–84]). Dante's meaning arises from a complex interaction among semantic factors: the large ethical structure derived from the *Ethics*, the specific exemplifications of that structure implicit in the sinners punished in hell, and the significance assigned to the monsters by previous commentary, especially Fulgentius.

Dante also changes Fulgentius by using the *Ethics* and the exemplary sinners. Fulgentius's Charon, etymologized as *ceron* or *cronon*, represents time that crosses the Acheron of the boiling emotions of youth; Cerberus, etymologized in Fulgentius's *Mythologiae* as "eater of flesh," becomes in his *Aeneid* commentary the flesh-eating power of contention and litigiousness.[77] Fulgentius's Tisiphone means "angry voice,"[78] and his city of Dis stands for pride and conceit.[79] Finally, his open pit of Tartarus is punishment for pride, and his Titans themselves embody this pride.[80] In Bernard Silvestris, much the same meanings are assigned: Charon means time again;[81] Cerberus means "devouring flesh" (*carnem vorans*), the verbal disciplines not necessarily used for litigious purposes;[82] Tisiphone is wicked speech and quarreling;[83] Dis is the city of temporal goods, connected to power, pleasure, and pride;[84] and the Titans are cupidity's proud drive to keep the soul from knowledge of the divine.[85] These interpretations are repeated in dozens of commentaries that are pieced together from Fulgentius, Bernard Silvestris, Servius, and other critics, as if they were the clichés of a modern college anthology. In Pietro Alighieri's commentary (Pietro was Dante's son), Charon remains time as in Fulgentius and Bernard, but Cerberus becomes "devouring flesh" as gluttony instead of litigiousness, because the *Inferno*'s ethical scheme requires that the upper Hades contain the sins of incontinence rather than fraud. Pietro understands Dante's Pluto as the patron monster of the fourth circle because he represents the incontinence of avarice that attaches to the earth. But this understanding surely also derives from something like Bernard Silvestris's rendering of Pluto as "earth." Tisiphone remains an aspect of rage; Dis is the city of riches and of sinfulness; and Dante's giants, substituted for Titans, are pride.[86] In short, the Fulgentian tradition has become a determinate and stable iconographic language informing the allegory of Dante's circles as Aristotle's *Ethics* controls that allegory and specific sinners modify it.

It is important to stress that the Virgil of Dante's *Commedia* is not simply the Fulgentian or Bernardine cartographer of the ages and educational stages of humankind, a poet who has left behind Roman imperial history. Dante's Virgil remains crucially the active-life poet of history, particularly the history of the Holy Roman Empire, and, like Servius's Virgil, he writes of that literal Italy for which Camilla gave her life (1.85–109). But Dante's Virgil also becomes the educator-Virgil created by Virgilian commentary, the guide through the learned world found in Fulgentius. Unlike Servius's Virgil, who appears to be captured by the assumptions of his own period and regime, Dante uses his learning to make one of the most devastating critiques that any poet has made of the ruling elites of his time. He rages with Cacciaguida and, yet, finds a place in the "ivory tower" castle of the seven liberal arts (*Inferno* 4.106ff.) implicitly celebrated in previous commentary on Virgil's book 6. Benvenuto's late fourteenth-century commentary on Dante explains the castle as follows: "The author believes philosophy and the arts themselves to be necessary and adapted to poetry, for poetry is, as it were, a veiled philosophy. It should be understood that a true poet ought to know all of the [liberal] sciences. Whence Aristotle and Horace in their poetics liken poetry to painting; for as one cannot be a good painter if one does not know about all things in some respects, so one cannot be a good poet if one has not mastered all knowledge, as is evident throughout this poem."[87]

Dante's dialogue with Virgil throughout the *Inferno* and *Purgatorio* fictionalizes what one does when one reads Virgil as a medieval reader – how one must anticipate the progress through the liberal arts that Bernard Silvestris celebrates *to be able to read him*. Virgil becomes the *Commedia's* surrogate for the *Convito's* examination of the seven liberal arts and reading of Cicero and Boethius as an introduction to the recovery of Wisdom.

Yet Dante's Virgil-guide is not all of the arts. As every student of the *Commedia* realizes, this Virgil knows almost nothing of theology or metaphysics or even the higher mathematical disciplines, and he does not soar, with Boethius's Lady Philosophy or Beatrice, above the heavens to the throne of Zeus. He is, to Pietro, simply rational philosophy,[88] a combination of logic, the natural sciences using logic, and the intermediate sciences between mathematics and physics (i.e., astronomy and music).[89] Generally his answers to Dante reflect rational philosophy's range of disciplines (cf. *Inferno* 23.25ff.; 7.54ff.; 12.121–25; 34.105; 2.97ff.; *Purgatorio* 6.61ff.; 9.88–93). Virgil stops before the river that keeps him out of the earthly paradise because he does not know those connections between number in the creation and number in the mind of the Creator that make the mathematical disciplines into noetic ones leading to God, disciplines whose insights Beatrice must mediate (see chapter 7).

Dante's higher guides, going beyond rational philosophy, also owe something to the *Aeneid* (cf. chapter 7). In the *Commedia*, the equivalents of Acates and Apollo who prepare the sibyl to guide Aeneas become a "donna gentil" who calls Lucia to her (*Inferno* 2.94) and Lucia, as Apollonian light-bearer, who comes to the Beatrice who secures Virgil to be Dante's guide (*Inferno* 2.97). The sibyl or her accoutrement – the golden bough of philosophy – become Dante's Virgil, the rational philosophy that performs the same function. Musaeus as poet becomes Statius, the poet who leads Dante to Eden, and Anchises, who tells of the mysteries, becomes Beatrice.[90] She tells the mysteries of a cosmos beautiful with Wisdom and number and ultimately delivered from human despoiling exactly as Augustine's natural world is. The succession of guides is simply a reminder that a series of cognitive levels and disciplines are part of the journey to Wisdom, and they play off against Boethius's similar guides (see chapters 6 and 7). Thus Dante consolidates what Servius, Fulgentius, and Bernard had set in motion – the creation of a language of symbol that can reflect history and yet rehearse the journey to Wisdom – and he does so in a way that many of his fourteenth-century readers understood (as the commentators make clear).

PETRARCH AND THE RETURN OF EDUCATION TO HISTORY

Petrarch makes history and the active life return to the epic using a method different from Dante's. In Petrarchan commentary on the *Aeneid,* the obvious figurative or allegorical structures, such as etymological allegory or the allegorizing of Virgilian books as the ages of life, disappear. In Petrarchan subcreation based on the *Aeneid* – that is, in the

Africa – history threatens to take over unless one reads carefully for the poem's clues to the notion that forces from beyond history have a shaping power in time. Yet, Petrarch's effort to limit the formless and useless in the educational process through the employment of the epic metaphor of the *Aeneid*-as-education remains vigorous. Once the *Aeneid* had become the story of the educational passage of the soul to cosmic light, one could present the struggle from two angles: in one, the heroic soul reaches toward scholarly illumination; in the other, illumination reaches toward the soul. Both angles are, to some extent, present in the earlier *Aeneid* commentary I have analyzed: the former perspective appears in Petrarch's commentary on the *Aeneid*, while some of the latter is to be found in Petrarch's own epic poem, the *Africa*.[91]

Petrarch sees the *Aeneid* as a practical and rhetorical guide to education in the higher truth, and he illustrates his understanding of it in his letters about education. In a full treatment of the education of the young in a letter to Gilberto, a Parmese grammarian and tutor to boys, he tells his correspondent that the young man whom Gilberto is educating is in Virgil's underworld at the dividing of the path of the Pythagorean Y, leading either to Tartarus or to Elysium (the equivalent of the biblical broad and narrow ways). Petrarch interprets the two paths leading from the Y as the paths of pleasure and virtue, hell and heaven, the multitude and the guide (*Aeneid* 6.539ff.). To teach the youth, the tutor must recreate, in daily life interactions, the antitheses that come after the Y. The tutor must oppose each of the child's emotional stances and attitudes with its opposite – joy with sadness, labor with rest, fear with friendship; he must administer words and physical punishments or rewards that are properly adjusted to the gravity of the student's deeds or misdeeds (*Fam.* 7.17).[92] He must show the child all of life's treacherous roads so as to represent the truth of Virgil's observation concerning the Elysian and Tartarean paths. Such a style of teaching, according to Petrarch, informs the young mind more fully than all of the liberal arts taken together.

Petrarch sees that Virgilian poetry can lead the student on the right road, since Aeneas's story tells of a man seeking perfection by setting forth toward the divine and leading his friends toward his goal. In other letters and comments, Petrarch interprets the *Aeneid* to make it represent the luminous path to truth and perfection. Aeneas is patently imperfect at the beginning because he is disturbed by the Venus of pleasure in his efforts to achieve the contemplation of God. In a letter to Federico d'Arezzo,[93] Petrarch writes that the Venus whom the hero meets at the beginning of the *Aeneid* (1.314ff.) patronizes the Trojans and the Trojan Paris, who chose the life of lust and license over Juno's power and wealth, and over Minerva's wisdom and study "among the lives described by the poets" (i.e., the voluptuous, active, and contemplative lives). Accordingly, this Venus – understood exactly as Fulgentius and Bernard would have understood her – leads Aeneas into his relationship with Dido. But when he escapes from this voluptuous Venus, he completes the perfective disciplines in his descent into Hades, and, unlike Gilberto's potential problem student, he takes the correct branch of Hades's Pythagorean y. Thereafter he contemplates, through Anchises, the mind flowing through all things to which humankind may return as fire after many purgations (6.722–48). Finally, the *Aeneid*'s three cities represent stages in his perfection – Troy, the voluptuous life; Carthage, the good civic life; and Rome, the contemplative one – so that Aeneas's journey takes him from the voluptuous to the active to the perfective or contemplative life in a rearranging of the Fulgentian progress from pleasure to contemplation to action.[94]

To make this interpretation work, Petrarch has to change the interpretation of book 1 as birth and make that book's storm leading to shipwreck on the Libyan coast (after which Aeneas meets the Venus who stands for lust) mean the windy power of passion loosed from the control of reason (Aeolus). Passion, in turn, leads to temptation and fall in Venus's *selva oscura,* the Libyan forest. At Dido's banquet (the conviviality of any proper human community), Iopas, representing a royal mastery of the trivium (eloquence) and quadrivium (knowledge), tells of the secrets of nature and combines the offices of poet and philosopher. In contrast, Dido's other banquet speaker, Bitias, represents all the negative aspects of human community summarized in greedy commercial activity. At the same banquet, Aeneas, the heroic, active man, tells of Troy's decadent life and of its destruction of the citadel of the soul, a destruction that allegorically makes the good man flee. Troy falls before the Greek intellectual arts – skill in navigation (Neptune), military strength (Juno), and general learning (Minerva). It also falls before Greece's reception of divine favor from God (Jove). As the old Troy falls and Aeneas loses his first Epicurean Venus, the clouds lift from his eyes, he sees the wrathful

Grecian deities destroying the city of lust (2.588ff.), and a new Venus – humankind's delight in fulfilling the harmonies of a divinely created nature – helps him on to the descent, to Anchises, and to the mind flowing through all. Thus, in its totality the *Aeneid* celebrates the perfective passage through the voluptuous, active, and contemplative lives (the three lives confronting Paris when he chooses between Venus, Juno, and Minerva) on the way to human completion in the divine (*Fam.* 1.2).[95]

While Petrarch uses letters and comments to reveal his understanding of the meaning of the *Aeneid* and to make it a little less schematic than had earlier medieval Virgilian commentators, he also uses his conception of the *Aeneid* to give both an educational and a civic structure to his *Africa.* The work builds on Virgilian interpretation while recovering Servius's interest in the surface of ancient history and its capacity to reflect contemporary events.[96] In the *Africa*, unlike in the poet's *Aeneid* commentary, Petrarch gives the active life a more prominent role by making his hero, the elder Scipio, represent the active life. Its Ennius is a poetic contemplative, and its Sophonisba is a new and very voluptuous Dido (*Fam.* 3.12).[97] However, both Ennius and Sophonisba play second fiddle to the Scipio who conquers Carthage. The work's beginning seems to make Hannibal's Carthage, the descendent of Troy, follow Petrarch's version of Virgil's Troy in that Hannibal's Carthage represents the excess of pleasure and passion that makes a city fall. In contrast, Libya represents a wholesome version of the active life, especially Syphax's Libyan banquet. The *loci* and contents of Scipio's and Ennius's dreams concerning the future suggest how contemplation informs destiny and action in the active world (cf. *Fam.* 3.12).[98]

The plot structure of the *Africa* inverts the sequence that Petrarch uses in his Virgilian interpretation. The early books tell how the contemplative life ideally rules and gives meaning to the active life, and how it must rule the voluptuous world if civil society is to exist at all.[99] The middle books show the voluptuous life successfully subverting destiny's intention that Rome should conquer Carthage and, thereby, fuse action and contemplation. Petrarch apparently did not complete book 4 of the *Africa*, but in book 5, he presents Sophonisba, Syphax's voluptuous wife, seducing Scipio's ally, Masinissa, by overwhelming him with a tempest of passion that parallels Aeneas's allegorical passion during the tempest near Libya's coast.[100] Like Dido, Sophonisba endeavors to prevent her lover's purposed service to Rome, and, like Dido, she destroys herself at last. Thus, the first five books of the *Africa* offer an emblematic historical structure parallel to that which Petrarch finds in the *Aeneid,* a structure asserting how the contemplative must control the active life and the active reign over the voluptuous.

The last four books mirror the first five in reverse order by portraying the triumph of the active over the voluptuous life and its fulfillment in peacetime's contemplation and poetry. In book 6, the voluptuous Sophonisba descends into an inferno of lovers that vaguely recalls the Paolo and Francesca episode, and an active Scipio conquers a passionate Hannibal in word in book 7 and in deed in book 8: two victories that permit Ennius in book 9 to announce his relationship as a poet to Scipio as a conqueror and to dramatize poetry's triumph over time.

The primary celebrations of the power of Wisdom poetry in books 5 through 9 come in the prayers of Carthage and Rome to Jove in book 7 and Ennius's discussion of the rule of the poet in book 9 (framed by the earlier visit to the Palace of Truth). Both concern the relationship between history and the formation of the soul. Carthage's and Rome's prayers announce the powers of the voluptuous and active lives. Carthage elevates Hannibal to the status of a new Turnus: an overreaching defier of the gods, given to bloody courses, and destroyed by rage and verbal deception. In contrast, Rome calls for Jove's protection against Hannibal in order to create the *pax romana.* Because it believes that the entrance of the Logos into the scholar-statesman is crucial to his success, Rome prays that Scipio's mind may be inspired by "divine intelligence" (7.841–48). In reply, Jove tells of the defeat of the spoiler beast through such prayers: His pleasure in His creation of the pearls of the stars and their choirs (7.912–13), His love of dwelling in virtuous souls, and His Logos-purpose, given in John 1, to dwell in human flesh and restore light to the earth. Rome's *raison d'être,* in Petrarch's logic as in Augustine's, is to create the temporal conditions necessary to the realization of Christ's and the creation's purpose. Petrarch's Rome, as the agent of the incarnation, avoids verbal deception and private passion while appealing to cosmic order and natural law, a development natural enough in a poet who draws much of his inspiration from Cicero's *De Re Publica.*

Throughout the *Africa,* Scipio as conqueror prepares for Christ's incarnation of divine intelligence in history – first by his being empowered by his dream in books 1 and 2, then by his visit to the palace of Truth, and finally by his receiving Ennius's revelation that God plans to make him an examplar of eternal virtue. The palace of Truth episode, often placed in modern texts in book 3 after the scene at Syphax's palace, should probably, as Aldo Bernardo believes, be placed at the end of book 4, so that Scipio's journey to the Atlas mountains culminates in his visit to Truth prior to his main actions.[101] The visit to Truth's palace thus informs Scipio's great civic actions exactly as does Aeneas's visit to the sibyl's temple of Apollo and his related underworld descent prior to his battle for Latium. Virgilian commentary's picture of Aeneas's visit to Apollo's temple and the underworld gives humanity to the educational process; the *Africa*'s picture of the visit to Atlas's palace does the same thing. In Atlas's palace in Petrarch's *Africa,* the giant who built the palace has set seven gems to imitate the seven planets and placed about them the signs of the Zodiac. Around them he has placed the pagan gods, including Mercury with Philology and her dower of the seven liberal arts. The temple of truth thus contains the seven liberal arts signified by Mercury accompanied by Philology, the arts, and the seven planets.[102] The disciplines used to study language and cosmic reality enlighten the statesman, represented by Scipio, before he undertakes his historical mission in the same way that Dido's banquet enlightens Aeneas before he sails to found Rome in Petrarch's commentary, and in the way that the underworld trivium and quadrivium inform Bernard's Aeneas.

After Scipio's visit to the palace of Truth, the higher disciplines are further made persuasive – the Word is made flesh – in the poetic theology practiced by Scipio's poet, Ennius, on the basis of his knowledge of the same truth. In book 9, Scipio calls on Ennius to speak with the talent which Apollo-Wisdom has given him (*Fam.* 10.4),[103] to speak as Wisdom's representative and as a divine poet, and to build a cloudlike structure on the foundation of truth (9.25) by fabricating his poetry from the "clouds" that surround the liberal arts and the palace of Truth on Mount Atlas. Ennius includes, among the disciplines he mentions, the threefold world of ethics, history (9.131–33), and the "hidden things of God" seen by the blind, contemplative Homer who in vision appears to him. He then rehearses the ascent from physics to metaphysics originated by the Platonists and Neoplatonists and included in Bernardine commentary. Since Ennius's kind of poetry is an encyclopedic art covering all of reality, it can celebrate what is best in humankind: those times when it consciously fulfills divine design.[104] Learning and poetry as constructors of civic and contemplative paradigms educate the soul to perform Wisdom's deeds and know its thoughts. Indeed, one can see in Dante and Petrarch the resurrection of a kind of hegemonic poetry in that both look to a new Rome. Dante looks to a new imperial Rome and Petrarch to a renewal of the republic. Yet they do not underwrite an extant order; instead they rehearse the possibility of a future order, not exactly what hegemonic poetry is supposed to do.

The appropriation of epic language that the classical commentators begin becomes, by the later middle ages, a formula for approaching the Virgilian epic as the adumbration of an education that moves beyond rhetoric and poetry to truth and the origin of things. The language becomes predictable across the centuries because the genre and plot structure of the epic predicate for medieval commentators and readers a language game that has become determinate and, yet, different from that which Donatus and Servius find in Virgil. The determinate meaning here is not entirely of a piece with that of Augustine's "Tolle, lege" garden or his "Enter into the joy" at Ostia, for it carries no assurance that the Logos speaks through historical events to direct a life. It tells us that a plot can map a life of learning. The allegorized epic, using a language-of-presence that does not, however, imply that the object is somehow "in" or simply labeled by the word, bases itself in the notion that the words of the epic ultimately refer to educational actions that can lead one to the Logos.[105]

This chapter began with Fulgentius's and Servius's epic allegories of education and action imposed on the Virgilian story, allegories written, respectively, as the Roman empire declines and after it has become moribund. The chapter ends with the stories of Dante and Petrarch adumbrating a similar fusion of study and action but for critical civic purposes. Having moved from its place as an underground in Origen's world, Christianity becomes the dominant religious power in the fourteenth-century world, but its believers, if they have the learning and critical sense of a Dante or Petrarch, can still place themselves outside the established political order and appeal to the order of Wisdom – Cassandras who foresee the burning of their city. One may at this point question whether the conventional periodization of medieval and early Renaissance humanism and classicism makes much sense. Period habits in reading the Virgilian epic and the shards of Homeric epic left to the middle ages, and period practices in making new creations based on Virgil, must certainly be central to any standard definitions of the differences between medieval and Renaissance humanism and classicism.

Yet the commentaries on Virgil's epic and the epics that grow out of them do not follow the standard period logic. In both the medieval and early Renaissance periods, the commentators and creators construct a substitute meaning for the Homeric and Virgilian epics that is wholly foreign to their original classical cultures. They do not wish to recover ancient times or to accomplish what Virgil does in celebrating Augustus or temporal rulership. Rather, they hold up to admiration a structured education and development that can serve as the basis for a critique of the temporal state. The epics as understood by medieval and early Renaissance people do not turn on the glorification of humankind or autonomous reason ("humanism") but on the celebration of humankind's capacity to be carried outside of itself through learning and love. Dante and Petrarch display as much interest in the understanding and glorification of the cosmos and its Author as in humankind. Though the Virgilian allegory begun by Fulgentius takes poetry away from history, Petrarch returns it there without entirely losing the Fulgentian tradition. Admittedly, Petrarch's allegory of the journey to truth in the *Africa* is no longer only a private, individual quest like that in Bernard's commentary on the *Aeneid* (perhaps the public nature of the *Africa* occasions Petrarch's questioning of it in the *Secretum*). But the center of his statement remains the journey to Wisdom and its uses in the construction of any future good temporal society. Petrarch, like Bernard and Fulgentius, faces a learned world made up of Gilberto's kind of students, a place lacking the compulsory tools that modern culture uses to mark benchmarks in education and force students to perform. He uses the epic to make vision substitute for compulsion.

When Fulgentius writes his commentary, learning controlled by the schools is under challenge and undergoing a transformation, and the collective learned institutions of the past are soon to become difficult to maintain. Fulgentius's picture of a journey to learning must have meant a good bit to the scholar buffeted by the various invasions that troubled European institutions and made the path to learning insecure. In contrast, Petrarch's world has a goodly number of fairly well-supported universities and schools that are relatively secure from the warriors of the time. However, if in Petrarch's world, the university or school offers some access to roles in the clergy and court, these roles are not guaranteed to the good scholar. As Petrarch often reminds his audiences, the scholar in his time has to live meagerly, without clear sources of subsistence, scrambling for manuscripts and often finding them in difficult places, if he finds them at all. In such a world, the central notion of the epic appears not to have been the celebration of the great historical figure, but the heralding of the mind that journeys to Wisdom by itself with only philosophy or the *Aeneid* for a guide. Such a mind journeys through pain to learn the disciplines and comes home to a vision of ultimate reality that makes clear the limits of the present political order. We have gone full circle from Servius to Petrarch. We have traveled from Rome to Rome. But in the passage, we have added to the Roman civic epic the picture of the heroic benchmarks of an education that the solitary soul passes through in order to know Wisdom and criticize the civic world. This extra meaning of the heroic intellectual quest suffuses Dante, Petrarch, and even the Renaissance scientists (as later chapters will demonstrate). It provides a much wider audience for the notion of a journey to Wisdom than Augustine's *Confessions* or his imitators, with their limited audiences, could ever provide.

It is not clear to me that there are lessons for our time in what medieval critics do with the epic of education. In many ways I do not like the late classical and early medieval exegetes' wrenching of the Virgilian epic out of its historical context and their displacement of its original language games, even for a good purpose. Medieval exegetes seem too often to play Humpty Dumpty to the medieval Alices who become neoepic poets. On the other hand, if we are to develop a less bureaucratized education, one suspects that we will have to make available some maps of the educational journeys that childhood might take into youth and adulthood. Bruno Bettelheim in *The Uses of Enchantment* argues that fairy tales do this. But even if one believes his Freudian argument, the tales do this only for the most basic parts of growing up, dealing with parents and authority, then leaving these behind. They do not treat of educational stages. In the Victorian period, the Dickensian picaresque novel and *bildungsroman* ground children and youth in what they have to face, or change, in the social reality of their time – what sort of self-education they need to survive that reality. These fictive worlds have now largely been replaced by the fantasies of television; but the greatest educational challenges now lie in understanding the scientific landscape that young people will face – what it is and what it means. The C. P. Snows of the world are not of much help in this effort. If Virgilian interpretation and subcreation have a use for us, it is in their demonstration that education can be mapped through fictions, their showing that the literary can point to the mathematical and scientific in cognition. This achievement is considerable, even if the interpretive procedure that leads to it is at best undisciplined and at worst irresponsible.

6

Boethius's Return to Plato and Wisdom

Boethius maps his version of the path to knowledge by using elements of the Platonic ascent, the Biblical Wisdom-road, and the epic journey. He does so to accomplish educational goals that this book has treated throughout. But his work derives its power less from originality than from its appearing at a moment when education that is primarily the hand-maiden of Roman cultural conditioning carries little long-term authority. New educational modes have to rise up because the educational bureaucracies of the empire have been weakened. It is also not accidental that Boethius becomes the primary source of educational theory in later figures as diverse as Alcuin, Hugh of St. Victor, John of Salisbury, Thomas Aquinas, and Dante.

In our own moment of cultural transition, Jeffrey Nealon has asked, "How does one make thought or action truly critical if the category that could ground such a criticism – *truth* – has been withdrawn?"[1] Bereft of the category of truth, Nealon poses a series of possible answers based on contemporary educational and literary theory – answers that present the academic disciplines as products of appropriations of power that lead to new subjugations of people. He argues that human beings create competing interpretations of the world to justify competing institutional practices that give power to their own group. To make an action critical, in his view, we must preserve a radical skepticism about the production of knowledge and the institutions that produce it.[2]

Nealon's view states succinctly what is implicit in much contemporary educational theory and in the position of the Sophists, namely, that power creates knowledge. However, whereas the Sophists sought to serve the powers-that-be, post-structuralist theory seeks to serve oppositional forces. The critic aims to create resistance against the conventional and the oppressive from within the system. Like most post-structuralist critics, Nealon ignores the answer that "traditional" critics, including Socrates and Boethius, give: that no serious criticism of the social order is possible without some grounding in "truth." The critique requires that one find where the present order is grounded in a lie or set of lies; the weakening of that order demands the communication of data (or data interpreted by theory) that shows the status quo to be founded on falsehood of a factual or theoretical sort.[3] Socrates and Boethius testify that criticism may, in circumstances of tyranny, require a willingness to die for the right to articulate a critique.[4]

A question comparable to Nealon's that contemporary educational theory poses is, "Can one find an education outside the constraining power of the institutions that 'construct' knowledge to serve the present order?" Some educational reformers in the twentieth century, such as Ivan Illich, would get rid of educational institutions altogether, especially at the lower levels.[5] Boethius addresses the question of the relationship between education and its institutions through his presentation of an educational (and imaginative) structure independent of bureaucracy that allows him to speak with critical authority from the margin. His tactic, like Socrates's, is to argue that, though he speaks from the social margin, he speaks for the center of the created order.

The histories of philosophy and literature sometimes treat Boethius as the last great Greco-Roman writer and sometimes as the first great medieval one. No one knows exactly when Rome fell and the "middle ages" began. One candidate for the beginning is Theoderic's Ostrogothic kingdom in Italy, which appears in A.D. 493 and gives life to Roman skeletons. A high official in this kingdom, Boethius is both the scion of one of the Roman Senate's chief families and for a time one of Theoderic's chief servants. His work reflects the influence of both traditions. In a time of transition, he fuses traditions about the shape and functions of self-directed education into a form that was to become academically popular and functional in the early, middle, and late medieval periods.

After the Germanic groups penetrated Italy in the late 400s, institutional education did not swerve from its primarily rhetorical content to any great extent (though it had a less secure municipal base in some areas in consequence of the political changes).[6] However, the need for an education to find a "truth" independent of Roman political power, as opposed to one imparting the literary skills necessary to cultivated life, must have become more apparent as the centers of conventional authority in Roman life were challenged. Boethius announces his theory of learning at a time when the Roman municipal schools are in decline and the new monastic schools are little more than a gleam in the eyes of persons like Cassiodorus. However, once understood, his sense of what learning should be comes to work for several kinds of people – for people in institutions that emphasize the group retreat from the world, for solitary learners that wander from institution to institution or study on their own, and for court laity. Perhaps they work because post-Roman educational conditions require a more personal or religious pursuit of truth, separated from state concerns.

Jean Leclercq, writing of monastic learning as a composite of the love of learning and the desire for God, asserts that "the monks did not acquire their religious formation in a school, under a scholastic, by means of the *quaestio*, but individually, under the guidance of an abbot, a spiritual father, through the reading of the Bible and the Fathers, within the liturgical framework of monastic life."[7] In the interior schools for youths preparing to be monks, one found something more like the ordered school of our day. But there was also an element of close personal attention directed to the students, especially to the ablest of the students – an effort to get children to see the spiritual reason for their labors, even for mechanical tasks.[8] Boethius laid the theoretical foundations that made such individualized clerical education feasible, but he also gave clear guidance as to the acquisition of learning to many nonclerical students, the source of his great influence with later medieval and Renaissance vernacular writers located at secular courts.

Boethius's central problem in the *Consolation* is the same as that which Socrates confronts when he criticizes the Sophists: to find a noncivic basis for his intellectual authority when the ruler grows tyrannous, to find a critical space for himself. To do this he resurrects Plato's mathematical road to truth and to Wisdom's final rulership and combines it with Aristotle's interest in the collection of particulars (or inductive research) while demonstrating in his own person that a willingness to suffer and to

pursue scientific learning can collaborate to move him from an "attachment to self and to things and to persons" to a detachment that makes
study possible. In the Homeric *Consolation*'s first scenes, he is (metaphorically) the person captive to the Calypso-island exile grief occasioned
by his political fall; in its end, he returns, like Odysseus, to the true country
of detachment, where he commands the intellectual and spiritual authority that secular government cannot overthrow (cf. chapter 5).

PHILOSOPHER-KING AND TYRANT:
BOETHIUS'S *REPUBLIC, TIMAEUS,* AND *PARMENIDES*

The *Consolation*'s structure reconstructs the pathway of Plato's three major works and does not flee the history of its own time any more than do
Plato's *Republic* and Augustine's *Confessions*.[9] The work achieves its authority, as a piece of prison protest literature set against the backdrop of
Theoderic's late reign and Boethius's confinement, by kissing the steps
where Plato and the Wisdom literature walked between the topical and
the permanent and by appealing to the possibility that humankind may
use the disciplines to mount to a truth that is independent of political
authority.

At the beginning of book 1, Boethius reconstructs the battle between
the philosophers and Sophists in the Boethius persona's "sophistic"
stance. He has been busy reading and writing tragic stories of mythic or
historical heroes that suffer as he does. Both readings and creations may
be either formal tragedies or works somewhat in the vein of Ovid's *Tristia*
(1.m.1).[10] In any case, their muses are strumpets, probably the muses of
the Sophists since Boethius's *In Ciceronis Topica* reveals that he knew of the
Sophists's characterization as persons who make tricky arguments.[11] He
certainly knew the *Republic*'s criticism of the Sophists's art as based on
emotionalism and self-indulgence, since he cites the *Republic* in the *Consolation*. But the empathy possible to the imprisoned Boethius can only be
the solipsistic empathy for himself of one who, as Philosophy observes,
forgets that his home is the permanent truth of eternity (1.pr.6); no one
outside the prison can empathize with him as an isolated prisoner feeling
self-pity, and in his solitude no community of empathy can exist, no use
develop for Gorgias's kind of tragedy. By placing himself in solitude in
the narrative of his work (as he presumably was placed in real life),
Boethius confronts what the nonsocial sources of authority and criticism

must be. Given the absence of effective literary consolation, the muse of Philosophy confronts him and his siren-muses (apparently dominated by the muse of tragedy) concerning his reaction to his fall.[12] She imitates Plato's exiling of the poets in the *Republic* (books 2, 3, and 10) by exiling the sirens (cf. 1.pr.1) with the charge that they feed Boethius only with the poison of his own emotion.[13]

The "objective" world is outside the prison walls: the world of Ostrogothic/Roman politics and beyond that the world of the creation. Boethius's intellectual task is to appeal from politics to creation for authority. Theoderic's civic realm, described in Boethius's first two books, represents a complex, sometimes straightforward and sometimes inverted, analogy for the *Republic*'s state ruled by philosopher kings. Behind the *Consolation*'s appeal in book 1 to the old senatorial Rome lies an appeal to the older civic order of Plato's ideal Greece, where the guardians are a senate of sorts. However, the *Consolation*, like the guardians, has also to appeal to the mathematically discerned order of the heavens. A polished member of the Roman senatorial class and a reader of Greek, Boethius tells us that, before his imprisonment, he had a private library containing philosophic treatises (1.pr.4) where he studied geometry, astronomy, and Plato's *Republic* and *Timaeus* (i.e., he studied how to order his life after the order of the heavens).[14] Given his emphasis on mathematical rather than rhetorical study in his home library, Boethius insinuates that his education has been unlike that of the majority of leaders in his time. Thus he begins to establish for himself a critical space, a legitimacy superseding that of Theoderic's state, and to suggest that only in prison has he become the victim of siren muses.[15]

The state that Boethius pictures has been altered from the Roman model by Theoderic's ascendancy (though its Senate survives). But Boethius recalls that, prior to his imprisonment when he was Theoderic's Master of the Offices (the most important office in the more or less intact bureaucracy left over from Roman times), he tried to rule as if he were Plato's philosophic guardian (1.pr.4).[16] From other histories, we know how Roman institutions decayed in the late fifth century, how, prior to Theoderic, Odovacar, the deposer of the last Roman emperor, had ruled Italy until 489 and had left many Roman nonmilitary institutions intact (institutions that Theoderic also left partially intact).[17] We know how Theoderic placed the *physis* of military power in the hands of his fellow

Ostrogoths, and how he appeased the Ostrogothic military by support-ing it with awards of land and other emoluments. When Boethius, the adopted scion of a powerful Roman family, took office as the most impor-tant bureaucratic official in Theoderic's largely Roman civilian establish-ment, he must have known that the divided rulership of the realm made his job hazardous; yet he claims that he tried to be Plato's philosopher king in this office (1.pr.4). His self-ascribed "crime" against Theoderic was the protection of the equivalent of Plato's "guardians," the legitimate Roman Senate, from the charges of treason leveled at it by Theoderic and his allies.[18] Boethius in prison, in a hardly objective apology for himself, pictures himself as a Socrates opposing Athenian tyranny, a Cicero oppos-ing Antony, the master of a rhetoric reaching to a Philosophy that rises above the tongues of civic persuasion as do Cicero's *De Re Publica* and *Hortensius*. Boethius's apology employs the *consolatio* genre, used in the Ciceronian *Hortensius* that so influenced Augustine's turning, to show that at the beginning the hero and his realm's institutions are at a turning point.

In looking at Boethius's apology for himself and at his imprisonment by Theoderic, Philosophy argues that a tyrant – by Platonic definition committed to the false goods of honor, delights, and possessions (*Republic* 8.543–48, 569) – remains impotent because he knows only the partial goods of the creation that he wishes to seize from the flux and possess permanently. Therefore, he is ignorant of the supreme good (or Wis-dom) that is the source of power in the creation. Quite simply, the ruler does not know the truth and must act out an assumption that the world can be created by *physis*. In contrast, the opposed subject can take the tyrant's punishment as a pedagogy, like that given to Augustine by his language teachers, free himself to rise above the tyrant's material ex-igency and the limited material goods he can offer, and contemplate a universe ordered by the "mighty and sweet" rule of Wisdom as the basis of his rule of conduct. He can act freely and declare his critical truth so long as he ignores the impediments of consequentialism. Of course, the price of such action may be death – as Philosophy's references to Socrates and Seneca make clear (1.pr.3) – but not impotent death. Boethius, like many a civil rights leader who illustrates the paradox of prison freedom, writes the *Consolation* as a political statement that anticipates medieval theory defining the tyrant as one who denies the good, violates natural law, and, as John of Salisbury advocates, deserves death. His power in this context depends on his ability to create a text that defines how one learns to know truth independent of political power, and to suffer or die in the cause of the discovery of that learning.[19]

As a philosophic ruler, Boethius claims that he has tried to be the just man – supporting the poor, protecting the justice system, and observing something like Ciceronian natural law, which guarantees rights to justice, rational discourse in assemblies, the fulfillment of contracts, and the protection of property and life.[20] Philosophy later reaffirms what Boethius says about himself and also reminds him of his Roman family satisfactions in the consulship of his two sons, in his standing between them to distribute gifts to the multitude, in his father-in-law's (Symmachus's) remaining a good man (2.pr.3), and in his wife's remaining faithful and temperate (2.pr.4). Philosophy thus situates Boethius's true community outside Theoderic's court and in the natural family structures that he later attributes to a universal love that preserves law, marriages, and friendship – structures that both the *Symposium* and New Testament commentaries also hymn ("*Hic et coniugii sacrum/Castis nectit amoribus*" [2.m.8]). Thus, Philosophy begins to redefine the fundamental social unit to which Boethius's life ought to have reference.

If the siren muses represent sophistry and its ally, tragedy, they reflect realities found in the institutionalized education popular in Boethius's period and not just in Boethius's attempts while in prison at self-consolation. Ennodius, a contemporary deacon and intellectual leader who lived in Milan from 499 to at least 511, mediates the predominant language-oriented view of a proper education.[21] His letters, representing an understanding of learning not greatly different from that Augustine attributes to the Roman schools of his day,[22] give his students encouragement in the verbal arts rather than in the critical logical, mathematical, and philosophic disciplines that Boethius had mastered and written about.[23] Boethius may attack the siren muses to express more than his own turning away from tragedy and rhetoric; he may wish to attack Ennodian and similar rhetorical views of education as largely language-based. But though Boethius rejects rhetoric and literary studies, his Philosophy is initially not ready for oppositional work either, for her clothes, torn by the long history of controversy between Stoic and Epicurean (1.pr.1; 1.pr.3), and perhaps by the obscuring of metaphysics and theology in institutionalized Roman education,[24] reflect their mistress's decline under Rome. Noetic mathematical study had not been thoroughly pursued after Augustine, and in one of his letters, Boethius's contemporary at Theoderic's court, Cassiodorus, emphasizes only the utilitarian value of the geometric sciences for surveying.[25] According to him, theoretical studies in arithmetic, geometry, music, and astronomy do not have any public support or supervision but, as he condescendingly remarks, appeal only to those who wish to probe the mysteries (Cassiodorus was later to take the noetic position, however, when he wrote his *Institutiones*).[26] Since Boethius, in his early treatise on arithmetic, puts forth the "mysterious" suggestion that the mathematical disciplines have spiritual uses as paths to Wisdom (*De Inst. Arith.* 1.1),[27] he (or a similar thinker) probably is the target of Cassiodorus's remarks.

If rhetoric and literature are impotent and philosophy is torn, the question becomes: "How does one critique the tyranny of the status quo?" On the basis of Plato's *Republic* and the works that follow from it, Boethius attacks the political and educational culture of Theoderic's regime. As the Virgil that comes to Fulgentius represents what Fulgentius could discover in reading the *Aeneid,* the Philosophy that comes to Boethius represents what he can recall from Plato and the other philosophers in his library. But this Philosophy, though torn, is also more than the philosophy to be found in books: she embodies Boethius's sense of divine Wisdom and its contrarian authority.[28] In book 3, prose 12, Philosophy, following the Wisdom 8.1 passage that says that Wisdom "reaches from end to end and mightily and sweetly orders all things," asserts that "the *Supreme Good* mightily and sweetly orders all things."[29] Philosophy's "Supreme Good" is that Wisdom that animates natural law, before which even tyrants are impotent. When Philosophy substitutes the phrase "Supreme Good" for the biblical word "Wisdom," she invites us to think of the biblical and Platonic simultaneously, Plato's Supreme Good as biblical Wisdom. Throughout the *Consolation,* Philosophy explains to the Boethius persona what Wisdom is to one who suffers, how it can elucidate historical failure and tragedy, and what the real meaning of philosophic kingship is. The passage from Wisdom 7–8, from which Boethius takes his "mighty and sweet ordering," makes its Wisdom rise like an effluence or mist from God's power, permeating things, reflecting flawlessly its source, and surrendering itself to sciences commonly listed in the Pla-

tonic and Neoplatonic *gradus* toward God – physics, the mathematical
sciences, and metaphysics – as well as to the more uncommon zoology
and botany (Wisdom 7.17–26). These sciences appear to be the sources
of Boethian truth, the platform that gives him critical authority, and the
path through which one reaches the Wisdom or Supreme Good that
makes tragedy meaningful.[30] Philosophy's garment (1.pr.1) contains
what medieval readers saw as the symbols for the practical and theoretical
sciences and points to the disciplinary ascent to Wisdom. Boethius specifies in *De Trinitate* (section 2) that the theoretical sciences are divided
into physics (or natural philosophy), studying motion in bodily forms;
mathematics, studying the static form of bodies independent of matter;
and, finally, theology, studying the static ultimate Form independent of
matter.[31] These three levels of theoretical understanding relate respectively to rational, disciplinary (or pedagogically trained), and intellectual
(or synthetic) learning.[32] Presumably their practical counterparts apply
these disciplines to active life problems. Theology, the highest form of
learning, surmounts the mind's interest not only in disciplinary thought
but in the images or imaginations that characterize mathematics (*De.
Trin.* 2).[33]

Plato quarrels with the Sophists because their social world does not
ground itself in anything beyond itself – never reaches beyond tyranny to
truth. Following this line the *Consolation* moves toward a ground of being foundational to its ethical republic. After its reflections on *Republic*
themes in its first two books, the *Consolation* moves upward through an
ascent that reflects the usual Neoplatonic disciplinary ascent,[34] through
Philosophy's three heights. Joachim Gruber relates these heights to the
appearance of the Eris in the *Iliad* (4.442ff.), who is at first little,[35] then
taller, and finally heaven-tall. But they probably also characterize the speculative or theoretical side of the Philosophy that climbs to the Logos.[36]
They are heights that adumbrate, for the later medieval reader, the ascent
from practical ethics to the highest theoretical study of nature and Wisdom that makes a critical engagement with the active life possible. Boethius's conversation with Philosophy thus represents a cognitive religious experience and not the purely technical study represented by
Victorinus's kind of interpretation of the philosophic disciplines, a perspective attacked by Boethius in his *Dialogue on the Isagoge*.[37]

Obviously disciplinary knowledge as Boethius understands it has nothing to do with any institutional control of the construction of knowledge. Rather, he understands it as a means towards an individual discovery and critique of the established order. Boethius's Philosophy is an essentialist figure, to use the current jargon, and her essentialism requires no apologies. For what she envisages is not that there are verbal essences to be found in scholastic or literary critical debate, but that the employment of her tools may lead to the discovery of genuine paradigms, natural laws, or foundational patterns in the cosmos. She receives her illumination from the divine Wisdom, who leads her followers back to her through the mathematical disciplines that ascend to the stars.[38] She is thus the center of the critical disciplines.

The structure of Boethius's ascent comes from the ascent through the *Republic, Timaeus,* and *Parmenides* that was projected on Plato's three great works by the Neoplatonists.[39] Boethius probably follows after the Neoplatonists who had identified the growth from correct citizenship to mathematical and dialogic discipline to contemplation of the One with the successive study of ethics, mathematics, and theology to be found in specific Platonic works thought to embody these disciplines. Specifically, the *Republic* encapsulated ethics, the *Timaeus* encompassed the physical sciences (especially mathematics), and the *Parmenides* comprised theology.[40] Proclus, at the end of his comment on the *Timaeus,* book 1, says that the *Republic* comes first among the educational group of Plato's dialogues because education must first present the formulation of verbal hypotheses and the social preparation of people for the contemplation of reality through the disciplines. Then, according to Proclus, the *Timaeus* can present instruction – to a person who is ready to learn – about the generation of the universe, astronomy, and divine law. Finally, since the world requires a divine origin, theology comes last,[41] and the *Parmenides* encapsulates theology. Boethius's logic in imitating Plato's works recuperates Proclus's logic in describing them. This Neoplatonic structure may be anticipated somewhat in the *Republic,* books 2 and 3, where Plato assumes that children and young people will receive an education in proper civic behavior or justice (42C–466D) – that is, ethics – and in book 7, where he argues that the state's guardians should concentrate on mathematics until they become fifty, work on dialectic for the next five years, and, thereafter, spend time in the contemplation of the transcendent ideas (*Republic* 533E–540B).[42] But when Boethius presents his version of this progress, it is "deschooled," taken away from the *Republic*'s state-sponsored schools and into a prison where it can be used by the critic of the state.

Following Proclus's structure, the *Consolation*'s first two books present a dystopian *Republic* – actually a tyranny – that educates Boethius in the meaning of his failure to achieve the ideal state through the philosophic kingship discussed in the *Republic* (5.473). While the *Republic*'s Socrates claims that the combination of power and philosophy in the leaders of the state can create true happiness for the individual, Boethius has tried and failed with Socrates's formula and, therefore, reminds Philosophy that Plato, wishing philosophers to seek public office, promised happiness to commonwealths governed by them ("studiosi sapientiae": 1.pr.4). When he sought to forge for Theoderic a public rule that conformed to what his private philosophic study told him, he did what Plato could not do. Though the *Republic* constructs a social order in the imagination, Boethius writes a work whose narrative mode is like that of Cicero in his *Republic* in that it deals with a real history and a social order that does not conform to Plato's utopia. The historical equivalents of Plato's guardians, the Roman senators, are accused of treason; the "Republic" has come to be ruled by Nero-like figures, Theoderic and his minions (2.m.5; 2.m.6; 3.m.4); and the philosophic ruler is in prison. The de facto rulers concern themselves with honors, riches, and delights, the goods of fortune that propel society's decline into tyranny in *Republic* 8 and 9 (cf. *Consolation* 2.pr.5ff.; 3.pr.2). But however self-serving the *Consolation* may appear to be, it is not without a serious self-criticism of its author as a person that, in expecting that philosophic rule would lead to particular consequences, suffers from the precise consequentialist faults he assigns to the tyrants whom he criticizes. Throughout books 1 and 2, the Boethius persona does not understand that Plato's ethical system is a deontological, not a consequentialist one, and that neither the *Republic* nor the *Timaeus* promises material returns for good deeds. Plato offers no payoff to the individual for good civic rule and neither does Philosophy. In Plato, the ethical individual cannot expect fixed consequences for ethical actions but only knows that temperance, courage, wisdom, and reason must rule the concupiscible and irascible appetites, whatever the circumstances (4.427C–434D, 441C–445B).[43] Boethius-the-author, as opposed to the persona within the work, similarly praises whoever builds on the middle ground and respects the spirit of the "Platonic communism" of the first ages of humankind (2.m.3; 2.m.5): "Happy was that early time /, satisfied with their steadfast fields, not wrecked by lazy luxury" (2.m.5; 11.1–3).

Yet Boethius's chief antidote to tyranny in the first three books is not the *Republic*'s temperance but the *Symposium*'s and the Gospel of John's cosmic love: a love having the potential to order human communities, friendships, and marriages (*Consolation* 2.m.8; 3.m.9).[44] Restraint, satisfaction with limits, and love are more the rewards of right conduct than riches, honor, or pleasure: "This (love) binds peoples together by an inviolable compact; it binds holy wedlock together in chaste love; it speaks its rule to faithful friends. O happy human race – if only the love that rules the heavens ruled your minds" (2.m.8, 11.22–30). Boethius, unlike Plato dreaming of ideal states, cannot look to philosopher kings; he cannot appeal to Plato's *Laws*, where a constitution is the substitute for the philosopher-king (he has no clear avenue of appeal to a constitution, though he does reassert the importance of many of the beliefs whose denial is heresy to the Plato of the *Laws:* belief in marriage, providence, and in a world of natural laws or "numbers" that should be the basis of human social life).[45] In short, no utopian option exists, no clear opportunity to "imagine a future society that conforms to the exigencies of human nature" as he and his time might understand them.[46] As the *Laws* is less utopian than the *Republic*, so the *Consolation* is less utopian – more "Augustinian" – than the *Laws*, promising instead of physical security from the state only Fortune's uncertain futures and a possible Socratic death (1.pr.3).[47] The ascent to Wisdom through sciences whose precise content Boethius cannot fully know becomes for him the alternative both to Plato's utopian compulsory education and to the subscription to power as the author of knowledge that the Germanic invasions appear to make inevitable.

As Boethius presents his own ascent above his prison-emptying, he recreates the three stages of the *Republic, Timaeus,* and *Parmenides* by picturing what Plato might have done in writing his three books concerning the relationship between the state and the cosmos had he really known Wisdom and philosophized as a Socrates condemned. Later medieval political theory calls this exploration of the state and cosmos relationship a study of the dependency of positive law on natural law.[48] The first book's prose describes the philosopher-persona's misery at losing his "Republic" and sets forth some propaedeutic observations from Philosophy. But its contrasting poetry offers a hope not dependent on philosophic republics. It asserts that Boethius once knew the sun – in the *Republic* "the good" – or Wisdom (1.m.2) and affirms that the general creation's numbered chain of order, held by the Maker, could include mankind among its links (1.m.5). In the poetry of book 1, the cosmic ground already begins to substitute for the failed republic, and the two meters of book 1 that come after meter 5 make Philosophy reinforce meter 5's position by asserting the existence of a divine order and the emotional human being's limitation in perceiving this order. Thus Book 1 ends with an implicit statement of the need for a cognitive transformation of the narrator so that he can find himself within the proportionate order that governs the universe. It thus becomes an *Apology* and *Republic/Laws* looking for a *Timaeus.*[49]

Book 2, treating of fortune or the moving domain of the false goods that in the *Republic* create tyranny, establishes that suffering persons can resist attachment to and domination by fortune, can detach themselves from fortune's wheel. They can get beyond Derrida's vanishing world of reference – the world that becomes the object of desire – by looking for more permanent cycles or patterns (i.e., the world that physical science eventually describes). Philosophy tells the Boethius persona that a resistance to attachment and the assumption that changes in things are orderly must become basic in his intellectual quest (2.m.8).[50]

The *Consolation*'s third book concerns the cosmic ground of existence and dissent by describing how physical change conforms to rules ordered by number and how Wisdom authors the numbered cycles of nature's change. In this concern, it closely follows Plato's *Timaeus*. That is, the *Timaeus* begins with the ideal political structure described in the *Republic,* ascribes it to an antediluvian period, and then pictures the cosmos to which human states must relate if they are to aspire to ideality, implying that understanding requires that one study mathematics, cosmic music, and astronomy. The *Timaeus*, like the *Consolation*, begins with a review of the essential matter in the *Republic*. Solon tells of an ancient Athens organized like the *Republic*'s ideal city, with an educational program based on an understanding of the sensible world's creation and ordered by the intelligible principles on which it is based. These principles are constructed according to rules of geometry, arithmetic, and music. Only institutions based in natural law possess the strength and justice that extends beyond their institutionalization. Reviewing this section of the *Timaeus*, Proclus remarks that if "the *Republic* is inferior to the *Timaeus*, [it is so] because it is conversant with that which is partial, and to discuss mortal affairs is to dwell on an image, yet the universal prevails in it" since "the same form of life exhibits indeed in the soul justice, but in the city a polity, and in the world, fabrication."[51] Justice in the soul perceives the numbered basis of the creation, and the ideal city exhibits the fabricational structure of the cosmos. Thus, the elimination of repression is no subjective task separated from making the numbered architecture of the world the foundation of the civic unit's polity and of the soul's justice.

The relationship between justice, polity, and fabrication is also the concern of book 3 of the *Consolation*. In book 1, prose 4, Boethius anticipates that he will move from *Republic* to *Timaeus* concerns when he describes his earlier philosophic study in his library and asks Philosophy whether she thinks that his prison house resembles the domestic library where, before his imprisonment, he and she together studied the "secrets of nature" and delineated the "paths of the stars" with a geometer's rod. This *Republic*-to-*Timaeus* kind of study led his Philosophy to relate the human order ("mores nostros totiusque vitae rationem") to the patterns of the celestial order ("ad caelestis ordinis exempla"). However, prior to his imprisonment, Boethius has only studied Plato academically and has retained an anachronistic, consequentialist position since he has not known serious pain.

Book 3, meter 9 commonly receives a footnote labeling it Boethius's Timaean passage. But in truth the whole of book 3 and parts of book 4 render what Wisdom might say through the *Timaeus*. The early discursive portions of book 3 examine again the imperfect goods that make up fortune and obsess the tyrant, and its poems show, in hymnic language, the cyclical character of all natural processes (3.m.2), the laws underlying their change, and the insufficiency of human reliance on the products of such processes for permanent beatitude (3.pr.3 to 3.pr.8).[52] Then, at the end of book 3, prose 9, Boethius knows that he must pray to the Author of all goods, as the original Timaeus says that his group must do prior to his discourse on the creation (*Timaeus* 17c–d). Philosophy, having summarized the essential points that both the *Timaeus* and the *Republic* make about contingent and limited goods, prays on behalf of Boethius by singing a Timaean prayer (3.m.9) that describes the Supreme Good that guides nature later defined as Wisdom (3.pr.12).[53] Critics have always noted book 3, meter 9's dependence on the *Timaeus* but scoffed at medieval interpretation's Christianization of the hymn as an address to the Logos. But the hymn precisely celebrates the noetic mathematical road to the Logos coming out of study and prayer that Augustine and Origen earlier celebrated.

In Timaeus's discourse in Plato's work that bears his name (27c–92c), Timaeus argues that the Demiurge (or God) makes the world on the basis of an eternal archetype or model, Plato's equivalent of the Logos. While using the model to make physical order from chaos, the Demiurge providentially acts as a mind (Nous) for the physical order and makes a World-Soul, or animating power, in which that mind can rest.[54] This World-Soul, in turn, mediating between the eternal Mind and the temporal physical cycles, consists of three circles that connect, at various levels, the eternity of the Nous with the temporality of the physical cosmos: what astronomy and the other mathematical disciplines study. The outermost circle of the World-Soul controls the movement of the fixed stars; the innermost controls the motion of the then-known seven planets, arranged in relative distances that reflect the Pythagorean musical intervals; and the middle circle mediates between outermost and innermost. Within the visible world, controlled by the governing soul with its three circles and by the mind placed within it, one finds the four substances: fire, air, water, and earth. By employing a series of geometrical analogies, Plato argues that fire is to air as air is to water as water is to earth. This is not the place for a full explanation of the *Timaeus* cosmology, but suffice it to say that *Timaean* cosmological study, as appropriated by Boethius, requires for its full comprehension a knowledge of arithmetic, geometry, music, and astronomy.[55] Philosophy summarizes all of these Timaean concepts by singing both as a cosmic force and a force growing up within Boethius and uttering her prayer to discover the source of the world's form:

> O Thou who dost by everlasting reason rule,
> Creator of the planets and the sky, who time
> From timelessness didst bring, unchanging Mover,
> No cause drove thee to mould unstable matter, but
> The form benign of highest good within Thee set.
> All things Thou bringest forth from Thy high archetype:
> Thou, height of beauty, in Thy mind the beauteous world

> Dost bear, and in that ideal likeness shaping it,
> Dost order perfect parts a perfect whole to frame.
> The elements by harmony Thou dost constrain.
>
> (3.m.9)[56]

What is translated as "harmony" in the above translation could also be translated as numbers ("numeris"). The elements are bound together by love as book 2, meter 8 puts it. Both wisdom and number give form to love's attractive powers, as book 3, prose 12 soon stipulates. Hence, medieval commentaries recognize both the *Timaeus* and John 1 in the poem's description of an archetype, Logos, or Demiurge that orders the visible world through its geometrically defined circular moving World-Soul that mixes the four elements to produce the natural sequences.

Book 3, meter 9 ends with an appeal to the Creator-Logos to reveal himself through John 1's transcendent light:

> Disperse the clouds of earthly matter's cloying weight;
> Shine out in all Thy glory; for Thou art rest and peace
> To those who worship Thee; to see Thee is our end,
> Who art our source and maker, lord and path and goal.
>
> (3.m.9)[57]

The remainder of book 3 simply represents how God as chief good supersedes the partial goods that tyrants crave; it also illustrates how all human beings knowingly or unknowingly seek His goodness, the Wisdom that "mightily and sweetly disposes" all things (cf. Wisdom 8.1). What is crucial about book 3 is that it assumes, beyond the vanishing world of fortune and reference, a world of describable regularities originating with Wisdom, which language and mathematical language can accurately describe.

The last two books of the *Consolation* ascend above consideration of the connection of the Creator and creation through mathematical forms and address the nature of God *in ipso*, the matter of the *Parmenides* as interpreted in Proclus's version of Plato's ascent. At the end of book 3 (3.pr.12), Boethius goes to the *Parmenides*, the expected signifier of the ascent to theology/metaphysics. To mark his next stage, he first quotes Parmenides himself from fragment 8.43, a passage about God's or Being's existing like a well-rounded sphere: "Πάντοθεν εὐκύκλου σφαίρας ἐναλίγκιον ὄγκῳ (In substance resembling a sphere that is properly rounded on all sides)."[58] Boethius uses this Parmenidean quote to argue that God is the unmoved Mover (3.pr.12). Then, in books 4 and 5, he describes the nature of the divine cognition that moves all and, yet, does not destroy human freedom.[59]

Proclus supplies Boethius with his immediate idea of the theological discourse necessary in the next stage of his ascent, for Boethius's quote from the *Parmenides* does not appear in Plato's *Parmenides* but in Proclus's comment on it.[60] Proclus, citing the passage from Parmenides (fragment 8.43) that Boethius cites in book 3, prose 12, also makes a full account of what can be said about the unmoved Mover, turning the *Parmenides* from a work fundamentally about the nature of the One-and-the-many to a full-fledged theological speculation. His interpretation of the *Parmenides* represents Plato's third level of work, theology. Boethius's books 4 and 5 also investigate God *in ipso* by using many of the topics found in Proclus's analysis of the *Parmenides*.[61] In book 4, Boethius argues that providence is universal, that the divine power extends to all things, and that God knows everything. Since the divine mind simultaneously knows all things, it suffers no injustice to occur to things. The universal knowledge of God does not make human beings slaves caused to act by God's knowledge; rather, as book 5 has it, the difference between divine and human cognition permits God to know all without suspending human freedom. Boethius's books 4 and 5 follow Proclus's version of the *Parmenides* in taking up the significance, to one's understanding of the human condition, of a belief in divine providence, cognition, and foreknowledge. His book 5 (meters 4–5 and prose 5) also concerns the ascent from sense to imagination to reason to intellection that Proclus treats at some length. Proclus, like Boethius, uses his faculty psychology to describe different ways and levels on which the Forms may be apprehended and to show that divine foreknowledge does not resemble cognition as humanly conceived. Anyone seeing the *Consolation* through eyes like Proclus's would see theology as the predominant discipline treated in Boethius's books 4 and 5 – in their concern for foreknowledge and free will and their presentation of Hercules and Odysseus as heroes of the ascent who rise to the level of the intellect's apprehension (see *infra*).[62] Significantly in book 5 (prose 4 and meter 4), Boethius's description of how we know things – combining Aristotle's empiricism with Plato's search for models abstracted from the material world – begins to lay out a relationship between the Stoic's tabula rasa perception and the shaping of that perception in terms of theoretical constructs that can be seen as anticipating the forms of scientific inquiry developed in the Renaissance (see chapter 8).

BOETHIAN EPIC AND THE PHILOSOPHIC FUNCTIONS OF POETRY
The third strain of the tradition traced here, the tradition of the epic symbolic of education, appears in the hymns found in the *Consolation*'s book 3 and thereafter. As the *Consolation* rises in intellectual level, the tragic or epic muse driven out by Philosophy reappears in a transformed state to treat of divine matters. The poetry that Philosophy drives out at the beginning of the *Consolation* is of the "Sophistic" or kinetic kind that Plato had condemned, and the meters in the first three books mostly contain straightforward exemplary or didactic poetry of a kind acceptable even to Plato. However, once Philosophy finishes the hymn contained in book 3, meter 9, heroic poetry returns accompanied by glosses that make it more the marker of an educational progress than the vessel of self-pity. The mythic and "tragic" symbolic poetry that Philosophy creates as her own muse begins at the end of book 3 and continues through books 4 and 5; it rehearses aspects of the ascent to God by using such figures as Odysseus and Hercules as metaphors for it (Odysseus and Hercules are somewhat similar symbols in Proclus's comment on the *Parmenides,* where Hercules's conquest of the Stymphalian birds becomes a conquest of the lower knowledge provided by sensory perception and opinion and an ascent to the sciences [i.e., mathematics to reality conveyed by intellect]).[63] Both heroes, in Proclus and Boethius, are associated with educational growth. Though Boethius constructs much of the symbolic poetry in books 4 and 5 out of mythic patterns suggested by Proclus, he finally ends all construction and, like Augustine, achieves silence before the "speech" of Wisdom[64] and in the presence of the Judge who beholds all things.[65]

At the beginning of the *Consolation,* Philosophy comes into Boethius's place of "exile" to alter his indulgence in the poetry that reflects his situation and to challenge his feeling that Symmachus's Rome – the here and now – is his true country. To understand his situation, Boethius does not need the inspiration of words but the sight of reality. Philosophy's function, like that of the allegories of Homer's Athena and Penelope, is to guide and woo her hero home to a permanent metaphysical Wisdom: Porphyry's inland region where the soul looks on contemplative reality

(*De Ant.* 34–35).[66] Her guidance of Boethius requires that she redefine poetry not as that which she condemns when she attacks the strumpet muse, but as that contemplative art of which she is the muse. The poems that she sings are the tragic and epic accounts that Plato would have removed from the libraries of his ideal state, stories of Odysseus or Hercules or of a later Nero. But though Philosophy's rejection of tragic poetry from Boethius's prison sounds Platonic, her acceptance of her own kind of poetry depends on Plato's children, the stabilizing Neoplatonic commentators on Homer. The Homer who had been rejected from Plato's educative state becomes in Neoplatonic criticism Plato's defender; thus the poet can be used to make Neoplatonic Christian sense of the world. Boethius's Philosophy rejects the sophistic muses in order to recreate a muse through which principle can speak to pain in appropriate style and in appropriately numbered prosody.[67]

As Alison White has persuasively argued, the notion that the quadrivium was the basis of understanding the creative design of God derives both from Neoplatonic tradition and from the verse, "Thou hast ordered all things in number, measure and weight" (Wisdom 11.21).[68] If, as Chamberlain has indicated, Boethius completes his treatise on music in the *Consolation* by treating of divine music,[69] he also makes the *Consolation* a three-stage educational progress (from the ethical through the physical and mathematical to the metaphysical) that depends on number in poetry for its weight and grandeur. At the heights of the *Consolation*, Boethius and Philosophy look at time through the eyes of the One and see His structured eternal copresent (called foreknowledge by human beings). They can, therefore, affirm divine providence and human ethical responsibility based on the freedom of the will in the choosing of goods and cognitive modes. If Plato is, in the three treatises that are the *Consolation*'s supporting texts, the dispassionate intellectual, Boethius is the passionate pioneer whose poems, however philosophically controlled, have the radiance and numerosity of the mosaics that, ironically, Theoderic was placing at about the same time in the church of San Apollonare Nuova.

MEDIEVAL BOETHIAN COMMENTARY'S EDUCATIONAL THEORY AND THE NEW EDUCATION

Boethius insures a relatively stable, determinate reading for his *Consolation* by glossing it from within and by making explicit what works are his foundation; this work of stabilization continues in Boethius's commentators and the educational theorists who derive from him. The interpretation of Boethius represented by his own reference to Plato's works of ascent and to Wisdom theology reappears in all of his major medieval commentators: Remigius of Auxerre from the ninth-century Carolingian Renaissance, the anonymous commentator edited by Silk from between the ninth and the twelfth centuries (sometimes called the Anonymous of Erfurt), William of Conches from the twelfth-century revival of education, and Nicholas Trivet and Pseudo-Thomas from the fourteenth-century schoolmen's culture. Though these men did not know the *Republic* and the *Parmenides* directly and only knew the *Timaeus* in Chalcidius's translation, enough of Platonic tradition was left for them to make sense of the *Consolation,* a sense that reappears in the major medieval educational theorists to be discussed later: Cassiodorus, Alcuin, Hugh of St. Victor, and Dante. It may not be too much to argue that Boethius, coming at the crucial period of cultural change when he did, changed the assumptions of medieval education from those of the Roman rhetorical schools, directing it to an examination of the nature of things. Certainly he helped in the process. Educational theories stated by his commentators or by theorists who derive from him dominate medieval educational discourse, whether at the ninth-century court of Charlemagne, in twelfth- and thirteenth-century Ile de France, or in fourteenth-century England.

One can organize the commentators' assertions about the *Consolation* in relation to four cruces: (1) Lady Philosophy's appearance establishing what the ascent through the disciplines ought to be for a suffering Boethius; (2) the myths of intellectual ascent contained in the meters' celebration of the same ascent; (3) the work's theology of Wisdom asserting that the creation is luminous and ruled by love, number, and scientific law; and (4) the Timaean hymn (3.9) showing those undertaking the intellectual climb how Wisdom's print is imposed on the world.

Philosophy's Appearance Establishes that the Consolation Concerns the Ascent through the Disciplines

All of the commentators define Philosophy as the love of divine Wisdom, whose three heights emblemize the learner's initial concern with earthly studies, then with mathematics and heavenly studies, and finally with metaphysics and theology.[70] To look at the commentators in historical order: for Remigius the heights represent, respectively, from lowest to highest (1) common sense, (2) astrology, and (3) divinity; for the Pseudo-Erigena (1) ordinary philosophy such as Socrates's, (2) knowledge of the heavens such as Plato's, and (3) metaphysics or theology; for William of Conches (1) ethics, economics, and politics, (2) astronomy, and (3) divinity; for Pseudo-Thomas (1) natural science, (2) mathematics and astronomy, and (3) divine science; and for Nicholas Trivet (1) ethics, economics, and politics, (2) astronomy, and (3) theology.[71] The commentators do not perfectly agree in terminology. But they agree in concept when they make the three heights anticipatory of a disciplinary ascent in the whole work that moves from the mundane to the mathematical-astronomical to the metaphysical/theological. The commentators treat the ladder of the Pi and Theta on Philosophy's garments as representing an analogous climb from the active to the contemplative, from the practical to the theoretical life. William of Conches, for instance, says that the ladder represents an elevation from the ethical and economic concerns of earth by means of mathematics to the stars, an ascent that ends with the Creator. Nicholas Trivet makes the ladder progress from the practical concerns of ethics and economics to a more elevated interest in politics to the speculative study of forms in matter (i.e., mathematics), and finally to the study of forms without matter, metaphysics.[72]

The same commentators make the fine threads of Philosophy's clothing her subtle sentences and disputations in the liberal arts,[73] an interpretation recalling Neoplatonic remarks on Penelope/Philosophy's weaving. Philosophy's books and scepter represent her concern to relate detached study to the administrative life.[74] Later (1.4), when Boethius asks ironically if Philosophy thinks his prison is the library where she discoursed with him of divine and human things (searching the secrets of nature, the geometry of the stars, and the celestial patterning of human life), the commentators assert that rule cannot have a simply conventional (or positivistic) basis but must be grounded in the study of physics, geometry, astronomy, ethics, and natural law.[75]

The disciplinary distinctions given by the interpreters of the library scene reappear in other sections of the commentaries. For instance, William of Conches says that Philosophy's fresh color in book 1, prose 1 demonstrates that she comes in her natural color, not with the pallor of fear, the red of blushing ("erubescent"), or the color of make-up. The reasons given by Philosophy are beautiful and natural to the wise without any addition of rhetorical colors.[76] When William describes the letters signifying the active and the contemplative lives, he indicates that knowledge is divided into eloquence – grammar, rhetoric, and dialectic – and wisdom, which includes both the practical arts of ethics, economics, and politics and the theoretical arts of physics, mathematics (the quadrivium), and theology.[77] However, rhetoric is not so entirely rejected as it is in Plato. For example, though the earlier commentaries, Remigius's and Pseudo-Erigena's, simply refer Philosophy's clothing to the seven liberal arts,[78] later ones include the range of disciplines, including those in the trivium. They also include disciplines beyond the quadrivium that were later encompassed by the medieval university. For example, William of Conches and Nicolas Trivet see the practical arts – ethics, economics, and politics – represented in Philosophy's symbol of the active life, and they find the theoretical arts of physics, mathematics, and metaphysics in her symbol of the contemplative life.[79] Before the foundation of the medieval university, Boethian "education" amounts to more than Cassiodorus's trivium and quadrivium and includes the whole range of subjects later systematized in the thirteenth- and fourteenth-century university, subjects that had to be pursued primarily through the study of texts or conversations outside of the educational establishment.

The Major Myths Celebrate the Intellectual Ascent

Boethius founds his meters after book 3, meter 9 on the Neoplatonic assumption that heroic poetry metaphorizes an education, and the commentators refine his notions by establishing how movements in space stand for movements among the disciplines. Though Pseudo-Erigena makes Boethius's version of the Orpheus myth (3.m.12) speak only of the person who escapes from and then falls back into carnality,[80] William of Conches turns Orpheus into the man made eloquent by the trivium disciplines and made wise by physics, the mathematical disciplines, and metaphysics. Eurydice, his natural concupiscence, flees from the divine goods offered by Aristaeus until bitten by the serpent of a natural desire for temporal goods. Given this dissociation of sensibility, Orpheus must descend into Hades as the educated mind going down to observe the fragility of material things so as to draw natural desire away from the carnal. The mind does so through the pedagogy of song and teaching, passing beyond the Hades monsters described in the *Aeneid* (interpreted almost exactly as Fulgentius interprets them in his commentary) and drawing natural desire away from its concern for the temporal and toward the eternal. Orpheus's ascent should culminate with a glimpsing of the light of the true good, with Wisdom, and with the cognition and love of the Creator.[81]

To follow up on this poem, the commentators' Philosophy, flying with her wings (4.m.1), ascends from astronomy to divine contemplation[82] or, alternately, from cognition of the creature to divine Wisdom.[83] William of Conches says that when Hercules (4.m.7) ascends to the stars after his labors, his actions metaphorize his conquest of the vices and his mastery of the disciplines that arrive at celestial contemplation.[84]

In short, the commentators make the major mythic journeys of the *Consolation,* beginning at the end of book 3 and continuing through books 4 and 5, into metaphors for immersion in carnal ignorance and ascent to Wisdom through the academic disciplines.

The End of the Journey, Wisdom, Generates a Universe on the Edge of Science,
One Governed by Love, Number, and Law

The commentators see Boethius's creation as structured by love, a sort of attractive force in all things, and by law. Remigius says of the "amor" in book 2, meter 8 that it means God who made and rules all things.[85] The Anonymous of Erfurt calls this "amor" divine love and the Son of God, presumably the Wisdom that creates harmony in the universe since it is the force that binds the elements, moves the sun and stars, and maintains harmonious marriages and friendships.[86] William of Conches calls this same force the love or concord of God that appears in the divisions of time, the mixing and harmonizing of the elements, the control of the seas, and, potentially, in man.[87] Pseudo-Thomas and Nicholas Trivet, while making a fairly strict periphrasis of the meter, regard the love mentioned in the poem as the divine love that rules all physical things and that creates and keeps alive virtuous human friendships.[88] Throughout the commentators' interpretations of book 2, meter 8 runs the notion that, while divine love automatically rules the nonhuman world in its regular cycles, love's regency in the human world extends only as far as human willing allows.

Law is as important as love. The cosmological regularities of a natural law created by Wisdom reappear in the commentators' version of book 3, meter 2, in the examination of *natura potens*, perhaps the ancestor of nature in Alanus, the *Roman de la Rose*, and Chaucer. *Natura potens* in book 3, meter 2 may either be God, as the source of nature, or His creation informed by rules that direct the animals to follow species law. These latter rules also direct a self-conscious mankind back to its divine origin.[89]

The Timaean Hymn Shows the Seeker Where Natural Law Comes from and How Wisdom's Print Is Imposed on the World

From the Carolingian period on, the commentators regard the hymn at book 3, meter 9 as derived from Plato's *Timaeus* and from Wisdom theology. Remigius makes the "ratio" of "O qui perpetua mundum ratione gubernas" become the Logos – the *Verbum Dei* or *Filius Dei* – who fills space and time with his majesty (3.9.1–3), a Wisdom that created the world for no extrinsic reason but out of endless love or benevolence. This "ratio" or Wisdom becomes the exemplar or Form in the mind of God through whom all things were made: it is the repository of Plato's ideas or, showing the close association of Platonic and Johannine theology, the "life" in John 1.4 that is the light of men. As Forms and metaphysical light impose themselves on matter, they create the "triple nature" in the Ptolemaic scheme comprised by the planets above the sun, the sun, and the planets below the sun ("triplicis . . . naturae" [3.m.9]). They also create the vegetable, animal, and rational nature in the world or the concupiscible, irascible, and rational in man. Pseudo-Erigena makes pretty much the same moves, identifying the archetype ("exemplo") with God's plan for the world, Plato's idea, John 1.4's "life," Boethius's "providence of God," and the ideas located in the Nous, or the Logos. He equates Wisdom with Boethius's whole providence that rules history and nature. To explain 3.9's Timaean picture of the creation and ordering of the world, he engages in the numerous mathematical or pseudo-mathematical explanations of the elements that make mathematics one of the milestones on the road to God. Finally, he argues that the *perpetua ratione* of the first line of the poem represents the Wisdom through which the world was made, that the fire (1.21) that conducts souls back to the One is the Holy Spirit, and that the conclusion of the prayer shows how the mind moves from its normally unfocused state to concentrate itself on the Platonic/

Johannine "light" coming into the world that enlightens every man in his metaphysical darkness.[90]

William of Conches's commentary makes book 3, meter 9's drawing together of "law" and "love" even more clearly a hymn to Wisdom. His God, who is the center of a circle or the hub of a wheel ("stabilisque manens das cuncta moveri"), anticipates Dante's later *Commedia* God, who is the center of the wheeling of the natural world, and John 1's light coming into the world that illumines all. William's nature in this poem creates species on the basis of divine plans and makes human beings self-conscious so that they can love and comprehend the divine; it creates human beings, the crown of the world, who are dependent on the creatures below and the lights above that are capable of contemplating the divine archetype, or Wisdom. William's elements bound by number ("tu numeris elementa ligas") come together in divinely appointed musical proportions and have a relationship to one another analogous to the relationship among plain, solid, and linear numbers; his archetype (l.5–9) is the form or divine Wisdom of things while his "anima mundi" (l.14) represents the love of God or, implicitly, the Spirit. Since the only aspect of the deity that can be known through the creation is Wisdom, the ascent to the divinity at the poem's end explicitly transforms human knowledge from a sensory base to an imaginative, rational, and, finally, to a divine intellectual one (i.e., weds it to the disciplinary ascent).[91] Pseudo-Thomas and Nicholas Trivet continue much the same conception with the elimination of some Timaean concepts and the addition of some scholastic ones.[92]

The commentators keep alive Boethius's faith in the study of and respect for the laws governing the creation as the source of intellectual authority and criticism in a troubled world. The educational universe that Boethius's Philosophy, as the love of Wisdom, reveals to the commentators is a world where the mind naturally seeks to learn the patterns and laws governing things and the universe seeks to unmask itself through scientific and metaphysical disciplines that reveal it as system and law, love and providence.

BOETHIAN EDUCATIONAL THEORY APART FROM THE COMMENTATORS

The *Consolation*, given stability by the glosses as a book about the intellectual ascent that culminates in a new view of Wisdom, helped to restructure the West's educational assumptions, moving education from its school-and-culture center to a greater emphasis on self-direction and mathematics.

Boethius's contemporary, Cassiodorus, a theoretician of monastic education, seems to have owed much to Boethius (though they were probably political adversaries). Cassiodorus's monastery at Vivarium symbolizes the transformation of Roman learning in late antiquity from civic, culture-centered learning to learning centered in religion, and, of course, in the number disciplines of the quadrivium. In the *Institutiones,* Cassiodorus asserts that, early in his life (possibly around A.D. 535–36),[93] he wished to found a school at Rome, apparently a rhetorical school dedicated to the Christian writers, but that the troubles of the time prevented his doing so.[94] However, late in his life Cassiodorus wrote the *Institutiones*[95] for a monastery, creating a work that does not emphasize drill, structured learning, or a formal *regula* at all but the more independent formation that Leclercq describes (cf. notes 7 and 8, this chapter). The *Institutiones* is neither a workbook for students whose teachers have all the answers nor, like Quintilian's *Institutes,* a methods text for teachers. Instead, it tells the monks how to study on their own when they seek to "improve" themselves.

In developing this viewpoint, the *Institutiones* asserts that the seven liberal arts are the seven pillars of Wisdom described in Proverbs 9.1, and it extends Boethius's notion that the quadrivium supports Wisdom's study. Though Cassiodorus's idea that the disciplines move upward toward Wisdom is not new, his formulation of it in terms of Proverbs 9.1 appears to be.[96] For him, the seven arts comprehend God as numerical definition, structure, and harmony in the creation,[97] and God's mind creates this numbered order and limit, weighing the fountains of creation and measuring the heavens: all attributes of Wisdom. Later Cassiodorus describes evil's world as a world independent of number. As his quadrivium sciences proceed through number to Wisdom, they progress from understanding the creation's pattern to understanding the Creator.[98] Even as Boethius's heavenly Philosophy rises from the mundane to the celestial in the contemplation of things, Cassiodorus's human mind rises from earth to heaven by studying the trivium and quadrivium, concluding its quest with the vision of God.[99]

Alcuin at the court of Charlemagne also apparently holds to the ideology of a Logos within and of a self-initiated journey to Wisdom. In his eulogy to his teacher, Ælberht, Alcuin says that Ælberht did not try to teach all of the disciplines to all of his students but fostered them, "watered parched hearts with diverse streams,"[100] took his pupils to him to "teach, cherish, and love,"[101] and, just before he died, dedicated the Church that he built to "holy Wisdom."[102]

Alcuin develops this view of education in more detail in his prologue to *De Grammatica*, a work that draws on both Boethius's *Consolation* and Cassiodorus's *Institutiones*. The prologue presents a dialogue between Alcuin and his pupils and has the pupils quote or paraphrase *De Consolatione* (1.pr.3). The students assert that they have heard Alcuin say that Philosophy is the teacher ("magistra") of the virtues, the one among all the earth's rich gifts that will not leave her possessors; but they, too weak to learn untutored, wish to know the fullness of Philosophy-as-teacher and climb to her heights.[103] Hence, they wish Alcuin to teach her to them. As the outer mind can receive light from the sun, so, in their opinion, the inner mind can receive Wisdom if some source of light will provide its radiance.

The students' request, full of echoes from the *Consolation*, clearly invites Alcuin to substitute himself for Lady Philosophy. However, the master turns aside from the requested pedagogical role and interprets Philosophy as the love of Wisdom or the Logos, assuring the students that the light coming into the world mentioned in John 1.9 can illumine and guide their minds.[104] Unfortunately, *De Grammatica* does not fulfill the promise of its prologue, and the Wisdom rhetoric addressed to Charlemagne in *De Rhetorica* shows none of Boethius's sense that the state may become a tyranny and education a mere mechanical exercise when it is wholly beholden to the prince and his institutional order.[105] Charlemagne's pure mastery of political power and his rhetoric of a Christian empire must have made Erastianism a temptation even to thinkers, like Alcuin, who tried to place themselves in Boethius's lineage.

After the Carolingian "renaissance," the next important developments in education come in the twelfth-century Parisian schools that lead into the medieval university system. Their most important theoretical work, Hugh of St. Victor's *Didascalicon*, represents the culmination of prescholastic Boethian theory. For Hugh, all of education directs itself toward divine Wisdom and toward the pursuit of Wisdom as divided into linguistic-logical disciplines and the theoretical ones conforming to Lady Philosophy's three heights (physics, mathematics, theology). The *Didascalicon*'s first section echoes the *Consolation* (3.pr.12) by asserting that Wisdom is the form of the Supreme Good.[106] In general, the book respects the fundamental Boethian division of the disciplines into logic (rhetoric and dialectics); physics, mathematics, and metaphysics; and theology. It adds the mechanical arts that relate to Philosophy's practical functions, and, like the *Consolation,* emphasizes the fundamentally spontaneous and contemplative (mystical) direction of study based on a Boethian and Augustinian assumption that the souls of fallen human beings are restless until they contemplate divine Wisdom, seek the Logos in the structure placed upon things, and, in a restoration of Eden, contemplate the ideas in the mind of God, the structure placed upon things.[107] Hugh, in contrast to post-Baconian atomists, does not see the mind as made up of the same stuff as what it knows. He regards a mind that forgets its superiority to the material world it knows as seduced out of itself – as acting as a mind that does not know itself as mind, becoming subject to change (i.e., Boethian fortune) and losing its place in the hierarchy of being. Hugh's form of education does not create any of the edenic physical states promised by later applied scientific thinkers from Bacon onward. It is rather constituted by a state of detachment much like that sought by Buddhist thinkers in our time.

Hugh claims to be self taught.[108] In his statement of how he learned as a child, he describes how he taught himself the basics of the trivium as a schoolboy through learning "the names of all things that my eyes fell upon or that came into my use" or "propos[ing] cases and, when the opposing contentions were lined up against one another, . . . diligently distinguish[ing] what would be the business of the rhetorician, what of the orator, what of the sophist." He initiated himself as a child in the basics of quadrivium, beginning with arithmetic and going on to geometry, astronomy, and music:

I laid out pebbles for numbers, and I marked the pavement with black coals and, by a model placed right before my eyes, I plainly showed what difference there is between an obtuse-angled, a right-angled, and an acute-angled triangle. Whether or not an equilateral parallelogram would yield the same area as a square when two of its sides were multiplied together, I learned by walking both figures and measuring them with my feet. Often I kept watch outdoors through the winter nights like one of the fixed stars by which we measure time. Often I used to bring out my strings, stretched to their number on the wooden frame, both that I might note with my ear the difference among the tones and that I might at the same time delight my soul with the sweetness of the sound.[109]

One suspects that this representation is more a schematization of what Hugh thought should have been in his childhood than a representation of what actually happened, for to create the models that Hugh creates one would already have to know a good deal about them. But what is crucial is the change in representation. Hugh's child, working through a step-by-step process, is a radically different creature from Quintilian's empty vessel into which the teacher pours rhetorical knowledge. Hugh's picture of learning explains why students in the high middle ages, whether in monastery or in school, become wandering scholars or study by themselves in "cells," rather than drilling in collective groups in a large room. In the later middle ages worship has largely become the central collective process for the clerk or monk and learning has become a radically individualistic business.

After Hugh come the university theoreticians, such as Thomas Aquinas, who partly depended on Boethius (cf. chapter 7). After Hugh also comes the thirteenth-century reintroduction of Aristotle on a grand scale, the creation of the university and the development of an educational practice more complex, more bureaucratized, more concerned with offering degrees and licensure. Prior to the foundation of the French and English universities in the thirteenth century, John of Salisbury's meandering education, guided by a moral imperative, strongly suggests that deviation from the path laid out by the general map was allowed.[110] After this time, things appear to be more carefully structured by the medieval university. Dante tells us of the fusion of the old practice and the new. But before Dante could write his grand cathedral of education, Boethius had to lay the foundations for the medieval house of education, the glossators had to sketch its blueprints, and the theoreticians had to assemble the materials for it.

We return to the question with which this chapter began: "How can one create a criticism of the present order without access to what is fundamental to criticism, namely, the possibility of finding truth or truths that undercut the present order's foundations?" Boethius, and the Boethian tradition in education and social policy, would argue that one cannot make such a critique without resort to some search for a truth that counters the fictions created by the state's *physis* or political power. Clearly Boethius is dependent on canonical works (i.e., the Bible, Plato, and the epic), but he appropriates them in his subcreation not because they are "classics" and "prescribed" (as the conservative educational critics of our day would have us appropriate them). He appropriates them because they are necessary to his sanity and "salvation" in his prison. He appropriates them less as a gesture of overreaching a previous writer than of underwriting a new order, since he cannot find in the present order the elements that would make the canonical texts that he loves meaningful. He does not have the stable social order that makes the proverbial advice of the Wisdom books functional. He does not have Plato's philosophical rulers or even a just constitution. He cannot regress to an epic or heroic society, literally conceived.

Therefore, it is not accidental that Boethius is so concerned with verification – in *De Arithmetica* with arithmetic verification, and in the *Consolation* with judicial verification and the relationship between sensory experience and the formation of species conceptions (a view derived from Aristotle's conception of induction and a primitive formulation of the relationship between inductive and deductive science). Boethius's view is precisely that truth counts, that each species obeys its own laws, that the universe is orderly and gives a mandate to human beings to behave justly under conditions either of justice or of oppression. If his view is foolish, then the tradition of education and opposition that emerges from him is also mistaken both in its method and in its results.

7

Boethius's Wisdom and Dante's Architectonics of Desire

Dante's *Convito* and *Commedia* present Boethius revisited and revised from the schoolmen's perspective. His new ascent retains much of the old mythos but makes a more elevated place in it for ethics and the psychology of desire. Dante consistently uses Boethius to give us a sense of how we are to read his "autobiography" – his guides, epic journey, and threefold *Commedia* structure.[1] But he also alters Boethius to conform to Aquinas and Aristotle, emphasizing that ethics, the lowliest of the disciplines in earlier writers, should belong to the heights informed by Christian theology and control the process of education. His ethics replaces the old mathematical disciplines in this role. Dante's sense of the divine derivation of ethics grounds his sense of what the Christian political and social vision must be. It makes him more the sermonizer, more the indoctrinator in "values," that contemporary conservative educators would have teachers be than are the earlier writers treated in this book. But Dante is a "values educator" that conservative educational theorists would hardly find acceptable, for his didacticism emerges from a respect for the best knowledge available in his time as to how the universe is constructed. It is a didacticism of the redirection of passion, not of its repression.[2]

Dante assumes throughout his work that the autodidact learns through the redirection of desire. The older writers in the tradition described in this book speak of the redirection of desire from the goods of fortune to those of Wisdom. Except for Augustine, however, they do not say much about how this redirection can be accomplished. Augustine's autobiography makes so much of the effect of the redirection depend on nonordinary events that it fails to speak to an age without miracles. In contrast, Dante endeavors to set forth an ethics, an ethical psychology, that speaks to the redirection of desire as it might operate in anyone.

Allan Bloom offers a contrasting modern view that may give focus to what Dante does with Boethius and with ethics. Bloom characterizes the issue of ethics and desire as it exists in one wing of contemporary educational discussion by examining Nietzsche's view of the religious impulse and the creation of values. According to Bloom, Nietzsche and the post-Heideggerian Nietzscheans of our day emphasize how humankind created its gods and its values out of the id – out of unconscious, uncontrollable desires of the culture-makers that create peoples: "Since values are not rational and not grounded in the natures of those subject to them, they must be imposed."[3] Bloom continues:

God is myth, Nietzsche taught. Myths are made by poets. This is just what Plato says in the *Republic,* and for him it is equivalent to a declaration of war between philosophy and poetry. The aim of philosophy is to substitute truth for myth (which by its very definition is falsehood, a fact too often forgotten in our post-Nietzschean fascination with myth). . . . Socrates, as depicted in the Platonic dialogues, questioning and confuting the received opinions, is the model of the philosophic life; and his death at the hands of his countrymen for not believing in the myths epitomizes the risks of philosophy. Nietzsche drew precisely the opposite conclusion from the same facts about myth. There is no nature and no such freedom. The philosopher must do the contrary of what Socrates did. . . . The tragic life, which Socrates defused and purged, is the serious life. The new philosopher is the ally of the poets and their savior, or philosophy is itself the highest kind of poetry. Philosophy in the old mode *demythologizes* and *demystifies.* It has no sense of the sacred; and by *disenchanting* the world and *uprooting* man, it leads into a void. The revelation that philosophy finds nothingness at the end of its quest informs the new philosopher that mythmaking must be his central concern in order to make a world.[4]

The dichotomy between poets and philosophers is not a classical one after the rise of the Neoplatonists (see chapter 5). Nor is it significant among medieval literary critics. Dante does not, like Bloom, attribute values either to an enlightened reason that opposes religious experience or to a religious experience that emerges from a nonrational id. He does not oppose subjective and objective knowledge as Bloom does when he tells us that Nietzsche has, in anguish, delivered us from the gods that we have made and that we await a journey within that will give us a new decalogue while we turn outward to a revived enlightenment for a new sense of natural rights.[5] Dante presents us with a notion of education in values that relates what we must desire if we are to be ethical people to what we must know.

Dante's address to the issue of values in education also differs from that of educational reformers, such as Chester Finn, who propose a return to the idea of ethical education as family, or family-like, socialization to right social behavior.[6] Dante's sense of the relationship of ethics and education does not point to bourgeois conformity. It comes in the context of a fresh relating of the study of ethics to the study of theology or the sacred.[7] For him no unmalleable id exists. The transformation of cognition implies a transformation of desire (and conduct); in turn, the transformation of desire can free the individual for new cognition and new conduct.[8] Dante's greatest contribution as an educator is his modification of the Boethian tradition to make a new representation of the role of ethics and mythmaking.

Dante's capacity to make things new depends partly on the historical context in which he writes. After Boethius fused the Platonic, Wisdom, and epic representations of the educational journey, his map of it remained relatively unchanged for nearly eight centuries for those persons who began with the Wisdom assumptions of the *Consolation*. The major theoretical documents for the period A.D. 525–1300 include the glosses on the *Consolation* and the discursive works of Boethian educational theory (cf. chapter 6) that are basic to school and monastic practice in the period. The devastation of western Europe by its Islamic and Viking invaders probably did not leave much time for the elaboration of commentary concerning the Wisdom books or theory-making about the process of education beyond the glossing and reworking of Boethius. Even epic interpretation and creation take secondary roles (though they include a heavy dose of Boethius, at least in Bernard Silvestris). Indeed, it can be argued that minimal attention was given to developing the quadrivium in the period 525–1200, save for the work of Gerbert of Aurillac,[9] Thierry of Chartres,[10] William of Conches,[11] Gerard of Cremona,[12] William of Moerbeke,[13] and the translators of medieval Arabic documents in the quadrivium disciplines. Theology and metaphysics, concentrated in the monastery, were directed more toward acts of worship and adoration than formal disciplinary exploration.[14] The pictures of the "journey to Wisdom" included in previous chapters of this book inspired the individual efforts of such persons as Boethius's glossators to achieve mastery of the higher learning. Yet there is little evidence that they made actual "advances" in the disciplines, formed communities of scholars dedicated to learning outside the monastery, or wrote sophisticated works to create new kinds of schools (except for the schools in the Paris region in the twelfth century). Perhaps the chief symbol of the sophistication of medieval mathematical pursuits dedicated to the noetic way are the geometrically designed Gothic buildings created in proximity to Paris in the late twelfth and thirteenth centuries.[15]

But with the rise of the thirteenth-century university and the recovery of a fuller representation of Aristotle's corpus, the sense of the direction of studies changes because of the work in optics of Robert Grosseteste,[16] the translations of Aristotle by Albertus Magnus,[17] Roger Bacon's works on Aristotle and on scientific studies in general, Thomas Aquinas's works on the nature of the world and on the problem of the relationships between faith and reason,[18] and the scientific works of John of Holywood,[19] Gerard of Brussels,[20] and John Pecham.[21] With the new work, the ascent does not so clearly go from physics and ethics to the mathematical subjects to metaphysics and theology. The ambit of studies becomes wider. In the process of recovering Aristotle, the schoolmen invent different ascents from those found in Boethius. Following Aristotle, they draw a sharp line between physics, which considers material substance on the earth, and the mathematical subjects, which consider earthly abstractions and measure the heavens.[22] This line is only gradually breached in the scholastic world, and only Copernicus, Galileo, and Kepler breach it altogether. Many of the scholastic thinkers deny noetic force to mathematics because, for Aristotle, mathematics was not a noetic subject halfway up the ascent but a tool discipline to be learned early in the curriculum. With the change in the place of mathematics came also a change in the place of ethics. For Aquinas, at least, ethics (what we would call psychology) does not have its place at the mundane beginning of study, as it does in the Boethian commentaries, but is an adjunct to the highest study of the Logos or God. It may not be an exaggeration to say that the medieval study of ethics prior to the foundation of the universities in the thirteenth century falls largely into two classes of study: (1) the study of various moralistic treatises that might tell one what one's practical obligations are in various life situations, the stuff of fables and sermons; and (2) the study of the meaning of loving God as the highest good and one's neighbor as oneself. The recovery and study of Aristotle's *Nichomachean Ethics* and its various Greek and Arabic commentaries in the twelfth and thirteenth centuries leads to a view of ethics as a highly systematic study that examines the general principles of right action, based on natural reasoning or on revelation, and the ethical decision-making appropriate for "me" in "my circumstances," matters to which the individual conscience normally speaks.[23] Dante uses Aristotle's *Ethics* and Virgil's explanation of it to speak to the first category of ethical problems in the *Inferno*. He uses Statius and the siren to speak to the second category, the psychology of desire as it relates to ethical decision-making by the persona of Dante in the *Commedia*.

While Dante's general quest is, like Boethius's, a quest to know God as a gardener and the garden of the creation as a sacred place, it differs from it in dealing with the architecture of desire. It also differs from the modern quest for education in the canonical that seems to distance reading, to emphasize the acquisition through reading of a series of trophies: the Olympian liberal encounter with the "best that has been thought and written" advocated in different ways by Matthew Arnold, and contemporary promoters of the canon.[24] Dante is not primarily interested in a canon. He is interested in the help with his own desire that he requires to be a good man. He turns to Virgil and Virgilian epic not for any general ennobling but for specific directives concerning his and mankind's understanding of the physical and ethical world (see chapter 5). He does not read Statius as a model of the "best that has been thought and written" but as a model of how to direct his own desire and take the steps beyond the siren. He approaches Arnaut and the other troubadors in the *Purgatorio*'s circle of the lecherous, but not as "great writers" who have set down the best that has been thought and written. Rather, he sees them as examples of lechery who happened to know the craft of poetry. Arnaut "[f]u miglior fabbro" (*Purgatorio* 26.117). Dante always distinguishes among reasons for approaching previous writers – whether as ethical teachers, as craftspersons, as educators, as negative or positive examples, or as friends. And many of the writers whom he addresses are not canonical in his period.

THE *CONVITO'S* ROAD TO WISDOM: ETHICS AND EDUCATION

The *Convito* anticipates the *Commedia* in using aspects of the *Consolation's* form while arguing with aspects of its content. If the *Consolation* is a medley of prose and poetry (a *satura*), the *Convito* is a medley-banquet whose poems (many of which may have been originally erotic in content) were written prior to Dante's encounter with philosophy. In their recycled form, the *Convito's* poems recall the *Consolation's* "tragic" poems recycled from Boethius's period of Senecan compositions. Both *Consolation* and *Convito* shape poetic meaning through prose commentary.[25] While the *Consolation's* poems suggest metaphorically how heroic scholarship surmounts the loss of beatitude to recover it through Wisdom, the prose in its determinacy requires that we see this poetic meaning. Similarly, the *Convito's* love poetry leads to prose commentary that transforms the "sophistry" of love poetry concerned with the loss of Beatrice into praise of the higher scientific disciplines that recover the beatitude of Wisdom. The *Convito's* prose commentary does to its canzone what the *Consolation's* prose (and later commentary on it concerned with the disciplinary ascent) does to its meters.[26]

The *Convito's* equivalent for Boethius's fall, imprisonment, and expectation of death is the death of "Beatrice" defined as "the first joy of my [i.e., Dante's] soul" (*Convito* 2.12).[27] The joy may be an autobiographical Beatrice Portinari or a fable for other loss; no one can know whether Beatrice was a real woman whose beauty delighted the historical Dante or was another happiness experienced prior to its being destroyed. All that one can say is that "Beatrice" dead is the soul's delight lost, whatever the delight. In the *Convito,* Dante recalls the loss of this delight at the same time as he brings back *La Vita Nuova's* Lady-at-the-Window, the one who comforted him after he lost Beatrice, remembering her in the *Convito* as an allegory for philosophy. Dante asserts that he first followed this lady by reading Cicero and Boethius (*Convito* 2.12), understanding them by an ability that allowed him to see "quasi come sognando" ("as it were dreaming a *somnium*"), a fact that, he says, is clear in *La Vita Nuova.*[28] "Quasi come sognando" may imply that the *Vita Nuova* Dante read Boethius and Cicero with the lower level abstractive faculties located in the imagination that allowed him to see the shape of events surrounding Beatrice's death apart from her physical presence.[29] However, in the *Convito,* Dante finds meanings in Boethius and Cicero expressed in the more "virile" mode of philosophic explanation as the Lady-at-the-Window, philosophy, becomes an intellectualist reading from Boethius's *Consolation* and Cicero's *De Amicitia*.[30] This reading involves an imitation of the *Consolation* that makes Dante's loss of the earthly Beatrice in the *Convito* resemble Boethius's loss of his political position,[31] his meeting with the Lady-at-the-Window follow after Boethius's encounter with Lady Philosophy,[32] his affair with the Wisdom-Lady when he reads Boethius and Cicero as part of his search for the allegorical silver of consolation for Beatrice's death, a search paralleling Boethius's effort to gain consolation from the tragic muses. However, instead of finding consolation, Dante finds what he calls the gold of Wisdom, exactly what Boethius finds in the *Consolation* (book 3) when he discovers the exemplar of the universe (3.m.9) and the Supreme Good that "mightily and sweetly moves all things" (Wisdom 8.1; 3.pr.12). In the Lady-at-the-Window, Dante sees the Wisdom implicit in the etymology of *philo-sophia* (cf. *Convito* 2.12). He also discovers that this lady can lead him to the learning of Boethius and Cicero and visitations to "the schools of the religious orders and in the philosopher's disputations" (*Convito* 2.12.5–6).[33] Whereas Beatrice's death constitutes the *Convito*'s equivalent of Boethius's political disappointment and exile, the comparable disappointment comes to the *Commedia* Dante later and in the form of a "Boethian" political disappointment and exile from Florence, which he experiences in 1302 after his self-education and work in the friar schools.

The *Convito*'s Wisdom fuses with its philosophy and conjoins the visionary and civic in the same way that Boethius's Lady Philosophy joins them in her books and sceptre.[34] Desire is crucial. Book 3 of the *Convito* (chapters 14 and 15), playing with the standard medieval etymology of *philosophia*, asserts that love is the form of philosophy, and Wisdom is its substantial manifestation.[35] In the *canzone* that begins book 3, Dante describes this Wisdom:

> Cose appariscon ne lo suo aspetto,
>   che mostran de' piacer di Paradiso,
>   dico ne li occhi e nel suo dolce riso,
>   che le vi reca Amor com'a suo loco.
> Elle soverchian lo nostro intelletto
>   come raggio di sole un frale viso:
>   e perch'io non le posso mirar fiso,

mi convien contentar di dirne poco.
Sua bieltà piove fiammelle di foco,
animate d'un spirito gentile
ch'è creatore d'ogni pensier bono;
e rompon come trono
l'innati vizii che fanno altrui vile.
Però qual donna sente sua bieltate
biasmar per non parer queta e umile,
miri costei ch'è essemplo d'umiltate!
Questa è colei ch'umilia ogni perverso:
costei pensò Chi mosse l'universo.

(*Convito* 3.c.55–72)

[Things are evident in her face that show us the joys of Paradise – I speak of her eyes and her smile, which Love placed there as in their place. These surpass our intellect as the sun's ray surpasses our sight, and because I cannot admire them with focused eye, I have to be satisfied to speak a bit about them. Her beauty comes down as little flames of fire, animated by a gentle spirit that is the creator of all good thoughts; and they break apart as would thunder the innate vices that make people villainous. Therefore when any lady hears her beauty condemned for not appearing peaceful and humble, let her look on this one who is the exemplum of humility. She humbles all who are wrong: of her was He thinking that set the universe in motion.]

"Of her was He thinking that set the universe in motion" (l.72) echoes Proverbs 8.27–30 and stipulates that Wisdom, the object of the Creator's thought at the time of the creation and the object of Philo-Sophia's love, is the figure described (cf. *Convito* 3.14–15 and passim). Dante's prose commentary relates this line to the Proverbs passage where Wisdom plays before God during the laying of the foundations of the universe (*Convito* 3.15.15–17).[36] Thus what Dante seeks after the disappearance of his first beatitude goes beyond the trivial schooling to be found in "the schools of the religious orders" to the Wisdom that acted at the creation, whose beautiful eyes (or demonstrations) fuse with a smile (or persuasions) seen under a veil: logic and mathematics with rhetoric (Convito 3.15.1–2). With the Lady-at-the-Window's authors and books also go intellectual disciplines that are not necessarily pursued in corporate study: "authors, *disciplines* (scienze), and books" (*Convito* 2.12.6; italics mine). Dante mentions philosophy's (or Wisdom's) pursuit of the seven standard liberal disciplines, plus ethics, physics, and metaphysics/theology – the very studies implied by the combination of the ladder and heights attached to philosophy in the commented medieval Boethius discussed in chapter 6 (*Convito* 2.12–14).[37] These ten studies are precisely the "scienze" that Dante chooses to describe in *Convito* 2.13 when he makes the *Convito*'s disciplinary "heavens" include the Moon as grammar, Mercury as dialectic, Venus as rhetoric, the sun as arithmetic, Mars as music, Jupiter as geometry, Saturn as astronomy,[38] the fixed stars as physics and metaphysics, the *primum mobile* as ethics, and the Empyrean as theology.[39] Dante must have known a medieval commented version of Boethius, such as the one that William of Conches offers, as his son, Pietro, clearly did (see below). And from such a commentary, he must have developed the assumption that philosophy was a love of Wisdom reached by the ladder of the disciplines/stars that the *Commedia* translates into another form.[40]

But Dante changes how the planets relate to the disciplines from that in Martianus Capella, and he changes the Boethian order of the ladder on the basis of Thomas Aquinas's and Aristotle's revision of the Platonic order. He does so to accommodate the new interest in ethics and in explicit statement about how desire is directed. In Martianus Capella's old scheme relating the planets and disciplines, Mercury is rhetoric; in Dante's new one, it becomes dialectic. Similarly, in Boethius's and the Neoplatonists's old scheme, ethics comes near or at the bottom of the disciplinary scale and seems simply to tell the child, "Be a good boy or girl now," through fables and proverbial sayings. Dante has no truck with such primitive moralism. While he places most of the disciplines in the ladder according to the normal order of Boethian ascent, attaching them to the planets placed in the Ptolemaic order, he makes physics and ethics (in the old schemes the lowliest of disciplines) appear on the celestial levels immediately below a theology analogous to the empyrean heaven. Physics is paired with metaphysics, and ethics is placed on the rung immediately above them.[41] He does so, I believe, to root ethical education in a simultaneous exploration of the structure of the universe and its Creator.

The shifting upward of physics and ethics is not accidental. When the poet puts physics and metaphysics near the top, he puts them there to be, as he says, the visible and invisible poles of the Milky Way: to represent the paired study of the corporeal and the incorporeal governing it. This shift suggests that the scientific and the metaphysical understanding of the nonhuman aspects of the creation are related (cf. *Convito* 2.14.1–14),[42] that the study of the transcendent clarifies our understanding of material reality and vice versa as the views of some twentieth-century scientists such as Einstein suggest.[43] The structure of the universe in medieval thought is always related to the structure of ethical obligation; hence the interest in natural law throughout the period.[44] Ethics controls the whole scheme below it in the ladder. The placing of ethics derives from Thomas Aquinas and Aristotle and involves yet another effort to relate the transcendent and the visible, but now in relationship to the human world.

Dante draws on Thomas and Aristotle for his conception of ethics as a discipline falling between earthly studies and the celestial study of theology. However, he changes the basis of the Boethian ascent from one in which the faculty used and the reality cognized are correlative to each other (e.g., the senses to material reality, imagination to the mathematicized version of material reality, and so forth) to one in which the journey is inward and then upward but not correlative to external reality in a one-for-one way: the mind goes from cognizing material reality to knowing its inner self to reaching for the transcendent.[45] Boethius's Neoplatonic picture of the standard sequence of studies derives from his interest in the increasingly abstractive power of the disciplined human mind: in the *Consolation* and other works, he studies the mind's capacity to see sensory objects first; its subsequent examination of a phalanx of the imagined forms of the individual species to create a species idea; its later mathematicizing of its investigations through descriptions of the proportions, laws, and constancies underlying created things; and finally its pulling together of these mathematical descriptions in systemic pictures of the relationships among the natural laws that govern systems. In contrast, the Aristotelian-scholastic thinker commonly makes the mathematical subjects mere tools that one learns early, that accompany one throughout one's investigations, and that are useful primarily because of their utilitarian applications.[46] Because Thomas Aquinas views the mathematical subjects as tool subjects apprehended by the imagination, he sees them as properly encountered and understood by the imaginative young at the beginning of their studies.[47] He sees the study of "things" as coming next: the study of physics, or the natural philosophy, which orders human beings' natural observations of plants, animals, the heavens, human anatomy, and so forth.[48] Next he places ethics, which studies how the "soul" knows the external material world and the natural and eternal laws that bind (or should bind) human conduct in society – what later ages called psychology. In the final position he places metaphysics/ theology, which studies the governing systems, spiritual and material, that control the creation. As he moves the mathematical disciplines to the role of a tool subject on the lower disciplinary rungs, he replaces them with ethics moved up to the mediatory position.[49]

The importance of this Aristotelian destruction of the earlier medieval period's faith that mathematics has a noetic power to lead one to God should be carefully noted. Before astronomical science can receive its sixteenth- and early-seventeenth-century formulations based on mathematics and Wisdom theory, this change must be reversed and the mathematical ascent made central. The divine and visionary and the physical sciences relate to the civic through the study of ethics (i.e., psychology). Dante follows Thomas in placing ethics next to theology to make ethics more than the ethics of private life, a kind of ethics cum politics. Thomas and Aristotle regard ethics as an architectonic science that determines which liberal arts should be studied, how they should be studied, and how they should be used to construct civil society.[50] This ethics derives from the architecture of the universe. As the *primum mobile* gives order to the movement of the lower planets, so ethics gives order to study by mediating between theology's stable "empyrean heaven," where resides the peace left by John's Logos (*Convito* 2.14.19–20; John 14.27),[51] and the moving corporeal spheres of the lower liberal arts (*Convito* 2.14.14ff.).[52] The study of ethics gives structure to study and order to society; it gives the poet the power necessary to the poetic pursuit of reform in the active world. This view of the study of ethics also gives the poet, as the creator of rationally controlled myth, a power over reform never visualized by Allan Bloom's Nietzsche as he peers into the id to find the next culture-creating stories. It is this view of ethics that Dante epitomizes in the figure of Statius who, according to Pietro Alighieri, represents ethics and prepares for Beatrice as theology. The *Convito* Dante anticipates the *Commedia*'s relating of ethics to theology in the garden of the reconstituted society where he says that without ethics there would be no "generation" or "life filled with joy" – in short, no metaphorical Eden or Beatrice as beatitude.[53]

The disciplines lead to Wisdom in the *Convito* as Statius leads to Beatrice-as-Wisdom-figure in the *Commedia;* both Wisdoms, empowered by ethical study, transform the active life.[54] The *Convito* Wisdom-figure's demonstrations or eyes represent studies in logic and the traditional quadrivium (the contemplative subjects), and her smiling mouth represents the trivium subjects that, by persuading, transform the active life and, together with quadrivium studies, lead one to the highest beatitude ("altissimo di beatitudine" [*Convito* 3.15.2]).[55] When Dante praises the Boethian god-within realized by Philosophy (*Convito* 3.2 passim; cf. 3.11.10–12), he does not praise any specialized study such as music or rhetoric that might reform a portion of the active life. He does not advocate the utilitarian pursuits that seek profit or office – the activities of doctors, lawyers, or members of the orders (with whom Dante studied [*Convito* 3.11.10]). Dante rather praises the Logos-like god-within of the autodidact, "a divine love of that which is to be understood" (*Convito* 3.11.13) that redirects humankind's attention toward the intellectual Sun that reveals the actions of Wisdom in the creation while seeking to change the active world (*Convito* 3.12 passim):

The divine power without any mediation draws this love (i.e., of Wisdom) into a semblance with itself without an intermediary. . . . [A]s the divine love is altogether eternal, so its object is necessarily eternal, since eternal things are those that it loves. And hence this love (i.e., of Wisdom) causes us to love, for Wisdom – which is struck by this love – is eternal. Hence, it is written of her, "From the beginning before the world I was created, and in the ages to come I shall not fail" and in Solomon's Proverbs the same Wisdom says "I have been ordained from everlasting." And at the beginning of the Gospel of St. John, her eternity can be plainly seen. (*Convito* 3.14.6–7)[56]

As in Origen, Augustine, and the Boethian commentaries, this Wisdom and the Logos are one and draw all things to themselves.[57] Dante's eternal Wisdom is a holistic source of the reforming motive, sending down flamelets of fire to her earthly lover in the form of right desire culminating in right acts. She becomes thereby the author of natural law and right love among people (*Convito* 3.15 passim) and informs both the contemplative and the pragmatic active life. She is the Beatrice of the *Commedia*.

THE *COMMEDIA* LADDER OF LEARNING:
ETHICS AS THE NEW MIDDLE DISCIPLINE

The *Commedia*'s Dante continues his revision of Boethius while focusing on ethics as the architectonic discipline undergirding the good society.

Again, he represents autobiographical events similar to those that befell Boethius – exile from the good, suffering, and a search for the good – as the sources of his *Commedia* journey, making his guides like Boethius's guides and his ascent like his. But whereas in the *Convito* it is Beatrice's (or beatitude's) death that sends Dante off to study, the *Commedia* focuses on Dante's later political exile, the figures related to it, the political and religious traditions that led to it, and the sense of meaninglessness that it created in him – all phenomena that have their parallel in Boethius's life.

The *Commedia*'s Aquinas – appropriately Aquinas – presents Boethius in the circle of the Sun's first twelve theologians:

> Per vedere ogne ben dentro vi gode
> l'anima santa che 'l mondo fallace
> fa manifesto a chi di lei ben ode.
> Lo corpo ond' ella fu cacciata giace
> giuso in Cieldauro; ed essa da martiro
> e da essilio venne a questa pace.
>
> (*Paradiso* 10.124–29)

[The holy soul that makes clear the falseness of the world to anyone who hears him correctly rejoices there in seeing the All Good; the body from which his soul was driven lies below in Cieldauro whence the soul came from his martyrdom and exile to this peace.]

Here Boethius's life of exile from Theoderic's court implicitly parallels Dante's exile from Florence, and Boethius's vision of the All-Good anticipates the *Paradiso*'s vision of the "Love that moves the sun and the other stars." Later, Cacciaguida's portrait of Dante's future and Dante's reply to Cacciaguida (canto 17) recapitulate Dante's career in Boethian terms by asserting Dante's exile, his eating others' bread, losing his allies, and becoming his own solitary faction (cf. *Purgatorio* 30.13ff.; *Paradiso* 33.79–81).

The parallelism between the *Commedia*'s Dante and the poem's Boethius goes beyond similarities between their lives to theme-and-variation similarities in the basic structures of their educational journeys. Pietro Alighieri, in one of his exegetical formulations, explains his father's guides by using a system that both recalls the *Convito*'s system and reflects Boethius and the kind of Boethian commentary discussed in chapter 6.[58] Pietro first affirms that the guides in *Inferno* 1.52–102 recall Boethius's

Consolation, where Philosophy's three heights (her natural, mathematical, and metaphysical/theological parts) appear. He also indicates that these three subdivisions can be further subdivided into rational (or objective) and moral (or applicative) categories. Though Pietro does not present us with guides from the *Commedia* that correspond to all six of these categories, he does tell us that Dante imitates Boethius's Philosophy's natural height, natural philosophy, in the gentle lady (*Inferno* 2.94); Philosophy's height of the heavens, the mathematical disciplines speaking to the intellect and imagination of abstract things separated from the material, in Lucia (*Inferno* 2.97); and Philosophy's height penetrating the heavens, theology and metaphysics, in his heaven-ascending Beatrice. Pietro argues further that, in his father's work, rational and ethical philosophy claim a lower subdivision of philosophy than theology, and that, therefore, both Virgil and Statius appear in purgatory: the former as learned information – rational philosophy, the "demonstrative and syllogistic" study of the effects of the vices and virtues (see chapter 5); the latter as information applied to conduct – ethics, the conscience's process of constructing an ideal active life that facilitates Beatrice's appearance as theology and metaphysics.[59] Pietro does not bother to reconcile the difficulties in his scheme that derive from his making both mathematics (Lucia) and ethics (Statius) lead to theology (Beatrice), but the difficulties are probably implicit in Dante's retention of Boethius's old scheme while imposing on it the new path described by Aristotle and Thomas. This imposition on the new on the old may also account for Dante's use of Aristotle's naturalistic ethics and physics to explain the ethical scheme of the *Inferno* (canto 11) and his return to a religious ethics based in scholastic psychology to explain the direction of desire in the *Purgatorio*.

Statius, the equivalent of Virgil's Musaeus, is a guide found only in the purgatorial realm, and particularly in the sections of it where excessive desire is redirected. Statius and his realm are, as Pietro claims, ethics. (Pietro is not alone in relating the *Purgatorio* to the formal discipline of ethics; the possibly spurious "Epistle to Can Grande" does so in interpreting the meaning of the *In exitu de Israel de Egypto* psalm sung in canto 2 of the *Purgatorio*.[60] And Guido da Pisa asserts humankind's subservience to rational and natural law from the beginning of time to Moses, to moral law or ethics from Moses to Christ, and to spiritual law from Christ's time on: three eons that parallel Dante's three realms and make purgatory the realm of moral law.[61] None of the commentators explicitly makes Statius ethics, aside from Pietro.)[62] In making Statius into the representation of ethics, Pietro most clearly reflects the *Convito*'s Thomistic revision of the Boethian ascent. A poet and mythmaker, Statius tells Dante what the soul is and how it functions and, thus, represents ethics as scholastic psychology. He also shows how one can make the myths and the decisions that surmount the id – in Dante's terms, the sirens of instinct (Aquinas argues that ethics studies the soul's actions through its effects and that the passionate and incontinent cannot be students of this subject because their emotions destroy their understanding of their own effects).[63] Statius first appears in the middle of the *Purgatorio,* having just been cleansed of the evil effects of his last sins, avarice and prodigality. As a poet constructing fictions that represent a choice of desires, he can lead Dante through the circles of gluttony and lechery and into the earthly paradise's utopian model of the upright active life, where church and empire properly collaborate to lead humankind.[64] Ethics is again the architectonic study.

Dante shows, in the Boethian "siren" passages associated with Statius, how the poet may become the architect of an inner Eden, how the psychology of the imagination's operations can be transformed through the poet's art. Dante prepares for these passages in the antepurgatory when the eagle, the Lucia, of cooperative grace or mathematical study, moves him upward like Ganymede above the temptations of the valley of the princes (*Purgatorio* 8–9).[65] Thereafter, he wills some good because fewer *phantasmata* distract his imagination, because mind and imagination together encounter, in the *Purgatorio,* a world of art – sculpture, emblem, statement – that solicits the upright choice shaped by the bridles and whips. However, in these early sections of the purgatory proper, Dante's imagination remains partially bound as Augustine's imagination remains bound through much of the *Confessions,* until, in the upper purgatory, the poet-pilgrim experiences a nocturnal phantasm functionally similar to Augustine's nocturnal erotic dreams, a wet dream in the form of the Boethian siren becoming more beautiful as she is gazed upon (*Purgatorio* 19.17–24) – a siren that represents what Boethius's siren also represents, the last phantasm standing between Dante and an objective sight of reality as medieval psychology would understand the matter.

The siren of desire comes just after Statius has liberated himself from the "siren" of prodigality. Responding to her, the holy dream-lady whom the commentators identify as a returned Lucia – reason, conscience, or intellectual power, but surely some form of grace (*Purgatorio* 19.26)[66] – calls to Virgil to rip open the siren's belly, awakening Dante with her stench. Rational philosophy destroys the siren's power as Philosophy does that of the Boethian sirens (*Purgatorio* 19.19–36).[67] Statius represents ethical poetry or poetic ethics, the poet-as-ethical-philosopher whose very existence Allan Bloom's Nietzsche denies. But as we observed in chapter 5, epic commentary in the late Roman period redeemed rhetoric and poetry from the exile to which the philosophers had consigned them. Dante's late Roman Statius does the same thing. He prompts the Christmas *Gloria in Excelsis* and recollects the appearance of the resurrected Christ to James and John on the way to Emmaus (*Purgatorio* 21). More than a model or psychologist, he is the poet whose teaching elaborates the psychological principles empowering moral choice.

Statius's power involves both his capacity to explore psychological principles and his capacity to make myths that embody them. When Dante asks Virgil how disembodied souls can suffer hunger, Virgil turns to Statius as a master of ethical psychology for the explanation, namely, that God placed the possible intellect in the body to allow for human choice based on the possible intellect's receiving of images, its self-consciousness, and its ethical discernment of its own effects ("vive e sente e sé in sé rigira" [*Purgatorio* 25.75]).[68] Pietro says that Dante assigns the possible intellect discussion to a Christian Statius because this topic covers matters both of faith and of morals – how human beings can imagine possible futures and choose among them according to divine commandment.[69] Choice, in the human soul, creates the architecture of all societies, especially the architecture of the good society, and Statius's iconology, like the realm of purgatory itself, emphasizes the importance to ethics of the artistic creation and emulation reconstructed in Dante's scheme.[70] Statius's art is not the middle mathematical art through which the creation's architecture is known, the art that Augustine and Boethius praise and that both classical and medieval architecture embody. It has to do with a new imagination of things that derives from allegory and has to do with the structure of human willing. Statius says that he converted to Christianity (1) after reading a pagan Virgil's condemnation of humankind's rage for gold, a rage also his in the form of prodigality (*Purgatorio* 22.31–

45), and (2) after seeing Christians martyred during the Domitian persecutions (*Purgatorio* 22.67–69). A pagan negative exemplum and a Christian positive one combine to recommend detachment. In conformity to this model of fusing pagan and Christian in an ethical myth, Statius allows himself to be baptized, seemingly in the waters of his own poem (*Purgatorio* 22.88–90), as his own *Thebiad*'s Greeks come near to the rivers of Thebes.[71] As a mythmaker who leads himself with his own myths, Statius (like Cicero in the *Confessions* and *Convito*) also leads Dante through the waters so that, working with Matilda, he acts as Dante's guide into and after his "baptism" in the waters of Lethe (cf. *Purgatorio* 31–32) and through the time of his confession to Beatrice (*Purgatorio* 22.88–90).[72] Like the discipline of ethics during the scholastic period, Statius is both pagan and Christian, the product of Virgil and the martyrs' actions,[73] and he goes with Beatrice and Dante across Eden to its tree and the cleansing waters of Eunoe, where the innocence revives (*Purgatorio* 33.115–46). Matilda, as the upright active life, and Statius, as moral philosophy, together follow the chariot of the Church across the recovered Eden, across the sacred and unpolluted wood lost to the serpent and recovered by penitential choice.[74]

Dante's *Convito* shows how the love and study of ethics leads to theology/metaphysics and to the generation of the kind of felicity and peace that are embodied in the name of the *Commedia*'s Beatrice (*Convito* 2.14.19). The *Commedia*'s Statius leads to Beatrice – right desire to joy, ethics to theology/metaphysics. Beatrice in the *Purgatorio* is a figure fusing "real" or fictive experiences with echoic texts that construct a picture of desire refined by ethical discipline. For example, Dante's Virgilian memory reappears when he sees the new "living" Beatrice come down from above and detects in himself the Virgilian old flame of love that Dido felt. His Boethian side is dramatized when Beatrice reproaches him, as Lady Philosophy reproaches Boethius, for turning to siren substitutes (*Purgatorio* 31.45; *Consolation* 1.pr.1). Beatrice reminds Dante that for some time she sustained him with her face and youthful eyes until, at the time that she arrived at the beginning of the second age, or adolescence, she died ("e mutai vita" [*Purgatorio* 30.125ff.]) and so increased her beauty and virtue (or power).[75] She also observes that, when she changed form, her lover regarded her as less dear and turned his steps to a false way ("per via non vera") until even her dream appearance to him in sleep ("sogno") did no good and Virgil had to show him the damned to turn him to other ways ("le perdute genti").[76] Like the God of the *Consolation,* the *Purgatorio*'s Beatrice makes all second loves of goods other than her good become false images, perhaps like the images of false poetry ("imagini di ben seguendo false" [*Purgatorio* 30.131]). Since she alone represents the true good, she, as a discipline, must be what Pietro says she is, namely theology/metaphysics, "scientia Dei et beatorum."[77] She comes down from heights that reach to God and beatitude as, apparently, does Boethius's Philosophy (1.pr.1).

That the new Beatrice supersedes the Lady-at-the-Window, philosophy, may be puzzling. But the Lady-at-the-Window in the *Convito* supersedes the dead Beatrice by providing Wisdom instead of consolation for the physical Beatrice's death. Now the *Purgatorio* Beatrice supersedes the *Convito*'s Lady-at-the-Window – generic philosophy and Wisdom – by replacing the study and love of lesser goods reflective of God with theology as the direct study of God.[78] As the *Convito*'s physics must give way to higher studies in metaphysics, ethics, and theology, so the Lady-at-the-Window (and all other "false" ladies representing lesser goods) must give way to Beatrice. Beatrice differs from Boethius's Philosophy/Athena, the pre-incarnate Logos,[79] but her sapience is crowned with the olive, Athena's tree.[80] She attacks the sirens, displays the *Convito* Lady Philosophy's lucent eyes revealing truth (*Consolation* 1.pr.1; *Purgatorio* 31.118–23), and repeats many of philosophy's reproaches to Boethius.[81] The women or goods that Beatrice says she supersedes would include goods studied by any lower form of philosophy, whether Virgil's natural philosophy or Statius's ethics – goods that may, of course, be embodied in the pursuit of a real woman as well as in other efforts.[82] Beatrice thus represents the love of the incarnation of the Logos that opens the door to the permanent good temporal state in Eden and ultimately to the celestial paradise. Education in "values" in the *Commedia* ultimately is education in the choice of the least selfish, the most cosmic of loves.

BEATRICE AND THE *PARADISO*'S PICTURE OF THE CREATION: HEAVENLY ARCHITECTONICS

For the purgatorial Dante directed by Virgil and Statius, art and suffering redirect desire and make ethical choice possible. For the paradisal Dante directed by Beatrice, the beauty of light, music, and mathematical proportion keep desire fixed on the good. Though in the *Purgatorio* Statius, as ethics, replaces the mathematical disciplines that normally constitute the middle of the ascent, these disciplines return as a kind of background in the *Paradiso* (the placement of Lucia/mathematics in *Inferno* 1 suggests that they should). Lucia, whom Pietro has earlier glossed as mathematics, represents the last sight that Dante has before Bernard's prayer leads to Dante's beatific vision (*Paradiso* 32.137–39). The *Paradiso* Beatrice consistently offers Dante insights from the mathematical disciplines of astronomy, music, and optics. She also functions as the metaphysics that looks at the sources of nature and directs Dante's vision to the intelligible things that must be the goal of his love affair with the creation and Creator.[83] When the *Paradiso* begins, the poet expresses his awe and love for Wisdom's work directly in the "La gloria di colui che tutto move" passage that praises the divine imprint on the universe experienced by "nostro intelletto" (*Paradiso* 1.1–12), a passage that attributes Dante's new study in the *Paradiso* to the intellectual faculty (*Paradiso* 1.6–9) and probably ultimately reflects Boethius's *De Trinitate* assignment to theology of the study of intellectible static structures.[84] In the upper reaches of the *Paradiso*, Dante comprehends God-created unmoving or cyclical structures that create motion in other systems (e.g., the love that moves the sun and the other stars [*Paradiso* 33.143–45]).[85] Yet beneath the stasis of the *Paradiso*, the flux of time bespeaks its problems; the saints, until the last few cantos, lament time's problems – broken vows, corrupted empire and papacy, depraved Dominican and Franciscan, faithless Florentine and monastic. Each speech about a partially failed institution represents a freely willed human misappropriation of the *virtu* or power that the planets offer to those born under them. Thus, the *Paradiso* creation and desire for Beatrice offer what natural law theory says that the creation should offer to the human polity – a set of models of what just civic life should be. Beatrice, acting as an Anchises in his role as the *Aeneid*'s "dweller in the heavens,"[86] facilitates Dante's examination of the fields of the blessed and of the all-Father reflected in the created universe as Anchises does when he shows the souls (who are about to go to the upper light) that the sky, the moon, the sun, and all of the stars are moved by a single spirit and mind. While Dante is not as pantheistic as Virgil, his paradise has the unity of a continuous metaphor in which light, music, and proportionality in the celestial motions all reflect the imprint of Wisdom on the world system. Image, imagined form, and imagination itself take second billing to the light symbolic of the divine Wisdom that illumines the intellect and creates new desire: the love/light celebrated in the *Convito* and now in the *Paradiso*.[87] The intellect discerns the light, radiating out from divinity, that gives a form to things that the writer can neither record nor his memory recapture (*Paradiso* 1.7–9).

In treating of the mathematical disciplines and the redirection of desire, the *Paradiso* speaks primarily about optics, about light – the planets' light related to the souls' light, the emblematic light with which God writes on Jupiter or Mars, the light that sets forth the relationship between the divine and the various ideal human orders represented as formed light, the river of light, the rose of light, the knotted form of substance and accident leading to the universal form. As the sun of this light, Christ-the-sun (or the Trinity-as-source-of-the-forms) radiates intelligible form to the universe, the kind of notion that almost certainly prepared the way for the heliocentric scientists discussed in the next chapter.[88] Beatrice's eyes, which represent the theological and metaphysical powers given to reason and intellect, mediate to Dante their sense of system.[89] With each ascent, Beatrice's eyes burn brighter, and her smile becomes more beautiful. In Saturn's sphere of the contemplatives, she tells her student that he, Semele-like, will burn to ashes if he sees her Saturnian smile. Commentary has it that Beatrice says this because Dante's intellectual power is as yet inadequate to true contemplation of eternal beauty and can see it only through its symbols (*Paradiso* 21.1–12).[90] When Beatrice (*Paradiso* 23) looks toward the arising of the sun as a bird waiting for the sun so that she may feed her young, the commentators suggest that Beatrice is theology looking toward the divine as she prepares to educate her scholars, in this case Dante.[91]

With light goes the quadrivium's music that forms the knower to what is known – to the order of things – a music more permanent in its effects than the purgatorial music of humanly formed song and poetry:

> Quando la rota che tu sempiterni
> desiderato, a sé mi fece atteso
> con l'armonia che temperi e discerni,
> parvemi tanto allor del cielo acceso
> de la fiamma del sol, che pioggia o fiume

lago non fece alcun tanto disteso.
La novità del suono e 'l grande lume . . .

(Paradiso 1.76–82)

[When the wheel which You, being desired, make everlasting, held me, concentrated on it, through the harmony which You tune and send forth, it appeared to me then that the sky was fired with the flames of the sun so that neither rain nor a river ever made a lake so wide. The newness of the sound and the great light . . .]

Benvenuto, commenting on this passage and citing Albertus Magnus, assures us that the heavens do not make real music but, instead, make the silent harmony of the proportionality governing the skies.[92] Light and sound, studied by the middle quadrivium discipline, complement each other as tokens of the illumination given by the divine plan and its systemic harmony awakening delight and love. The joy implicit in self-initiated study – the attractive power of light and music and proportion among the celestial bodies – makes Dante into a scholar who has gone to the school of his own poem, as the bachelor's oral scene cited at the beginning of this work suggests. Dante says that he armed himself as would a bachelor of arts preparing for an oral examination (*Paradiso* 24.46–51), and he returns to this university-based metaphor in the next canto (*Paradiso* 25.64–66). Some of the fourteenth-century commentators are aware that these passages make the form of Dante's examination resemble that of the university, and the variety of the disciplines reflect those in higher education:[93] logic ("silogismo" [*Paradiso* 24.94]), proofs physical and metaphysical (*Paradiso* 24.133–41),[94] discourse theological and scriptural (*Paradiso* 24.136–38), and philosophic arguments and celestial authority (*Paradiso* 26.37–39).[95] That the examination opens the empyrean to Dante suggests that the university of the autodidact can reach to ultimate truth.

It is difficult to write the poetry of mathematical cognition. Modern physicists have difficulty describing the desire that leads to an increasing cognition of beauty in their understanding of the system of the universe. To counter this difficulty while dealing with medieval cosmic understanding, Dante turns to repeated images that tell of Wisdom's system, images that center in a single focus: wheelings, rivers surrounded with flowers and bees, the petals of a rose (*Paradiso* 28–33). Beatrice speaks as a representative of the creating Logos, announcing the structure of the first creation and describing its angelic wheeling, a truth beyond what the schools know (*Paradiso* 29 passim). The poetry has to use either images of system or Beatrice's speaking of systems and unities discovered by the higher forms of the liberal arts disciplines, especially metaphysics, to make us sense the "form that makes the universe resemble God." Dante, as the lover of the *Commedia*'s Beatrice, resembles the *Convito*'s lover of Wisdom. Through the study of Beatrice as the Theos-Logos in the *Purgatorio*[96] the lover learns the right action and desire found in Eden. Similarly, through the study of Beatrice as metaphysics in the *Paradiso* he learns to desire, to love the beauty of created things and their transcendent models. Beyond this lies the vision of the universal Form, the "geometric" wheel of love where things fall silent:

> A l'alta fantasia qui mancò possa;
> ma già volgeva il mio disio e 'l velle,
> sì come rota ch'igualmente è mossa,
> l'amor che move il sole e l'altre stelle.

[To the high fantasy to be found here my power is lacking, but already my desire and will were turned *as a wheel is moved in symmetry by the love* that moves the sun and the other stars. (*Paradiso* 33.142–45; italics mine)]

Love is here truly the form of philosophy, Wisdom its substance, and geometry its art.

The *Paradiso* is not a cold poem, but it is a very demanding one with respect to the disciplines of desire and the apprehending of form. Beatrice's explanations of the freedom of the will hold the pilgrim responsible for what he wills and for what he does in thought (*Paradiso* 4). This includes the apprehending of form. By implication, the reader is held responsible for knowing the form of the poem: the form that, by way of analogous structure, celebrates the threefold structure of the universe – inferno, purgatory, and paradise – pure potency, mixed potency and act, and pure act reflected in the same life; sensory vision, imaginative vision, and intellectual vision. Dante ends his poem seeing the form and meaning of Wisdom's mirror as reflecting all created things tied into the divine essence:

> Oh abbondante grazia ond' io presunsi
> ficcar lo viso per la luce etterna,
> tanto che la veduta vi consunsi!
> Nel suo profondo vidi che s'interna,

> legato con amore in un volume,
>   ciò che per l'universo si squaderna:
> sustanze e accidenti e lor costume
>   quasi conflati insieme, per tal modo
>   che ciò chi'i' dico è un semplice lume.
> La forma universal di questo nodo
>   credo ch'i' vidi, perché più di largo,
>   Dicendo questo, mi sento ch'i' godo.
> Un punto solo m'è maggior letargo
>   che venticinque secoli a la 'mpresa
>   che fé Nettuno ammirar l'ombra d'Argo.
>
> (*Paradiso* 33.82–96)

[O grace abounding whereby I presumed to fix my sight through the eternal light so great a distance that my sight was consumed in distance. In its depths I saw, bound by love in one volume, that which is scattered through the whole universe: substances and accidents and their connections, as it were brought together in such a way that what I speak of is but a single light. The universal form of this knotting together I believe that I saw, because, as I say this, I feel my joy grow large. A single instant creates greater forgetfulness in me than twenty-five centuries have made of the journey that made Neptune wonder at the shadow of the Argo. (*Paradiso* 33.82–105)][97]

Dante's fiction is that he remembers the structure of the universe. In his hands, Augustine's Book of Memory becomes the Book of the Universe because he claims to remember the whole architecture – the whole architectonic – that should inform human action. While Dante's structure reflects the later fourteenth-century scholastic university's elevation of ethics and theology to the highest spheres,[98] it also construes the final journey with theology/metaphysics in such a way as to recall the older sense of the importance of the mathematical disciplines in the redirection of desire.

Dante's poem is a vernacular poem, a vernacular university for readers who do not have full access to Latin learned institutions. It is one poem for which readers, from the beginning, have welcomed introductions and notes and references sending them off in a hundred different directions to read. It is also a poem that should have sent its readers off to look at the creation. One does not become educated in reading Dante, but if one truly reads him – if one enters into dialogue with him and his speakers – one has to educate oneself. As Charles Singleton has said, "the fiction of the *Comedy* is that it is not fiction."[99] As a vernacular poem in a Latinate age, the poem invites lay learning. Yet, no lay person reading the poem, by that mere action, will change his or her cognitive level. On the other hand, no one reading with understanding can fail to grasp intuitively that differing levels of cognition exist – levels that, to a greater or lesser degree, permit service to the species and to the natural system. When Dante wonders why Thomas Aquinas describes Solomon as the wisest of people, the saint explains that when an individual affirms or denies an idea hastily without distinguishing among ideas (as Dante does in misunderstanding Thomas) "then the emotions may bind the intellect" ("l'affetto l'intelletto lega" [*Paradiso* 13.120]). Thomas goes on to explain that to fish for the truth without the art of fishing for it – an art taught by those learned in the liberal arts – is to fish in vain. By implication, to fish with the arts taught by those in the know (e.g., Augustine, Boethius, and Virgil) is to throw out with a chance of catching. Thomas's metaphor is important. One fishes because one wishes to fish, because one needs it, or because one takes joy in it. But fishing, though a self-initiated art, is not a self-centered one. The goal is always to be "out there," attuned to the movement of wind and weather, the habits of the schools, the feeding places. So also with learning: one must have at least an intuitive grasp of the whole system of the water and shore where one fishes.

Finally, Dante's vision of an effort to know the whole system of the creation is an effort to escape from evil – the evil that despoils nature and humankind – through the contemplation of what the order of the system has to say to human disorder. The system is not to be known so that it can be changed. In explaining *Paradiso* 16.73–75, Pietro says that Augustine observed in the *Confessions* that sin is everything which is not congruent to the whole, that it is impossible that a person should be good unless properly "proportioned" ("bene proportionatos"). Proportion is what the *Commedia* celebrates in its form, in the content of its journey, and in the redemption to which it tends. The aesthetic and moral system of the *Commedia* are finally one and they contribute to further fishing on the part of early Renaissance scientific thinkers.[100]

Dante's contribution in the creation of representations of education is complex. One may argue that his use of the vernacular, his enormous learning, and the power of his poetry made his revision of the Boethian educational journey something that made people sit up and listen. However, Dante also turns education toward ethics (or psychology) and, to some degree, away from noetic mathematics, and one may wonder about the efficacy of that move. Despite Dante's skill in presenting the optical, astronomic, and musical insights of his time, he does not make these insights the sine qua non of the educational journey. Rather, ethics is – ethical teaching. It has been argued that, whereas Romanesque architecture is a prayer, Gothic architecture is a sermon. Something like this shift has occurred with Dante in the development of the idea of an educational journey. Whereas Boethius journeys to the One to know the mind of the One, Dante journeys toward the Trinity with Virgil, Statius, and Beatrice to purge his soul of the vices that would prevent full contemplation – but also to look back in rage on a misgoverned world and to preach about it. There is often some straining in his looking back. However, as an ethical teacher, Dante offers an important vision: he attaches his ethical teaching to a view of human psychology that argues that we can surmount the imaginations of the id and a view of the structure of the universe that asserts that cognition can lay hold on natural regularities or laws that tell human beings how to act. Bertolt Brecht has parodied a Renaissance know-nothing version of this sort of attachment in *Galileo*, and existentialist thinkers from Kierkegaard on have argued that the cosmos has nothing to say about how we ought to behave. On the other hand, environmental thinkers have not been slow to draw sermons and fables for our time from the Book of Nature. In the process of creating fables about the natural world for our own youth, we may wish to look to Dante's concern to envision a human relationship to the natural world that listens more to Apollo's lyre than to the flutes of Dionysus.

Plato Revisited:
The Florentine Platonists
and the Astronomers

The appearance of the scholasticism that influences Dante means, for much of the learned world, an emphasis on natural philosophy and inductive research (though developments in the area of induction are largely confined to more exact classificatory schemes).[1] The interest in induction to some extent focuses intellectual interest away from the longing for mathematical exactitude in the description of nature characteristic of the Wisdom tradition. The old Platonic and Wisdom visions of what the search for reality might be like are not as alive in the learned world of the fourteenth and early fifteenth centuries as they were in the twelfth century. However, the late fifteenth, sixteenth, and seventeenth centuries in Western Europe see the Wisdom vision come to life again. The nearly 2000-year-old literary/scientific models that this book has discussed reappear in the work of the Florentine and other Renaissance Platonists, and these revived models become basic to scientific investigation in the quadrivium subjects pursued by Copernicus, Galileo, and Kepler. As such, they achieve a payoff in unexpected discoveries that are neither wholly implicit in the original versions of the models nor quite possible without them.

The reconfiguring of the empirical evidence occurred only after contradictions in the Ptolemaic account could no longer be easily resolved, after the gradual discovery of ancient heliocentric accounts of the planetary system, after the discovery and use of trigonometry to achieve more accurate planetary measurements, and after several Renaissance thinkers had fused physics and mathematics into a single discipline. The Ptolemaic configuration of physical evidences lost credibility gradually, and its disintegration threw both scientists and literary figures back on basic quasireligious notions – that Wisdom made the universe, that the universe is undergirded by a system of proportionate numbers or "music," and that understanding the universe requires a climb from the study of lower things to the examination of higher ones. Persons of extraordinary persistence and courage, such as Copernicus, Galileo and Kepler, were required to make this old heuristic work so as to produce useful new formulations. But without the old heuristic, their discoveries would not have been possible at all.

The Florentine Platonists – especially Ficino, Pico della Mirandola, and Cristoforo Landino – work to develop the Platonic mathematical notion of the ascent and to create or recreate metaphors of the educational journey supposedly imbedded in the texts of Virgil and Dante. They base their efforts on the literary / scientific work of many of the earlier authors we have studied. The new view of the physical universe still finds it expressive of sacred Wisdom and worthy of a personal journey to that Wisdom through learning, but it is less detailed in its didacticism and concern for ethics than is Dante's vision. Present arguments about the continuity or discontinuity of seventeenth-century physics and astronomy with the medieval tradition largely concern the scientific procedures used in each age.[2] In the area of procedures, powerful arguments can be made both for continuity and for discontinuity. But what may be more important than procedure to the issues of continuity and discontinuity may be world view, the fundamental set of assumptions about the world that makes the labor of detailed scientific measurement and formulation of new hypotheses bearable and defensible. In that area, the picture of the architecture of creation that comes down from Plato, Origen, Augustine, and the "interpreted" Virgil and Dante undeniably works to make the research effort bearable and even wonderful at times. One emblem of the antiquity of the epistemological foundations of the new view appears in Kepler's *Tertius Interveniens*, which mentions Wisdom as the basis of Kepler's geometric searches and makes a periphrasis of the Proverbs 8.30–31 Wisdom passage (i.e., where Wisdom claims to have been with God forming all things and playing before him and in the world): "As God the Maker played; so He also taught Nature, His Image, to play at precisely the same game that he had played before her."[3] To Kepler, all plants, rocks, and heavenly bodies are part of God's geometric play. This sense of Wisdom as describable by mathematical research and as playing, making music, or creating geometry while structuring the world's beauty remains a dominant metaphor underlying the discoveries of the three significant sixteenth- and early seventeenth-century mathematical astronomers (i.e., Copernicus, Kepler, and Galileo). Through these astronomer-physicists, the Wisdom tradition produces what it had claimed to seek from the beginning: "truth" as opposed to "poetry."

This book's view that the appearance of Renaissance astronomy and physics has a partially literary basis is not entirely new. More than twenty-five years ago, E. A. Burtt argued that the Florentine Platonists, especially Pico, through their renewed emphasis on the mathematical-Pythagorean element in Plato, contribute to the revolution in scientific thinking that led to Copernicus, Kepler, and Galileo. As Burtt saw it, the Platonists' mathematical and Pythagorean ideas spread out from Florence to all of the important intellectual centers in Italy – especially Bologna, where Dominicus Maria de Novara, Copernicus's teacher in mathematics, is affected.[4] By defying the pervasive theoretical empiricism and Aristotelianism of the schoolmen, the Platonic revival, in Burtt's view, returns mathematical measurement to a significant place in investigation and empowers the subsequent revival of an epistemology based on mathematics and skeptical of immediate sense experience. This epistemology, according to Burtt, creates the new science.[5]

Although Burtt's theory may attribute too much to the Platonists,[6] it is on the right track. While study subsequent to Burtt has shown that Copernicus and his teachers did not get their mathematics from the Florentine Platonists,[7] the texts that these men edited and wrote influence the astronomers not so much in the area of technical mathematics as in the approach to knowledge that undergirds their work. The Platonists of Florence do not go it alone but proceed in relation to the tradition described in this book, and Ficino himself is aware of the many streams of Platonism emphasizing mathematical verification that reach his age and influence his group. In a letter to Martin Prenninger, he lists – as the significant works in his tradition – Chalcidius's version of the *Timaeus*, the works of Pseudo-Dionysius, much Augustine, Boethius's *Consolation of Philosophy*, Macrobius's *Dream of Scipio,* and other late medieval and Renaissance works.[8] As Klibansky has shown, even the fifteenth century, prior to the appearance of the Florentine Platonists, was not entirely dominated by Aristotelians but had a strong Platonic tradition.[9] Ficino and Pico and, ultimately, Copernicus, Galileo, and Kepler become parts of this broad tradition. Indeed, the primary difference between the fifteenth-century leaders of the Platonic movement in Florence and the sixteenth- and seventeenth-century astronomers stems from the Florentine academicians' interest in civic symbolism based on number, in contrast to the scientists' interest in the astronomical and physical reality that can be defined by number. By and large, the former constructs ideological symbols based in numerology while the latter pursues empirical investigations based on the search for the system of Wisdom and number.

One can find the scientists referring to works in the Platonic and Wisdom traditions often enough. Copernicus cites Ficino at crucial turns; Galileo both analyzes Landino's commentary on Dante and uses Augustine's *Timaeus,* his *De Genesi Ad Litteram,* to justify his greatest discoveries; and Kepler uses the Old Testament books that deal with Wisdom theology plus the *Timaeus,* Proclus on Euclid, and Proclus's hymn to the sun to propel his work (see chapter 6 for Proclus).[10] What is more important than these specific sources is the general use of the Wisdom model as a sort of free-floating basis for exploration. To understand what the Wisdom tradition was like when the new scientists came on the scene, one should look at the relevant Florentine work reshaping the tradition.

THE REVIVAL OF WISDOM AND NUMBER AMONG THE FLORENTINE PLATONISTS

Ficino's most interesting analysis of the ladder to Wisdom appears in a letter to Bernardo Bembo praising philosophy and Wisdom. Following the tradition of the Sophists, he says that rhetoric, though the lowest of subjects, creates love and unity in society and serves to found human communities, determining their geographic locations, their marriage practices, their languages, and their laws. Ethics appears at a point only slightly higher on the scale; contrary to Dante and Aquinas, it returns to one of the lower rungs on the ladder of learning, and it acts as the "love of truth and devotion to wisdom" that enables poets to speak. In the same cluster of subjects, dialectic teaches, through its distinctions, the inferiority of nonhuman to human bodies, of bodies to the soul, of the senses to reason, and of the "active" to the "contemplative" life. Furthermore, dialectic permits the mind to distinguish among the qualities of physical things, so that it progresses from physics to the mathematical analyses of physical things (i.e., astronomy) and, finally, to metaphysical studies that reach the throne of Wisdom. This progress, in turn, empowers the mind to construct, through poetry, artistic representations of the divine order and Wisdom, a passage that seems to echo Petrarch's assignment of poetry to one of the highest realms.[11] Indeed, throughout Ficino's work on number, his central concerns seem to be poetry and artistic representation, forms of cultural life rather than investigations of truth.[12] Hence, for the trivium disciplines of grammar, rhetoric, and dialectic, he sometimes substitutes grammar, rhetoric, and poetry; at times he makes the old quadrivium disciplines into music, orphic singing, architecture, and painting.[13] However much Ficino may emphasize number, his thought in its unadulterated form clearly cannot be the basis of a scientific revolution.

Another Florentine, Pico della Mirandola, seems to elaborate Ficino in describing the ascent but does not come very close to the science that Burtt attributes to him; Pico's 1488 oration, *De Hominis Dignitate,* praises an ascent to Wisdom through the liberal and theoretical arts, but it is mostly a work of mystical theology. Fusing several traditions, *De Hominis Dignitate* divides the world into three zones: the lower sublunary one of the animals, the upper planetary and stellar one where the souls guide the stars, and the supracelestial one composed of minds or angels.[14] The work assumes that humankind, through learning, can escape the animal level (i.e., the voluptuous life) to rise above the stellar world and invade an angelic layer that has the three tiers of the active, contemplative, and unitive lives. The active life has support from angelic thrones that give right judgment to the ruler; the contemplative life belongs to cherubim that encourage an ascent to contemplation and a descent to intervention in the active life; and the unitive life emulates the seraphim, who are one with God. For humankind, the crucial ascending stage occurs in the cherubic life, where the active, contemplative, and unitive lives join together so that divine insight can inform civic judgment. The cherubic life becomes, for Pico, a Jacob's ladder, a scaling place like the active to contemplative ladder in medieval Boethian illustration.[15]

However, unlike the Boethian ladder, Pico's scale also ascends to unity with the One. The cherubic life also contains (somewhat inconsistently, given the function assigned to the seraphim) the pseudo-Dionysian stages of purgation, illumination, and even union with the deity – stages that are equated, in turn, with academic disciplines: purgation comes through grammar, rhetoric, and dialectic (together treated as ethics!); illumination through natural philosophy and the quadrivium; and union through theology. In the purgative stage, grammar and rhetoric combine to lead the mind to the dialectic that "calm[s] the turbulence of reason as it is tossed around between the battles of oratory and the sophistry of the syllogism."[16] Reason then goes from dialectic to the illuminative natural philosophy that calms the soul divided by conjecture and, as Pico implies later, permits the student to contemplate the quadrivium disciplines: the stars, planets, and elements as the adornments of the divine temple.[17] Finally, reason hears the music of the muses who create the harmony of the spheres – and of Bacchus, who leads the muses – as a harmony that makes possible a perception of the invisible things of God through visible objects and natural laws.[18] After such a natural revelation, Pico's theology, like Dante's Beatrice, comes down from above to help the initiate to look on the One and to burn with the divine fire of a love that apotheosizes the self.[19] Thus the disciplines return to the noetic functions that they had in Platonic medieval thought.

Pico agrees with the pseudo-Platonic *Epinomis*'s placement of the numerical sciences as the chief of the liberal arts. Yet no serious mathematical investigation, such as that done by Boethius, appears in his writing, and what appears to be an advocacy of "science" in his work becomes primarily a promotion of individual mystical ecstasy and collective civic celebration. In this respect, Pico resembles Ficino.

A more precise anticipation of the astronomers may appear in Landino, whom Field represents as developing a "poetic theory" that is "the concrete application of Ficino's philosophical principles."[20] Landino resembles both Ficino and Pico in his conception of the ladder, but he applies this conception to the epics of the Wisdom journey that we have studied, specifically to the *Aeneid* and the *Commedia,* and he does so in a way that seems to justify mathematical study as an end in itself rather than as a route to the improvement of fine art in the city of the Medici. Landino's conception of the relationship between the number-based ascent and the construction of the good city resembles Ficino's and Pico's in that he regards poetry and the arts as tools that enact the reversal of the voluptuary's fall.[21] Ficino retains the traditional interpretation of the judgement of Paris as a preference of the life of pleasure to that of power and wisdom,[22] and Landino builds, in his commentaries on Virgil and Dante, on this interpretation and on what appears to be Petrarch's inter-pretation of Virgil (see chapter 5). To achieve the knowledge of God, Landino's hero, whether Aeneas or Dante, makes decisions that oppose Paris's choice placing of Venus before Minerva and Juno. Each hero puts behind Paris's voluptuous life and chooses first Juno's active life and then Minerva's contemplative one, including mathematics as a component of the latter.[23]

In commenting on the *Aeneid*, Landino says that "mind," represented by Aeneas, first descends from the heavens, following Platonic ideology, and later reascends to the stars through the astronomical and mathe-matical disciplines learned in Hades, traveling above the stars to the supramathematical realm where the mind of the ruler can know the cosmic order and apprehend what civic rule requires.[24] Landino repre-sents Dante as embodying the same "Virgilian" mythos. In the *Camaldu-lensian Dialogues,* Landino's character, Lorenzo de Medici, argues that, superficially, Dante borrows little from Virgil, but that careful examina-tion reveals that Dante gets almost everything from the Roman poet.[25]

Although the *Commedia* pilgrimage described in Landino's commen-tary on Dante follows the pattern of Landino's understanding of the *Aeneid* journey, the purgations he finds in the Christian poet are more elaborate than those discovered in Virgil. Following the Fulgentian pic-ture of the *Aeneid* as a kind of life journey through the world of learning, Landino posits that Dante begins his descent in the middle of the journey of his life because discretion comes when the developing person recog-nizes that he stands at the midpoint between the voluptuous and con-templative lives,[26] at the point when the human spirit begins to desire to purify itself from earthly things and to return to its origin in the One. In the infernal descent, the poet-pilgrim only contemplates the effects of the vices created by earthly appetites and voluptuousness. But in the purgatorial ascent, he purges himself of those things that stand in the way of his helping to establish the just civic or active life symbolized by Eden. In the *Paradiso,* he prepares himself for the full contemplative life by adding the intellectual virtues – intellectual passion or Venus, practical reason or the sun, and so on – until he reaches the cognizance of God. In his analysis of the *Paradiso,* Landino argues that the mathematical disciplines advance by the power of a higher *virtu speculative* or *intelligenza* that ascends beyond the power of ordinary pragmatic science or wisdom.[27] This analysis of the *Paradiso* seems to be new, but it has some basis in Dante's return to mathematically based knowledge as a backdrop in the *Paradiso* (see chapter 7). By envisioning a paradisal, intellectual purgation that he adds to the moral purgations achieved in the *Purgatorio,* Landino elevates mathematical mastery to the highest realms that come just before the unitive experience.

Landino also fills Dante's "imaginary garden" with real toads that interest later scientists. For example, he takes seriously the *Convito's* notion that the world has a circumference of 20,400 miles and a radius of 3,245 and 5/11ths miles.[28] From this, he derives the precise measurements for the inferno and sets the stage for Galileo's discussion of the same measurements in one of his earliest essays. Thus, though he makes Dante into a kind of number mystic, he seems also to assume that he is a scientist who works at measuring accurately the circumference of the world.

WISDOM AND THE NEW ASTRONOMY: COPERNICUS AND THE SUN AS COSMIC STAGE DIRECTOR

The Florentine Platonists' chief accomplishment in remapping the journey to truth comes in their recovery of and commentary on ancient and medieval Platonic and Neoplatonic texts celebrating mathematics as the middle discipline on the road to Wisdom. They recreate the mythos of a mathematical road to truth, though they know little about mathematics. The physicist-astronomers, whom Burtt links to the Florentine Platonists, share the Platonists' interest in the journey to Wisdom and in mathematical studies as the middle disciplines, but they transform this interest. For them, the study of numbers does not work to decorate the city with numerological symbolism but to explore the cosmos. However, the astronomers can look to mathematical studies as a cognitive tool partly because they have more than the thoughts of the Florentines. They have the books that the Florentines translated and interpreted: Ficino's *Timaeus* edition,[29] the poetry of Dante as commented on by Landino, and the Neoplatonic Augustine, to whom Ficino traces his academic ancestry in the letter to Martin Prenninger cited above.[30] Specifically, Copernicus uses a Timaean model, cites Ficino's edition of the *Timaeus,* and uses Ficino's commentary on Plato's *Laws.* Galileo mentions Ficino in his juvenilia, employs Dante in his first lectures responding to a critique of Landino, and uses Augustine's heavily Platonic *De Genesi ad Litteram* to describe his understanding of the creation and to defend himself against his Vatican opponents. Kepler uses the *Timaeus* constantly, probably in Ficino's edition, and he employs Proclus repeatedly, particularly the commentary on Euclid's geometry that contains Euclid's allegorization of the *Odyssey* as a journey through the mathematical to the One (see chapter 6). Finally, Kepler sings his own Wisdom songs with the fervor of a Ficinian rhapsodic singer.

Copernicus keeps alive the notions that the universe is sacred and that truth requires a journey. The first work to explain Copernicus's views, Rheticus's *Narratio Prima* (1540),[31] assigns to Copernicus a position that appears to be derived from Ficino's edition of and commentary on the *Timaeus,* a book found in the library of Copernicus's canonry chapter at Frauenburg.[32] Rheticus asserts that Copernicus's theory begins with the observation that all of the planets conform themselves to the motion of the sun, but that Copernicus remains uncertain, at this point, whether the sun administers the planetary system as an unmoved mover, like God moving the total cosmos, or whether it is a moved mover, both moving itself and administering the other planets. According to Rheticus, Copernicus sees God's making and ordering of the cosmos as like a playwright's creation of a play or entertainment and believes that the sun may play the role of the choral leader in the dance of the planets.[33] Copernicus's debt to the translation of and commentary on the *Timaeus* by Ficino implicitly appears, in this account, in the former's assigning of roles to the sun and to God. In Ficino's commentary, the Timaean Demiurge equates with the Christian God the Father, the Platonic Nous (or exemplary, intellectual reason), with Christ the Son or the Logos, and the World-Soul with the Holy Spirit.[34] (This Platonic Trinity parallels the Platonic Trinity that William of Conches discovers in Boethius's Timaean hymn in the *Consolation* [3.m.9]). In Ficino, the World-Soul pours forth intellectual light that, by degrees of emanation and fusion with matter, becomes light, fire, the source of creation and cause in the physical universe.[35] For Ficino, the World-Soul is implicitly a kind of cosmic stage director, and the firmament conveys this director's vital force to the physical universe. Copernicus probably found little difficulty in shifting this part of the World-Soul's symbolism and power to the sun, since Plato and most Platonists had also assigned a special place to the sun by making the Demiurge directly create the sun that fills the world with light and number (*Timaeus* 39b), and Ficino also gives a preeminent place to the sun in his commentary.[36] Since Plato's *Republic* had, in the myth of the cave, made the sun's illumination stand for what makes it possible to see reality, or the Forms, it was natural for Copernicus to make the physical sun occupy the place in relation to physical reality that the Unmoved Mover occupies in relation to all reality. Given what the sun is metaphorically in Plato, it was easy for Copernicus to convert the material sun into a Neoplatonic vivifying power that conducts the "numbered" dance of the cosmos.[37]

Within this metaphor, the dance occurs in a grand theater where the eighth sphere, containing the fixed stars, becomes the static backdrop against which the great planetary dance or drama plays. At the center, God, like a hidden playwright or choreographer, stations the sun and gives its rhythms power to govern the motions of the gods (i.e., the planets named after the classical gods), as Pontanus's *Urania* asserts.[38] Rheticus's Copernicus changes slightly the traditional conception of the journey to God when he argues that the mind should respect the stage-setting and stage as sacred while looking to the scriptures for the final revelation of truth about God (an opinion that seems to leave astronomy's relation to the study of divinity ambiguous to a degree that it is not in Boethius or, later, in Galileo and Kepler). Rheticus says that Copernicus takes astronomy back to the heights and to her palace where she once reigned as the queen of the mathematical disciplines (just as Atlas took the heavens on his shoulder from a wavering Hercules).[39] But he does not say where Copernicus thinks that the palace might be in relation to God. Without saying where Copernicus's trip to the heavens ends, whether at the sphere of the fixed stars or at the throne of God,[40] Rheticus recreates Copernicus as "Plato's" astronomer in the *Epinomis* (recall the important place that the *Epinomis* had in Pico's scheme), as one who acts under God's guidance to reveal things.

Both numbers-philosophy and poetic conceptions inform much of Rheticus's description. For example, Rheticus's Copernicus counts the number of the six planets – Saturn, Jupiter, Mars, Earth, Venus, and Mercury – and he sees them as fulfilling the perfect biblical and Pythagorean numbers that reveal God's Wisdom and number.[41] Copernicus is also the epic hero who journeys, like Orpheus in his *descensus*,[42] carrying in his hand his "golden bough," the staff of geometry or mathematics, while led along the road by a God that allows him to recall Urania, the patroness of astronomy, from the underworld. Rheticus's Copernicus never claims to see God directly and sees Wisdom only indirectly, but he configures himself as a surrogate Aeneas in his allegorical descent into Hades or a surrogate Boethian Orpheus (3.m.12) in the land of learning, one for whom all phenomena are linked together as by a golden chain.[43]

Copernicus's linking of the phenomena together appears to dictate his other change in the ladder of learning understood by ancient and medieval Aristotelians. While they separate physics and mathematics, Copernicus makes physics and the mathematical disciplines become one. Hence, in the preface to *De Revolutionibus*, he complains that those who believe only that the planets move in homocentric motions cannot obtain results that agree with the phenomena, while those who add the Ptolemaic eccentrics can create a picture that agrees with the phenomena but disagrees with the laws of motion.[44] Since the laws of uniform motion are parts of the study of physics, previously thought to apply only to terrestrial things, their citation in the context of an astronomical discussion signifies that Copernicus presumes physics and astronomy (earthly and heavenly phenomena) to be governed by a single set of laws and to give rise to a single discipline.[45]

De Revolutionibus, published as Copernicus lay dying, represents his definitive work on planetary motion,[46] a work less speculative than Rheticus's earlier account of Copernicus's thoughts, but one that uses metaphors that tend to confirm Rheticus's *Timaean* representation of his cosmology. In *De Revolutionibus*, Copernicus says that, when he began his research, human beings had not described the motions of the world machine created by the most systematic of craftsmen, God.[47] Beginning with the *Timaeus*'s assumption that the heavens are a visible model of a god (a phrase suggesting that they reveal Wisdom to the Christian writer),[48] Copernicus makes astronomy study this visible model through a contemplative art that draws human minds from vice to wonder at the divine disposition of things and that gives grounds for rejoicing in the works of God's hands (Psalm 92.4).[49] When *De Revolutionibus* asserts that the earth moves and has several motions and that the sun is the universe's

center, it supports its assertions with Wisdom-tradition assumptions concerning the divine principles governing the general order of things. First,
it assumes that the planets, in following each other in circles, follow
divine providence. Second, it assumes that the universe, or planetary
system, is a harmony.[50] As Thomas Kuhn puts it, Copernicus's argument
rests on the sense of harmony, on the "aesthetic sense . . . alone,"[51] an
aesthetic sense enforced by Augustine's view of the harmony of the world
and by common Wisdom tradition and Florentine Platonic representations of what beauty, harmony, proportion, and Wisdom are. Copernicus
reminds us that his work came out of problems in the geocentric system
and out of possibilities contained in an ancient tradition of scientific
inquiry postulating heliocentrism or leading toward it: Hicetas, certain
thinkers cited by Plutarch, and certain Pythagoreans.[52] But these problems and the support of background readings in ancient astronomy
would not have come to anything for Copernicus had they not been com-
bined with his assumption that, in its core logic, the universe represents a
harmony moving in circles that reveals Wisdom. In this assumption, he
shows his roots in Plato, in the Florentine Platonists, and in the Wisdom
tradition.

GALILEO'S USES OF WISDOM, DANTE, AND AUGUSTINE

Since Copernicus dies shortly after *De Revolutionibus* (1543) was published, the defense and the modification of his theory to fit precise astronomical measurements and experiments falls to Galileo (1564–1642)
and Kepler (1571–1630). Both of these men are more explicit about
their intellectual roots in the Wisdom tradition than Copernicus and
more ambitious to claim that the wisdom and number they find bespeaks
God.

Galileo includes most of the meditations on his world view in polemical
writings that defend his scientific works against ecclesiastical efforts to
silence him. Nonetheless, his positions are sufficiently consistent to suggest that they are no mere fluff spun out in moments of polemical need.
They reveal a writer committed to the notion that Wisdom lies behind
natural law, that one must make an ascent to Wisdom to understand
nature, and that the work of ascent is an epic work.

Galileo's earliest writings reflect his relation to the Florentine Platonists, especially his juvenile writings from about 1590 that examine Aris-

totle's *De Caelo* and other works of natural speculation, and that several times quote Ficino on the nature of the sky and the elements;[53] his early fragments attached to his *Discourse on Floating Bodies,* which cite the Bible to the effect that God made all things to have number, weight, and measure (thereby showing that measurements are from the beginning important to him as indicative of God's thought);[54] and his first public lectures on "the location, arrangement, and dimensions of the places described in Dante's *Inferno.*"[55] The lectures defend Manetti, against Vellutello's animadversions, for his support of Landino's commentary on the *Commedia* and, in particular, Landino's picture of the measurements of hell.[56] The early Galileo is a geocentrist. The idea developed in his Dante lectures (i.e., that God put the earth which contains hell under the moon and at the center of the universe so that the infernal region would be as far from the heavens as possible and spare the celestial beings the sight of the infernal ugliness) recurs in the first version of his first scientific treatise, *De Motu.*[57] Such a flow back and forth between scientific and literary disciplines reappears throughout Galileo, with literature flowing into science in the early work, and, in the later work, "literary" conceptions from the Wisdom literature, Augustine, and certain exegetes contemporary with Galileo flowing into his apologies for his scientific efforts.

When the great controversies about Galileo's discoveries arise, he provides himself with a defense by calling on Augustine's Neoplatonic work on creation, *De Genesi ad Litteram,* in his 1615 letter to the Grand Duchess Christina of Lorraine. Arthur Koestler dismisses Galileo as "devoid of any mystical, contemplative leanings" and "wholly and frighteningly modern,"[58] but he does so by looking at Galileo's method and ignoring his assumptions. If the Wisdom tradition that inspired the writers studied in this book is in any sense a "mystical, contemplative" one (however often it uses mathematics to achieve contemplation), Galileo is as indebted to it as are Copernicus or Kepler or Boethius and Augustine.[59] Galileo writes his letter to the Grand Duchess following attacks on his *Discourse on Floating Bodies* and his "Copernican" *Letters on Sunspots* by followers of Lodovico delle Colombe and Cardinal Bellarmine.[60] In his letter, he argues that both scriptures and creation emerge from God but that, where these appear to differ in their message about the physical world, preference must be given to the creation. The scripture is divine Wisdom dictated to writers by the Paraclete,[61] but the creation is the product of God's command, given through the Logos ("Verbo divino").[62] Whereas the scriptures address the limited understandings of human beings and contain much that, taken literally, accommodates the truth to the dictates of popular culture, the created world follows the divine dictates without deviation or vulgarization.[63] The infallibility of the creation's revelation of the ideas in the mind of Wisdom corrects the possibility of any exegetical misunderstanding of scriptural passages. If an issue of authority arises, the problem for human understanding is to know the creation accurately (i.e., mathematically) and to penetrate beyond any accommodative vulgarizations that might lead to an interpretation of scriptural locutions inconsistent with what the creation reveals. In this process one must use one's sense, reason, and intellect fully.[64] Indeed, for Galileo the text of the Bible and the text of creation have separate spheres of authority; the creation testifies to the character of the Logos as Creator, while the scriptures testifies to His redemptive actions in history.

As Galileo himself mentions, his position derives both from Augustine's Neoplatonic *De Genesi ad Litteram,*[65] and from Augustine's less well-known letter to Marcellinus. *De Genesi ad Litteram* purports to explain the first book of the Bible literally, but Augustine makes even his reading of the literal sense of Genesis into a figurative, Christianized *Timaeus* that explains the creation of the world by an equivalent of the Nous, the Word, or Wisdom, and speaks of an intellectual creature mediating between the Word and matter that appears to be the equivalent of the World-Soul (2.8).[66] Admittedly, *De Genesi'*s account of *Genesis* is more literal than that in the last few books of Augustine's *Confessions* (discussed in chapter 3), but it is not a very literal interpretation.[67] The Wisdom/Word, Augustine says, is the reasonable force shaping all things, the perfect original light that initiates the "speaking out" that made things, the number, weight, and measure beyond all physical number, weight, and measure (*De Genesi ad Litteram* 1.2–5; 1.14).[68] Contrary to Greek philosophy, Augustine's matter did not exist before the Word, but God constructed it in a form that allowed the Word also to evolve it into a complex design, a design neither fully nor adequately reflected in the nonscientific sections of a Bible adapted to common understanding. Because *De Genesi* assumes that the creation represents a divine speaking out, it tells us that what is demonstrated by scientists or specialists in physical things cannot contradict scripture (though mere scientific opinion may and should be refuted [1.21]).[69]

Augustine asserts a similar position in the letter to Marcellinus. There, as Galileo observes, he argues that the scriptures may be misunderstood to contradict reason,[70] but the scripture should never be understood to deny the testimony of reason for, where that contradiction appears, either reason is faulty or the scriptures have been misunderstood.[71]

Eileen Reeves has argued that Galileo's letter to the Grand Duchess subordinates scripture to the authoritative testimony of the heavens, while Augustine, particularly in *De Genesi,* subordinates the varying testimony of science to the unchanging authority of the scriptures.[72] However, as I have mentioned, Augustine in *De Genesi* itself does not give a "matter-of-fact" account of the text of *Genesis.*[73] Rather, he presents a highly interpretive version of it that assimilates it to the *Timaeus,* to Neoplatonic writings, and to Wisdom texts from other parts of the Old and New Testaments. In short, he makes *Genesis* conform to scientific and philosophic understanding as it existed in his time. Galileo understands that Augustine does this, doing the same thing himself by making Augustine's precept concerning the testimony of reason apply to what he has discovered concerning the testimony of the heavens.

Galileo's sense of the Creator's Wisdom appears in his admiration of the complexity found in the created universe, a complexity that invites one to ascend through investigations open to sense, reason, and intellect to discover Wisdom's craft. To do less than a full investigation of the phenomena is to reject the power of the hierarchy of the senses, reason, and intellect to travel toward God in areas where the scriptures do not speak definitively.[74] It is, so to speak, to do less than the highest possible justice to the intellectual faculties that human beings possess. Galileo's argument that the senses, reason, and intellect must all be used in the understanding of the creation relates to his general understanding of the ladder to learning and his traditional awareness of the place that theology occupies on the ladder. Galileo's opponents, departing from the tradition of the ascent, had argued that theology is, by ascription, so completely the queen of the sciences that findings in the other disciplines inconsistent with her precepts should be rejected.[75] Scholars in the subordinate sciences, practicing a form of self-censoring intellectual exploration that we may think of as characteristic of modern totalitarian states, should, on their own, discover and correct any of their findings inconsistent with theology's precepts without any nudging from the theologians. In contrast, Galileo denies such authority to theology and makes her depend on the lower disciplines made available to her through the ascent. Here he follows the whole Wisdom tradition treated in this book from Augustine and Boethius onward. To him, theology is the queen of the sciences by virtue of her synthesis of the other disciplines. With a bow in the direction of earlier understandings of the ladder of the disciplines, he tells the Grand Duchess that theologians who have studied geometry, astronomy, music, and medicine will not argue that the Bible replaces Boethius, Ptolemy, Archimedes, or Galen.[76] Though theology is the study of contemplation and eternal blessedness (Galileo's Dantesque definition of theology in Beatrician terms), it cannot properly order an intellectual to become a Sophist or command the disciplines to deny findings which the creation (as agent of the Logos) announces in the book of creation.[77]

With a sweeping literary flourish, Galileo tells the Duchess what kind of authoritative bookmaker God is, the God whose grandeur may be read in the open volume of the heavens ("nell' aperto libro del cielo"). This God's text speaks beyond the radiance and movements of the sun and stars and reaches to the fundamental mysteries of creation yet to be comprehended by human faculties.[78] It is this grandeur that the scientist studies, the truth about nature, and he does so without basing himself in the authority of opinions or in that of the rhetorical professions, law, and merchandising – perhaps one more reminder of the centuries-long battle between rhetoric and philosophy.[79]

In bringing in exegesis to support his argument, Galileo also implicitly pursues Augustine's observation (in the letter to Marcellinus) that where the scriptures seem to deny rational authority, they have been misunderstood. He endeavors to show that, even in the realm of exegesis, the weight of the scriptures and the exegetes does not point to a geocentric system. He sees Job 9.6 as speaking of a God that moves the earth from its place (Didacus of Stunica explains this as referring to the Copernican theory).[80] He recalls that Dionysus the Areopagite in his epistle to Polycarp, Augustine in *De Mirabilius Sacra Scripturae*, and Bishop Alfonso Tostado of Avila, in their respective commentaries on the Joshua story, show that Joshua's feat of making the sun stationary refers to his making the *primum mobile* stop so that the always-stationary sun appears to stand still against the background of temporarily stationary stars.[81] And he reminds his opponents that Pseudo-Dionysus the Areopagite's *De Divinis Nominibus* argues that the sun converts to its own purposes everything that moves, and that it carries out God's will in shaping the universe, implying that the *primum mobile* was stopped by Joshua.[82] Even St. Ambrose's *Caeli Deus Sanctissime,* in Galileo's view, asserts that God put the sun in the center and rotated it like the hub of a wheel, turning the planets in their courses:

> Caeli Deus sanctissime,
> Cui lucidum centrum poli
> Candore pingis igneo,
> Augens decoro lumine;
> Quarto die qui flammeam
> Solis rotam constituens,
> Lunae ministras ordinem,
> Vagosque cursus siderum . . .[83]
> [Most holy God of Heaven
> Who paints the brilliant center
> of the (heaven's) axle
> With firelike brightness
> Enhanced by beautiful light;
> Who created on the fourth day
> The fiery spindle of the sun
> And governed the successions of the moon
> And the wandering star courses . . .][84]

Finally, Galileo reminds the Grand Duchess that in Proverbs 8, Wisdom implies that the earth turns on hinges or poles (Prov. 8.26).[85]

While the letter to the Grand Duchess gives the fullest account of the epistemological and exegetical bases of Galileo's scientific work in pursuit of Wisdom, other writings of his confirm this letter's positions. For example, his *Assayer* (1623) argues, in a manner worthy of Plato's attacks on the Sophists and poetry, that philosophy (i.e., science) is not a fiction like *Orlando Furioso* or the *Iliad*.[86] Philosophy is written in the book of the universe and is recorded in the transparent language of mathematics (however, here Galileo seems either to deny the allegorical journey-to-Wisdom aspect of these epics or to be speaking only of their literal fictions).[87]

Again, Galileo's *Dialogue Concerning the Two Chief World Systems* (1632), his ironic defense of the Copernican as opposed to the Ptolemaic system, speaks of the Book of Nature as the object of all philosophy and as written by the universal Artisan, meaning exactly what the *Assayer* means when it speaks of the book of the universe. Salviati, one of Galileo's spokespersons in this work, advocates the science of number advanced by the Pythagoreans and Plato.[88] At the end of the dialogue of "The First Day," Salviati also asserts that, though the scientific, geometric study of the natural world gradually reads the Book of Nature, the reading never will be complete:[89] although human beings can know some "intelligible" things accurately through the intensive study of geometry, "Divine Wisdom" knows these and all other mathematical relations intuitively and instantly. In short, Galileo founds his mathematical and physical discoveries on a belief that the mind can ascend from the sensory to the intelligible, but that the intelligible system that can be known by human beings represents only a portion of the whole known to Wisdom.

KEPLER'S PURSUIT OF THE TIMAEAN MODEL IN GEOMETRY, COSMIC MUSIC, AND EPIC

While Copernicus writes only a few laconic passages that reveal his framing assumptions and Galileo reveals his basic frame of reference primarily when under attack, Kepler (roughly Galileo's contemporary) carries the Wisdom model with him constantly and shows precisely how it operates in his research. Kepler is a man more dependent on philosophy and philosophic poetry than either Copernicus or Galileo, a man more fully "emptied" by the sufferings in his life, and a more complete mystic. One can trace his steps following Wisdom better than in either of the other two great astronomer/physicists because he tells of his literary models, of his false starts, and of the emotion with which he greets his work. Kepler's first scientific work, the *Mysterium Cosmographicum* (1596), sets him on the path charted by Plato's *Timaeus* and by the Wisdom literature, but it contains little of lasting scientific value. When the solutions in the *Mysterium* prove to be incomplete, he goes back to the planetary problem and writes his greatest scientific works, the *Astronomia Nova* (1609) and the *Harmonice Mundi* (1618). These two works formulate his three planetary laws: (1) that the planets move in ellipses rather than circles, and that the sun is placed at one of their foci; (2) that the radius vector of a planet sweeps past equal areas in equal times so that a planet moves most quickly when it is closest to the sun; and (3) that the square of the time that each planet takes to go around the sun is equal to the cube of the planet's mean distance from the sun (i.e., there is a harmonic, proportional relationship between a planet's distance from the sun and its circumnavigation around it).[90]

If Kepler's God plays (as Wisdom does in Proverbs) in making the creation, Kepler also plays in his discovery of the Maker. In the *Mysterium*, he says that when he discovered the similarity between the proportions among the five regular solids when they nest inside each other and the proportions among the orbits of the planets circling around the sun in the Copernican scheme,[91] he experienced such a wonder in discovery that he plowed ahead day and night to "make public in print this wonderful example of His [i.e., God's] wisdom" so that he might sing the glory of the "All-wise Creator."[92] His preface to the second edition (1621) of the *Mysterium* claims an oracular inspiration that strikes the seven stringed psalter of the Creator's Wisdom, finding Wisdom and number embodied in the seven "strings" of a lyre that includes the six planets then known plus the sun.[93] For Kepler, scientific inspiration is related to worship. The dedication of the first edition (1596) of the *Mysterium* asserts that an exact knowledge of God the Creator leads to an exact worship of Him and cites, for support, the Psalms' statements on the beauty of the heavens as praising God (this dedication also repeats Origen's and Augustine's comparison of God the Creator to an architect creating order and pattern, so that studying his works will nourish the human sense of beauty and increase human desire for divine knowledge). The process of studying the heavens, Kepler says, can move one from earthly care to tranquil celestial contemplation.[94]

Kepler's effort to create an exact model of the physical universe centers in the sun even as his spiritual universe centers in God the Father. As in Copernicus, the sun is the image of God the Father, but Kepler's works extend this Copernican symbology to make the universe, as conceptualized in the new cosmology, represent the Trinity (see chapter 6). The preface to the reader in the second edition of the *Mysterium* (1621) develops the ideas that the sun resembles God the Father; the curved surface of the sphere of the fixed stars, God the Son; and the intermediate space, God the Holy Spirit.[95] Though the idea partially originates with Nicholas of Cusa's *Complementum Theologicum* and has some precedent in

Copernicus, it also belongs in the tradition of Ficino's Timaean Trinity and William of Conches's Boethian version of God as the three Timaean divine forces.[96] For Kepler, the Son or Wisdom provides the forms of things, conceived of as a geometry and a music, that the students learn for themselves when they become autodidacts who climb the ladder to God, moved on by the beauty or symmetry of what they find.

The notion of Wisdom as revealed in the creation appears further expanded in Kepler's emblemology of light and optical measurement. In the *Ad Vitellionem Paralipomena* (1604), he says that the universe takes a form like that of the Trinity, a sphere having three parts: center, spherical cortex, and space between central point and cortex.[97] Since bodies emit nonmaterial but corporeal forces (e.g., light or the magnetic forces) that act according to geometric rules, they can be described by geometry.[98] The light seen by the writers of the first chapters of *Genesis* expresses the life given to all things within created matter (Kepler's redefinition of John 1's notion of the light of the Logos as the life of the creation).[99] Light to him is the noblest thing in the corporeal world, the link between the world of matter and the world of spirit, that which energizes the animal faculties.[100] At the center of this universe of real and symbolic light (like Ficino, Kepler consistently mixes the two) sits the sun whose actions Kepler's optical work unfolds in its analysis of the laws of reflection and refraction. Everything that the sun does is lawful, purposeful, directed to revealing the Creator. For example, the Creator writes his signature even through the eclipse that invites that spirit of humankind to investigate the divinity behind the signature and to feel awe before Him.[101] The world's beauty, according to Kepler, derives both from physical light and from a Johannine intellectual light awaiting discovery.

Kepler's world is also beautiful because it is full of geometric and musical proportions that require all of Kepler's adult life for their discovery. In chapter 2 of the *Mysterium,* Kepler turns to Timaean forms of Christianity when he tells us that his Creator conceived of the Idea of the universe as the most beautiful work possible in his mind. The Creator – a spherical shape with center, cortex, and space between reflecting Father, Son, and Spirit – constructed the universe in His own image in the "most beautiful" shape of the sphere, giving it quantity so that, within this sphere, the primary regular solid geometric figures could be inscribed: the cube, pyramid, dodecahedron, icosahedron, and octahedron. Kepler appropriates to his mathematical purposes Plato's Timaean "physics" of the elements as the regular solid geometric figures,[102] and he argues that between the center and the sphere of the fixed stars comes the space in which these imaginary solids set the courses of the planets, a concept of interplanetary space to which the remainder of the *Mysterium Cosmographicum* is dedicated.

Kepler continues this biblical-Timaean synthesis throughout the *Mysterium*. In chapter 10, he remarks that the physicists (i.e., those trained in Aristotle's *Physics*) will oppose him because he deduces the characteristics of the planets from nonmaterial things and mathematical figures ("ex rebus immaterialibus et figuris mathematicis"). But this opposition does not bother him. He responds that God or Founding Wisdom ("Conditricis Sapientiae") does create on the basis of immaterial and imagined things because He has had the mathematical figures as archetypes with Him from eternity, a position reminiscent not only of the *Timaeus* but also of Origen's discussion of John and of Augustine's various discussions of the creation.[103] Though Kepler modifies some of the positions of the *Mysterium* later in his career, he holds consistently to his notion that God creates on the basis of geometric archetypes.[104]

In the *Ad Vitellionem Paralipomena,* a work on optics written at about the same time as the *Astronomia Nova* but published earlier (1604), Kepler turns again to major metaphors of the Wisdom (or Logos) literary tradition. He dedicates the work to the Emperor Rudolph, who, he says, has fought long with the Turks but who also serves the liberal arts that promote peace. In pursuing those arts that Rudolph honors, Kepler says that he does not imitate those abstract geometers who spend all of their time on speculations. Rather, he studies geometry where it is real – in the body of the world where the traces of the Creator are to be found.[105]

Platonic (or Neoplatonic) assumptions about light and geometry are part of Kepler's heuristic. Music is the other part, and musical assumptions are basic to the *Astronomia Nova,* published in 1609 but written earlier in the decade. Kepler turns to the epic mode to start this book's mediation of its discovery. In his "epic" dedication of the book to the Emperor Rudolph II, he writes that he, through his *Astronomia Nova,* has made a prisoner of Mars, the planet placed in the heavens to awaken people from intellectual sloth and ignorance. Mars should stimulate them to seek the praises of the Creator and Architect of the world in the

sky.[106] By this, Kepler means that he formulates his first and second planetary laws to explain the orbit of Mars in relation to the sun and to the
orbit of the Earth. While Copernicus is in some ways as old-fashioned as
Dante and still shares Dante's vision of universal movement in circles,
Kepler, using Tycho of Brahe's data, finds that the planets move in ellipses. However, even after that discovery, Wisdom assumptions push him
in the direction of finding, beneath the ellipses, a harmonious music of
proportions. These he discovers in his second law, showing that the radius vector of Mars, though defining an ellipse, sweeps past equal areas in
equal time periods. Underlying his project of finding these proportional
relations in the ellipses is a faith that the universe has a musical, numbered organization relating the Creator and creation, that it is ruled by
laws, and that it is not some unpredictable cosmic animal or organism
governed by creatures of mind and will or by "planetary minds."[107] Kepler, as much as Galileo, breaks down the divisions between physics and
the mathematical disciplines because "he [is] not satisfied with a geometrical theory until he ha[s] further reduced it to physics," verifying his
hypotheses with natural investigations.[108]

Kepler's final major work, the *Harmonice Mundi,* uses the framework
developed in the *Mysterium Cosmographicum* to arrive at the last of his laws,
the one that makes possible Newton's astronomical discoveries. In the
process, Kepler reformulates Ptolemy's and Cicero's conceptions of the
harmony of the universe. The third and most complex of Kepler's planetary laws, it states that the proportion of the squares of the period of
revolution of two planets is equivalent to the cube of their mean distance
away from the sun.[109] The earth revolves around the sun in a year, and
Saturn does so in thirty years. The cube root of one is one and one
squared is one; the cube root of thirty is a little above three, and three
squared is nine. Therefore, the law implies, Saturn's mean distance from
the sun should be about nine times the Earth's mean distance from the
sun. This is, in fact, the correct distance. The formula is pure mathematics, but Kepler could not have found the formula had he not begun with a
harmonic assumption and searched until he found its correlative in the
material world.[110]

At the beginning of book 5 of the *Harmonice,* Kepler describes himself
as St. Augustine describes the good exegete, that is, as one who plunders
the vessels of the Egyptians, the ancient mathematicians, to display the

universe as a tabernacle to God.[111] His version of the nature of the harmony to be discovered in the heavens is based on that to be found in the
Pythagorean analysis of music: the octave uses the 1:2 ratio in the length
of vibrating strings, the fifth the 2:3 ratio, the fourth the 3:4 ratio, and so
on. Kepler assumes that, since the circle is the perfect form, perfect
harmonies reflect proportions that can be inscribed into a circle by a
compass and ruler alone. Thus, compass and ruler can be used to in-
scribe a triangle, a square, and a pentagon into a circle, and the sides of
such figures produce ratios that, when used in vibrating strings, produce
musical harmonies. Ratios that cannot be inscribed in a circle with a
compass and ruler are disharmonious and cannot be intuitively grasped
as music; therefore, they cannot underlie harmonious music, the prosody
of poetry, the proportions of good architecture, or the movement of the
planets. Furthermore, ratios that do not produce a figure that can be
constructed by compass and ruler, if one side is related to the remaining
sides according to ratio, are also not harmonious. Thus, if the relationship of one side of a square to the other three sides is 1:3, the ratio that
can be constructed in a circle with compass and ruler is a triangle.[112] As
Caspar says, "If this principle is followed through, the result is the group
of seven ratios: 1:2, 1:3, 1:4, 1:5, 1:6, 2:5, 3:8" plus their complements
"1:2, 2:3, 3:4, 4:5, 5:6, 3:5, 5:8."[113] The complement ratios account for the
harmonious sounds: the octave, fifth, fourth, major third (4:5), minor
third (5:6), major sixth (3:5), and minor sixth (5:8).

Kepler intuits that these ratios must also be present in the sky's sound-
less music and makes a variety of efforts to find them in the movements,
distances, and other features of the planets. He fails in these efforts.
Finally, he looks at the angle velocity, when viewed from the perspective
of the sun, of each of the planets at its perihelion, when it is closest to the
sun and has the highest angle velocity, and at its aphelion, when it is most
distant from the sun and has the lowest angle velocity. He discovers that
the ratio between lowest and highest velocity of each of the planets is a
harmonious ratio. By a process of musical calculation, he finds that each
of the planets plays its own "tune" in the ratios among their angle ve-
locities, and that together they play a polyphonic music.[114] Seeking the
cosmic harmonies, Kepler finds his third law, the basis for Newton's development of the general theory of gravitation.[115]

All of this "music of the heavens" material in the *Harmonice Mundi* appears in the context of general aesthetic and learning theories firmly affixed to Wisdom tradition assumptions. However, Kepler shapes the ladder of learning anew, making it a structure that moves from the mathematical disciplines back to their physical embodiment – his physics – and then back to the Creator. He writes in book 1 of harmony in regular abstract geometric figures, in book 2 of harmony in solid geometric figures, in book 3 of the embodied mathematics of music (including the music of poetry), in book 4 of metaphysics and epistemology (including his mild version of astrology), and in book 5 of metaphysics and astronomy. In this last book, the third law is announced. Like other members of the tradition traced here, Kepler argues that the human mind teaches itself the basic mathematical relationships, that children being instructed only recognize what is already within them, and that this "autodidactic" view of knowledge, drawn from Plato and Proclus, is preferable to the Aristotelian *tabula rasa* view.[116] According to Kepler, the Platonic equivalent of Wisdom – the Archetype – constitutes the place where all of the mathematical ideas and harmonies that make up creation and human art exist in their pure, full energy, and these ideas and harmonies are communicated as a sense of archetypal harmony into the higher regions of the soul. The soul only discovers what it already knows when it woos itself to find numbered proportions and harmonies in the sensible world and in the world of art.

The whole ecosystem is dominated by these proportions: crystals and plants and the heavens. We reawaken to such proportions by self-instruction as if from sleep. And so the sense of the harmonic appears not only in the learned but also in children, novices, farmers, primitive people, and even wild beasts. The purpose of study and science is to clarify – to awaken fully – the sense of the cosmic harmonies in the faculties of the soul not touched by the first communication of divine knowledge.[117]

Kepler finds the divine harmonic proportions implicit in regular and solid geometric forms imitated in the artful human productions of music, dance, architecture, and poetry, and he organizes his sense of learning in reverse sequence from the abstract to the concrete – from music and the harmonic arts to sublunary nature to the heavenly creation and God. As Kepler would have it, "Geometry is as eternal as God himself . . . and she passed within humankind with the image of God."[118] The sensible harmonies are received by the senses, judged in terms of the inner geometry and so analyzed.[119] The process of moving upward on the intellectual ladder is a process of making conscious that which is within.[120]

Kepler suffered incredibly during his life from disease, loss of family, political turmoil, and the like, and some of his more autobiographical writing reflects that suffering. But the discovery of music in the movement of the planets leads Kepler to an "O altitudo." His conclusion to the *Harmonice Mundi* suggests the sublimity of the early writers studied in this book – Plato or Origen or Augustine – and it summarizes his sense of scientific discovery, the discovery of Wisdom, as worship, contemplation, and joy. Kepler begins his investigations in the *Harmonice* by using Proclus's commentary on Euclid, a work that begins with the kind of allegorized version of the *Odyssey* on which Boethius draws.[121] At the end of the *Harmonice Mundi*'s calculations, Kepler, like the old philosopher who appears at the beginning of the *Timaeus*, offers up a prayer to the Creator that leads him back to Proclus's hymn to the sun. The prayer reads as follows:

> You [i.e., God] who foster in us, through the light of nature, a desire for the light of grace, so that through it you may carry us up to the light of glory, I thank You, Lord, Creator. You have rejoiced me with Your creation and made me exult over the works of Your hands. Look! I have just completed the work that my vocation gave me to do, using the power of mind that You gave me. To those who read my proofs, I reveal the glory of Your work, to the degree that its infinitude can be comprehended by my finite intellect. My mind has been committed to exact philosophy. If I have set forth anything beneath Your designs – worm as I am, born and bred in a sty of sins – blow Your breath into me with whatever You wish humankind to know that I may correct what I have done. If I have been seduced into hastiness by the wonderful beauty of Your work, or if I have loved my own fame among men, while I have gone forward with a work designed for Your glory, treat me with kindness and mercy and forgiveness.[122]

Kepler follows his Timaean prayer with a reglossing of Proclus's hymn to the sun as a tribute to the Wisdom/Word that has inspired his work. According to his interpretation, Proclus wrote his hymn to a sun-symbol for God, neither the sun-god Titan of the pagans nor the incarnate sun of justice of the Christians, but the Neoplatonic Logos. The hymn sings to the Logos, the light coming into the world that lightens every man, because Proclus glimpsed that light sufficiently to hymn it in ways that might attract the Christians back to his form of Platonism. In the poem, the sun as the dancer and leader of the dance in the cosmic theater sends out its lovely harmonies, sun spots and flames, toward the planets to keep the world in order. These powers are in turn pulled back to the sun so that it will remain the throne room through which God rules the physical universe. The sun here images both the Father/sun who stops the chaos of the elements and the Logos/Christ who first acted in creation to separate divine light from darkness and make all things, including the harmony of the world. Even as the world of matter requires that the planets circle about the sun, so the world of mind requires that discursive reason be integrated and made systematic in the world of intellection that both begins discursive reasoning and gathers discursive reasoning into a synthesis that reveals God's power to the scientist.

As Mind can act as a whole, the world is a whole. The "ecosystem" has system and music not only in the heavenly polyphony. All things in the universe have their place: the white bears and white wolves of the north, the whales as food for the white bears, and birds' eggs as food for the wolves.

Finally, the great astronomer ends with a psalm made up of a pastiche of passages from Psalm 143, Psalm 148, and the typical "wisdom and number" passages from the Old Testament. But the psalm, like the whole tradition described in this book, also includes Neoplatonic assumptions about the relation between the sensible and intelligible world:[123]

Great are you, our Lord, and great your power and your Wisdom is beyond number; you skies, praise Him, you – sun, moon and planets – with whatever senses you use to perceive and whatever tongue you use to praise. Praise Him, you heavenly harmonies; praise Him my soul, praise the Lord, your Creator, for as long as I shall be. For out of Him and through Him and in Him all things exist, both those things sensed and those things intellectually understood; for those things that we know are insignificant in comparison with those that we are wholly ignorant of, for there is more beyond. To Him be praise, honor, and glory, world without end.[124]

Kepler and Galileo are the end of one tradition and the beginning of another. Newton's *Principia*, though written by a man who had religious interests, is not in itself a statement about the journey to Wisdom. As scientists, Galileo and Kepler change the tradition by emphasizing the consistency of natural law and down-playing the element of special providence and miracle in ordering phenomena.[125] They do not dwell, in their scientific treatises, on the autobiographical accounts of suffering, emptying, and death of the self (though their work by modern scientific standards retains a remarkable element of autobiography and personal religion). The world remains a "Thou" for them as an object of contemplation but, as an object of examination, has become an "It." Both scientists could have written volumes on their lives and their emptying, but they are a kind of new/old breed that begins to distance the self from the journey. However, for them, the spaces are not yet infinite nor are they silent in Pascal's sense. They are music and mathematics and architecture and a token of the design in the mind of Wisdom, a suggestion of the abyss of thought that is to be found in the mind of God. Comprehending them is not part of an endless process that leads to nothing, but part of a fairly carefully staged, though epic, journey. Understanding them does not suggest (as Lynn White claims Christian thinkers argue) that the system of nature ought to be changed or that the plan of Wisdom is anything other than wise.[126]

Galileo and Kepler are both lonely autodidacts, drawn to the journey to find the structure created by the Wisdom/Logos figure both by the Wisdom model and by the inconsistencies apparent in the evidence available to their own time. The beast of formless education does not frighten them because they have a sense of where they are going in their self-education. They are looking for an explanation that both preserves the Wisdom model and that handles the inconsistencies in the evidence available in the versions of the cosmic system circulating in their own times. The freedom to explore within the model creates their strength. There is little of the chameleon in their language in that their essential texts refer to physical observations that other observers can check out; the texts have a clear reference and a determinate meaning. Nowhere do the physicist/astronomers advocate or seek the radical manipulation of the natural world that Lynn White attributes to the despoiling proclivities in Christendom. Kepler even appears to believe that the white wolves and bears of the north reflect Wisdom's speech. It may well be that the phrase "Be fruitful, multiply . . . subdue" had somewhere the kind of influences that Lynn White attributes to it, that some philosophies of nature in the patristic, medieval, and early Renaissance period allowed for a radical alteration of the ecosystem; but this book has not found evidence of such philosophies. The spoiler tradition is certainly not to be found in the works of the Wisdom journeyers.

The hope for alteration of the system remains with the marginal alchemists and white magicians, the latter group having been given a certain intellectual legitimacy in the Florentine Platonists' writings on magic. However, it was for Francis Bacon, that servant of the same King James I to whom Kepler dedicated the *Harmonice Mundi,* to dismiss Wisdom as merely the matter and motion of the atoms.[127] In Bacon the atoms and the rest of the natural process are malleable, and they can be changed drastically for human benefit. The applied science that he proposes includes the extension of the "bounds of Humane Empire, to the Effecting of all Things possible."[128] The vision includes the changing of weather, the altering of plants and animals, the transformation of the ecosystem, and the reconstruction of a physical Eden fitted to human desire.[129] None of these supposed benefits is to be found in the more contemplative sciences of the earlier Wisdom writers. It is with Bacon that the vision of subduing the earth is announced. It is with his students in the Royal Society that it is given a measure of practical realization in the late seventeenth and eighteenth centuries.[130] That is matter for another study that includes the rehearsal in literature of the process of subduing the earth and making education toward such subduing compulsory.

Conclusion: Fables for Our Time

The model of learning initiated by Plato and continued by Neoplatonic, Jewish, and Christian thinkers makes five assumptions: (1) education that seeks and finds "truth" can give intellectual authority to opposition to tyranny (since tyranny thrives on the suppression of truth); (2) students, especially those driven by suffering, dissatisfaction, and their own inner Logos, will learn without schools or set bureaucracies; (3) cultural knowledge is secondary to "objective" (or mathematical) and dialectical knowledge; (4) "truth" consists of definitive natural description and a definitive mandate for one's life; and (5) the beauty of the universe invites the knower to understand it – its sacred character and structure reflecting God. The canonical texts and commentaries that work with this model across the centuries give it an imaginative and, ultimately, an institutional force that culminates in the beginnings of the modern scientific project. The centuries-long stability of a project that extends from Plato to Kepler, secured by efforts to achieve a stable mathematical and theological language that makes the project rigorous and communicative, is necessary to its eventual production of scientific and other insight. Currently the efficacy of the project is under attack.

THE NATURAL WORLD, THE DESPOILING BEAST, AND LOGOCENTRIC EDUCATION

Since Heidegger it has been fashionable to consign the educational assumptions discussed in this book to a repressive Christian or humanistic culture (labels that conceal more than they reveal). The pre-Socratics have become models of intellectual power.[1] Since we know little about the pre-Socratics, the switch is easy. However, some brief argument against the abolition of knowledge – even Western knowledge – in the interest of promoting Dionysian force may be worthy of our consideration.

Many of the putative evils of Western civilization come from the works described in this book, evils to be expelled by the virtues of postmodernism. For example, William Spanos, in *The End of Education,* attributes to Plato and his descendants the creation of advanced Western knowledge about, and power over, "nature" and the development of the Western world's sense of hegemony over non-Western cultures:[2]

Since Plato's allegory of the cave, but especially since the Roman appropriation of Greek thinking, the purpose of Western education . . . has been to lead Man (*ex ducere*) out of the darkness and depths of his fallen / temporal condition and into the universal light. . . . The historical continuity, which begins with Plato's "correction" of Heraclitus is what Heidegger implies in calling the Western tradition ontotheological. Whether Greek (onto-), medieval (theo-) or humanist (logo-), the theory and practice of education in the West, like philosophical and literary discourse, has been logocentric: a process oriented by a fixed, abiding and luminous Word willfully devoted to the reduction of time to a totalized circle, the center of which, as Derrida puts it, "is elsewhere" and thus "beyond the reach of play" – and criticism. . . . [T]he theory and practice of education in the ontotheological tradition has been Apollonian, its purpose the domestication of the obscure Dionysian force by bringing it to light, identifying its parts within a comprehensive and visible structure, and putting it to social use.[3]

One ought not to defend evil lightly, and Spanos purports to tell us about the evil created by precisely the tradition described in this book (though he mistakes the role of Rome's primarily rhetorical and not Platonic schools and describes the effort to discover scientific law as mere "logocentrism"). Yet is Spanos right? The question as to whether Plato or his model, Socrates, shows much love of hegemony (e.g., the hegemony of the Athenian regimes) is certainly worth asking. Did they advance the use of language in the interests of tyrannical power? Where do we find in the tradition that comes from the Neoplatonists and Boethians and ends with Kepler much interest in putting Apollonian knowledge to social uses? Where and when is the Platonic tradition directed toward practical hegemony over nature? Such matters surely need to be demonstrated to give validity to Spanos's representation and those like his. Spanos finally argues that the representation of non-Western peoples in such a way as to permit Western domination over them is a product of the Platonic tradition.[4] Such a representation, superficially considered, would appear to be more suited to the East India Company, its guns, and the stereotypes generated by its politicians and press than to Plato. One does not find much concern for Western domination in a Plato that can hardly conceptualize anything beyond the city-state, and one can only know if a representation is a misrepresentation in the cultural or the natural world if one has tools such as Plato admires for determining the difference between an accurate representation and a representation generated by the sophistry and self-interest of one's social group. The initial quest for an education based on accurate or, at least, mathematical representation in the area of natural things begins with Plato and the Wisdom tradition. Without such a quest, it may be hard to determine the differences among representations and misrepresentations. Of course, the notion, misread out of Thomas Kuhn, that knowledge – even scientific knowledge – is only a subjective social construction has made it possible for contemporary theory to regard the works of the natural scientists as constructions from which questions of accuracy and reference disappear.[5]

Spanos's attribution to the Platonic-Christian educational tradition of the origins of domination over nature requires fuller documentation than he gives it. The idea of self-emptying as basic to learning that develops with Paul, Origen, and Augustine gives little space for the domination of nature. Even Kepler and Galileo have little dominative impulse. However, it may be that the destruction of the environment by contemporary culture requires that we find a teleological movement of history and a historical scapegoat to explain our error: Lynn White's and Spanos's arguments that Platonism, Judaism, and Christianity are environmentally destructive religions seem to fill the bill perfectly. We cannot blame the Coketowns of the nineteenth century because we, who live in the ivy-covered towers of the modern university, know that our standard of living derives from the existence of such Coketowns. But if we wish to tell the truth, we will recognize that the patristic and medieval authors studied in this book raise questions about the accuracy of White's and Spanos's environmental arguments that are as forceful as those raised by the contemporary environmentalist and poet, Wendell Berry:

The ecological teaching of the Bible is simply inescapable: God made the world because He wanted it made. He thinks the world is good, and He loves it. It is His world; He has never relinquished title to it. And He has never revoked the conditions, bearing on His gift to us of the use of it, that oblige us to take excellent care of it. . . . [T]hose who see in Genesis 1:28 the source of all our abuse of the natural world (most of them apparently having read no more of the Bible than that verse) are guilty of an extremely unintelligent misreading of Genesis 1:28 itself. How, for example, would one arrange to "replenish the earth" if "subdue" means, as alleged, "conquer" or "defeat" or "destroy"? . . . We have in fact in the biblical tradition, rooted in the Bible but amplified in agrarian, literary, and other cultural traditions stemming from the Bible, the idea of stewardship as conditioned by the idea of usufruct. George Perkins Marsh was invoking biblical tradition when he wrote, in 1864, that "man has too long forgotten that the earth was given to him for usufruct alone, not for consumption, still less for profligate waste."[6]

Although medieval civilization gave rise to many evils when viewed from a modern perspective, these are centered in its militarism, inquisitorial repression, unnecessary differentiation in wealth between the bottom and the top of society, and chaotic rule. They are not sins of subduing the earth. Berry accurately characterizes the Bible and medieval ideology in this passage. The medieval sense of the right of property remains generally a usufruct sense. The belief that God made the world in beauty and loved it for its loveliness grows primarily out of the Wisdom tradition. While medieval people did not always treat the natural world carefully, Lynn White and others, in studies of medieval farming and treatment of the natural world, demonstrate the common medieval concern, under the open field system, for the protection of common forest, meadow, and wetland that must have contributed to the stabilizing of soil, a care for wild species and encouragement of game that prevailed at least until population pressures distorted the system, probably in the fourteenth century.[7] People who held land from an overlord in many parts of Europe could be removed from it for failing to keep the land and ditches in good shape. Medieval common land was clearly governed by a customary culture that protected it, if only in part, from the environmental degradation that Garrett Hardin finds in the nineteenth-century "tragedy of the commons."[8] On the other hand, what is not clear is the degree to which the ethos described in this book informs actual practices in agriculture and craft in medieval culture. That would require a more intense investigation of the relationship between thought and practice than this study allows. One place where such a relationship should be found most obviously would be in the monasteries where Wisdom study and occasional intervention in the practice of farming and crafts may have been related through the monastic chapters' development of craft and manor farm policy for the stewards and outriders. Another place might be in the practical effects of medieval rules against usury as contrary to both nature and charity.

The writers in the Wisdom tradition do not envision the Sierra Club's wilderness world set aside from human beings but a human community fitted to the models and constraints of the natural and "supernatural" community.[9] Consider, for example, how Dante makes the models of the right use of the power (*virtu*) in each planet imply a critique of out-of-control human communities.[10] Augustine says that he would not wish for a better natural world than the one that is, and the same notion is expressed in various ways by Boethius, Aelred of Rievaulx, Dante, Petrarch, some of the writers of epic and epic commentary, and the Renaissance astronomers who build on the Wisdom tradition. To find in the middle ages and early Renaissance an intellectual tradition that argues for a very serious manipulation of nature beyond a basic agricultural shaping of arable land, one has to turn to marginalized intellectual groups – magicians and alchemists who did promise that they could create a natural world more conformed to human desire. It is on this tradition that Bacon builds in the *New Atlantis,* the *Advancement of Learning,* and the *Novum Organum.*

If, as some students of the relationship between education, technology, and religion have argued, no religion can control the impulse to exploit and destroy the environment once a culture has the technological tools to use and, therefore, to exploit its natural surroundings,[11] then we have to ask how we got the tools. The question comes to be, "Why, in the seventeenth and eighteenth centuries, did Western culture come to visualize the absolute domination of the environment and create institutions of collaborative normal science capable of doing so?" Plausible answers to this question may be various, given the present state of research. But if ideas do not exist until they are formulated, Bacon deserves a great deal of the credit and the blame. Historical research might usefully explore how Bacon's project gained credibility from his followers' repetition of his proposals for a land-grant style collaborative normal science designed to transfigure the physical universe in the context of the Thirty Years' War and the Cromwellian religious wars. Europe's subsequent weariness with religious wars and debates based only on religious opinion seem to have turned Comenius and the leaders of the Royal Society in the direction of proposing a science and education that envisages the domination of the natural world. In their writings, Bacon appears as a new Moses.

To envisage the new experimental science, based in corporate research institutions that would change the face of nature, Bacon has to assume that "wisdom" is the matter and motion of the Democritan atoms and no more.[12] The world, he believes, can be shaped to do new things – the "bounds of Human Empire" can be "enlarg[ed]" – without our harming its general system.[13] The Baconian vision became, in the late eighteenth and early nineteenth century, the basis of the massive educational effort created by the early Utilitarians, an effort that ultimately issues in public schools that direct their primary attention to science and technology of the sort that purports to "improve" on nature.[14] Our culture is now concerned about the efficacy of that effort as it is reflected in today's public schools and universities and in the transformation of the environment.

In any proposals for changing education, we should recognize that the Wisdom tradition's respect for the natural world differs from the natural respect to be found in cultures other than the Western patristic and medieval one. The Wisdom writers display none of the skill in the discovery of useful wild plants that one finds in the Native American traditions (where the discovery of such plants becomes an art form based in vision-seeing, a form intended to produce minimal change in the climax eco-system).[15] One also does not find in the Wisdom writings any basis for the emulation, in human dances, of natural forms and creatures, the emulation that produces so much of the awe and wonder in Native American religions. One does not find the common Native American conception that the human species is simply one of a series of brother species, all of them equally interdependent. One would go on to other religious systems – Zen Buddhism, Pure Land Buddhism, Hinduism, the Confucian odes – demonstrating how each implies, in its basic values and modes of knowing the world, its own form of cherishing and using the natural system.

Some proper and useful effort has been made in recent years to educate children and youth to respect the natural world by using Native American or Zen Buddhist or other non-Western materials. Though the Wisdom tradition's assumptions lead to a study and love of aspects of the natural world that differ from those examined by other religious cultures, in environmental matters it is not better than – simply different from – other traditions depending on pre-Enlightenment technologies. Given its difference from (and yet vestigial relationship to) the dominant culture in this age, it deserves to be represented in the contemporary educational process, lest those students who come from European-based cultures be led to feel that their heritage is only the creation of consumerism and garbage. No harm would be done if we were to look at what pre-Enlightenment, preindustrial Western writers have to say about the sanctity of the natural world and the iconic uses of theoretical science.

Finally, of course, teachers and mentors need to address the contemporary equivalents of the foundational questions that the Wisdom thinkers address. Our education ought to be in touch with what cosmologists and evolutionists say about the structure of the universe and the origins of things and what their discoveries mean, if anything, for our sense of what we are doing as human beings.

FORMLESSNESS, STRUCTURE, THE CANON, AND INSTITUTIONS

The present scientific/technological structure of education arises from the Baconian project, but the structure is not inevitable even where natural studies are pursued, as the examples of Kepler and Galileo demonstrate. The compulsory eight- or twelve-grade school given over to several subjects studied simultaneously appears first in the Protestant principalities of Germany, especially in Strasbourg. In these school systems the emphasis goes, as it does in Quintilian's form of education, to the learning of language skills that the reformers thought would allow people to know the words of the scriptures, not to the study of material evidences that might bespeak the preincarnate Logos. The eight- or twelve-grade structure has increasing scientific and technological content in Enlightenment Germany and is used to define how much time the student spends on each subject (many subjects being studied at the same time). In medieval schools and patristic/medieval accounts of lives given over to learning, each subject is studied intensively for a period. Ariès points to John of

Salisbury's meandering educational program, in which "dialectics, grammar, review of the trivium, the quadrivium, review of rhetoric, logic" are studied one after another.[16] This intense scrutiny of subjects one at a time and one after another goes by the board in the Protestant and, later, the Jesuit schools. Gradually, as the scientific revolution takes place, the subjects implied by this revolution find some place in the school and university. The drastic change from compulsory word-centered education to compulsory scientific and technological education comes with the "Baconian" Utilitarians of the nineteenth century. The goal of the Utilitarians is to minimize or eliminate the verbal and humanities studies altogether in favor of the scientific and technological studies that can make the scientific and industrial projects work.[17]

Since the sixteenth century, when the German Protestants' revival of compulsory education embraced a higher percentage of the population than in the Roman cities, what is called education has been asked to take on more and more of the burden of social formation and social reform. Guided by the mythos of progress, we ask the schools to make each generation of people wiser and better than its predecessor. In response to the range of demands that we place on the schools, contemporary critics of education on the right argue that education should have clearer and fewer goals: (1) education in reading, writing, arithmetic, and a few other basic skills, and in the socially acceptable conduct once thought to be communicated by the family ("values") at the lower levels;[18] (2) education in the more advanced skills necessary to obtaining a job and in the canonical writings of members of Western culture conceived of as a culture that extends from Greece, Rome, and Israel to modern European-based groups.[19]

It is as difficult to argue with "basics" rhetoric as it is to make it mean anything. No culture can survive without giving basic skills to its next generation, though it may not be clear about what those skills are. The medieval trivium dedicates much of its curriculum to education in "basic skills" in Latin; arithmetic and geometry, which had practical implications in the medieval world, are a basic feature of the quadrivium. Furthermore, medieval institutional education – in the guild, school, and university – directly or indirectly equips people for the vocations available in the medieval world.[20] However, that is not all that the academic education described in this book promises. What is basic in this education is knowing – knowing as Origen describes it, sheer knowing. When twentieth-century Western governments design their educational systems, they frequently have trouble designating what is "basic" for the future. They do not value knowing for its own sake, and they cannot be confident that the technological future will be a linear extension from the past and present, requiring skills that can be transmitted to students now.[21]

The instability and secularization of industrial societies has inspired people with the wish to educate or indoctrinate youth in what are called traditional values. Too often what is meant by values education bears a striking resemblance to the education in the routines of marketplace citizenship that Socrates criticizes in the education provided by the Sophists. The figures studied in this book seek a type of learning that will help them make sense of their lives and the psychology of their ethical choices (Dante is particularly important in this regard). Such learning may not serve Main Street and may make little sense vocationally or from the perspective of economic or social advancement. These figures find what they need more in experience than in books, more in books than in teachers – perceptions that are particularly important in a society as rootless as ours. The wildness, the exploratory power, of self-directed education from Gregory Thaumaturgos to Kepler emerges from the conviction that there is a vision to be gained from autodidactic exploration that institutionalized education rarely communicates to its clients. This vision has both active and contemplative content.

A prescribed canon did not create Western culture in the periods described in this book. An attitude did – an attitude of exploration. The defense of the canon of Western "great works" has frequently been identified with a defense of Western education. For example, Dinesh D'Souza speaks, in *Illiberal Education*, of the "animus against the Western civilization course" of Clayborne Carson, member of the Stanford African-American Studies department and leader in the late 1980s of an effort to shift the Stanford core curriculum away from readings in Homer, Plato, Virgil, Aquinas, Dante, Machiavelli, Voltaire, Marx, and Freud and studies in Greece, Rome, medieval Christianity, and so forth. The actual changes in the curriculum, as Gerald Graff has shown, were fairly moderate.[22] Yet D'Souza vehemently criticizes Carson for arguing that the curriculum must always change as new "canonical texts" appear. He attacks Stanford for surrendering to pressures from third-world people to make the curriculum more reflective of the historical experience of their many cultures. In particular, D'Souza is angered by the appearance on the new Stanford reading list of *I, Rigoberta Menchu*, a work reflecting the experience of Nobel prize-winner Rigoberta Menchu, which D'Souza sees as mediating doctrinaire Marxist and feminist views.[23]

But is D'Souza correct? Does education in "Western Civilization" depend on the old Stanford canon or Robert Hutchins's Great Books program or the old sophomore surveys in British and American literature? How does one learn to understand a civilization other than that before one on the television tube? Ironically, D'Souza seems to vest the defense of Western culture in a list of books and according to a set of principles that the patriarchs of Western culture included on the list – at least those animating this book – would hardly have defended. Of course, there was a canon of sorts that medieval people who went through the trivium encountered; Cato's *Distichs*, the fables of Avianus, Ovid's *Metamorphoses*, and Virgil's *Aeneid* were often on the list. But these are not central fare on the Stanford or Chicago lists. Moreover, the medieval lists did change. The text for grammar at the University of Paris was at first Priscian, then Alexander of Villedieu's *Doctrinale Puerorum*, then Despautère.[24] The books used to teach the various subjects in medieval and Renaissance Europe's schools and universities altered as new material came in from the Arabic world and new Roman and Greek texts were discovered. Patristic and medieval readers recognized that the Jewish biblical books, Roman texts (and Greek ones where they were known), and Arabic texts came from "dispensations" different from their own. But even they, in ages of the Inquisition and heresy-hunting, did not reject teaching the texts of other cultures so long as they did not propose, or were not taken to propose, a belief in strange gods. Allegory destroyed the strange gods. D'Souza does not establish why a Homer who writes of a semitribal society should automatically be read and a Rigoberta Menchu, who also writes of a semitribal society, should not. D'Souza seems to object to Carson's view that different historical epochs may require a different set of canonical texts.[25] But a culture such as ours that has no official gods can hardly afford to reject the intellectual products of other cultures, particularly since those products may give insights into our problems.

D'Souza also attacks Carson's opposition "to the very idea of a canon or principle of selection that determines which books undergraduates should read."[26] Yet the canonical writers studied in this book did not find the study of the canon consistently meaningful: Augustine rejects Virgil and turns to a noncanonical *Hortensius* and life of St. Antony; Boethius leans on a Greek *Republic, Timaeus,* and *Parmenides* that were not common in Roman education in his time; although Dante has a canon of folks whom he meets in the castle of the liberal arts in the *Inferno,* he is actually guided by a Virgil that has been radically changed by commentary, by a Statius that would never appear on a modern list of canonical writers, and by a St. Bernard who is on precious few contemporary reading lists.

On the other hand, it is romantic folly to attribute our evil to education in the canonical writers. The critical theorists who attribute, for example, pollution to Genesis or imperialism to Virgil have a responsibility to show that these books were read as they say they were read in the periods in question.

We may not require a canon, but we do need teachers. The mentor's search for books to recommend should be about finding books that, through their statements and through their ambiguities, permit students to make decisions about where they are going. This does not depend on a list of required readings but on a sense of what the student needs to read and when, given the inscape of his or her experience. This, in turn, will require that we know our students a great deal better than we do, that we know the literature better, and that we adopt a more consultative role than we currently do.

One area where a "canon" of sorts might be useful is that of books offering young people a rehearsal of a structure – or alternative structures – for education. The present use of very large anonymous schools and universities, their overwhelming bureaucratization, and our culture's compulsion to make students stay in school for more and more time each day and more and more years across a lifetime cannot be productive.

We have tried two modes of education in recent years, one advocating the student's absolute dependence on the sequences of the educational system, the other advocating absolute autonomy from them. The former mode is represented, at its most extreme, by a behavior modification and programmed learning that attempt to make the student the product of a "teacher-proof system." The call for a subversive or oppositional pedagogy from the critical theorists may actually arise as much out of sheer weariness with institutions that threatens to engulf all of life as out of impatience with the dependence of the institutions on conservative or "hegemonic" ideology. A large bureaucracy or a programmed curriculum could not recognize the legitimacy of what Boethius learns in his lonely prison. Though Plato, as I. A. Richards argues, may believe that the just society creates the just man and the just man the just society,[27] after Origen, and especially after Boethius (from Boethius through Galileo), the Wisdom writers assume that learning is a singular enterprise, that the construction of a just society begins with the just person working outside or against conventional institutions.

The second mode, the mode of autonomy, appears in the last forty years' movement toward preferring "development" to education, a movement based on Piaget's psychology, Illich's proposals for a deschooled society, and some forms of the free and home school movements. Too often when it has been executed badly, it has been characterized by the aimlessness and ennui of people who do not know where they are going and have not set a direction for themselves or their group.

Between the ideals of total institutionalization and total autonomy, the individual teacher in contemporary state-supported classrooms has to work out some neither comfortable nor easy middle ground. They often do a remarkable job of it. Education does need to be deschooled to give teachers and students, especially during the high school and college years, more opportunity to decide what they need to learn from each other, and what from experience or "autobiography." But education cannot be deschooled if we cannot provide the young with an imagination – or alternative imaginations – of what education might be for them. If this study points to anything lacking in the contemporary system, it is our failure to present to the student an imagination of what education is for and where it goes. The Wisdom tradition, especially in its epic versions, appears to have offered a powerful imagination of education capable of inspiring intellectual effort across a lifetime, an art of the highest order independent of an all-encompassing institutionalization. Most of the works in the tradition held out the promise that the end of the educational journey would be worth the effort, whatever the institutional context. And that tradition did not entirely die with the rise of vernacular or popular literature.

Much of the power of nineteenth-century novels (e.g., those by George

Eliot and Charles Dickens) for the industrial and middle classes in early Victorian England may have derived from an imagination, communicated to the child and youth in family reading, of what maturation and life outside the home would be like. Nowadays, after the fairy tales go down the road from the child's sensibility and after Pippy Longstocking no longer performs heroic deeds, our culture too seldom offers children or young adults serious or comic imaginings of where education and development will go. This may be partly because we have so little sense of where they should go. To have such a sense, we would need to have a sense of the kinds of adulthood, in our various cultures, that we are seeking; we would need to have the sense of what we are looking for at the highest levels of intellectual achievement (e.g., that of the Keplers in our society). Absent an imagination of education, or a set of alternative imaginings, deeply internalized, the student is thrown back on the institutions of education that promise more and more counseling, more and more coercion, more and more behavior-modification and goal-setting, and ever larger bureaucracies.

TRUTH AND THE CHAMELEON

We may not know where we are going because we are less inclined than are the Wisdom writers to assume that we are part of an intellectual culture that extends from generation to generation – a culture that has an ongoing textual and educational project. Plato, Boethius, and the thinkers and poets who follow after them argue that the path of resistance to tyranny requires access to truth. They did not have access to scientific methods of verification in most areas outside of astronomy in the patristic period, and the growth of the higher mathematics and inductive science is very slow throughout the middle ages until the fifteenth century. The later part of the period witnesses a probing for more definitive methods of understanding and verification. One can see Plato and the Wisdom writers as myth makers (witness the geometric myths of the *Timaeus*) as surely as are those who write and teach in the rhetorical tradition. But the difference is that, whereas for the Sophists and their successors the goal is the creation of empathy and social consolidation, for the writers and scientists in the Wisdom tradition the goal is the creation of a heuristic – a set of assumptions to guide investigation – that will lead to certainty on the model of the certainties expressed by the Ptolemaic system.

A second kind of certainty sought by these writers is knowledge of the Creator and of the Creator's design for one's life. Of course, the search for this second kind of certainty has been moved from the arena of study to the realm of subjectivity since Kierkegaard's time. Moreover, the general search for certainty based on the formulation of hypotheses, the gathering of evidence, the organizing of evidence in terms of hypotheses – the whole thrust toward verification in research and education – has come into question in literary and educational circles. Thomas Kuhn's paradigm argument in *The Structure of Scientific Revolutions* has been interpreted (particularly from its first edition) to say that even in matters of scientific investigation the mind makes up its own reality (or rather that the paradigm community makes up its own reality).[28] At a more general level, Foucault has argued that truth is essentially constructed by power:

Truth is a thing of this world. . . . Each society has its regime of truth, its "general politics" of truth: that is, the types of discourse which it accepts and makes function as true; the mechanisms and instances which enable one to distinguish true and false statements, the means by which each is sanctioned; the techniques and procedures accorded value in the acquisition of truth; the status of those who are charged with saying what counts as true.[29]

We need to recognize that disciplinary societies, societies that function according to Foucault's prescription, do not create certainty; scholars do, students do. Disciplinary societies create funding. Foucault's picture suggests that power creates knowledge. It does not explain how Galileo ever triumphed over his inquisitors or Boethius over Theoderic or heliocentrism over geocentrism. In this regard, one needs to look carefully not only at the politics but at the processes by which new ways of establishing certainty – formulating hypotheses, gathering evidence, verifying it, using it to confirm one's hypothesis over alternative hypotheses – are created. Stephen Toulmin's accounts of how this happens are helpfully detailed and careful.[30]

The subjectivizing of knowledge and education becomes a fetish when the university and school substitute intensity for evidence and replace learning with various nationalisms – a process that has gone on for a long time in Europe and America. On a more sophisticated level, the subjectivizing of knowledge has meant that the disciplines of literary scholarship have become subjective disciplines. The sense of a necessity for accurate description, for the creation of hypotheses and the gathering of historical evidence to verify hypotheses, undergirded the work of nineteenth-century historical philology, however much its rhetoric may have been tarnished by nationalistic ambition or Enlightenment political purposes. The same may be said, in more recent times, for descriptive linguistic studies and the historical study of literature. Studies in these areas may have been as naive in their sense of the relationship between a word and its referent as is the statement by Augustine quoted by Wittgenstein and examined in chapter 3. However, such studies did, at their best, endeavor to describe the relationship between the words that they studied and what Wittgenstein calls the "forms of life" in which the words were used (which includes also the things handled and seen by a people – the world of reference – that is part of that form of life).[31] At present, however, Derrida speaks of the recontextualizing of texts, or to quote a more defensible position of his, he argues that "no meaning can be determined out of context but no context permits saturation."[32] This means, according to Nealon, that one cannot turn to a historical context to "rein in the significations of a statement or a text."[33] Alice has no right to query Humpty Dumpty's definitions. One may ask how one learns the significations of a text save by learning the language of the text and by looking at the forms of life in which the words of the text have uses. Critical theory based on this sort of view is either banal or solipsistic. It is banal if it suggests that people, "seeing a text as," can make a text mean different things in different times – as do the readers of Homer and Virgil described in chapter 3. It is solipsistic if it means that the art of reading texts from the past is the art of saying about them "any old thing that one wants to say," as Humpty Dumpty does. For Harold Bloom such saying is the mark of greatness, essential to genius (see Introduction and chapter 5). But that is not Kepler's way, and it should not be the way of scholarship or teaching in the verbal or mathematical arts. Indeed, patristic and medieval authors and scholars go to great pains to create texts in which the crucial sections are not indeterminate, texts that can be understood in the same, or similar, ways by different readers in differing times. They do this, first, by providing a life context for their works (in the case of autobiographical texts), a context that tells one how the words and sentences in the texts are being used. They do it, secondly, by attaching their work to genres that give one a larger sense of the work's place in a system of communication. Finally, to insure a determinate reading, they provide glosses for the texts that tell one what they mean. It is, of course, possible to "find" meanings in the text that are not part of the language game of the time or of the writer, but one does this as one finds dragons in a Rorschach or as Polonius finds figures in the clouds.

To avoid saying "what one wants to say" in the interest of objective discovery, the role of the self – the individual self or the nationalistic pseudoself – is crucial. To go to Bloom's hypothesis and the issue of the emptying of the self for objective work: one does not detect the "anxiety of influence" in Augustine or Boethius or Aelred of Rievaulx. The epic writers and commentators remain nearly anonymous up through Dante. They build on each other in obvious and self-deprecatory ways. Though Dante carries his burden of pride until nearly halfway through the *Purgatorio,* he is not proud of his burden. In fact, the role of patristic and medieval imitation, allusion, or subcreation is to place oneself in a tradition and under the authority of a previous author's text. Frequently that author, or group of authors (Fulgentius's Virgil, Boethius's Philosophy, Dante's Virgil and Statius, Petrarch's Augustine) becomes a guide-within-the-work that asks the author-within-the-work to reexperience the anguish and the ascent that the guide has experienced and rediscover its pertinence for his life, shifting the emphasis for the purpose of personal identification. No logocentrism appears here; no preferring of speech to writing. At the end of the ascent the burden of self may seem to disappear altogether, as in Dante or the *Confessions.* Alternatively, the self may be diminished in the presence of a larger picture drawn by a philosophic or religious messenger such as Boethius's Philosophy or Petrarch's Augustine. The sense of a self diminished in the presence of cosmic understanding appears in Kepler's last statements in the *Harmonice Mundi.* The presence of the shaping self is precisely the issue in contemporary education and research outside of the sciences. Our culture does not have available the disciplines that Augustine or Kepler had for self-emptying, though one does find incredible stories of self-discipline in the discovery of knowledge in the contemporary world. One does not know how such stories are possible, but clearly they are worthy of study, of emulation, and of our attention in the process of educating the young and the mature.

Notes

INTRODUCTION

1. Cf. *Paradiso* 24.46–51 in Dante Alighieri, *The Divine Comedy,* translated with a commentary by Charles S. Singleton (Princeton: Princeton UP, 1975); all quotations and citations, unless otherwise noted, are to the Singleton edition. Cf. Benvenuto da Imola and Giovanni della Serravalle on *Paradiso* 24.46–51 [Dartmouth Dante Project]. Cf. Hastings Rashdall, *The Universities of Europe in the Middle Ages,* ed. F. M. Powicke and A. B. Emden (Oxford: Clarendon Press, 1987), 1:450–62.

2. The view explored in this book must be distinguished from "design" arguments for the existence of God such as those discredited by David Hume. In the authors explored here, faith that God exists and creates always precedes the exploration of the physical universe.

3. Cf. Karl Morrison, *The Mimetic Tradition of Reform in the West* (Princeton: Princeton UP, 1982), 42–43. Morrison speaks of Paul's advocating a mimesis centering in the human nature of Christ where the rite of baptism imitates Christ's death and resurrection (cf. Rom. 6.1–11), perhaps a model for medieval autobiographies described in chapters 3 and 4.

4. For example, Dinesh D'Souza in *Illiberal Education* (New York: Random House, 1992), 249–51, says that we cannot talk about "reform without reference to form" though his discussion of liberal education in ancient times shows little understanding of the history of the concept. Cf. Allan Bloom, *The Closing of the American Mind* (New York: Simon & Schuster, 1987), 336–47, which shows equally little understanding of ancient and medieval traditions in the liberal arts.

5. The works of Antonio Gramsci, Ivan Illich, and Paolo Freire begin this analysis in modern times. More recently this sort of analysis has been continued by Jim Merod, Noam Chomsky, Michel Foucault, Edward Said, Paul Bové, and others.

6. Ian McHarg, *Design with Nature* (Garden City NY: Doubleday, 1969), 26. There have been numerous Christian apologetic responses to White's and McHarg's arguments, but the significant ones trace reader response to the Genesis passage in patristic and medieval times.

1 THE JOURNEY TO SOPHIA

1. For the Right, see Chester E. Finn, *We Must Take Charge: Our Schools and Our Future* (New York: Free Press, 1991), 140, 251–57. Allan Bloom speaks more generically of the necessity that the university have the goal of offering a "distinctive visage" to young people and sees the goals of the modern university as

properly defined by the Enlightenment (*The Closing of the American Mind,* 336 and passim).

2. Paolo Freire, *Pedagogy of the Oppressed* (New York: Continuum, 1993), 52–67; William V. Spanos, *The End of Education: Toward Posthumanism* (Minneapolis: U of Minnesota P, 1993), argues that "the institutions of higher learning are collectively the Western capitalist state's essential agency for the reproduction of the sovereign individual and the transmission of the repressive hypothesis" (24).

3. Ariès asserts that "nobody thought of having a graduated system of education, in which the subjects for study would be distributed according to difficulty, beginning with the easiest" in the Middle Ages. His examples are the teaching of Priscian or the *Doctrinale,* difficult philological works, to boys of ten, and John of Salisbury's cycle of studies. See Philippe Ariès, *Centuries of Childhood* (New York: Alfred A. Knopf, 1962), 33, 145–48. Cf. *The Metalogicon of John of Salisbury,* trans. Daniel D. McGarry (Westport CT: Greenwood, 1982), 95–100 and passim.

4. For the early middle ages, see Pierre Riché, *Education and Culture in the Barbarian West: Sixth Through Eighth Centuries,* trans. John J. Contreni (Columbia: U of South Carolina P, 1976); also Pierre Riché, *Les écoles et l'enseignement dans l'Occident chrétien* (Paris: Aubier Montaigne, 1979). Riché, *Écoles,* 249, notes that a few texts for grammatical study remained fairly constant, but others were added and removed across the centuries; the other disciplines also changed, as did the disciplinary order.

5. The modern analogy to the medieval idea of development is Jean Piaget's sensory-motor, preoperational, concrete operational, and formal operational stages.

6. Charles M. Radding, *A World Made by Men: Cognition and Society, 400–1200* (Chapel Hill: U of North Carolina P, 1985). For the classical influence on medieval science, see David C. Lindberg, *The Beginnings of Western Science: the European Scientific Tradition in Philosophical, Religious, and Institutional Context, 600 B.C. to A.D. 1450* (Chicago: U of Chicago P, 1992).

7. Radding places an impossible demand on medieval thought: that it always be formal in Piaget's sense. Few of us use formal operational procedures in all our doings. The very existence of such a complex, systematic discipline as geometry in the patristic and medieval periods, its employment in medieval astronomy and architecture, and its importance in the thinking of many of the figures in this book testifies to the limitations in Radding's hypothesis.

8. W. B. Yeats, *The Variorum Edition of the Poems of W. B. Yeats,* ed. Peter Allt and Russell K. Alspach (New York: Macmillan, 1957), 563.

9. Cf. Lindberg, *The Beginnings of Western Science.*

10. *Herodotus,* ed. A. D. Godley (Cambridge: Harvard UP, 1966). Loeb Library editions hereinafter are generally cited in text by section and subsection numbers.

11. Jürgen Gebhardt, "The Origins of Politics in Ancient Hellas: Old Interpretations and New Perspectives," *Sophia and Praxis: The Boundaries of Politics,* ed. J. M. Porter (Chatham NJ: Chatham House, 1984), 5–6.

12. Arthur W. H. Adkins, "Cosmogony and Order in Ancient Greece," *Cosmogony and Ethical Order* (Chicago: U of Chicago P, 1985), 39–67. For a good account of Eleatic and Ionian philosophers, see David Furley, *The Greek Cosmologists* (Cambridge: Cambridge UP, 1987), esp. 31–48, 51–53.

13. G. S. Kirk and J. E. Raven, *The Presocratic Philosophers* (Cambridge: Cambridge UP, 1957), 188, 204ff.

14. Spanos, *The End of Education,* 15. Spanos (119) regards such journeys to origin as relegitimizing the dominant culture, though Plato is clearly at odds with the dominant culture.

15. For a critique of postmodernist efforts to reduce scientific methods of knowing, see Paul R. Gross and Norman Levitt, *Higher Superstition: The Academic Left and its Quarrel with Science* (Baltimore: Johns Hopkins UP, 1994), a work with which I am not entirely comfortable.

16. For good treatments of the *Protagoras* and *Gorgias* as well as useful citation of recent scholarship, see Samuel Scolnicov, *Plato's Metaphysics of Education* (London: Routledge, 1988), 21–42, 126–32. The *Gorgias* and *Protagoras* are cited in the Loeb edition.

17. I cite *The Republic* throughout by section and subsection from the Cornford translation; *The Republic of Plato,* trans. by Francis Cornford (New York: Oxford UP, 1945).

18. The claim to teach virtue may be a bit of Socratic/Platonic irony, since Gorgias in his own writing treats 'virtue' as a social construction.

19. Some post-Freudian rhetoricians treat rhetoric as a defense of what one believes on affective grounds. Plato would obviously regard such a rhetoric as sophistic.

20. Henry Teloh, *Socratic Education in Plato's Early Dialogues* (Notre Dame IN: U of Notre Dame P, 1986), 129–51.

21. Scolnicov correctly presents Plato's metaphysics of love in the *Symposium* as also a metaphysics of education, a matter to which I will refer in chapter 5. Cf. Scolnicov, *Plato's Metaphysics,* 73–82.

22. T. Rutherford Harley, "The Public Schools in Sparta," *Greece and Rome* 3 (1934): 129–39; W. Knauth, "Die spartanische Knabenerziehung im Lichte der Völkerkunde," *Zeitschrift für Geschichte der Erziehung und des Unterrichts* 23 (1933): 151–85; Ephraim David, *Sparta Between Empire and Revolution 404–243 B.C.* (Salem NH: Ayer, 1981), 59–65. Xenophon is cited from *La République des Lacédémoniens: Xenophon,* ed. and trans. François Olliér (New York: Arno Press, 1979); Plutarch is cited in the Loeb edition. Cf. Friedrich Solmsen, *Plato's Theology*

(Ithaca: Cornell UP, 1942), 112–19; cf. C. J. Classen, "The Creator in Greek Thought from Homer to Plato," *Classica et Mediaevalia* 23 (1963): 1–22. Paradoxically, the Plato of the *Republic* is not the Plato of the more fully deschooled tradition examined in this book (the *Symposium* and other Platonic works do suggest a more inward picture of the sources of motivation to learn).

23. Morriss Henry Partee, "Plato's Banishment of Poetry," *JAAC* 29 (1970): 209–22. Whatever one wishes to say about the accuracy of Plato's picture of the Sophists, they certainly did not pursue ideas like Herodotus's or Plato's. Nor did they have an interest in the nonhuman world that forms the basis of the study of earlier *philosophia*, especially in the Eleatics and Ionians whom they mocked.

24. For a history of the relationship between humanistic and scientific education, see Kimball, *Orators and Philosophers*. Classical scientific study and its Christian successor included a personalism and interest in the meaning of suffering foreign to modern science.

25. Untersteiner, *The Sophists*, esp. 119–21, 194–202, 311–12, 321–42.

26. Untersteiner, *Sophists*, 143ff.; H. D. Rankin, *Sophists, Socratics and Cynics* (Totowa NJ: Barnes & Noble, 1983), 81.

27. Rankin, *Sophists, Socratics,* 81–91.

28. For an account of Thucydides's understanding of the art of rhetoric, see Cole, *The Origin of Rhetoric,* 104–11.

29. Untersteiner, *Sophists,* 324.

30. Untersteiner, *Sophists,* 119–24, 194–202, 323–24, 328–31; Rankin, *Sophists, Socratics,* 98–121; G. B. Kerferd, *The Sophistic Movement* (London: Cambridge UP, 1981), 111–30. I do not, in this chapter, distinguish extensively between what the Sophists actually said and what Plato attributed to them, an important topic but not significant to my argument.

31. Thomas Cole, *The Origins of Rhetoric in Ancient Greece* (Baltimore: Johns Hopkins UP, 1991), argues that for rhetoric to be conceptualized the notion of a difference between medium and message had to be developed (ix–xi) and a sense of a permanent, verifiable truth had to be created (139–58).

32. Untersteiner, *Sophists,* 112–18. Plato also objects to the Sophists' educational cynicism, to the Gorgian use of tragedy for the subjective creation of social norms, and to the use of rhetoric for "sophistic" purposes in the modern, popular sense: Plato, *Republic* 8.568; 6.491d–493d; 10.595–608b; 2.376e–383c.

33. For Isocrates's career as an educator, see James Bowen, *A History of Western Education* (London: Methuen, 1972), 1.91–97; Frederick A. G. Beck, *Greek Education: 450–350 B.C.* (London: Methuen, 1964), 253–300; H. I. Marrou, *A History of Education in Antiquity,* trans. G. Lamb (New York: Sheed & Ward, 1956), 79ff.; Isocrates is cited from the Loeb edition.

34. This may appear to be an unduly negative view of Isocrates; in some of his

arguments he assumes that his art should only be learned by those aristocratic persons who have proper character. I agree with Untersteiner, who treats Isocrates as being essentially a Sophist.

35. Isocrates, "Antidosis," *The Educational Theories of the Sophists*, ed. James L. Jarrett (New York: Teachers College Press, 1969), 225–27.

36. Bowen, *Western Education*, 94ff., 110–11, 152–66; Marrou, *History*, 102–16; 142–75; 194–205; 274–92. For a useful account of Isocrates, see Werner Jaeger, *Paideia: The Ideals of Greek Culture*, trans. Gilbert Highet (New York: Oxford UP, 1944), 3.46–155.

37. For the Platonic sense of Logos, see John Sallis, *Being and Logos: The Way of Platonic Dialogue* (Atlantic Highlands NJ: Humanities Press, 1975), esp. 527–31, 533–34. For a useful account of later Platonic responses to the conflict between Plato and Homer, see Robert Lamberton, *Homer the Theologian: Neoplatonist Allegorical Reading and the Growth of the Epic Tradition* (Berkeley: U of California P, 1986), 97–229 and passim. Cf. Scolnicov, *Plato's Metaphysics*, 112–19. Cf. Porphyry, *De Antro Nympharum* 55.14–18; Porphyry, *Platonici Opuscula*, ed. Augustus Nauck (Leipzig: Teubner, 1886). For Plato's belief in absolutes, see *Gorgias*, 523a–527e, *Republic* 10.614ff. The belief in absolutes in the *Gorgias* and *Republic*, intended to put to flight the Sophists, obviously appealed to those Christian fathers, influenced by Neoplatonism, who had their own eschatology; cf. Plato, *Gorgias*, ed. E. R. Dodds (Oxford: Clarendon Press, 1959), 63, 397–98.

38. Marrou, *History of Education*, 79–91, 197–205; Beck, *Greek Education*, 282–84, 261–63.

39. Marrou, *History*, 95–313.

40. Marrou, *History*, 102–15.

41. For an account of the continued rivalry between Sophists and philosophers, see G. W. Bowersock, *Greek Sophists in the Roman Empire* (Oxford: Clarendon Press, 1969), 11. Aristides says that philosophers "do not speak or write *logoi*, adorn festival assemblies, honour the gods, advise cities, comfort the distressed, settle civic discord, or educate the young," characteristics that Bowersock sees Aristides using to define what Sophists in the second century did (11). Such thinkers as Plutarchus (A.D. 350–443), Proclus (A.D. 410–85), Ammonius (c. A.D. 500), and the sixth century A.D. "pagan," Olympiodorus of Alexandria, analyzed the *Gorgias* in the Neoplatonic schools. Scholia directed against the *Gorgias*, possibly deriving from Plutarchus's commentary, also exist. Plato, *Gorgias*, 58ff.

42. For Aristides's religious system, see C. A. Behr, *Aelius Aristides and the Sacred Tales* (Amsterdam: A. M. Hakkert, 1968), 148–61. After his first illness, he turns into a fanatical hypochondriac in the service of Asclepias, and his pantheon exists to make him healthy.

43. All quotations and citations from Aristides are from the Loeb Classical Library.

44. For the relationship between cosmology and ethical system in ancient Greece, see Adkins, "Ethics and Breakdown of the Cosmology in Ancient Greece," 279–309.

45. For an account of Cicero's *De Republica* and its influence in the Middle Ages, see Macrobius, *Commentary on the Dream of Scipio*, trans. with introduction by William Harris Stahl (New York: Columbia UP, 1952), 3–55; for an account of the use of the book in defining medieval parliamentary government as based in cosmological harmony and natural law, see Paul A. Olson, "*The Parlement of Foules:* Aristotle's *Politics* and the Foundations of Human Society," SAC 2 (1980): 53–69. All references to Cicero are from the Loeb Classical Library.

46. Granville C. Henry, *Logos: Mathematics and Christian Theology* (Lewisburg PA: Bucknell UP, 1976), 73–147, describes some of the issues raised by the fusion of Greek and Hebrew thought about the Logos and mathematics, though in a polemical form.

2 PHILOSOPHY, THE CREATION, AND LEARNING

1. For an account of environmental problems in the ancient world, see Vernon Gill Carter, *Topsoil and Civilization* (Norman: U of Oklahoma P, 1974).

2. Cf. Lynn White Jr., "The Historic Roots of Our Ecologic Crisis," *Science* 155 (1967): 1203–7, for the view that, for classical and medieval Christianity and their descendants, "no item in the physical creation had any purpose save to serve man's purposes" (1205) and that Christianity is "the most anthropocentric religion the world has seen" (1205). Jeremy Cohen supports Richard Hiers's view that White "confront[s] the text of Scripture in a 'critically illiterate' manner" and ignores Genesis exegesis which overwhelmingly represents humankind as the steward of nature, required to subdue his own sin rather than external nature. Jeremy Cohen, *"Be Fertile and Increase, Fill the Earth and Master It": The Ancient and Medieval Career of a Biblical Text* (Ithaca: Cornell UP, 1989), 2–5, 15–18, 224–31, 259–69 and passim; cf. Walter Brueggemann, *Genesis* (Atlanta: John Knox Press, 1982), 32. Cf. Olson, "*The Parlement of Foules:* Aristotle's *Politics* and the Foundation of Human Society," cited above. For White's later views, see "Continuing the Conversation," *Western Man and Environmental Ethics: Attitudes Toward Nature and Technology*, ed. Ian G. Barbour (Reading, MA: Addison-Wesley, 1973), 55–65.

3. White, "Historic Roots of Our Ecologic Crisis," 1204.

4. White, "Historic Roots of Our Ecologic Crisis," 1203, 1205.

5. John Macquarrie, "The Doctrine of Creation and Human Responsibility," in *Knowledge and the Future of Man*, ed. Walter J. Ong (New York: Holt, Rinehart & Winston, 1968), 132–38.

6. Cf. note 2, this chapter. Conventional religious and philosophic polemics against the White-McHarg view are represented by the following works: Francis A. Shaeffer, *Pollution and the Death of Man – The Christian View of Ecology* (Wheaton IL: Tyndale House Publishers, 1971); Albert J. Fritsch, *Environmental Ethics: Choices for Concerned Citizens* (Garden City NY: Anchor Books, 1980); John Passmore, *Man's Responsibility for Nature: Ecological Problems and Western Traditions* (New York: Charles Scribner's Sons, 1974). Passmore's emphasis on the contributions of the Western analytic tradition are important, but his xenophobia concerning other traditions is unfortunate.

7. David Ehrenfeld, *The Arrogance of Humanism* (New York: Oxford UP, 1978), 17–18, 247, and passim.

8. For Asian cultures, see J. Baird Callicott and Roger T. Ames, eds., *Nature in Asian Traditions of Thought: Essays in Environmental Philosophy* (Albany: State U of New York P, 1989). For Native American and other indigenous cultures, see Paul A. Olson, ed., *The Struggle for the Land* (Lincoln: U of Nebraska P, 1990).

9. Wendell Berry in *Remembering* uses *Paradiso* 1.1–3 as the touchstone of his environmental ethic. White argues that the medieval invention of mining tools, spinning machinery, and other simple technology set the world on the way to industrialism, but it did not do so more than comparable technology in other cultures.

10. Augustine's belief that the creation had been in some measure upset by sin in the realms beneath the moon did not prevent him from also asserting that the whole creation as a system is good; cf. chapter 3, and Michael Macklem, *The Anatomy of the World* (Minneapolis: U of Minnesota P, 1958), 9–10.

11. All citations and references to Augustine's *Confessions* are to the *Patrologia Latina* (hereinafter PL), checked against the *Corpus Christianorum* edition. For the present quote, cf. Augustine, "Confessionum," in PL 32: col.803.

12. For a further discussion of this aspect of Augustine's theory of perception and the abuse of beauty, see D. W. Robertson Jr., *A Preface to Chaucer* (Princeton: Princeton UP, 1962).

13. For Philo's understanding of mathematics and the mathematical sciences, see F. E. Robbins, "Arithmetic in Philo Judaeus," *Classical Philology* 26 (1931): 345–61; David T. Runta, *Philo of Alexandria and the "Timaeus" of Plato* (Leiden: E. J. Brill, 1986), 226.

14. Scriptural citations and quotations are from the Jerusalem Bible in this chapter, since it takes cognizance of the early texts.

15. Georg Misch, *A History of Autobiography in Antiquity*, trans. E. W. Dickes (Cambridge: Harvard UP, 1951).

16. Late antique Jewish and early Christian thought is, in Jacques Derrida's terms, incurably "logocentric," and it is such at the most basic level of the concep-

tion of creation. But it does not privilege speech over writing: in fact texts are crucial. For a more structured and controlled form of Christian education of the younger child, see John Chrysostom, *Sur La Vaine Gloire et L'Education des Enfants,* ed. Anne-Marie Malingrey (Paris: Éditions du Cerf, 1972). For *hokmah* as *sophia,* see Elias J. Bickerman, *The Jews in the Greek Age* (Cambridge: Harvard UP, 1988), 166.

17. Reider denies that "word" and "wisdom" are here one or that Philo's Logos doctrine is present, and he may be correct. However, later writers identified Word and Wisdom. Joseph Reider, *The Book of Wisdom* (New York: Harper, 1957), 126. Cf. David T. Runia, *Philo of Alexandria and the "Timaeus" of Plato* (Leiden: E. J. Brill, 1986), 449–51, which sees Philo's Logos as like Plato's World-Soul. Biblical quotations in this chapter are from the Jerusalem Bible, which reflects the earliest manuscripts; thereafter, quotations come from the Vulgate-Douay.

18. Anne Freire Ashbaugh, *Plato's Theory of Explanation* (Albany: State U of New York P, 1988), 56–71.

19. Robert M. Berchman, *From Philo to Origen* (Chico CA: Scholars Press, 1984), 29–30.

20. Berchman, *From Philo to Origen,* 119–20.

21. Kirk and Raven, *Presocratic Philosophers,* 187–215.

22. Scholars do not know whether the two fuse on the basis of Wisdom 9.1–2 or on the basis of general structural similarities between the two figures perceived by later thinkers such as Philo or Origen.

23. In the book of Proverbs (300–200 B.C.), Wisdom first appears as woman and divine theophany (8.22–30). In most later Old Testament literature, she is a beautiful woman calling her seekers, sons, and lovers to know God and the structure of nature (Ecclus. 24; Wisdom 7–9). She is the lady at the window of Proverbs 7.6ff. who calls to the senseless man going after the harlot; at the same time, she is a structure that is "the object of thought," "imminent in creation," that brings "order to the whole of life in God's eyes." (Gerhard von Rad, *Wisdom in Israel* [Nashville: Abingdon Press, 1972], 171–72). In Wisdom 7.22–8.8 (20 B.C.–A.D. 54) and Ecclesiasticus 24.1–22 (ca. 180 B.C.), one finds her slightly transformed from the Proverbs woman. For a discussion of the tradition of Wisdom in Proverbs 8 and elsewhere and of the Logos in Stoicism and Gnosticism in relation to John 1 1ff., see Rudolf Bultmann, *The Gospel of John; A Commentary,* trans. G. R. Beasley-Murray (Oxford: Basil Blackwell, 1971), 22–31.

24. Bickerman, *Jews,* 165ff. In a "Platonic" vein, Ben Sira's sage claims a divine "light" that allows humankind to know the structure of living things so that it can "praise [God's] holy name" and "tell of his magnificent works" (16.24–17.20). To him, pursuing Wisdom and her light is a lifelong meditative quest that disciplines the intellectual and moral faculties, as the work of the plowman and sower disci-

plines the body (14.20ff.). Cf. Harry Austryn Wolfson, *Philo* (Cambridge: Harvard UP, 1968), 1.286–89; 1.259–60; 1.266–69. In most of the later Wisdom works, she manifests God, as Plato's middle figure or Antiochus's Logos manifests Him, by tying the material universe to the ultimate. Cf. Wisdom 7.25; Philo, "De Fuga et Inventione," 51, in *Philo*, trans. F. H. Colson and G. H. Whitaker (Cambridge: Harvard UP, 1934), 5.37; Berchman, *From Philo to Origen*, 25–53, 113–66.

25. Cf. Henri de Lubac, *Exégèse Médiévale* (Paris: Aubier, 1961), 2.48–49. For a list of some Origenian citations of Ben Sira, see Hans Ur von Balthasar, *Origen: Spirit and Fire*, trans. Robert J. Daly (Washington DC: Catholic U of America P, 1984), 406. Ecclesiasticus and Wisdom and the earlier Wisdom books, Proverbs, Job, and certain Psalms, were accepted as fully canonical by Origen, Chrysostom, Ambrose, Augustine, Gregory, Rabanus Maurus, Hincmar, Peter Damian, and Peter Cantor.

26. Cf. John D. Turner, "The Feminine Principle in Platonic and Gnostic Metaphysics," forthcoming, for a review of various transformations of this feminine figure from Plato on in Greek thought. Cf. Berchman, *From Philo to Origen*, 29–31, 57–59, 117–21. Cf. Bickerman, *Jews*, 165–73; Rad, *Wisdom in Israel*, 240–62; Edmond Jacob, "Wisdom and Religion in Sira," *Israelite Wisdom*, ed. John G. Gammie (Missoula MT: Scholars Press for Union Theological Seminary, 1978), 247–60.

27. Bickerman, *Jews*, 166–67.

28. Bickerman, *Jews*, 164; 167.

29. Rad, *Wisdom in Israel*, 24–50. See also Henry A. Fischel, "The Transformation of Wisdom in the World of Midrash," *Aspects of Wisdom*, 67–102. For some samples of Stoic teaching in the marketplace mode, see Hans von Arnim, ed., *Stoicorum Veterum Fragmenta* (Leipzig: Teubner, 1903), 3.146–71.

30. Philo, "De Vita Mosis," 1.23, in *Philo* 6.

31. Philo, "Legum Allegoria," 1.53–87, in *Philo* 1.181–205. See also Philo, "Questiones et Solutiones in Genesin," 1.57, in *Philo*, Supplement 1.35; "De Plantatione," 7.28–46, in *Philo* 3.227–37. Cf. Jean Laporte, "Philo in the Tradition of Biblical Wisdom Literature," in Robert L. Wilken, ed., *Aspects of Wisdom in Judaism and Early Christianity* (Notre Dame: U of Notre Dame P, 1975), 125–27. The Wisdom books of Proverbs, Ecclesiastes, the Canticle of Canticles, Wisdom, and Ecclesiasticus were often as a group attributed to Solomon, though sometimes Wisdom and Ecclesiasticus were excluded from the Solomonic corpus and simply attributed to a wise man. Lubac, *Exégèse Médiévale*, 2.48; Marrou, *History of Education*, 80–91, 194–216.

32. Justin Martyr appears to have been the first Christian to have written a dialogue, that with Trypho, and he also suggested the identity of the philosopher's Logos and Christ in his two *Apologies*. Wilken, "Wisdom and Philosophy in Early Christianity," in *Aspects of Wisdom*, 159.

33. Cf. for Christ-as-Wisdom sending out his followers, Fred W. Burnett, *The Testament of Jesus-Sophia* (Washington DC: UP of America, 1979), 43–45.

34. J. C. M. Van Winden, *An Early Christian Philosopher; Justin Martyr's Dialogue with Trypho* (Leiden: E. J. Brill, 1971), 22–48; Marrou, *History of Education*, 326–27.

35. Wilken, "Wisdom and Philosophy in Early Christianity," in *Aspects of Wisdom*, 160.

36. The distrust of words uninformed by a sense of the knowledge of the structure of things in the *Gorgias* also informs Ben Sira; Ben Sira "counts on sapience and not on Greek rhetoric to develop the skill of his students" (Bickerman, *Jews*, 174). Similarly, Clement condemns "sophists" in "Stromata," 1.3, in *Patrologia Graeca* (hereinafter *PG*) 8: cols.712–13, and Origen condemns his human teachers who teach only grammar, rhetoric, or dialectic in "In Leviticum Homilia," in *PG* 12: col.458. Later Augustine repents his own rhetorician's past, and Boethius his prostitute tragic muses in the *Consolation*.

37. Gustave Bardy, "Philosophie et 'philosophe' dans le vocabulaire Chrétien des premiers siécles," *Revue d' Ascétique et de Mystique* 25 (1949): 97–105; Anne Marie Malingrey, *"Philosophia"; Étude d' un groupe de mots dans la littérature grecque, des Présocratiques au IV siècle après J-C* (Paris: C. Klincksieck, 1961).

38. For Christianity and ancient schools, see Marrou, *History of Education*, 318–29.

39. Gregory Thaumaturgos, "Oratio Panegyrica in Origenem," in *PG* 10: cols.1051–104. Subsequent quotations and citations will be in the text by section. For a useful introduction to the background of this chapter, see Werner Jaeger, *Early Christianity and Greek Paideia* (New York: Oxford UP, 1961). For some account of the kind of circle in which Origen taught, see Peter Brown, *The Body and Society: Men, Women and Sexual Renunciation in Early Christianity* (New York: Columbia UP, 1988), 104ff.; cf. John Clark Smith, *The Ancient Wisdom of Origen* (Lewisburg PA: Bucknell UP, 1992), 132–46.

40. For Origen on mortality and the Logos, see Hans Urs von Balthasar, *Origen: Spirit and Fire*, trans. Robert J. Daly (Washington DC: Catholic U of America P, 1984), 37–59.

41. It is not clear to me how Gregory distinguishes human reason from the individual Logos that dwells in him. Perhaps human reason is conceptualized as a prudential reasoning power while the Logos within is conceptualized as a faculty capable of cognizing the cosmos and its divine origin. In that case the distinction would be like the later medieval distinction between the lower reason and the higher reason.

42. For Origen's account of "Know thyself," as meaning "Know yourself made in the image of God," or "Know your own soul," see Origen, "In Cantica Canticorum," in *PG* 13: col.123.

43. James Olney, *Metaphors of Self; the Meaning of Autobiography* (Princeton: Princeton UP, 1972), 6.

44. For a list of Origenian quotations from Heraclitus, see Kirk and Raven, *The Presocratic Philosophers,* 182ff.

45. I assume that the emphasis on friendship in education owes something to the *Symposium* or other works in its tradition; however, I am unable to establish this.

46. For an account of the beauty of the natural system based on visible paradigms, see Origen, "In Cantica Canticorum," in *PG* 13: cols.172–75; cf. D. S. Wallace-Hadrill, *The Greek Patristic View of Nature* (New York: Barnes and Noble, 1968), 120–21.

47. For the dependence of 1 Corinthians on Jewish Wisdom literature, see Andre Feuillet, *Le Christ, Sagesse de Dieu d'après les Épîtres Pauliniennes* (Paris: J. Gabalda, 1966), 25–112. Feuillet also argues that Paul attributes to Christ the principle of cohesion in the universe, a principle labeled "love" in Boethius's *Consolation;* cf. Feuillet, *Le Christ, Sagesse de Dieu,* 213–17.

48. Birger A. Pearson, "Hellenistic-Jewish Wisdom Speculation and Paul," in *Aspects of Wisdom,* 43–66; Robin S. Barbour, "Wisdom and the Cross in 1 Corinthians 1 and 2," *Theologia Crucis, Signum Crucis,* ed. Carl Andresen and Günter Klein (Tübingen: Mohr, 1979), 57ff.; see also Feuillet, *Le Christ, Sagesse de Dieu.*

49. Baptism reenacted crucifixion/martyrdom in the early church; cf. Anton Mayer, *Vom Christlichen Mysterium* (Düsseldorf: Patmos-Verlag, 1951), 115–34. Resurrection is the birth of a new self, capable of a *gnosis* that obeys cosmic law and loves things properly. For Pauline antecedents, see Robin S. Barbour, "Wisdom and the Cross," 57ff. For the Origenian aesthetics of the natural world based on the notion that "spirit," structure, and proportion are above matter and the sources of its beauty, see Wallace-Hadrill, *The Greek Patristic View of Nature,* 101–30.

50. Origen, "ΠΕΡΙ ΑΡΧΩΝ," 3.3.2, in *PG* 11: cols.314–15. Origen speaks here of poetry, grammar, rhetoric, geometry, and music as the wisdom of the world.

51. Quoted in Balthasar, *Origen: Spirit and Fire,* 275.

52. Clement holds to the same view; cf. Berchman, *From Philo to Origen,* 181, 189ff.

53. Berchman, *From Philo to Origen,* 172–200, esp. 174.

54. Berchman, *From Philo to Origen,* 201–14. Cf. Origen, "In Cantica Canticorum: Prologus," in *PG* 13: col.73.

55. Clement of Alexandria, "Stromata," 6.10–11, in *PG* 9: cols.300–17; "Stromata" 1.28 in *PG* 8: cols.921–25.

56. Origen, "In Cantica Canticorum: Prologus," in *PG* 13: cols.73–80.

57. Origen, "In Cantica Canticorum: Prologus," in PG 13: cols.73–75. Origen bases his three disciplines on his three worlds of physicals, mathematicals, and theologicals – created world, Holy Spirit, and Father; Berchman, *From Philo to Origen*, 140.

58. In the *Republic*, Plato does not locate the Forms in the One; in the *Timaeus* the Forms are received by the Mother (also called Nurse and Receptacle) and communicated to the sensible world (sections 48–51). Later Platonists propose a variety of solutions as to how the Forms are communicated to the middle figure and from it to the material world.

59. Chalcidius, "In Timaeus," 272, 335, in *Platonis Timaeus interprete Chalcidio cum eiusdem Commentario,* ed. I. Wrobel (Leipzig: Teubner, 1876); Proclus, *In Platonis Timaeum,* ed. Ernest Diehl (Leipzig: Teubner, 1903–6), 202. Cicero makes the progress Ethics, Physics ("de natura et occultis rebus"), and Dialectic, in Cicero, "Academica," 1.5, in *De Natura Deorum; Academica,* ed. H. Rackham (London: W. Heinemann, 1933), 428. For a progress similar to that in Origen and Gregory from Hebrew tradition, see Philo, "De Congressu Quaerendae Eruditionis Gratia," 14.74–81, in *Philo* 4.74–80. Cf. Origen, "In Cantica Canticorum: Prologus," in PG 13: col.73 and Origen's commentary on Proverbs, "Fragmenta ex Libro de Proverbiis Salomonis," in PG 13: cols.17–34, which emphasizes the figurative element in Proverbs and its use of Christ's techniques. Origen's not-so-obvious interpretation of Ecclesiastes as a work of Physics probably derives from its proposition that repetitive times and seasons define both the rhythms and the vanity of human life, and its assertion that the movement of the sun, moon, and stars remind one that the Creator should be remembered (12.1–8).

60. Berchman, *From Philo to Origen,* 126–34. I do not endeavor in this section to treat all of the complexities of the middle figure in Greek, Hellenistic, and Hebrew philosophy.

61. Rad, *Wisdom in Israel,* 172.

62. Origen explains how the Logos within or the "life" in John 1 is what is added upon the completion of reason in human beings. "Commentariorum in Evangelium Joannis," 2.19 and 1.27, in PG 14: cols.156–57, 73.

63. Clement downplays the Pauline elements of "fear of God," the death and resurrection of the self in the process of *gnosis.* He does emphasize selfless love and martyrdom as basic. (Clement of Alexandria, "Stromata," 4.21–23, in PG 8: cols.1340–61.) He attacks rhetorical decoration, the tendency of rhetoric to seek the hearer's delight rather than truth ("Stromata," 1.3, in PG 8: cols.712–13). He affirms the vision of Plato's *Republic* as a vision of a proper inward Republic or divine kingdom ("Stromata," 4.26, in PG 8: cols.1372–82). In him, learning does have to answer to an external standard. In his "Paedagogus," he attacks the

Sophist rhetoricians while his "Stromata" defends philosophy as leading to God and argues that true *Sophia* represents objective truth (6.8, in PG 9: cols.284–92).

64. Clement of Alexandria, "Paedagogus," in PG 8: cols.249–61, 311–24.

65. Clement of Alexandria, "Paedagogus," in PG 8: cols.262–80.

66. Clement of Alexandria, "Paedagogus," in PG 8: cols.280–311.

67. Clement of Alexandria, "Paedagogus," in PG 8: cols.313ff.

68. Though his Logos directs its instruction to conduct, Clement occasionally extends its activity to philosophy's traditional topics – Ethics, Physics, Metaphysics, and Dialectics. Clement of Alexandria, "Stromata," 6.10–11, in PG 9: cols.300–317.

69. Based on Proverbs 8 and the other passages attributing creative functions to Wisdom, and also based on the Logos's function in transmitting the ideas to the creation, John 1 and several passages in Matthew make the intermediary figure become Christ, the Wisdom or Logos of the new dispensation. For a succinct summary of scholarship on the Logos in the gospel of John, see *The Jerusalem Bible*, ed. Alexander Jones (Garden City NY: Doubleday, 1966), 2.1447 (note a), 140–41; J. Rendel Harris, "Athena, Sophia, and the Logos," *BJRL* 7 (1922): 56–72. Bultmann places more emphasis on Gnostic sources for the Logos hymn in John than do some recent commentators. See Bultmann, *The Gospel of John*, 22–23; for a critique of Bultmann, see William Baird, "The Problem of the Gnostic Redeemer and Bultmann's Program of Demythologizing," *Theologia Crucis, Signum Crucis*, 39–55. For scholarship on Matthew, see James M. Robinson, "Jesus as Sophos and Sophia: Wisdom Tradition and the Gospels," in Wilken, *Aspects of Wisdom in Judaism and Early Christianity*, 1–16; M. Jack Suggs, *Wisdom, Christology, and Law in Matthew's Gospel* (Cambridge: Harvard UP, 1970); cf. Burnett, *The Testament of Jesus-Sophia*. For an account of the movement in the ancient world from *Sophia* to *Logos*, see Burton L. Mack, *Logos und Sophia; Untersuchungen zur Weisheitstheologie im hellenistischen Judentum, Studien zur Umwelt des Neuen Testaments* 10 (Göttingen: Vandenhoeck & Ruprecht, 1973), 63–170 and passim. The ancient Chaldean cultures posited a high God who spoke to create the universe, whom Hellenism made to stand for Wisdom; Athena as Wisdom leapt from the head of Zeus and was allegorized to stand for the ideas. Cf. Berchman, *From Philo to Origen*, 29 and Felix Buffière, *Les Mythes d'Homère et la Pensée Grecque* (Paris: Sociéte d'Edition "Les Belles Lettres," 1956), 282, 458.

70. In Origen, the middle figure apprehended through human thought as the structure behind material reality is the Logos. Wisdom relates the middle figure to God, the Logos aspect of the same figure relates it to the creation intellectually apprehended. Origen, "Commentariorum in Evangelium Joannis," in PG 14: cols.56–60. Origen here develops Philo's ideas; cf. Mack, *Logos und Sophia*, 133–53; cf. David T. Runia, *Philo of Alexandria and the "Timaeus" of Plato* (Leiden: E. J. Brill, 1986), 206–7; 446–51.

71. Smith, *Rhetoric in Alexandria*, 90.

72. Origen, "Commentariorum in Evangelium Joannis," 1.16ff., in *PG* 14: col.49ff. For analogous traditions, see John D. Turner, "The Gnostic Threefold Path to Enlightenment: the Ascent of Mind and the Descent of Wisdom," *Novum Testamentum* 22 (1980): 324–51.

73. Origen, "Commentariorum in Evangelium Joannis," 1.19–1.20, in *PG* 14: cols.53–56.

74. For the rule of the mathematical sciences in Roman architecture, see Vitruvius, *De Architectura*, ed. Frank Granger (New York: G. P. Putnam's Sons, 1934), 8–23, 158–67.

75. Origen, "Commentariorum in Evangelium Joannis," 1.22, in *PG* 14: cols.56–57. This passage containing the architectural analogy strongly suggests that Augustine knew either Origen's commentary on John or knew works derived from it, for he develops an almost identical analogy in explaining the hymn to the Logos at the beginning of John; for further explanations of Origen's theory of Wisdom and the Word, see Berchman, *From Philo to Origen*, 118ff.

76. Origen, "Commentariorum in Evangelium Joannis," in *PG* 14: cols.72–73.

77. Berchman, *From Philo to Origen*, 158.

78. Bickerman, *Jews*, 171. Ben Sira's emphasis on providential history seems to relate more to the epic tradition of such works as the *Iliad* where the gods guide with a personalistic concern for the individual hero. Some scholars argue that Ben Sira quotes Homer.

79. For brief accounts of Origen's influence on Augustine, see Henri de Lubac, *Exégèse Médiévale* (Lyon: Aubier, 1959), 1.213–15; 1.294. For an account of early Christian imitation of the dialogue mode of the philosophers, see Bernd Reiner Voss, *Der Dialog in der Frühchristlichen Literatur* (München: Wilhelm Fink, 1970), 26–186.

80. Religious thinkers may have sought to encourage an ascent through the scientific search because of *emic* factors intrinsic to Judaism and Christianity or their theories of Wisdom and the Logos. Rival religions also made scientific claims. For a study of Origen's Greek-based theories of the stars, see Alan B. Scott, *Origen and the Life of the Stars: A History of an Idea* (New York: Oxford UP, 1991); for Mithra and science, cf. David Ulansey, *The Origins of the Mithraic Mysteries* (London: Oxford UP, 1989).

3 AUGUSTINE'S *CONFESSIONS*

1. For contemporary discussions of issues of determinacy and indeterminacy in language, see Horst Ruthrof, *Pandora and Occam* (Bloomington: Indiana UP, 1992). For a deconstructionist argument for a kind of unconscious indeterminacy in Augustine's statement, see Ralph Flores, *The Rhetoric of Doubtful Authority* (Ithaca: Cornell UP, 1984), 44–65.

2. Cf. Flores, *The Rhetoric of Doubtful Authority,* 44–65 and note 3, this chapter.

3. Ludwig Wittgenstein, *Philosophical Investigations,* trans. G. E. M. Anscombe (New York: Macmillan, 1958), 2e. For a useful discussion of Derrida's commitment to the notion that all language is self-referenced in contrast to Wittgenstein's notion that some language refers to objects and situations outside language, see Newton Garver and Seung-Chong Lee, *Derrida and Wittgenstein* (Philadelphia: Temple UP, 1994), 32–33, 45, 121, 207–19.

4. Garth Hallett, *A Companion to Wittgenstein's "Philosophical Investigations"* (Ithaca: Cornell UP, 1977), 73.

5. Though Wittgenstein, in the *Investigations,* attacks the picture theory of meaning set forth in the *Tractatus* and by Bertrand Russell and regards many words as not having naming functions, he still recognizes complex naming functions for many sentences that depend on one's understanding both the language game and the form of life of which the functions are a part. He recognizes procedures for verification. Augustine's assumptions about language-as-name seem to be derived from Plato's *Cratylus,* a work with whose doctrines Wittgenstein struggles in the early sections of the *Investigations.* For a useful discussion of these matters in relation to literature, see Bernard Harrison, "Imagined Worlds and the Real One: Plato, Wittgenstein, and Mimesis," *Philosophy and Literature* 17 (1993): 26–46. Cf. Hallett, *Companion to Wittgenstein's "Philosophical Investigations,"* 118–19, 465–67.

6. Patricia H. Werhane, *Skepticism, Rules and Private Languages* (London: Humanities Press, 1992), 115–33.

7. See George Pitcher, "About the Same," in *Ludwig Wittgenstein: Philosophy and Language,* ed. Alice Ambrose and Morris Lazerowitz (London: Allen & Unwin, 1972), 120–39.

8. This is an abbreviated account of a complex critical theory set forth in Harold Bloom's primary works in this area: *The Anxiety of Influence: A Theory of Poetry* (New York: Oxford UP, 1973); *A Map of Misreading* (New York: Oxford UP, 1975); *Kabbalah and Criticism* (New York: Seabury, 1975); *Poetry and Repression: Revisionism from Blake to Stevens* (New Haven: Yale UP, 1976). For Augustine as doubling himself and predecessors and seeking to inspire a doubling of himself in others, see Flores, *Rhetoric of Doubtful Authority,* 55–56.

9. Lamberton, *Homer the Theologian,* uses the strong misreading theory. Flores, *Rhetoric of Doubtful Authority,* 44–65, struggles with the issue of whether Augustine transcends himself and/or his predecessors and inspires genuine doubling in those who imitate him (such as Alypius).

10. Morrison, *Mimetic Tradition of Reform in the West,* xiv.

11. For a deconstructionist treatment of Augustine, see Flores, *Rhetoric of Doubtful Authority,* 44–65. For Augustine's understanding of autobiography, see Au-

gustine, "Epistola 231.6," in *PL* 33: cols.1025–26; Augustine, "Retractationum, 2, 6," in *PL* 32: col.632. In writing a narrative about learning in the tradition of Gregory Thaumaturgos's account, Augustine does not offer a file of proprietary memories assembled into an "I" while assigning to that "I" a raison d'être uniquely its own, since such a narrative would have no educative function given his world view. Weintraub correctly observes that Augustine saw in "the story of *one* Christian soul, the one he could know best, the *typical* story of all Christians." This chapter endeavors to trace the roots of Augustine's so seeing. Cf. Karl J. Weintraub, *The Value of the Individual: Self and Circumstance in Autobiography* (Chicago: U of Chicago P, 1978), 45.

12. Robert J. O'Connell and Robert McMahon have both shown that the *Confessions* represent the soul's journey as understood by the Neoplatonists. However, the Neoplatonists did not write autobiography but accounts of the soul's journey into matter and its reascent above it, a travel that can be anyone's or everyone's. Robert McMahon, *Augustine's Prayerful Ascent: An Essay in the Literary Form of the "Confessions"* (Athens: U of Georgia P, 1989); Robert J. O'Connell, *St. Augustine's Confessions: The Odyssey of Soul* (Cambridge MA: Belknap, 1969). Cf. Kenneth Burke's treatment of Augustine's interest in the relationship between words and the Word in *The Rhetoric of Religion: Studies in Logology* (Berkeley: U of California P, 1970), 43–171; cf. Marcia L. Colish, *The Mirror of Language* (Lincoln: U of Nebraska P, 1968), 7–54, especially 41–43. Henry Adams understood that the *Confessions* is a work designed to model an education; Augustine "wrote a heavy dissertation on modern education and fill[ed] up the background with moving figures that will carry the load. . . ." Henry Adams, *The Education of Henry Adams*, ed. Ernest Samuels (Boston: Houghton Mifflin, 1973), 513. George Howie correctly argues that the *Confessions* are "an educational document of great sensitivity" and a "primary source for the study of Augustine's educational theory," showing "how much the learner must perform by his own unaided effort" without the aid of formal teachers and, simultaneously, the "necessity . . . of divine illumination." George Howie, *St. Augustine: On Education* (Chicago: Henry Regnery, 1969), 7–8.

13. Augustine's *Confessions* represents a response to political pressures that he, in his role as bishop, came under from the Donatists, who mounted a criticism of his hedonistic past and former Manichaean leanings. One must recognize that the *Confessions* reconstructs a life, and that it may not fully or accurately represent that life and may in part apotheosize the ego that Augustine seeks to control; however, this chapter endeavors to give an *emic* interpretation of the *Confessions* as part of the tradition traced in this book. Quotations and citations from the *Confessions* refer in the text to book and section in the *Patrologia Latina* edition, in *PL* 32: col.659ff., checked against the *Corpus Christianorum* edition. Biblical quotations translate Augustine's Latin.

14. Marrou, *History of Education*, 95–313.

15. Marrou, *History of Education*, 102–15.

16. Marrou, *History of Education*, 301.

17. Marrou, *History of Education*, 294–95.

18. Marrou, *History of Education*, 306–7.

19. Marrou, *History of Education*, 305.

20. Marrou, *History of Education*, 304.

21. The notion that Roman education was insistently imperialistic or hegemonic and that early Greek education was not – a notion propagated by Nietzsche, Heidegger, and Spanos – mistakes the distinction between philosophic and Sophistic education for the distinction between Greek and Roman education. Greek education was never predominately philosophic, and a philosophic underground always existed in Roman times among the Stoics, late Platonists, and philosophic Christians. For an opposing view, cf. Spanos, *The End of Education*, 106–17.

22. Ariès's claim that protective education comes into being after the Enlightenment is incorrect; cf. Philippe Ariès, *L'Enfant et La Vie Familiale sous l'ancien régime* (Paris: Librarie Plon, 1960), 102–33.

23. *The Institutio Oratoria of Quintilian*, trans. H. E. Butler, 4 vols. (Cambridge: Harvard UP, 1963). It is cited in the text by book, section, and subsection. Cf. Stanley F. Bonner, *Education in Ancient Rome* (London: Methuen, 1977), 115ff.

24. Augustine's embrace of the Gregorian-Origenian tradition also sets him apart from many other Christians of note, and the *Confessions* may partly be directed against the rival pedagogical traditions within Christianity itself. Jerome represents a rival tradition. Chrysostom (A.D. 347–407) advocates an education at least as protective and conventionalized as Quintilian's. Cf. Chrysostom, *Sur La Vaine Gloire et L'Education des Enfants*. Though Tertullian censures Roman teachers for worshipping Minerva, soiling their lips with Roman gods, and misleading students, he recognizes the necessity that Christians go to Roman schools ("De Idolatria," 10, in *PL* 1: cols.673–75). Later, fourth-century Christian Roman education emphasizes Virgil, Cicero, and Seneca and enables the laity to create some Christian doctrine and culture; cf. W. H. C. Frend, *The Rise of Christianity* (London: Darton, Longman, & Todd, 1984), 555. Early Christian nonviolence possibly aroused some Christian opposition to the Roman schools, which sanctioned corporal punishment. Cf. Roland Bainton, "The Early Church and War," *Harvard Theological Review* 39 (1946): 189–212, for an account of the early church and violence.

25. J. N. D. Kelly, *Jerome: His Life, Writings, and Controversies* (London: Duckworth, 1975), 10–14. For Donatus's grammatical manuals, see *Grammatici Latini*, ed. H. Keil (Leipzig: Teubner, 1857–80), 4.356, 359–62, 392–94, trans. in W. J.

Chase, "The Ars Minor of Donatus," *University of Wisconsin Studies in the Social Sciences and History* 11 (1926).

26. Jerome, "Epistola 107," in PL 22: cols.867–78. Citations in the text are from this edition. Cf. Harald Hagendahl, *Latin Fathers and the Classics* (Göteborg: Almqvist & Wiksell, 1958), 199–201. Contrast Jerome's picture of a protective education with Augustine's of the self-disciplined education of the youthful aspirant to philosophy: "De Ordine," 2.8, in PL 32: cols.1006–7.

27. Cf. Jerome, "Epistola 22, 30," in PL 22: col.416; Jerome, "Epistola 70," in PL 22: cols.664–68. For useful discussions of the meaning of the dream accusing Jerome of being a Ciceronian, see Neil Adkin, "Some Notes on the Dream of St. Jerome," *Philologus* 128 (1984): 119–26, and by the same author, "Gregory of Nazianzus and Jerome: Some Remarks," *Institute of Classical Studies: Bulletin Supplement* 58 (1991): 14–17. After the dream, Jerome clearly did not give up his interest in reading the pagan authors and engaging in rhetorical pyrotechnics, though he sometimes condemns eloquence while indulging in its devices to the full; see Neil Adkin, " 'Adultery of the Tongue': Jerome, Epist. 22.29.6f.," *Hermes* 121 (1993): 104–6.

28. Cf. Jerome's "Epistola 128," in PL 32: cols.1095–99. Jerome taught the pagan authors to boys in his "school" at Bethlehem and defended his basically rhetorical pedagogy in his controversy with Rufinus.

29. Augustine distinguishes between good rhetoric and the Sophists' version, contention for the sake of contention: "Contra Cresconium Grammaticum," 1.2, in PL 43: col.448. Flores, *Rhetoric of Doubtful Authority,* 48, 57, argues that Augustine exchanges pagan for Christian rhetoric; while this is partially true, his significant change is toward an interest in logic, the mathematical subjects, and metaphysics – a new episteme.

30. Augustine, "Epistola 28," in PL 33: cols.111–14.

31. Augustine, "Epistola 40," in PL 33: col.155.

32. Augustine, "Epistola 71," in PL 33: cols.241–43.

33. Augustine, *Confessions,* ed. O'Donnell, 3.387, commenting on 13.20.

34. Augustine writes about education off and on throughout his career, from the very early *De Magistro* (A.D. 387) to the late *De Doctrina Christiana* (A.D. 397–417). In his educational writings, he endeavors to separate education from Roman *mythoi* and to give it a place that relates it to Christian belief and to the objective exploration of the creation. His position with respect to education here is not unlike that in the later *City of God,* where he tries to separate Christianity from the political fate of the Roman empire. In *De Magistro,* Augustine argues that education is a learning that comes from a truth (Logos) within that teaches one about the objective order.

35. Kelly, *Jerome,* 16–17.

36. Though Misch speaks of Roman autobiography as life-story stylized to model civic or military virtue and separates Augustine from the mode, Augustine simply offers us the warfare of the spirit. Georg Misch, *A History of Autobiography in Antiquity,* trans. E. W. Dickes, 2 vols. (Cambridge: Harvard UP, 1951). For history and "fable" in the *Confessions,* see Pierre Courcelle, *Recherches sur les Confessions de S. Augustin* (Paris: Boccard, 1968), 188–202; Stephen A. Shapiro, "The Dark Continent of Literature: Autobiography," *Comparative Literature Studies* 5 (1968): 422–25 and 421–54 passim. The Augustine of the early section of the *Confessions* does not match the respectable Augustine praised by Vincentius in the same period (Augustine, "Epistola," 93.4, section 13, in PL 33: col.346). Brown notes that the word "confession" means, for Augustine, "accusation of oneself" or "praise" of God, after *Serm.* 67.2; cf. Peter Brown, *Augustine of Hippo: A Biography* (Berkeley: U of California P, 1967), 175. However, the word also has the sense of beginning the movement toward health or reform; cf. Augustine, "Enarratio in Psalmos," 99.16, in PL 37: cols.1280–81. For the epistemological aims of the *Soliloquies,* see Colish, *Mirror of Language,* 15–16; Augustine, "Soliloquia," in PL 32: col.869ff. For the Logos both as objective reality and as dwelling in the interior man, see Augustine, "In Joannis Evangelium Tractatus 124," 9–10, in PL 35: cols.1541–42; Augustine, "De Trinitate," 9.7, in PL 42: col.967. For Word as writing with visible events in the creation, see Augustine "Enarratio in Psalmos," 44.5, in PL 36: cols.496–97. For Origin and Augustine, see de Lubac, *Exégèse Médiévale,* 1.294. Augustine also uses, in his commentary on John, the Origenian ideas of the Christ/Logos/Wisdom as (1) God's design or architectural plan expressed in the building of creation; and (2) the Platonic "light" apprehended by human reason. Origen's *De Principiis* argues for the conception of the relationship of the Wisdom/Logos figure to the creation found in Origen's commentary on John. Augustine knew the *De Principiis.* Cf. Origen, *Traité des Principiis,* ed. Henri Crouzel and Manlio Simonetti (Paris: Éditions du Cerf, 1978), 1.111–43, 2.32–56.

37. For Allan Bloom on the canon, see *The Closing of the American Mind* (New York: Simon & Schuster, 1987), 62–68; for Bennett's proposals, cf. William J. Bennett, *American Education: Making It Work* (Washington DC: Government Printing Office, 1988), 26.

38. For an excellent discussion of this principle in Augustine, see Marjorie O'Rourke Boyle, "Augustine in the Garden of Zeus: Lust, Love and Language," *Harvard Theological Review* 83 (1990): 117–39.

39. Athanasius of Alexandria, "Life of Antony," translated by A. Robertson in *Nicene and Post-Nicene Fathers* (Grand Rapids: Eerdmans, 1957), second series, 4.195–221; Karl Morrison, *The Mimetic Tradition of Reform in the West* (Princeton: Princeton UP, 1982). I am indebted to Professor Morrison's *Mimetic Tradition* throughout this book and to his personal commentary on this chapter.

40. For Victorinus's theology, see Pierre Hadot, *Porphyr et Victorinus*, 2 vols. (Paris: Études Augustiniennes, 1968), 1.475–78.

41. Athanasius, "Life of Antony," 196–97, 198–99, 210, 213–14, 219.

42. Dante knew the *Confessions;* he probably derived the title of *La Vita Nuova* from Augustine's "novae vitae."

43. For a balanced view of Augustine on asceticism and sexuality, see Pierre J. Payer, *The Bridling of Desire* (Toronto: U of Toronto P, 1993).

44. The "Tolle, lege" scene is replete with recollections of previous scenes in which Augustine engaged in playful activities; cf. Karl Morrison, "*I am You*" (Princeton: Princeton UP, 1988), 73.

45. O'Rourke argues that the garden imitates the garden of Eden, but the more likely imitation comes from the story of Ponticianus's friends. O'Rourke, "Augustine in the Garden of Zeus," 121–22. For the truthfulness of the scene, see Flores, *Rhetoric of Doubtful Authority*, 47–48.

46. Cf. Alypius's experience at 6.8. For the psychology of the imagination's leaving one in the power of its imagery, see Augustine, "Epistola 9," in *PL* 33: cols.71–73.

47. For the spouse/Christ in the Canticles, the *Verbum dei* married to the flesh, see Augustine, "In Joannis Evangelium Tractatus 124," 8.4, in *PL* 35: col.1152.

48. The scene of "rebirth" is a breaking of habit represented in the former mistresses. Augustine, "Contra Julianum," 4.103, in *PL* 45: cols.1398–99) argues that habit is a second nature; cf. Augustine, "Enarrationes in Psalmos: in Psalmum 30, Enarratio 2: 13," in *PL* 36: cols.237–38. Augustinian education correctly conquers whatever custom or habit makes one nonconformable to the pattern of Wisdom.

49. Augustine, "Enarrationes in Psalmos: in Psalmum CX," section 9, in *PL* 37: col.1466; cf. Brown, *Body and Society*, 387–427.

50. Augustine's remark that he could not remember hearing children chanting such a chant implies that the voice may well be inside of him (8.12).

51. This chapter does not attend to the importance of the Bible and biblical exegesis to Augustine's development because that has been treated superlatively by many other scholars. Suffice it to say that the gaming table experience with the Bible is only one of numerous crucial experiences with it.

52. Karl Morrison, letter to author, 9 Dec. 1991.

53. Radding's argument that Augustine's search for meaning in the events that occur to him is a regression from Cicero and, by implication, from earlier Roman thought, is misleading. The *Aeneid* and most other major Roman literary works that have a narrative structure include various divine revelations that announce the meaning of past or future events. Cf. Radding, *A World Made by Men*, 48–55.

54. Jacques Derrida, *Of Grammatology,* trans. Gayatri Spivak (Baltimore: Johns Hopkins UP, 1976), 1–94.

55. To remind us of the power of the liberated mind, Augustine asserts that Adeodatus, a relatively untutored youth, actually said what *De Magistro* assigns to him (9.6). *De Magistro* itself emphatically comes to the position that no one can teach anyone else anything, only the Logos. Cf. Augustine, "De Magistro," 11–13, in PL 32: cols.1215–20; Colish, *The Mirror of Language,* 39–41.

56. For the *Hortensius,* see Harald Hagendahl, *Augustine and the Latin Classics,* 2 vols. (Stockholm: Almquist & Wiksell, 1967), 1.486–97; for the significance to Augustine of Cicero's and the African Manichaeans' Wisdom, see Brown, *Augustine of Hippo,* 40–45.

57. Augustine regards Cicero's *Hortensius* as answering the view that happiness consists in having what one wants; it insists that happiness also requires wanting the good; cf. "De Trinitate," 13.5, in PL 42: cols.1019–20. The Neoplatonists, as represented by Marius Victorinus, also had a doctrine of the Logos that in many respects mediates between that of Origen and Gregory and that of Augustine: cf. Mary T. Clark, "A Neoplatonic Commentary on the Christian Trinity: Marius Victorinus," *Neoplatonism and Christian Thought,* ed. Dominic J. O'Mara (Albany: State U of New York P, 1983), 24–33. The *Hortensius,* coming from Cicero as the greatest of Roman rhetoricians and philosophers, influenced Augustine to pursue Wisdom, but he later found what Paul emphasizes – that Wisdom was crucified, that the divine Christ-Wisdom stooped to humanity and mortality (7.9). Cf. Augustine, "Ennarrationes in Psalmos," in PL 36: cols.269–70.

58. Augustine, "Epistola 118," 4.24, in "Epistolae: Secunda Classis," PL 33: col.443–44; Augustine, "De Diversis Quaestionibus Octogenta Tribus," section 79, in *De Diversis Quaestionibus Octoginta Tribus: De Octo Dulcitii Quaestionibus,* ed. Almut Mutzenbecher (Turnholt: Brepols, 1975), 226. Contrast Radding, *A World Made by Men,* 46–47.

59. Augustine, "De Trinitate," 14.8–17, in PL 42: cols.1044–55. For Augustine's use of the Bible in the *Confessions,* see Georg Nicolaus Knauer, *Psalmenzitate in Augustins Konfessionen* (Göttingen: Vandenhoeck and Ruprecht, 1955).

60. For a good discussion of these sections that does not focus on the role of Wisdom in mediating between the structure of creation and the individual life, see Colish, *Mirror of Language,* 47–49.

61. H. I. Marrou, *St. Augustin et la Fin de la Culture Antique* (Paris: de Boccard, 1958), 248–73, 277–98. James J. O'Donnell says that "detachment and objectivity are not to be found in the *Confessions,*" but "objectivity" in the Platonic sense is precisely what Augustine learns through absorption in the creation and Creator and through self-transcendence. Cf. James J. O'Donnell, *Augustine* (Boston: Twayne, 1985), 81.

62. Robert J. O'Connell, *St. Augustine's Confessions: The Odyssey of Soul* (Cambridge: Belknap, 1969), 32; *St. Augustine's Early Theory of Man* (Cambridge: Belknap, 1968), 191–96; cf. "De Ordine," 2.53–4, in PL 32: col.1020. Colish does not treat Augustine's interest in the numerical disciplines as studies that relate to Wisdom. Cf. Colish, *The Mirror of Language*, 29–30.

63. Augustine, "De Magistro," sections 11–13, in PL 32: cols.1215–20.

64. Both Manichaeanism and Neoplatonism originate evil with the imprisonment of the soul in the body (*Enneads* 4.8 [6]). Cf. A. Hilary Armstrong, "Man in the Cosmos: a Study of Some Differences between Pagan Neoplatonism and Christianity," in *Romanitas et Christianitas*, ed. W. den Boer et al. (Amsterdam: North Holland, 1973), 5–14.

65. Augustine did not believe that all people could ascend from the examination of number, measure, and weight in created things to an examination of them as they exist in God. Cf. "De Genesi ad Litteram" 4.3–5, in PL 34: cols.299–301.

66. O'Connell, *St. Augustine's Confessions*, 47, says that Monica becomes, in the *Confessions*, "the maternal presence of God himself," perhaps more biblically described as a reflection of Sophia. In *De Ordine* (1.11), Augustine includes Monica among the students of philo-Sophia (*amor sapientiae*), in PL 32: cols.992–94.

67. Cf. Augustine, "De Libero Arbitrio," 8–11, in PL 32: cols.8–11.

68. Augustine regards Wisdom as the same as number. Cf. "De Libero Arbitrio," 2.10, in PL 32: cols.1257–58.

69. Augustine, "De Genesi ad Litteram," PL 34: cols.299–301.

70. Cf. Augustine, *Confessions*, ed. James J. O'Donnell, 3 vols. (Oxford: Clarendon Press, 1992), 2.10.

71. Augustine, "De Genesi ad Litteram," in PL 34: cols.299–300.

72. Cf. Augustine, "In Joannis Evangelium Tractatus 124," 1.17 and 2.10, in PL 35: cols.1387–88, 1393.

73. Augustine, "In Joannis Evangelium Tractatus 124," 1.9–17, in PL 35: cols.1383–88.

74. For Augustine on the Fall, see Augustine, "De Trinitate," 12.12, in PL 42: cols.1007–8; cf. Robert J. O'Connell, *The Origin of the Soul in St. Augustine's Later Works* (New York: Fordham, 1987), 260–66; O'Connell, *St. Augustine's Confessions*, 25–27, 135–57. Augustine in much of his writing assumes that original sin remains within human beings as a latent sting of concupiscence, but human choice must repeat the pattern of the Fall for the latent to become actual. Cf. in particular, "De Nuptiis et Concupiscentia Carnis," in PL 44: cols.414–27.

75. Augustine's "I wept for Dido slain who wept not for my own sin" depends on the sense that the Dido story is a tragedy within the epic of Aeneas. Augustine follows Plato in regarding such tragedy as permitting an emotional glut that detracts from responsibility. For Augustine's probable use of the *Aeneid* as refer-

ent in the *Confessions,* see Andrew Fichter, *Poets Historical* (New Haven: Yale UP, 1982), 40–69.

76. For Augustine's theory of the imagination, see Gerard O'Daly, *Augustine's Philosophy of Mind* (London: Duckworth, 1987), 106ff.

77. For Augustine's reaction to the Roman grammatical and rhetorical schools, see George Howie, *Educational Theory and Practice in St. Augustine* (New York: Teachers College Press, 1969), 3–7 and passim.

78. Cf. Marjorie O'Rourke Boyle, "Augustine in the Garden of Zeus," 125–31. Augustine in *Confessions* 1.16 appears to blame literary study for his difficulty in understanding the anthropomorphic God of the Bible in an allegorical sense and, hence, for his Manichaeanism, but he does not always reject objective literary study that presents fables as fables. Cf. Augustine, "Soliloquiorum," 9–11, in PL 32: cols.892–95; cf. Augustine, *On Christian Doctrine,* trans. D. W. Robertson (New York: Liberal Arts Press, 1958), esp. xiii–xix, 54, 75; Joseph A. Mazzeo, "St. Augustine's Rhetoric of Silence," *JHI* 23 (1962): 175–96; Marcia L. Colish, "St. Augustine's Rhetoric of Silence Revisited," *Augustinian Studies* 9 (1978): 15–24.

79. When Augustine writes his own rhetoric in *De Doctrina Christiana,* he idealizes simple, transparent language that conveys the "truth" and not the rhetoric and poetry that creates fantastic alternative worlds; cf. Phillip Arrington, "Reflections on the Expository Principle," *College English* 54 (1992): 320–22.

80. Augustine, "De Octo Dulcitii Quæstionibus," 3.6, in PL 40: cols.160–61; cf. "De Libero Arbitrio," 2.8–11, in PL 32: cols.1251–58.

81. Robert J. O'Connell, *Art and the Christian Intelligence in St. Augustine* (Cambridge: Harvard UP, 1978), esp. 1–49. To Augustine all arts and crafts possess a perfection that resides in their objects' "number" based on Wisdom's creative design (cf. "De Genesi ad Litteram," 4.3.7–7.14). The universe is God's work of art, the place where Wisdom's numbers and proportions order all things in heaven, earth, and sea, making them exist. God restores our human ruin through crushing and pain but also through the mathematical study and love of the creation and the arousal of the aesthetic sense by it. Augustine, "De Genesi ad Litteram," in PL 34: cols.299–301; cf. "De Ordine," 2.11–19, in PL 32: cols. 1009–19. Eugene Vance, *Mervelous Signals* (Lincoln: U of Nebraska P, 1986), 34–50.

82. James McEvoy, "The Divine as the Measure of Being in Platonic and Scholastic Thought," *Studies in Medieval Philosophy,* ed. John F. Wippel (Washington DC: Catholic U of America P, 1987), 102–4; cf. W. J. Roche, "Measure, Number and Weight in St. Augustine," *New Scholasticism* 15 (1941): 350–76. Augustine uses "number" as meaning the essential species definition or form that defines a species (Roche, 355–59). For the Augustinian tradition, mathematics, and "number" in the Middle Ages, see Russell A. Peck, "Number as Cosmic Lan-

guage," in *By Things Seen: Reference and Recognition in Medieval Thought,* ed. David L. Jeffrey (Ottawa: U of Ottawa P, 1979), 47–80.

83. McEvoy, "The Divine as the Measure of Being," 104.

84. McEvoy, "The Divine as the Measure of Being," 90–94; cf. Augustine, "De Ordine," 2.11–12ff., in *PL* 32: cols.1009–19.

85. Dante sees the *Confessions* as describing a perfective process; cf. "Convivio," 1.2.14–15, in Dante Alighieri, *Opere Minori,* ed. Cesare Vasoli et al. (Milano: Riccardo Ricciardi, n.d.), 1.2.19. He also sees human perfection as being the perfection of reason in Wisdom: "Convivio," 3.15.4–6, in *Opere Minori,* 1.2.473–75.

86. Augustine, "De Ordine," 2.11–18, in *PL* 32: cols.1009–17.

87. Augustine, "De Civitate Dei," 8.4.10, in *PL* 41: cols.227–35. Augustine, "De Civitate Dei," 11.25–27, in *PL* 41: cols.338–42.

88. I agree with Marcia Colish that "sign theory serves as the structural basis" of the *Confessions,* but that theory must include mathematics as describing realities accurately. It must also include events as signs revealing Wisdom. Cf. Colish, *Mirror of Language,* 17.

89. Colish's picture of Augustine's perfection as resting entirely on his learning linguistic discipline (Colish, *Mirror of Language,* 7–54) might be expanded to include the mathematical disciplines.

90. "Augustine understands that one may know a thing without knowing the word for it, that one may know the word for a thing without communicating the idea of the thing correctly, and that one may use the word for a thing to represent a fantasy or a lie rather than the thing itself" (note to the author from Karl Morrison). Cf. Colish, *Mirror of Language,* 25–26, 39; Morrison, "*I Am You,*" 177ff.; Augustine's *De Magistro* makes this argument very fully.

91. For Mani and art, see Hans-Joachim Klimkeit, *Manichaean Art and Calligraphy* (Leiden: E. J. Brill, 1982), 144ff.

92. For a brilliant account of Augustine's theory of the numerical disciplines and the mystical ascent and contemporary analogous theories, see Augustine, *Confessions,* ed. O'Donnell, 2.269–78.

93. Radding, *A World Made by Men,* 47.

94. Contrast the point made by Flores, *Rhetoric of Doubtful Authority,* 49.

95. Augustine, *Confessions,* ed. O'Donnell, 2.450 (on "laudandum te ostendunt"). For useful suggestions on the structure of the *Confessions,* see McMahon, *Augustine's Prayerful Ascent,* 137–38.

96. O'Connell's demonstration, in his *St. Augustine's Confessions* (Cambridge MA: Belknap Press, 1969), of Augustine's indebtedness to Neoplatonism for his conception of his own life history influenced this section greatly.

97. The Ostia experience represents Augustinian illumination. The mind sees

divine ideas contained in the Logos or divine intelligence and goes beyond them to the eternal Wisdom; cf. Bruce Bubacz, *St. Augustine's Theory of Knowledge: A Contemporary Analysis* (New York: Edwin Mellen, 1981), 133–55. For the relation of this kind of experience to Augustine's understanding of language's limitations in relation to things and the realities experienced at Ostia, see Margaret W. Ferguson, "St. Augustine's Region of Unlikeness: The Crossing of Exile and Language," *Georgia Review* 29 (1975): 842–64.

98. For Augustine's sense of the beauty and holiness of creation, see Henry Chadwick, *Augustine* (Oxford: Oxford UP, 1986), 30–37 and passim. For this and Neoplatonism, see John J. O'Meara, "The Neoplatonism of Saint Augustine," in *Neoplatonism and Christian Thought,* ed. John J. O'Meara (Albany: State U of New York P, 1982), 34–41. Flores's argument (*Rhetoric of Doubtful Authority,* 44–65) that the *Confessions* solves the problems of the relationship between time and eternity, old and new self, delusion and authority through an appeal to a vanishing chain of allegory does not deal with the work's progressively unfolding interest in Wisdom and in the relationship of Wisdom to number and the natural order.

99. Augustine's references to memory as organizing the scattered and arranging it (e.g., perceiving that *cogitare* comes from *cogo*) suggests the organizing of a file or oration or book; Dante picks up on this in speaking of the book of his memory in *La Vita Nuova. Cogo* especially is used for collecting or rolling up a book. For a useful interpretation of the uses of memory in relation to the knowledge of God, see Colish, *Mirror of Language,* 35–46.

100. Cf. O'Daly, *Augustine's Philosophy of Mind,* 131ff., 199ff.; Robert J. O'Connell, *St. Augustine's Early Theory of Man* (Cambridge MA: Belknap, 1968), 191–92. Cf. "Epistola 7," in *PL* 33: cols.68–71. For a fuller discussion of Augustinian memory and epistemology, see Bubacz, *St. Augustine's Theory of Knowledge,* 61–89.

101. Karl Morrison, letter to author, 9 Dec. 1991; cf. Morrison, "*I Am You,*" 74–75.

4 READING THE *CONFESSIONS*

1. Though this view appears in much recent feminist scholarship on Augustine, it is not the view of Peter Brown in *The Body and Society,* 386–427.

2. This chapter is indebted throughout to Pierre Courcelle, *Les Confessions de Saint Augustin dans la tradition littéraire: Antécédents et Postérité* (Paris: Études Augustiniennes, 1963), 201–351 and passim.

3. I do not treat one other candidate for this chapter, Guibert of Nogent's *Monodiae,* a superficial imitation of Augustine's plot that wholly misses his meaning and substitutes a pinwheel of miracles for an ascent through the orderly universe and its beauty. Cf. John F. Benton, "Consciousness of Self and Perceptions of Individuality," *Renaissance and Renewal in the Twelfth Century,* ed. Robert L.

Benson and Giles Constable with Carol D. Lanham (Cambridge: Harvard UP, 1982), 263–95. Cf. Guibert of Nogent, *Autobiographie*, ed. with translation by Edmond-René Lebande (Paris: Les Belles Lettres, 1981). Guibert often echoes Augustine without understanding.

4. For a useful contrasting discussion, see Jonathan Culler, *On Deconstruction: Theory and Criticism after Structuralism* (London: Routledge & Kegan Paul, 1987), 64–83.

5. This seems to me implicit in Bloom's understanding of the uses of intertextuality; Flores seems to avoid this problem, speaking as he does of Augustine's writing "referentially" and of the doubling process as a biographical rather than a fictive process. Flores, *Rhetoric of Doubtful Authority*, 53, 63.

6. Edmund Reiss argues that Boethius knew the *Confessions*. Edmund Reiss, *Boethius* (Boston: Twayne, 1982), 88–93; Seth Lerer relates the work more to *De Magistro* than to the later *Confessions:* Seth Lerer, *Boethius and Dialogue: Literary Method in The Consolation of Philosophy* (Princeton: Princeton UP, 1985), 46–56, 233–39. The light-surrounded figure of Continence who comes to Augustine in the "Tolle, lege" scene may be one basis of Boethius's Philosophy; Anna Crable, "Literary Design in the *De Consolatione Philosophiae*," in Margaret T. Gibson, *Boethius, His Life, Thought, and Influence* (Oxford: Blackwell, 1981), 254.

7. Petrarch recognizes that Boethius's life-story in the *Consolation* is a variant of the *Confessions* plot when he introduces into the *Secretum*, as his own instructor, a Truth who is like Lady Philosophy. She calls on the Augustine of the conversion scene of the *Confessions* to educate the Petrarch persona in the work.

8. The fact that Augustine is a bishop at the time of the writing of the *Confessions* and Boethius is a former bureaucrat in a temporal government makes little difference for this argument.

9. All quotations and citations from *De Consolatione* are from Boethius, *Theological Tractates*, trans. H. F. Stewart and E. K. Rand (New York: G. P. Putnam's Sons, 1918).

10. One translation of Aelred suggests that the inappropriate loves which Aelred sought were not Augustine's Lady Folly or Guibert's Ovidian poems but homophile attachments; Aelred of Rievaulx, *Spiritual Friendship*, trans. Mary E. Laker (Kalamazoo: Cistercian Publications, 1977), 21; cf. Aelred of Rievaulx, "De Spirituali Amicitia," in PL 195: col.659. Cf. John Boswell, *Christianity, Social Tolerance and Homosexuality* (Chicago: U of Chicago P, 1980), 221–26. For the analogous passages in Augustine that concern desiring nothing more than to love and be loved, see *Confessions*, 2.2 and 3.1.

11. Walter Daniel describes Aelred as "hav(ing) in his hands the *Confessions* of Augustine." Powicke adds that it "is not surprising that his own autobiography is a kind of *Confessions*." Walter Daniel, *The Life of Ailred of Rievaulx*, trans. F. M.

Powicke (London: Thomas Nelson, 1963), 49, lxv–lxviii; cf. Pierre Courcelle, "Ailred de Rievaulx à l'école des 'Confessions,' " *Revue des Études Augustiniennes* 3 (1957): 163–74.

12. Aelred of Rievaulx, "De Spirituali Amicitia," in PL 195: col.667.

13. Aelred of Rievaulx, "De Spirituali Amicitia," in PL 195: cols.679–702.

14. For a bibliography of recent accounts of Dante and Augustine, see Peter S. Hawkins, "Divide and Conquer: Augustine in the *Divine Comedy*," PMLA 106 (1991): 471–83. Hawkins's view of Dante's use of Augustine some of the time as a foil parallels my view in chapter 7.

15. John Freccero, *Dante: the Poetics of Conversion* (Cambridge: Harvard UP, 1986), 2ff.

16. Text of the *Commedia* is from *The Divine Comedy*, ed. and trans. Charles S. Singleton (Princeton: Princeton UP, 1970–75). Generally I make my own translations – under the influence of Singleton.

17. Freccero also uses a *Confessions* analogy when he argues that Dante enters the Inferno as if he were Augustine coming into the "region of unlikeness" described in *Confessions* 7.10. Cf. Ferguson, "Saint Augustine's Region of Unlikeness," 842–64. Cf. Freccero, *Dante: The Poetics of Conversion*, 11ff.

18. For an account of the staging of Augustine's perfective progress that parallels Dante's analysis of him, see Anton C. Pegis, "The Second Conversion of St. Augustine," *Gesellschaft, Kultur, Literatur*, ed. Karl Bosl (Stuttgart: Hiersemann, 1975), 79–95.

19. Cf. Sara Sturm-Maddox, *Petrarch's Metamorphoses: Text and Subtext in the Rime Sparse* (Columbia MO: U of Missouri P, 1985), 95–126.

20. " 'Et quando istuc erit? Amicus autem dei si volvero, ecce nunc fio.' . . . [E]t turbidis parturitione novae vitae, reddidit oculos paginis . . . et exuebatur mundo mens ejus." Augustine, "Confessiones," in PL 32: col.756.

21. Dante Alighieri, *La Vita Nuova*, ed. Tommaso Casini and Luigi Pietrobono (Firenze: Sansoni, 1968), 113.

22. Dante, *La Vita Nuova*, 9.

23. Dante, *La Vita Nuova*, 30–31, 138–42. Since the thought soars above the intellect's realm ("lo nostro intelletto") to achieve the "intelligenza nova," it enters the realm of the intellectibles, the pure Forms that are the subject of theology. Beatrice or Beatitude may become such a being. Boethius's commentary on Porphyry's *Isagoge* is the best introduction to the concept of the intellectible world. Cf. *Porphyrii Isagoge translatio Boethii*, ed. Laurentius Minio-Paluello and B. G. Dod (Bruges: De Brouwer, 1966), 1–31.

24. Augustine's acquaintances mention his relationship with Monica prominently and in terms that parallel Augustine's; but Dante's autobiography is so stylized that even his son, Pietro, in encountering the Beatrice experience in the

Purgatorio, says nothing of the "real woman" whom Dante putatively knew but only refers to symbolically.

25. Dante, *La Vita Nuova,* 7.

26. Dante Alighieri, *The Divine Comedy,* trans. John D. Sinclair (New York: Oxford UP, 1961), 400. Pietro and other medieval commentators on Dante call Beatrice the *theos logos.* Dante, in searching for a guide or Word, reads the *New Life* from his book of memory in the same way that Augustine, in book 10 of the *Confessions,* speaks of his thought as assembling the scattered items of memory to make an orderly file of remembrance (10.11).

27. As the *Vita Nuova* progresses, Beatrice increasingly represents beatitude as a kind of similitude to the Logos/Christ in history – a "Wisdom and number," a three-times-three preceded as she is by Primavera-Giovanna as Christ is preceded by John the Baptist, a reflection of the One where history begins rather than simply a creature of history, the source of Wisdom and number for whom the poet went in search as "Solomon" in Wisdom 8.1 went in search of Wisdom. Dante, *La Vita Nuova,* 7 and note 8, and 86–87 and notes. The highest human faculty, the intellect, pilgrimages to Beatrice in eternity in sections 41–42. Augustine explains such a pilgrimage in the *Confessions* when he says that the memory of the beatific life is not the memory of a "Carthage," since the beatific life is not a "body" perceptible to the human body, and not a memory of number alone – presumably the number that orders creation – but rather a memory engraved as desired and loved by all people because reflective of the ultimate source of good: "And this is the beatific life – to rejoice in you, through you, on account of you: it is there and nowhere else." (10.22): Augustine, "Confessiones" 10.22, in PL 32: col.793.

28. Augustine, "Confessiones" 3.11, in PL 32: cols.691–92.

29. Dante, *La Vita Nuova,* 32–34.

30. Leo C. Ferrari, "Monica on the Wooden Ruler," *Augustinian Studies* 6 (1975): 193–205, associates the ruler with measuring and with the *regula* of perfection but not with Augustine's emphasis on the number that governs the cosmos. Benvenuto, interpreting the "Donne ch'avete intelleto d'amore" from *La Vita Nuova* as concerned with "materia amoris," also explains that Dante's reference, in *Purgatorio* 24.52–54, to love's breathing in him, his listening and following his direction, should be understood to refer to lascivious love, not to divine grace as some have argued. Benvenuto on *Purgatorio* 24.52–54, in Dartmouth Dante Project.

31. Only in the "intelligenza nova" of the last poem of *La Vita Nuova* and the "mirabile visione" of the last prose section do we find anything comparable to the "Tolle, lege" or the Ostia experience, and Dante does not explicate it.

32. Dante, *Opere Minori,* 203.

33. Dante, *Opere Minori*, 842ff.

34. The *Convito* says that it presents Dante's autobiography seen under the aspect of a more "virile" reason. It takes the *Vita Nuova* episode of the Lady of the Window who comforts Dante after Beatrice's death and makes her the "new love" ("nuove amore": Dante, *Opere Minori*, 120ff.). The thought of Beatrice in the *Convito* is presumably a sentimental thought that made the poet long for death, and not the "new intelligence" of her described at the end of *La Vita Nuova*. Sentimental or suicidal thought appears to be opposed by the Lady at the Window.

35. Dante, *Opere Minori*, 201. Cf. Dante, *Opere Minori*, 205–10. In these schools and disputations, Dante gave himself over, at the rational level, to Wisdom studies. As Dante relates in treatise 3, Wisdom studies are analogous to those that Augustine undertakes in Cicero – not studies in this or that philosophical school but in Wisdom itself ("non illam aut illam sectam sed ipsam . . . [S]apientiam"). Augustine, "Confessiones" 3.4, in PL 32: cols.685–86; Augustine, "Confessiones" 7.10–21, in PL 32: cols.742–48; Augustine, "Confessiones" 7.9, in PL 32: cols. 740–42. Such studies come before the new life for both Augustine and Dante.

36. Dante's study of Cicero on friendship is also Augustinian; cf. John F. Monagle, "Friendship in St. Augustine's Biography," *Augustinian Studies* 2 (1971): 81–93.

37. The *Commedia* restates the significance of the life imitating Augustine's in which the writer uses his own name, but it transcends the *Convito* by including incarnational theology, an explicit account of the details of the creation as a partial revelation of God, and the complete revelation of the beatific vision. Francis X. Newman, "St. Augustine's Three Visions and the Structure of the *Commedia*," *MLN* 82 (1967): 56–78.

38. Augustine "Confessiones" 1.5, in PL 32: col.663.

39. Architecture in classical and medieval culture depends on mathematics; cf. Vitruvius, *The Ten Books on Architecture,* trans. Morris Hicky Morgan (New York: Dover Publications, 1960), 5–13; Otto von Simson, *The Gothic Cathedral* (Princeton: Princeton UP, 1974), 20–58.

40. Since Virgil's afterworld offers no similar emphasis on the ordering of architectural structures to signal educational and spiritual growth, the Augustinian context, given the echo in *Inferno* 1.61, must shape Dante's vision. Dante's furies probably come from Alypius's fury; Robert Hollander, *Allegory in Dante's Commedia* (Princeton: Princeton UP, 1969), 239–43. Here the referenced text is used straightforwardly. However, sometimes it is used ironically (e.g., when Augustine's "reading no further" to worship God after the *sortes* experience becomes Francesca's reading no further to worship Paolo); see Hollander, *Allegory in Dante's Commedia*, 112–13.

41. In the *Commedia,* as in the *Confessions,* a death becomes the turning point in the protagonist's movement from ruin to orderly architecture. For additional parallelism between Dante and Augustine, see Jesse M. Gellrich, *The Idea of the Book in the Middle Ages: Language Theory, Mythology, and Fiction* (Ithaca: Cornell UP, 1985), 152ff.; Robert Hollander, *Allegory in Dante's Commedia,* 11, 165, 179, 235; Giuseppe Mazzotta, *Dante, Poet of the Desert: History and Allegory in the Divine Comedy* (Princeton: Princeton UP, 1979), 164–80 and passim. The fourteenth-century commentators see the *Confessions* as a frequent referent in the *Commedia:* cf. Guido da Pisa on *Inferno* 8.19, 5.37, 4.134. Pietro explains the "aspra e forte" of *Inferno* 1.5 using Augustine's *Confessions* statement that he was bound not with the iron placed on him by others but by the iron of his own will. Cf. Pietro on *Purgatorio* 22.67–72, *Paradiso* 10.1–6, 16.73–75. Cf. Benvenuto on *Purgatorio* 2.118–23. Many other references to the *Confessions* appear in fourteenth-century Dante commentary. Citations from Dartmouth Dante Project files.

42. As Dante takes the title for *La Vita Nuova* from *Confessions* 8.6, Petrarch takes his for the *Secretum* from *Confessions* 8.8; this parallelism is not, I think, accidental despite Petrarch's general coolness toward Dante. Cf. Aldo S. Bernardo, "Petrarch's Attitude Toward Dante," *PMLA* 70 (1955): 488–517. The source passage is as follows: "Abscessi ergo in hortum, et Alypius pedem post pedem. Neque enim secretum meum non erat, ubi ille aderat" ("I went away into the garden, and Alypius followed after me step for step, nor was my solitude [*secretum*] lacking when he was present"). Augustine, "Confessiones" 9.1, in *PL* 32: col.763; Augustine, "Confessiones" 8.8, in *PL* 32: cols.757–58. For a useful discussion of the structure of the *Secretum,* see Charles Trinkaus, *The Poet as Philosopher* (New Haven: Yale UP, 1979), 52–89; Trinkaus also sets forth a useful picture of Petrarch's conception of philosophy, but it is one which ignores the idea of the love of Wisdom in the biblical sense.

43. Contrast the position of this chapter with that of Albert Rabil Jr., "Petrarch, Augustine, and the Classical Christian Tradition," *Renaissance Humanism: Foundations, Forms, and Legacy,* ed. Albert Rabil Jr. (Philadelphia: U of Pennsylvania P, 1988), 1.95–114.

44. Augustine, "Confessiones," 8.12, in *PL* 32: cols.761–64.

45. "Tuque ideo, libelle, conventus hominum fugiens, mecum mansisse contentus eris, nominis proprii non immemor. *Secretum* enim *meum* es et diceris": Francesco Petrarca, *Prose,* ed. Enrico Carrara (Milano: Riccardo Ricciardi, n.d.), 26. All quotations and citations come from this edition. I confine to the *Secretum* my analysis of the *Confessions* as "imprinting" subtexts on Petrarch; for a good analysis of similar issues in the *Rime,* see Sturm-Maddox, *Petrarch's Metamorphoses: Text and Subtext,* 95–126.

46. My argument in this section is indebted to Robert M. Durling, "The Ascent

of Mt. Ventoux and the Crisis of Allegory," *Italian Quarterly* 18 (1974): 17–22. However, the reader will also observe my differences with Durling. For a useful analysis of Ventoux, see also Marjorie O'Rourke Boyle, *Petrarch's Genius: Petimento and Prophecy* (Berkeley: U of California P, 1991), 19. For a useful analysis of the Augustinus and Franciscus figures in relation to the *Confessions* and of the structure of the *Secretum*, see Charles Trinkaus, *In Our Image and Likeness* (Chicago: U of Chicago P, 1970), 1.3–50.

47. Augustine, "Confessiones," 8.8–11, in PL 32: cols.757–61. Petrarch, *Prose*, 28; see chapter 5 for Virgil's "homunculus" address in Fulgentius. Bernardo notes that "[a]ny real or pseudo-ancients from whom [Petrarch] had learned had become part of himself." Aldo S. Bernardo, "Petrarch, Dante and Medieval Tradition," *Renaissance Humanism: Foundations, Forms, and Legacy*, 1.119.

48. Petrarch, *Prose*, 24. Petrarch's dialogues and commentaries on classical works frequently reveal more about his views on education than do his straightforward remarks about it. See Benjamin G. Kohl, "Humanism and Education," *Renaissance Humanism: Foundations, Forms, and Legacy*, 3.10ff.

49. After the garden scene, Augustine still laments his divided will (10.30–37), and throughout his life he struggles with the meanings of scriptures. The *Secretum* comes even before the "Tolle, lege" and Romans 13.13 experiences, and in *Confessions* 8.7, just before the *secretum* scene, Augustine still holds himself responsible for having failed to "read" the *Hortensius* correctly and for failing to pursue Wisdom fully nineteen years before the *secretum* scene. Augustine, "Confessiones," 8.7, in PL 32: cols.756–57. After the experience of Romans 13.13, he continues to admit the possibility of wrong readings later, in *De Doctrina Christiana* and the *Retractions*. For Augustine's general understanding of the problem of misunderstanding scripture, see Augustine, *On Christian Doctrine*, 30–33 and xi. Augustine points out frequent misreadings of scripture that he constructed after the *Confessions* (e.g., *Retractiones*, 2.7, in PL 32: cols.632–33; 2.15, in PL 32: cols. 635–36; 2.18, in PL 32: cols.637–38 and so forth). Augustinus should not, in any case, be expected to inspire a definitive reading of anything in the *secretum* since the "secretum" scene comes before his encounter with Romans 13.13. For a contrasting view, see Victoria Kahn, "The Figure of the Reader in Petrarch's *Secretum*," PMLA 100 (1985): 154–55.

50. Augustine, "Confessiones," 8.8, in PL 32: col.758 ("Nam non solum ire, verum etiam pervenire illuc nihil erat aliud quam velle ire, sed velle fortiter et integre").

51. Augustine, "Confessiones," 8.8–11, in PL 32: cols.757–61.

52. Petrarch, *Secretum*, 36.

53. Petrarch, *Prose*, 40.

54. Petrarch, *Secretum*, 42.

55. For Petrarch's final willing to achieve "perfection," cf. Hans Baron, *Petrarch's "Secretum": Its Making and its Meaning* (Cambridge: Medieval Academy of America, 1985), 20–248.

56. Dialogue 2 moves to Petrarch's purgatory, where Augustinus, in a confessional mode, probes Franciscus's immersion in the seven deadly sins, especially lust, avarice, pride in eloquence and appearance, the love of city comforts and honors, and idle incapacity to achieve spiritual discipline, Franciscus's greatest fault in dialogue 1. Augustinus's confessional ministrations now direct Franciscus's love away from the temporal, and dialogue 3 relates the direction of Franciscus's love, the concern of dialogue 2, to the direction of his learning, the concern of dialogue 1.

57. Petrarch, *Prose,* 136.

58. Petrarch, *Prose,* 146, 148.

59. "[M]edio sub adolescentie fervore" – "in the middle of adolescent heat": Petrarch, *Prose,* 152. More recently, plague has turned Petrarch to the icon of Laura's face as he finds that face reflected in the Simone Martini painting of her that he carries. And ambition has turned him to her when he merges her image with the image of the poetic laurel that is granted by the empire. Petrarch, *Prose,* 156–58.

60. Petrarch, *Prose,* 200ff. Of course, the Augustinus who can quote from Petrarch's *Africa* represents what Augustinus has always been in the *Secretum,* the Augustinus within Petrarch, the Petrarch partially recreated by reading the *Confessions* and other Augustine, an Augustinus that demythologizes Laura and reduces the aura of the poetic laurel that signifies service to the imperial city. At the same time, this Augustinus reminds Franciscus that true fame is the shadow of a virtue that flows from the One to whom Franciscus sails as Aeneas sailed to Rome. Petrarch, *Prose,* 204.

61. Augustinus warns Franciscus not to make sweet songs for others that he cannot listen to himself, a warning that parallels Augustine's warning to himself about reading Dido (Petrarch, *Secretum,* 212). With a touch of the Petrarchan irony typical of the *secretum* position, Franciscus responds to Augustinus that he has to get back to important practical business, expressing once more his impotency (Petrarch, *Prose,* 214); he ends with what appears to be another anticipation of his own version of "Tolle, lege" and Ostia – the hope that his mind's waves will be stilled and that the world will be silent in it (Petrarch, *Prose,* 214). Cf. Jerrold E. Siegel, *Rhetoric and Philosophy in Renaissance Humanism* (Princeton: Princeton UP, 1968), 3–98. For a useful analysis of the *Secretum* with which I do not wholly agree, see O'Rourke Boyle, *Petrarch's Genius,* 15–19.

62. Ehrenfeld, *The Arrogance of Humanism,* 269.

5 The Heroic Educational Journey

1. I disagree with Lamberton's use of Bloom's notion of "strong misreading" in his account of the allegorization of the epic in the ancient world, though I owe much to Lamberton in other portions of my argument; Lamberton, *Homer the Theologian,* esp. 145, 298.

2. For a critique of the idea of private languages that employs Wittgenstein's analysis of this area, see Patricia H. Werhane, *Skepticism, Rules, and Private Languages* (Atlantic Highlands NJ: Humanities Press, 1992), esp. 187–90.

3. Lamberton, *Homer the Theologian,* illustrates both the truth and the limitations of this idea.

4. Jacques Derrida, "Living on: *Border Lines,*" *Deconstruction and Criticism,* ed. Harold Bloom (New York: Seabury Press, 1979), 85; cf. G. A. Phillips, "Sign/Text/Différance," *Intertextuality,* ed. Heinrich F. Plett (New York: De Gruyter, 1991), 90–91.

5. W. J. T. Mitchell, *Iconology: Image, Text, Ideology* (Chicago: U of Chicago P, 1986), 160–208; cf. Lee Patterson, *Negotiating the Past* (Madison: U of Wisconsin P, 1987).

6. For a summary of this position as it appears in T. S. Eliot, see Spanos, *The End of Education,* 114–17 and 226, n.31.

7. Riché, *Education and Culture in the Barbarian West: Sixth Through Eighth Centuries.*

8. Radding's *A World Made by Men, Cognition and Society, 400–1200* assumes that medieval culture as a whole goes through Piagetian cognitive stages as it develops, and that it begins in an infantile state. However, Boethius and later educators clearly recognize, as do modern educators, that the developing human person goes through differing cognitive stages, the later stages involving the equivalent of formal operations, especially in the study and application of mathematics.

9. Lamberton, *Homer the Theologian,* 259. For useful background information, see also Pierre and Jeanne Courcelle, *Lecteurs paiens et Lecteurs Chrétiens de l'Eneide,* 2 vols. (Paris: Institute de France, 1984); Domenico Comparetti, *Virgilio nel Medio Evo,* 2 vols. (Firenze: La Nuova Italia, 1955).

10. Macrobius, *The Saturnalia,* trans. Percival Vaughan Davies (New York: Columbia UP, 1969), 9. The *Saturnalia* has been redated to ca. A.D. 430 by Alan Cameron, "The Date and Identity of Macrobius," *Journal of Roman Studies* 56 (1966): 25–38. Cf. Lamberton, *Homer the Theologian,* 263, n.119.

11. Harold Bloom, *Agon: Towards a Theory of Revisionism* (New York: Oxford UP, 1982), 16ff.

12. Olson, *The Canterbury Tales and the Good Society,* 17–18.

13. Cf. Servius, *Commentarii in Vergilii Carmina,* ed. George Thilo and Hermann

Hagen, 3 vols. in 4 (Leipzig: Teubner, 1881–1902), 3.1.3–4. Cf. Comparetti, *Virgilio*, 1.144.

14. Servius, *Commentarii in Vergilii Carmina;* J. W. Jones Jr., "Allegorical Interpretation in Servius," *Classical Journal* 56 (1960–61): 217–26.

15. Jones, "Allegorical Interpretation," 220–21.

16. Fulgentius, *Opera*, ed. Rudolf Helm (Leipzig: Teubner, 1898), 83–107.

17. Fulgentius, *Opera*, 89–90 and passim.

18. In spite of Ariès's assertions to the contrary, medieval thinkers did understand childhood and adolescence as separate stages, and adolescence was made to correspond to Aeneas's stay at Carthage.

19. Fulgentius, *Opera*, 90–102.

20. Fulgentius, *Opera*, 86.

21. Macrobius, *Les Saturnales*, ed. and trans. by Henri Bornecque and François Richard, 2 vols. (Paris: Garnier Frères, 1937), 2.46–52.

22. Though some of the early copies of Fulgentius attribute his interpretation to the influence of the Christian Neoplatonist, Chalcidius, no Chalcidian commentary on Homer or Virgil remains.

23. Heraclitus the Rhetorician, *Allegories d'Homère*, ed. and trans. Félix Buffière (Paris: Les Belles Lettres, 1962), 61–63, 67–68, 75–82; Jaeger, *Paideia: The Ideals of Greek Culture*, 1.34–54; Lamberton, *Homer the Theologian*, 115–32, 318–24.

24. Eustathius, *Commentarii ad Homeri Odysseam*, 2 vols. in 1 (Leipzig: J. A. G. Weigel, 1825–26), 1.17–19.

25. Robert Lamberton has pointed out to me that *De Antro* here refers not to Ithaca, a small island, but to a place considerably inland – the region to which Tiresias in book 11 says that Odysseus must travel to placate Poseidon.

26. Joannes Stobaeus, *Eclogarum physicarum et ethicarum*, ed. August Meineke (Leipzig: Teubner, 1860–64). Citation is by section. I owe this reference and much of this section on Porphyry to Lamberton, *Homer the Theologian*, 118ff.

27. Proclus, *In Primum Euclidis elementorum Librum commentarii*, ed. G. Friedlein (Leipzig: Teubner, 1873); *Commentarius in Platonis Parmenidem*, in *Opera Inedita*, ed. V. Cousin (Hildesheim: Olms, 1961). Citations are by section in the text.

28. See *Enn.* 5.9.1.20–21, in Plotinus, *Opera*, ed. Paul Henry and Hans-Rudolf Schwyzer (Paris: Desclée, de Brouwer, 1951–73). The *Enneads* are cited by section and subsection. See also, for Circe and the return in Porphyry, Lamberton, *Homer the Theologian*, 115–32.

29. At the beginning Philosophy wipes away Boethius's tears as Athena removes the mists from Diomedes's eyes in the *Iliad*.

30. Proclus sees Calypso as the *phantasia* and Hermes, who liberates Odysseus from her, as geometry leading the mind upward to the Nous (Proclus, *In Euc.* 54–55).

31. For Athena as divine Wisdom (which is the end of Philo-sophia), see Buffière, *Les Mythes d'Homère*, 282, 458. For Penelope as Philosophy in Eustathius, see Buffière, *Les Mythes d'Homère*, 96. In encouraging Boethius to return to his true home in 1.pr.5, Philosophy acts the role of Hermes who, together with his staff, may be identified with the Logos-within in several classical commentators; see Buffière, *Les Mythes d'Homère*, 289–96. Philosophia as philo-sophia is also philo-Logos. Ann Astell's useful discussion of Boethius and epic appeared too late for me to use it; cf. *Job, Boethius and Epic Truth* (Ithaca: Cornell UP, 1994), 41–69.

32. Eustathius, *Commentarii ad Homeri Odysseam*, 1.86.

33. Athena, in Cornutus's interpretation of Homer, is the mind of God and anticipates Boethius's Philosophy, as theology/metaphysics, what she becomes when she changes heights, to the "above the heavens." Cf. Cornutus, *Theologiae graecae Compendium*, ed. Carl Lang (Leipzig: Teubner, 1881), 35. Cf. Buffière, *Les Mythes d'Homère*, 280–82.

34. Lamberton, *Homer the Theologian*, 115–32.

35. Eustathius, *Commentarii ad Homeri Odysseam*, 1.17.

36. Fulgentius, *Opera*, 90–93.

37. Heraclitus, *Allegories d'Homère*, 75.

38. Fulgentius, *Opera*, 93–94.

39. Heraclitus, *Allegories d'Homère*, 86.

40. Heraclitus, *Allegories d'Homère*, 75–79; Heraclitus (pseudo), "De incredibilibus," in *Mythographi graeci*, ed. Nicola Festa (Leipzig: Teubner, 1902), section 16.

41. Eustathius, *Commentarii ad Homeri Odysseam*, 1.17.

42. Heraclitus, *Allegories d'Homère*, 77–80; Buffière (*Les Mythes d'Homère*, 292) quotes a similar interpretation in Cléanthes cited by Apollonius Sophista.

43. Buffière, *Les Mythes d'Homère*, 357.

44. Fulgentius, *Opera*, 95.

45. Eustathius, *Commentarii ad Homeri Odysseam*, 1.436; Buffière, *Les Mythes d'Homère*, 485–89.

46. Fulgentius, *Opera*, 95–103.

47. Fulgentius, *Opera*, 103–7.

48. Winthrop Wetherbee, *Platonism and Poetry in The Twelfth Century; the Literary Influence of the School of Chartres* (Princeton: Princeton UP, 1972), 267. Bernard's argument may suggest that I should have included Martianus in this analysis. However, though Martianus's work contains many of the themes that characterize works treated in this volume (i.e, the contemplative use of number, the importance of Wisdom or Phronesis, and the significance of the mathematical disciplines), it does not convey much sense of rehearsing an idea of individual development or indicating the limitations of conventional culture. Richard Johnson calls him the last exponent of " 'the religion of culture' "; cf. Johnson, "The

Allegory and the Trivium," in *Martianus Capella and the Seven Liberal Arts*, written with William Harris Stahl, 2 vols. (New York: Columbia UP, 1971), 1.88.

49. Bernard Silvestris, *Commentum super sex libros Eneidos Virgilii*, ed. Julian and Elizabeth Jones (Lincoln: U of Nebraska P, 1977), 3.

50. Bernard Silvestris, *Commentum*, 4–14.

51. Bernard Silvestris, *Commentum*, 14–15.

52. Bernard Silvestris, *Commentum*, 15–23.

53. Bernard Silvestris, *Commentum*, 24–25.

54. Radding, in *A World Made by Men* (247), sees Bernard Silvestris as assuming the existence of a natural law not assumed by patristic writers; however, Bernard's assumptions in this area are not different from those of Augustine and Boethius, and he generally accepts their sense of psychological development.

55. Bernard Silvestris, *Commentum*, 25–28.

56. Bernard Silvestris, *Commentum*, 28ff.

57. Bernard Silvestris, *Commentum*, 31.

58. Bernard Silvestris, *Commentum*, 31–35.

59. Bernard Silvestris, *Commentum*, 35–36.

60. Bernard Silvestris, *Commentum*, 43–44.

61. Bernard Silvestris, *Commentum*, 40.

62. Bernard Silvestris, *Commentum*, 40–41.

63. Bernard Silvestris, *Commentum*, 43–44.

64. Bernard Silvestris, *Commentum*, 52. The Pauline emptying that derives from suffering also appears in Hades (e.g., Charon carries Aeneas through Acheron because suffering is useful to learning to abandon vice). Bernard Silvestris, *Commentum*, 114.

65. Bernard Silvestris, *Commentum*, 114.

66. Only the Cracow manuscript goes beyond book 6, line 636. John of Salisbury's short account of the *Aeneid*, manifestly related to Bernard's and Fulgentius's, tells how Aeneas's journey moves the soul from childhood to death, from slavery to sensuality (Dido) to free beatitude. John follows Bernard Silvestris rather closely, but is less explicit than is Bernard Silvestris about the need for the quadrivium disciplines. His Aeneas's journey, like that of his Ulysses, goes through luxury and moral weakness to surmount bad fortune and come home to philosophy – the beatitude which dwells in the love of Wisdom (*Pol.* 7.9; 8.24). Cf. C. C. I. Webb, ed., *Ioannis Saresberiensis Episcopi Carnotensis Policratici* (Oxford: Oxford UP, 1909), cited by section in the text. Otto von Simson describes the probable relationship of John of Salisbury, as Bishop of Chartres, to the building of the cathedral with its tribute to Wisdom and number; Otto von Simson, *The Gothic Cathedral: Origins of Gothic Architecture and the Medieval Concept of Order* (Princeton: Princeton UP, 1984), 106, 189–92, 200, 206–7. Cf. Seth Lerer, "John of Salisbury's Virgil," *Vivarium* 20 (1982): 24–39.

67. Bernard Silvestris, *Cosmographia*, ed. Peter Dronke (Leiden: E. J. Brill, 1978), 97–120.

68. For further discussions of this topic, see Theodore Silverstein, "The Fabulous Cosmogony of Bernardus Silvestris," *MP* 46 (1947–49): 107–12, and Winthrop Wetherbee (ed. and trans.), *The Cosmographia of Bernardus Silvestris* (New York: Columbia UP, 1973), 39. Bernard may have avoided equating Nous with the second person of the Trinity partly to avoid subordinationist implications.

69. Bernard Silvestris, *Cosmographia*, 121–55.

70. Cf. Paul A. Olson, "The Dartmouth Dante Project," *Envoi* 3 (1991): 33–39.

71. Dante Alighieri, *Convivio* (Alpignano, Italy: A. Tallone, 1965), 241, 248ff. Citations in text are to treatise, chapter, and section in the Wicksteed translation.

72. I gather this from the Dartmouth Dante Project files.

73. Francesco da Buti says the time of the middle of the journey of this life is thirty-five years, or after childhood and adolescence have passed and the person has fallen into concupiscent ways. Francesco da Buti, *Commento sopra la Divina Comedia*, ed. Crescentino Giannini, 3 vols. (Pisa: Fratelli Nistri, 1858–62), 1.23–24. The *Ottimo Commento* also says thirty-five years (when people can leave vice); *L'ottimo commento della Divina Commedia*, 3 vols. (Pisa: Capurro, 1827–29), 1.5; cf. *Commento d'Anonimo Fiorentino*, ed. Pietro Fantani (Bologna: G. Romagnoli, 1866–74), 1.12.

74. The poet's scheme has been traced to Fulgentius (A. Pagliaro, "Simbolo e allegoria nella Divina Commedia," *L'Alighieri* 4 [1963]: 3–35). The commentaries used in the middle ages all, save for Servius, make the journey travel through the ages. For disapproval of Servius, see Benvenuto da Imola, *Comentum super Dantis Aldigherij Comoediam*, ed. W. W. Vernon, 5 vols. (Firenze: G. Barbèra, 1887), 1.48. Hereinafter cited as Benvenuto.

75. F. X. Newman argues, correctly I believe, that the *Inferno* represents the *visio corporalis*, the *Purgatorio* the *visio imaginativa*, and the *Paradiso* the *visio intellectualis* from Augustine's *De Genesi ad litteram*. Cf. Newman, "St. Augustine's Three Visions," 56–78. Natural philosophy (or physics) was thought to be the product of the senses (or the *visio corporalis*), mathematical knowledge of the imagination (or *visio imaginativa*) because mathematics abstracts forms from bodies, and theology of the intellect or *visio intellectualis* because theology is a system-building science reducing multiplicity to unity (Thomas Aquinas, *The Division and Methods of the Sciences*, trans. Armand Maurer [Toronto: Pontifical Institute of Medieval Studies, 1986], 58–87). This three-fold scheme of cognition dictates the guides used in the *Commedia*.

76. Obviously also the Boethian cognitive ascent.

77. Fulgentius, *Opera*, 98–99. For evidence concerning the kind of commentary on Virgil that Dante must have used, see Gian Carlo Alessio and Claudia Villa,

"Per Inferno I, 67–87," in *Vestigia: Studi in Onore Giuseppe Billanovich,* ed. Rino Avesani et al. (Rome: Storia e Letteratura, 1984), 1–21. See also Gian Carlo Alessio, "L'allegoria nei trattati di grammatica e di retorica," in *Dante e le Forme dell'Allegoresi,* ed. Michelangelo Picone (Ravenna: Longo, 1987), 21–41.

78. Fulgentius, *Opera,* 100.

79. Fulgentius, *Opera,* 100.

80. Fulgentius, *Opera,* 100–101.

81. Bernard Silvestris, *Commentum,* 107.

82. Bernard Silvestris, *Commentum,* 87.

83. Bernard Silvestris, *Commentum,* 107.

84. Bernard Silvestris, *Commentum,* 106–7.

85. Bernard Silvestris, *Commentum,* 80, 108. In addition, Bernard Silvestris makes Minos "wisdom" in his role as the judge of ethical conduct; Pluto is the earth. Bernard Silvestris, *Commentum,* 4, 59, 92.

86. For Charon, see Pietro Alighieri's comment on *Inferno* 3.82–87; for Minos, Pietro's comment on 5.1–6; for Cerberus, Pietro's comment on 6.13–15; for Pluto, Pietro's comment on 7.1–2; for the furies, Pietro's comment on 9.38–40 and 9.37–39; for Dis, Pietro's comment on 8.67–69; for the giants, Pietro's comment on 31.31. Further references to the Dante commentaries hereinafter drawn from Dartmouth Dante Project Database. The other fourteenth-century commentators assign much the same iconological values to these figures from the Virgilian underworld. Fulgentius is used twenty-two times by Dante's fourteenth-century critics, five times by Guido, twice by Pietro, fifteen times by Benvenuto. Servius is used only five times by the same group.

87. Benvenuto on *Inferno* 4.110. The Virgil of *Inferno* 4.110, the master of the seven liberal arts, comes from commentary on Virgil's book 6 but to Benvenuto he is not different from the historical Virgil who illumined Statius, prophesied of Christ, made Statius a Christian, and so forth (see Benvenuto on *Purgatorio* 21.82–87, 22.37–45, and 22.64–65). The Virgil who leads Aeneas into the Elysian fields under the auspices of the sibyl is, figuratively speaking, the same Virgil who leads Statius to the Theban stream and to baptism (*Purgatorio* 22.70–72; 22.88–90) and Dante to Lethe stream and Beatrice (Dartmouth Dante Project Database).

88. Pietro on *Inferno* 1.1–136 (Dartmouth Dante Project).

89. Thomas Aquinas elucidates what forms of learning this rational philosophy comprehends in his excellent explanation of Boethius's *De Trinitate.* Aquinas, *The Division and Methods of the Sciences,* 44–45, 63–74. Aquinas is generally a good guide to Pietro's disciplinary distinctions.

90. While some differences separate the Fulgentian and Bernardian interpretations, the commentary version of the sequence of guides posits in general that study leads the understanding from a contemplation of the "fragility" of

material or "earth-bound" things to a study of the theoretical sciences (Bernard Silvestris, *Commentum*, 28–30), until a "gift of the muses" can point to the all-Father from whence come the mental constructs that lead to liberation (Fulgentius, *Opera*, 95–102; Bernard Silvestris, *Commentum*, 105–6).

91. I am indebted in this and other sections concerning Petrarch to suggestions from Professor Thomas P. Roche.

92. Petrarch, *De Rebus Familiaribus*, 1.393–402.

93. Petrarch, *Opera*, 3 vols. (Basel: Sebastian Henricpetri, 1581), 2.785–90; other editions number this letter *Senilia* 4.4. Petrarch, "Secretum," *Prose*, 102–4, 122–26.

94. Surprisingly, this interpretation appears to have a less "humanistic" emphasis than Fulgentius, if, by humanism, we mean an emphasis on the active life.

95. Cf. Petrarch, *De Rebus Familiaribus*, 1.37–39. Petrarch drops the Fulgentian-Bernardian notion of Aeneas's progress through specific ages, but he has kept a less specified sense of the progress toward the divine through both learning and experience.

96. For a useful account of the fourteenth-century events that Petrarch was probably reflecting in the *Africa*, see O'Rourke Boyle, *Petrarch's Genius*, 131–46.

97. Petrarch, *De Rebus Familiaribus*, 1.165–67.

98. Petrarch, *De Rebus Familiaribus*, 1.165–67.

99. Citations from the *Africa* are from Petrarch, *Africa*, ed. Nicola Festa (Firenze: Sansoni, 1926).

100. This obviously parallels the standard interpretations of the tempest at the beginning of the *Aeneid*. Cf. *Sen.* 4.4.

101. Cf. Aldo Bernardo, *Petrarch, Scipio and the "Africa": The Birth of Humanism's Dream* (Baltimore: Johns Hopkins UP, 1962), 103–67. Much of this discussion is based on Bernardo. Nicola Festa, "Il 'Palazzo della Verita' e le lacune dell' 'Africa'," *Giornale Dantesco* 27 (1924): 97–101; cf. Festa, *Saggio sull' "Africa" del Petrarca* (Palermo: Sandron, 1926), 72. For parallel usage in Boccaccio see Victoria Kirkham, " 'Chiuse Parlare' in Boccaccio's *Teseida*," *Dante, Petrarch, Boccaccio: Studies in the Italian Trecento in Honor of Charles S. Singleton*, ed. Aldo S. Bernardo and Anthony L. Pellegrini (Binghamton NY: Center for Medieval and Early Renaissance Studies, 1983), 338–41, 50–55.

102. Festa, "Il 'Palazzo della Verita' e le lacune dell' 'Africa'," 97–101; cf. Wilfred P. Mustard, "Petrarch's *Africa*," *AJP* 42 (1921): 103; "Africa Francesci Petrarchae," ed. Francesco Corradeni in *Padova a Francesco Petrarca* (Padua: Seminario, 1874), 427.

103. Petrarch, *De Rebus Familiaribus*, 2.82–92.

104. For the memorial functions of poetry, see Petrarch, *De Rebus Familiaribus*, 1.215–18.

105. Contrast Derrida, *Of Grammatology*, 6–73.

6 BOETHIUS'S RETURN TO PLATO AND WISDOM

1. Jeffrey T. Nealon, *Double Reading: Postmodernism after Deconstruction* (Ithaca: Cornell UP, 1993), 5.

2. Nealon, *Double Reading.*

3. The classic artistic statement of this view, outside of Boethius's *Consolation of Philosophy,* is Bertolt Brecht's *Galileo.*

4. Nealon's discussion of Derrida's essay on Nelson Mandela's imprisonment and testimony concerning the force of law seems to allow for an ethical logic that bears some relationship to Boethian foundationalist conceptions of truth; cf. Nealon, *Double Reading,* 161–67.

5. Ivan Illich, *Deschooling Society* (New York: Harper & Row, 1971).

6. Riché, *Education and Culture in the Barbarian West: Sixth Through Eighth Centuries.*

7. Jean LeClercq, *The Love of Learning and the Desire for God,* trans. Catharine Misrahi (New York: Fordham UP, 1961), 3.

8. LeClercq, *Love of Learning,* 143, 152.

9. Lee Patterson, *Chaucer and the Subject of History* (Madison: U of Wisconsin P, 1991), 72–78 and passim.

10. Lerer, *Boethius and Dialogue,* 97, emphasizes that the opening scene reflects linguistic education but does not note the presence of the Sophist/philosopher controversy in the confrontation between the tragic muses and Philosophy. Cf. Lamberton, *Homer the Theologian,* 274ff.; Joachim Gruber, "Die Erscheinung der Philosophie in der *Consolatio Philosophiae* des Boethius," *Rheinisches Museum für Philologie* 112 (1969): 166–86.

11. Boethius, *In Ciceronis Topica,* trans. Eleonore Stump (Ithaca: Cornell UP, 1988), 25, 27, 49.

12. Plotinus seems to conflate Calypso and Circe in *Enneads* 1.6.8.16–21, in *Plotinus,* ed. with trans. A. H. Armstrong (Cambridge: Harvard UP, 1966), 1.256; cf. Proclus's commentary on Euclid's *Elements* cited in Lamberton, *Homer the Theologian,* 224–25; cf. Jean Pépin, "The Platonic and Christian Ulysses," in *Neoplatonism and Christian Thought,* ed. Dominic J. O'Meara (Albany: State U of New York P, 1982), 5–18. Boethius's knowledge of the Sophists may in part have come from his supposed translation of Aristotle's *Sophisti Elenchi,* for which see L. Minio-Paluello, "Les Traductions et les commentaires aristotéliciens de Boèce," in *Studia Patristica* ("Texte und Untersuchungen zur Geschichte der altchristlichen Literatur," 64) (Berlin: De Gruyter, 1957), 22.358–67. For Boethius's later use of Seneca in *De Consolatione,* see Lerer, *Boethius and Dialogue,* 237–53. For the sirens as courtesans, see Buffière, *Mythes d'Homère,* 384.

13. Professor Thomas P. Roche has called my attention to the fact that Plato places the sirens on the various heavenly spheres (*Republic* 10.617b), and that

Macrobius replaces the sirens with the muses, thus lifting the muses up to the heavens and implicitly identifying them with the sirens. However, Boethius's siren muses have nothing to do with the heavens to which only Philosophy can ascend.

14. Riché, *Education and Culture*, 58.

15. Theoderic's empire, as Riché has shown, allowed Roman elementary education in reading and writing to remain intact. The urban centers, such as Ravenna and Rome, encouraged people to attend school, since written documents were used in some common transactions, carrying the autographs of the interested parties and their witnesses. Riché, *Education and Culture*, 23. "[T]eachers of grammar, rhetoric, and law were listed in the public budget [for the city of Rome] under Theoderic." Riché, *Education and Culture*, 28; cf. pp.24–25.

16. A. H. M. Jones, *The Later Roman Empire, 284–602* (Norman: U of Oklahoma P, 1964), 368ff.

17. Thomas S. Burns, *A History of the Ostrogoths* (Bloomington: Indiana UP, 1984), 66–107.

18. For a discussion of the context and charges against Boethius, see Burns, *Ostrogoths*, 101–3; Reiss, *Boethius*, 80–87; John Moorhead, *Theoderic in Italy* (Oxford: Clarendon Press, 1992), 220–51.

19. Hans Liebeschütz, *Mediaeval Humanism in the Life and Writings of John of Salisbury* (London: Warburg Institute, University of London, 1950), 50–55, 28–33.

20. For Cicero on natural law, see Neal Wood, *Cicero's Social and Political Thought* (Berkeley: U of California P, 1988), 70–89. Cicero gives a good summary of his theory in *De Re Publica,* 2.43–44 and 3.22; cf. M. Tullius Cicero, *De Re Publica,* ed. K. Ziegler (Leipzig: Teubner, 1964), 79–80, 96.

21. Ennodius, *Opera,* ed. Frederick Vogel (Berlin: Weidmann, 1885), 236, 268 (*Monumenta Germaniae Historica: Auctores Antiquissimi,* vol. 7).

22. Cf. Riché, *Education and Culture,* 24–33.

23. For Ennodius's conception of education, see Ennodius, *Opera,* 8, 18, 111–12, 154, and 225–26. Ennodius himself wrote model pleading situations for orators in a vein that goes back to the Hellenistic schools and Quintilian (Marrou, *History of Education,* 277, 282), but his work shows little understanding of the quadrivium subjects that Boethius first named as such and seems to associate arithmetic with rhetoric and philosophy with medicine (Ennodius, *Opera,* 301–2, 314).

24. For the decline of metaphysics, even in the philosophic centers of study, see Aubrey Gwynn, *Roman Education from Cicero to Quintilian* (New York: Russell & Russell, 1964), 48ff., 53ff., 72ff.

25. Cf. Riché, *Education and Culture,* 68.

26. Cassiodorus, *Variae,* ed. Theodor Mommsen (Berlin: Weidmann, 1894), 12.107 or 3.52 (*Monumenta Germaniae Historica: Auctores Antiquissimi,* vol. 12).

27. Boethius, *De Institutione Arithmetica; De Institutione Musica,* ed. Godfrey Friedlein (Leipzig: Teubner, 1867). Abbreviated as *De Inst. Arith* and *De Inst. Musica* in text.

28. Lerer, *Boethius and Dialogue,* 94–123. Though Lerer does not fully specify the disciplines involved, he sees the *gradus* as moving through the Philosophy's disciplines to book 5, where Philosophy alone speaks and the persona experiences the "philosophical silence which demands no company save the self and God" (123). The *gradus* is both the product of objective study and Wisdom revealed through the objective order. Though previous commentators (Reiss, *Boethius,* 138; Lerer, *Boethius and Dialogue,* 94–123) have seen Philosophy as an internal/external figure, they have not observed how this relates to Sophia theory from Origen on. Cf. Michael Masi, "The Liberal Arts and Gerardus Ruffus's commentary on the Boethian *De Arithmetica*," *Sixteenth Century Journal* 10 (1979): 23–41.

29. I translate the Vulgate here. For summaries of the controversy concerning this verse, see Henry Chadwick, *Boethius: The Consolations of Music, Logic, Theology, and Philosophy* (Oxford: Clarendon Press, 1981), 237–38; cf. Joachim Gruber, *Kommentar zu Boethius de Consolatione Philosophiae* (New York: De Gruyter, 1978), 311; cf. Lerer, *Boethius and Dialogue,* 147–48. Cf. Chadwick's review of the Gruber work, *Journal Theological Studies* 30 (1979): 572–73. Wisdom 8.1 must be read in the context of Wisdom 7–8.

30. Boethius supports the Wisdom 7–8 view of Wisdom and Philo-Sophia in his *De Arithmetica* when he identifies Philosophy with the love of Wisdom but not in a terribly powerful definition, since the etymology of the word "philosophia" means "love of wisdom." However, his Porphyry commentary adds, after Wisdom 7–8 and Proverbs 8, that Wisdom is the fount of created things. Boethius, "In Porphyrium Dialogi," in PL 64: cols.10–11.

31. Boethius, *Theological Tractates,* 8; cf. Boethius, "In Porphyrium Dialogi," in PL 64: cols.11–12.

32. Boethius, *Theological Tractates,* 8. Thomas Aquinas's interpretations of this section of the *De Trinitate* are useful. For a summary of these, see Mark D. Jordan, *Ordering Wisdom: The Hierarchy of Philosophical Discourses in Aquinas* (Notre Dame: U of Notre Dame P, 1986), 80–83.

33. Boethius is not a secular writer. Though John of Salisbury correctly observes that the incarnate Word is not to be found in the *Consolation* (John of Salisbury, *Policraticus,* trans. Joseph B. Pike [Minneapolis: U of Minnesota P, 1938], 274), the commentaries find the preincarnate Word there. Early Christian art, like the *Consolation,* does not portray the Father directly as a person and emphasizes a "praexistente Christus-Logos" as central; Friedrich Wilhelm Deichmann, *Ravenna: Hauptstadt des Spätantiken Abendlandes: Geschichte und Monumente* (Wiesbaden:

Franz Steiner, 1969), 110. For fourteenth-century nominalism's attack on the *Consolation* for its omission of Jesus-the-man, cf. Jean Gerson, *De Consolatione Theologiae* (Leipzig: Stöckel, 1498). Cf. Boethius, *Theological Tractates*, 64–69, where Boethius appears to answer Arian and orthodox Erastian theories of kingship that depend on different conceptions of the creation's relation to God and to the ruler; cf. Rowan Williams, *Arius: Heresy and Tradition* (London: Darton, Longman, & Todd, 1987), 100–105. Arius's Logos governs the universe providentially but not manifestly as does Boethius's; cf. *Athanasius Werke*, 3.1: *Urkunden zur Geschichte des Arianischen Streites*, 69. Arius's theology does not permit one to ascend to the One and substitutes the ruler for natural temporal manifestations of God (Williams, *Arius*, 181–98 and 230); Eusebius Pamphilus, an ally of Arius, defines the emperor as a contemplative who sees the Logos and acts as the pedagogue of his commonwealth; cf. Eusebius of Caesarea, *De Laude Constantini*, 2–5, ed. I. Herkel, in *Die Griechischen Christlichen Schriftsteller der Ersten Jahrhunderte* 7 (Berlin: Akademie Verlag, 1975); cf. Arius, *Athanasius Werke*, 3.1.34; cf. Williams, *Arius*, 233–45, who compares Athanasius to Barth in the 1930s. For a general account of Theoderican Arianism, see Jacques Zeiller, "Étude sur l'arianisme en Italie à l'époque Ostrogotique et à l'époque Lombarde," in *Mélanges d'archéologie et d'histoire publiés par l'école française de Rome* 25 (1905): 127–46; cf. Frend, *The Rise of Christianity*, 131–34, 419–21, 318–24, 452–63, 534–43, and 790–815; cf. Burns, *Ostrogoths*, 151. For the possibility that Boethius was involved in a plot against Arianism, see Bark, "Theodoric vs. Boethius," 410–26.

34. Cf. Turner, "The Gnostic Threefold Path to Enlightenment: The Ascent of Mind and the Descent of Wisdom," 345. Turner cites Plotinus, Porphyry, Chalcidius, and Proclus, but the same patterns had been absorbed by Neoplatonic Christianity and writings commonly used by Christians in late antiquity: Origen, Gregory, Augustine, Macrobius, etc.

35. Joachim Gruber, "Die Erscheinung der Philosophie in der *Consolatio Philosophiae*," 166–86. Athena's "changing heights" through wing-sandalled journeys to Zeus were thought to show how Philosophy ascends to the One. Cf. Cornutus, *Theologiae Graecae*, 35; Wilhelm Dindorf, *Scholia Graeca in Homeri Odysseam* (Oxford: Oxford UP, 1855), 1.96.

36. Boethius, in his *De Trinitate*, divides speculative philosophy into physics, mathematics, and theology, and the three "heights" were so understood by the later medieval glossators. Ethics or physics or both may become Philosophy's lowest level. Philip Merlan, *From Platonism to Neoplatonism* (The Hague: Martinus Nijhoff, 1953), 53–77. The ladder from the practical (π) to the theoretical (θ) on Philosophy's garment then must figure educational stages since the theoretical sciences such as mathematics and metaphysics were thought to come after the more practical ones in the student's progress.

37. Luca Obertello, *Severino Boezio* (Genova: Accademia ligure di Scienze e Lettere, [1974]), 1.55off.; Reiss, *Boethius*, 31.

38. Obertello, *Severino Boezio*, 1.562ff. Most postmedieval scholars, including Obertello, do not identify Boethius's references to Sapientia in the *In Isagogen* as references to divine Wisdom, as represented in the Wisdom books, partly because sapientia is indistinguishable from Sapientia in Roman texts. However, the dependence on biblical Wisdom is clear.

39. Though Seth Lerer demonstrates in his recent book on Boethius the *Consolation*'s debt to the Latin dialogues of Cicero, Augustine (particularly his *De Magistro*), and Fulgentius, he does not examine Boethius's debt to the Greek Platonic and Neoplatonic dialogues where the educational *gradus* is defined. While I do not wish to contest Lerer's conclusions, I do wish to argue a primarily Greek referent for the *gradus,* one commensurate with Boethius's other appeals to the Greek side of the Greco-Roman tradition.

40. P. Hadot, "La Métaphysique de Porphyre," *Porphyre* (Geneva: Fondation Hardt, 1960), 127–29; Turner, "Gnostic Threefold Path," 345.

41. Proclus, *In Platonis Timaeum Commentaria,* ed. Ernst Diehl, 3 vols. (Amsterdam: A. M. Hakkert, 1965), 1.203–4.

42. *Republic* 7, 533E–540B, in Cornford, *The Republic of Plato,* 253–62.

43. *Republic* 4, 427C–434D and 441C–445B, in Cornford, *The Republic of Plato,* 119–29, 139–43.

44. I disagree with Cornelia J. de Vogel's ("Greek Cosmic Love and the Christian Love of God," *Vigiliae Christianae* 35 [1981]: 57–81) sharp distinction between Christian and Neoplatonic love as a basis for interpreting Boethius. Cf. Origen, "In Cantica Canticorum: Prologus," in PG 13: cols.73–80, which compares Christian love of the Word to the love spoken of in the *Symposium.* For a useful supplementary discussion, see Susan Ford Wiltshire, "Boethius and the *Summum Bonum*," *Classical Journal* 67 (1972): 216–20. The relation between the love described in 2.m.8 and Dante's love that moves the sun and the other stars has often been remarked.

45. Plato, *Laws,* esp. 2.298ff., 2.336ff.

46. Edward W. Said, *The World, the Text and the Critic* (Cambridge: Harvard UP, 1983), 246.

47. Boethius generalizes his life, using Aristotelian theory of generalization (5.pr.4) and referring his situation to historical/mythic similitudes: to Theoderic, he compares (1) those who killed the philosophers (1.pr.3); (2) Nero; (3) the unnamed tyrants of Book 1, meter 4; and (4) Diomedes of Thrace (2.m.6; 3.m.4; 4.m.21); to his own imprisonment he compares the philosophic sufferings of Anaxagoras, Socrates, Zeno, Canius, Seneca, and Soranus (1.pr.3).

48. For a summary of scholarship on natural law, see Olson, "*The Parlement of Foules:* Aristotle's *Politics* and the Foundations of Human Society," 53–69.

49. Boethius later learns to surmount his commitment to the folly described in the Wisdom literature: folly in the form of weeping, being a narrow consequentialist, and acting as fortune's fool or the "ass to the harp" (1.pr.4). Boethius's picture of himself as the "ass to the harp" juxtaposed against Philosophy probably owes something to the juxtaposition of Wisdom and folly in Proverbs 8–9 and to St. Paul's fool imagery in 1 Corinthians.

50. Proclus's commentary on the *Republic* does not seem to me to be so important to the understanding of Boethius's books 1 and 2 as are his *Timaeus* and *Parmenides* commentaries to books 3, 4, and 5. Proclus does establish in his *Republic* commentary that matter, like fortune, is not evil, and he develops a full-fledged attack on dramatic poetry that may underlie Boethius's attack on the tragic muses in book 1. For an edition of Proclus's commentary on the *Republic*, cf. *In Platonis Rem Publicam Commentarii*, ed. W. Kroll (Leipzig: Teubner, 1899–1901), 2 vols. For accounts of Proclus on the *Republic*, see Anne D. R. Sheppard, *Studies on the 5th and 6th Essays of Proclus' Commentary on The Republic* (Göttingen: Vandenhoeck and Ruprecht, 1980); Thomas Whittaker, *The Neo-Platonists* (Hildesheim: Georg Olms, 1961), 295–314.

51. *The Commentaries of Proclus on the Timaeus of Plato*, trans. Thomas Taylor (London: n.p., 1820), 1.169. For Proclus and Boethius, see Obertello, *Severino Boezio*, 1.430–33, 508–21. For evidence of Boethius's use of Proclus on the *Timaeus* in book 3, see Friederich Klingner, "De Boethii Consolatione Philosophiae," *Philologische Untersunchungen herausgeben von A. Kiessling und U. von Wilamowitz-Moellendorff* 27 (Berlin: Weidmannsche Buchhandlung, 1921), 51–73.

52. Proclus defines the *Timaeus*'s nature as a corporeal force that organizes the regularities and productive basis of the natural world; Proclus, *In Platonis Timaeum Commentaria*, 1.6ff. Boethius's description of limited goods in book 3 derives from Plato's description of the goods of tyrants in the *Republic* but also from Plato's and Proclus's contrasting of the eternal and the generated in book 2 of the *Timaeus* and its commentary.

53. The poems preceding 3.m.9 prepare for its Timaean argument. The "number" of musical poetry in the immediately preceding poems generally treats of the rhythms implied by natural laws and the patterns and mathematical regularities that underlie material fluctuation.

54. In the *Timaeus*, mind is a concept-forming power. Soul is an animating power.

55. Chapters 2 and 3 discuss the extent to which variations of the basic God-concept of this mythos appear as part of the tradition of interpretation of the Wisdom/Logos figure in Jewish and patristic Christian thought. It should be observed that the whole creation ideology of the *Timaeus* exercised a profound influence on Philo, Clement of Alexandria, Origen, and Augustine as well as on

Proclus, the Neoplatonic writer on whom Boethius most depended for much of his understanding of the *Timaeus*.

56. Boethius, *The Consolation of Philosophy*, trans. V. E. Watts (Baltimore: Penguin, 1969), 97. I use Watts's translation of the poetry.

57. Boethius, *Consolation*, trans. Watts, 97–98.

58. For the full context of the Parmenidean quote, see Kirk and Raven, *The Presocratic Philosophers*, 276.

59. Books 4 and 5 of the *Consolation* derive from the many sources in late Neoplatonism traced by Lerer and Courcelle; Proclus should be added to the list.

60. *Proclus' Commentary on Plato's "Parmenides,"* trans. Glenn R. Morrow and John M. Dillon (Princeton: Princeton UP, 1987), 470. Plato does use the general passage from 8.42–49 both in *Timaeus* 33B and in formulating his more general concept of Being in the *Parmenides*, but he never uses fragment 8.43 in its exact words. Cf. Mitchell H. Miller, *Plato's "Parmenides": The Conversion of the Soul* (Princeton: Princeton UP, 1986), 200–201.

61. The *Parmenides* investigates the One or the Demiurge *in ipso* and in relation to the patterns in eternity, not in relation to the Timaean creation. After being educated by Philosophy, the Boethius persona flies poetically with her toward the divine (4.m.1); Lamberton, *Homer the Theologian*, 276. Cf. Buffière, *Mythes d'Homère*, 281, 288. Lerer's *Boethius and Dialogue*, 9, 32–78, 86, 96–100, 174, displays Boethius's dependence on the dialogic Plato, Cicero, and Augustine. Cf. Edmund T. Silk, "Boethius's *Consolatio Philosophiae* as a Sequel to Augustine's *Dialogues* and *Soliloquia*," *Harvard Theological Review* 32 (1939): 19–39. For precedents in this pattern, see Turner, "The Gnostic Threefold Path to Enlightenment," 344–45, which cites Plotinus, Chalcidius, and Proclus.

62. Proclus, *Commentary on Plato's "Parmenides,"* 303–9, 314–18.

63. Proclus, *Commentary on Plato's "Parmenides,"* 372–73, 376–77.

64. In Neoplatonic theory, especially Proclus, three distinct kinds of poetry appear: (1) symbolic poetry which attaches to the life of the One; (2) didactic exemplary or instructional poetry that attaches to the Logos as it reveals itself through model forms; and, lowest of all, (3) sense-based poetry that has a "Sophistic" emotional base. Lamberton, *Homer the Theologian*, 189–93; cf. Sheppard, *Proclus' Commentary on the Republic*, 162–202.

65. Proclus on the *Parmenides* is certainly not Boethius's only source or control in books 4 and 5, but learned readers of these books would almost certainly have recognized their myths on the ascent to theology/metaphysics as paralleling similar myths in the disciplinary ascents to theology in Neoplatonism and, especially, in Proclus. This, of course, in no way violates Boethius's fundamental Christian commitments. It does bring back the waning muses of the stage and the epic poet to serve a new purpose.

66. Porphyry, "De Antro Nympharum," in *Opuscula Selecta*, ed. August Nauck (Leipzig: Teubner, 1886), sections 34–35, pp.79–81.

67. This book does not comment on Boethius's choice of metrical forms. The medieval commentators comment at length on their appropriateness – their ordering of their subjects.

68. Alison White, "Boethius in the Medieval Quadrivium," in Gibson, *Boethius*, 162–63.

69. David S. Chamberlain, "Philosophy of Music in the *Consolatio* of Boethius," *Speculum* 45 (1970): 80–97.

70. Cf. Remigius of Auxerre, "The Commentary of Remigius of Auxerre," in *Saeculi Noni Auctoris in Boetii Consolationem Philosophiae Commentarius*, ed. Edmund T. Silk (Rome: American Academy in Rome, 1935), 314; Pseudo-Erigena in *Saeculi Noni Auctoris*, 6 (Silk attributed this commentary to John Scotus Erigena, but the attribution has been generally disputed; cf. Alastair Minnis, "Aspects of the Medieval French and English Traditions of the *De Consolatione Philosophiae*," in Gibson, *Boethius*, 356). Cf. William of Conches, "Commentary on the *De Consolatione Philosophiae*," in B. M. Ms. Royal 15 B III, fol.5^r; cf. Pseudo-Thomas, in Thomas Aquinas, *Expositio Aurea in Quinque Libros Anicii Manli Torquati Severini Boetii* (Paris: n.p., 1641), 5; cf. Nicholas Trivet, "Commentary on Boethius' *De Consolatione Philosophiae*," in B. M. Add. ms. 19,585, 11^v–12^r. These explanations are generally surrounded by other theological assumptions derived from the Sapiental books and medieval Sapiental theology.

71. Remigius speaks of Philosophy as short "propter communis animi conceptionem" and taller as astrology and divinity. Remigius, "Commentary," 314; cf. Pseudo-Erigena, *Saeculi Noni Auctoris*, 13; William of Conches, "Commentary," fol.5^r–6^v; Pseudo-Thomas, *Expositio Aurea*, 6; Nicholas Trivet, "Commentary," fol.12^r.

72. William of Conches, "Commentary," fol.8^r; Nicholas Trivet, "Commentary," fol.12^v.

73. Remigius, "Commentary," 315; Pseudo-Erigena, "Commentary," 14; William of Conches, "Commentary," fol.6^v–7^r. Pseudo-Thomas, *Expositio Aurea*, 6; Nicholas Trivet, "Commentary," fol.12^r.

74. Remigius, "Commentary," 316; Pseudo-Erigena, "Commentary," 15–16; William of Conches, "Commentary," fol.8^v; Pseudo-Thomas, *Expositio Aurea*, 6; Nicholas Trivet, "Commentary," fol.12^v. The Pseudo-Erigenan commentary also makes the point that whoever rules without learning is a tyrant.

75. Pseudo-Erigena, "Commentary," 33–35; William of Conches, "Commentary," Royal 15 BIII, fol.18^v–19^r; Pseudo-Thomas, *Expositio Aurea*, 17–18; Nicholas Trivet, "Commentary," fol.18^r–18^v.

76. William of Conches, "Commentary," fol.5^v.

77. William of Conches, "Commentary," fol.7ʳ–7ᵛ. Jerome Taylor contrasts this scheme with the fourfold Aristotelian scheme that Hugh of St. Victor uses in the *Didascalicon:* theoretical, practical, mechanical, and logical. Hugh's schematum appears to me to be more like William of Conches's than Taylor allows. The logical arts essentially equal William's verbal arts, and the practical and theoretical are similar in both writers. Hugh's attention to the mechanical arts is very important. *The Didascalicon of Hugh of St. Victor,* trans. Jerome Taylor (New York: Columbia UP, 1961), 7–10.

78. Remigius of Auxerre, "Commentary," 315; Pseudo-Erigena, "Commentary," 13–14.

79. Cf. Nicholas Trivet, "Commentary," fol.12ʳ–12ᵛ.

80. Pseudo-Erigena, "Commentary," 217–19.

81. William of Conches, "Commentary," fol.87ᵛ–90ᵛ; cf. Pseudo-Thomas, *Expositio Aurea,* 108–10.

82. Remigius, "Commentary," 339; Pseudo-Erigena, "Commentary," 222.

83. William of Conches, "Commentary," 92ᵛ; Pseudo-Thomas, *Expositio Aurea,* 113–14; Nicholas Trivet, "Commentary," 64ʳ–64ᵛ.

84. William of Conches, "Commentary," fol.120ʳ–122ᵛ.

85. H. F. Stewart, "A Commentary by Remigius Autissiodorus on the *De Consolatione Philosophiae* of Boethius," *Journal of Theological Studies* 17 (1916): 29.

86. Pseudo-Erigena, "Commentary," 112–13.

87. William of Conches, "Commentary," 61ʳ–61ᵛ.

88. Pseudo-Thomas, *Expositio Aurea,* 69; Nicholas Trivet, "Commentary," fol.41ʳ.

89. Pseudo-Erigena, "Commentary," 124–25. William of Conches, "Commentary," 66ᵛ. Pseudo-Thomas makes Nature here the threefold Nature posited by the scholastics, *natura naturans* or God, *natura naturans et naturata,* the heavens that depend on God and control the lower world, and *natura naturata,* the natural laws controlling mundane reality. Pseudo-Thomas, *Expositio Aurea,* 74. Cf. Nicholas Trivet, "Commentary," fol.43ᵛ–44ʳ.

90. Remigius, "Commentary," 332–36; Pseudo-Erigena, "Commentary," 155–90.

91. William of Conches, "Commentary," fol.74ʳ–81ʳ.

92. Pseudo-Thomas, *Expositio Aurea,* 91–93. Nicholas Trivet, "Commentary," fol.51ʳ–54ᵛ; cf. Pierre Courcelle, *La Consolation de Philosophie dans la Tradition Littéraire* (Paris: Études Augustiniennes, 1967), for an account of the general transformations of Boethian commentary in the Middle Ages.

93. I owe to John Moorhead the suggestion that Cassiodorus here refers to the period of the pontificate of Pope Agapetus (i.e., around A.D. 535–536).

94. Cassiodorus, *Institutiones,* ed. R. A. B. Mynors (Oxford: Clarendon Press, 1937), 3 (1, praefatio, 1).

95. Cassiodorus, *Institutiones*, 73–75, 79–82.

96. Boethius earlier, in *De Arithmetica*, says that the quadrivium supports the search for Wisdom (1.1), and Lady Philosophy's ladder from the active to the contemplative was later made into the seven liberal arts by Alcuin in the eighth century. Courcelle, *Consolation*, 77–81.

97. Cassiodorus, *Institutiones*, 89 (book 2, praefatio, 1). Cassiodorus says that the number seven indicates what is enduring, continuous, and eternal and that he adds seven chapters, one on each of the liberal arts. In this context, he cites Proverbs 9.1 on the seven pillars of Wisdom. For Cassiodorus's dependence on Origen and Augustine, see James J. O'Donnell, *Cassiodorus* (Berkeley: U of California P, 1979), 208–9. Cf. John R. S. Mair, "A Note on Cassiodorus and the Seven Liberal Arts," *Journal of Theological Studies* 26 (1975): 419–21.

98. Cassiodorus, *Institutiones*, 89–90, 132–33 (2, praefatio, 3; 2, 4).

99. Cassiodorus, *Institutiones*, 158–63. LeClercq speaks of Cassiodorus as placing the "accent upon learning" rather than the search for God: LeClercq, *Love of Learning*, 26, 24–28. However, Cassiodorus's commentary on the Psalms does not show him to be indifferent to the latter (though he is admittedly less pietistic than the St. Benedict whom LeClercq praises at Cassiodorus's expense): O'Donnell, *Cassiodorus*, 131–76. Boethius and Cassiodorus share a philosophic piety.

100. Alcuin, *The Bishops, Kings, and Saints of York*, ed. and trans. Peter Godman (Oxford: Clarendon Press, 1982), 112–13. Quotation is from the Godman translation.

101. Alcuin, *Bishops, Kings, and Saints*, 114–15. Godman translation.

102. Alcuin, *Bishops, Kings, and Saints*, 120–21. Alcuin speaks of "Sophiae."

103. Pierre Courcelle, "Les Sources Antiques du Prologue d'Alcuin sur les Disciplines," 293–305.

104. Cf. Alcuin, "Commentariorum in Joannem," 1.1, in PL 100, cols.743–46. Unfortunately, Alcuin's practical work falls short of his Boethian ideal. The preface to *De Grammatica* accompanies a thin set of rote grammatical exercises. Alcuin, "De Grammatica," in PL 101, cols.849–902.

105. Alcuin, "Disputatio de Rhetorica et de Virtutibus," in *Rhetorica Latini Minores*, ed. Karl Felix Von Halm (Leipzig: Teubner, 1863), 525ff. For a good dose of Alcuinian Erastianism, see "Epistolae: Ad Carolum Magnum," in PL 100, cols.207–10. Cf. Riché, *Les Écoles et l'enseignement dans l'Occident Chrétien de la Fin du Ve siècle au milieu du XIe siècle*, 69–75, 352–53. Riché notes the connection of Charlemagne's and Alcuin's emphasis on writing to centralized, writing-centered bureaucracy. For a full account of Alcuin and schools, see Andrew Fleming West, *Alcuin and the Rise of Christian Schools* (New York: Scribners, 1909). Some of the same tendencies appear in Alcuin's student, Rabanus Maurus, who wrote *De*

Institutione Clericorum describing a more demanding monastic education while a member of the monastery at Fulda (A.D. 819). Rabanus Maurus, "De Clericorum Institutione," 3.2, in PL 107, cols.379–80. His division, in the *De Universo,* of education into physics (the quadrivium plus medicine and the mechanical arts), ethics (the four cardinal virtues), and logic (rhetoric and dialectic but also apparently theology) is unusual; Rabanus Maurus, "De Universo," 15.1, in PL 111, cols.413–19. The "De Clericorum Institutione" division is more conventional; cf. PL 107, cols.384–85, 393–404. Courcelle, *La Consolation de Philosophie,* 47–50, asserts that Boethius ruled over the minds and fostered the teaching of most of the intellectual leaders of the ninth through twelfth centuries, including Huctolda de Saint-Amand (ca. 930), Heiric d'Auxerre (850–63), Ermenich d'Ellwogen, and Hrotsvitha.

106. Hugh of St. Victor, *Didascalicon,* 46.

107. Hugh of St. Victor, *Didascalicon,* 60, 46–48, 29–30. For thought parallel to Boethius concerning Philosophy and the disciplines among the thirteenth-century Parisian masters, see Claude Lafleur, *Quatre Introductions à la Philosophie au XIIIᵉ Siècle* (Montréal: Institut d'Etudes Mediévales, 1988).

108. For a full account of Hugh's reliance on Boethius, see Hugh of St. Victor, *Didascalicon,* 25–39, 158–228. Taylor's edition handles the Boethian tradition in educational theory in relation to Hugh so well that I see no need to treat it here in any detail. The Boethian theoretical base is retained in most twelfth-century educational treatises, even though the substance of mathematical knowledge was being transformed; see Guy Beaujolais, "The Transformation of the Quadrivium," *Renaissance and Renewal in the Twelfth Century* (Cambridge: Harvard UP, 1982), 463–87.

109. Hugh of St. Victor, *Didascalicon,* 136–37.

110. Ariès, *Centuries of Childhood,* 145–50.

7 BOETHIUS'S WISDOM AND DANTE'S ARCHITECTONICS OF DESIRE

1. My argument about Dante here follows my earlier Dante arguments closely. Chapter 4 demonstrates that Dante represents his journey to Wisdom in the shadow of the *Confessions* through treating (1) the effect of his sojourn in the "land of unknowing"; (2) the despair created by the death of a friend; and (3) the effect of the study of philosophy and the following of a female guide to a beatific vision achieved partly through study. Chapter 5 shows how Dante turned Virgil's text in book 6 of the *Aeneid* into his own journey to Wisdom.

2. Cf. Francis X. Newman's argument that the three worlds of the *Commedia* represent sensory, imaginative, and intellectual modes of cognition: "St. Augustine's Three Visions and the Structure of the *Commedia,*" MLN 82 (1967): 56–78; cf. John Freccero, *Dante: The Poetics of Conversion* (Cambridge: Harvard UP, 1986), 93–109.

3. Bloom, *Closing of the American Mind*, 201.

4. Bloom, *Closing of the American Mind*, 207–8; cf. Spanos, *End of Education*, 148–49.

5. Bloom, *Closing of the American Mind*, 198–208, 157–72, 185–94. My paraphrase of Bloom is influenced by William Marty's review of Bloom in *Essays on the Closing of the American Mind*, ed. Robert L. Stone (Chicago: Chicago Review Press, 1989), 308–27, esp. 324–25.

6. Chester E. Finn, *We Must Take Charge* (New York: Free Press, 1991), 282–85.

7. Contrast Bloom, *Closing of the American Mind*, 198–99.

8. Jerome S. Bruner, "Notes on Divisive Dichotomies," in *The Alternative of Radicalism*, ed. Thomas R. Holland and Catherine M. Lee (Lincoln: Nebraska Curriculum Development Center, 1969), 48–61; cf. Jerome S. Bruner, *On Knowing: Essays for the Left Hand* (Cambridge MA: Belknap Press, 1979).

9. *The Letters of Gerbert with His Papal Privileges as Sylvester II*, ed. and trans. Harriet Pratt Lattin (New York: Columbia UP, 1961); Uta Lindgren, *Gerbert von Aurillac und das Quadrivium: Untersuchungen zur Bildung im Zeitalter der Ottonen* (Weisbaden: Franz Steiner, 1976).

10. Nikolaus Häring, "The Creation and Creator of the World according to Thierry of Chartres and Clarenbaldus of Arras," *Archives d'histoire doctrinale et littéraire du moyen âge* 22 (1955): 137–215.

11. Tullio Gregory, *Anima mundi: La filosofia di guglielmo de conches e la scuola di Chartres* (Firenze: G. C. Sansoni, 1955).

12. Richard Lemay, "Gerard of Cremona," *Dictionary of Scientific Biography* (New York: Scribners, 1970–80), 15.173–92.

13. Lorenzo Minio-Paluello, "Moerbeke, William of," *Dictionary of Scientific Biography*, 9.434–40.

14. LeClercq, *Love of Learning*. We need better histories of monastic metaphysical studies.

15. Otto von Simson, *The Gothic Cathedral*.

16. Cf. James McEvoy, *The Philosophy of Robert Grosseteste* (Oxford: Clarendon Press, 1982); William A. Wallace, *Causality and Scientific Explanation* (Ann Arbor: U of Michigan P, 1978), 1.28–47.

17. James A. Weisheipl, ed., *Albertus Magnus and the Sciences: Commemorative Essays, 1980* (Toronto: Pontifical Institute of Medieval Studies, 1980).

18. David C. Lindberg, *The Beginnings of Western Science* (Chicago: U of Chicago P, 1992), 231–34.

19. John of Sacrobosco, *The Sphere of Sacrobosco and its Commentators*, ed. and trans. Lynn Thorndike (Chicago: U of Chicago P, 1949).

20. Marshall Clagett, *The Science of Mechanics in the Middle Ages* (Madison: U of Wisconsin P, 1959), 184–97.

21. David C. Lindberg, ed. and trans., *John Pecham and the Science of Optics* (Madison: U of Wisconsin P, 1970).

22. Lindberg, *Beginnings of Western Science*, 85–86, 281–87, 92–93.

23. For a history of patristic and thirteenth-century study of ethics, see Vernon J. Bourke, *History of Ethics* (New York: Doubleday, 1968), 47–64, 87–110.

24. See Spanos, *The End of Education*, 50–55, 142–43.

25. Dante reflects the siren-sophist scene in Boethius's *De Consolatione* in *Purgatorio* 19.1–36. Singleton, on *Purgatorio* 31.45, compares this scene to the Boethian scene in 1.pr.1 where the "sirens of poetry must yield to the muses of philosophy" (Dartmouth Dante Project). Pietro, in his commentary, compares the antidote to the siren who appears in the dream to the power of intellect and to the siren's Boethian opponent, Lady Philosophy; cf. Pietro on *Purgatorio* 19.31–33 (Dartmouth Dante Project). Benvenuto relates the siren to the study of the liberal arts and poetry as opposed to sacred writings and poetry used for sacred purposes, such as that found in Boethius and his like: Benvenuto on *Purgatorio* 31.43–48 (Dartmouth Dante Project). Cf. the remarks in *L'Ottimo*, *Purgatorio* 19.16–24 (Dartmouth Dante Project). Cf. *Paradiso* 24.79–81. Dante knew of the Sophists from Aristotle's *De Sophisticis Elenchis*.

26. Colish, *The Mirror of Language*, 166, argues that the genre of *La Vita Nuova* is taken ultimately from "the style of Boethius's *Consolation of Philosophy*." The work is a *satura*, like the *Consolation*, and echoes the *Consolation*. Colish's description of the relationship of Dante's poetic theory to rhetoric as pure persuasion or sophistry is helpful (cf. Colish, *The Mirror of Language*, 152–220).

27. For the standard scholarship on Dante and Boethius, see Rocco Murari, *Dante e Boezio* (Bologna: N. Zarichelli, 1905); Luigi Alfonsi, *Dante e la "Consolatio Philosophiae" di Boezio* (Como: C. Marzorati, 1944). For the disciplines, cf. Guiseppi Di Scipio and Aldo Scaglione, eds., *The Divine Comedy and The Encyclopedia of Arts and Sciences* (Philadelphia: John Benjamin's Publishing Co., 1988), especially articles by Costa (43–64), Hardt (81–94), Kay (147–62), Peterson (163–80), and Seung (181–222). For Dante and Wisdom, see Margherita De Bonfils Templer, "Il Dantesco 'Amoroso Uso di Sapienza': sue radici platoniche," *Stanford Italian Review* 7 (1987): 5–27.

28. Benvenuto defines the phrase "che sognando vede" in *Paradiso* 33.58 as meaning "qui habet visione in somnio." Benvenuto on *Paradiso* 33.58–63 (Dartmouth Dante Project).

29. Dante exercises his abstractive symbol-making talents in *La Vita Nuova* when he interprets Beatrice as a dream or visionary personage, a 3 and a 9, and the reflection of beatitude in the good (cf. *Convito* 2.12, 19–21).

30. In each of Dante's early major literary works, the imagination discovers similar shapes for events in disparate texts: (1) the similarity between Beatrice

and Christ in *La Vita Nuova;* (2) that between Cicero's friendship with human beings and Dante's with Philosophy in the *Convito* (3.1); and (3) that between Boethius's loss of beatitude in office and discovery of Philosophy and Dante's loss of Beatrice and discovery of Wisdom in the *Convito* (2.12). Dante Alighieri, *Opere Minori,* 1/2: 201–12; cf. 1/2: 291–97. All subsequent quotations and citations from the *Convito* are from this edition and are by section and subsection as well as by pages.

31. The loss of the *Convito* Beatrice seems to be primarily a physical loss – the loss of a "diletto" – that requires Philosophy for its cure, as Boethius's loss of position does in the *Consolation*. In the *Convito*, Dante makes the woman who was *La Vita Nuova*'s enemy of reason become Philosophy, the source of reason; cf. *Convito* 2.12 in *Opere Minori,* 201–12.

32. Dante may have made the window-lady of *La Vita Nuova* become Lady Philosophy because she embodies much of the iconography of Philosophy and Wisdom; in *La Vita Nuova*, she looks down from a window and gazes on Dante with a pitying and loving look (*La Vita Nuova,* 36–37) somewhat as Philosophy gazes down in the medieval manuscripts of the *Consolation* (1.pr.1). Wisdom looks from her window in Proverbs 7.6ff. to lament the folly of the young man pursuing the errant ways of the prostitute and to appeal to him to learn sense and seek instruction (cf. *De Consolatione* 3.m.9).

33. Dante, *Opere Minori,* 1/2: 205–10. Dante says that he went "ne le scuole de li religiosi e a le disputazioni de li filosofanti."

34. Cf. Charles Singleton, *Dante Studies* (Cambridge: Harvard UP, 1958), 135, n.5, for the argument that the two are identical. However, cf. note 30 above.

35. Dante, *Opere Minori,* 1/2: 452–92.

36. Dante, *Opere Minori,* 1/2: 488–91.

37. Cf. chapter 6 and Pierre Courcelle, *La Consolation de philosophie dans la tradition littéraire* (Paris: Études Augustiniennes, 1967), plate 26, 2.

38. Dante uses the phrase "astrologia" here but probably does not mean judicial astrology. However, cf. Dante, *Opere Minori,* 1/2: 240 n.28.

39. In Boethius's *Consolation*, Philosophy also goes through the various heavens in 1.pr.1 and 4.m.1, where she comes to the throne of the King of Kings.

40. The disciplines mentioned in the text of the *Consolation* (1.pr.4) do not explicitly belong to Philosophy, except perhaps obscurely in the mention of Philosophy's discourse in Boethius's library.

41. This shift does not appear in all of Aquinas. Cf. Mark D. Jordan, Ordering Wisdom (Notre Dame: U of Notre Dame P, 1988), 93, 234 n.6; Aquinas, *The Division and Methods of the Sciences,* 77–78.

42. This fusion may be based on Thomas's commentary on Aristotle's *Ethics,* where he makes both natural philosophy proper (physics) and metaphysics part of natural philosophy; cf. Aquinas, *Division and Methods of the Sciences,* 94–95.

43. Iain Paul, *Science, Theology, and Einstein* (New York: Oxford UP, 1982).

44. Cf. Olson, "*The Parlement of Foules:* Aristotle's Politics and the Foundations of Human Society," 53–69.

45. Jordan, *Ordering Wisdom*, passim.

46. Jordan, *Ordering Wisdom*, 115–17; 77–82.

47. Thomas Aquinas, "Sententia Libri Ethicorum," *Opera Omnia*, Leonine edition (Rome: 1882–): 47², 358–59.

48. Aquinas, *The Division and Methods of the Sciences*, xx–xxi, 18–22, 41, 65–77, 101.

49. To put it another way, ethics/psychology studies the "boundary between the corporeal and incorporeal" as Mathematics does in Boethius. Cf. Jacopo della Lana on *Purgatorio* 1.13–18; Guido da Pisa on *Inferno* 2.94; *L'Ottimo Commento* on *Purgatorio* 1.15–18; Benvenuto on *Paradiso* 1.46–48; Fiorentino on *Inferno* 2.53 (Dartmouth Dante Project).

50. Dante, *Opere Minori*, 1/2: 256–57 n.15 and 258–60 n.17.

51. Theology is said, in *Convito* 2.14.19, to despise sophistry, another of Dante's reflections of Boethius's dichotomy between the sophistic muses and truth.

52. Cf. Dante, *Opere Minori*, 1/2: 255–57 n.14, 15, for useful explanations of Dante's implications here and his sources in Aristotle and Thomas.

53. The ascent to peace in the *Convito*, though an end in itself, also constructs an ethical civic vision or "architectonic" and unites Boethius's scepter and book. Dante, like Boethius, elevates the contemplative above the active life in the *Convito* and in the *Commedia*. Cf. Brian Vickers, ed., *Arbeit, Musse, Meditation* (Zürich: Verlag der Fachvereine, 1985), 87–108, 133–52. The *Convito* offers Dante's equivalent of Beothius's Pi and Theta, the active and contemplative lives (1.pr.1), when it asserts that the state totters when imperial power ignores philosophy and does not abide by Wisdom and the laws of nature (*Convito* 4.6.15–20; cf. *Convito* 4.16.1ff.). Cf. Dante, *Opere Minori*, 1/2: 593–95, 709ff. Earthly limitations mean that all desires, save that for knowledge, remain unsatisfied (*Convito* 4.12.13; 4.13.16); the latter transcends earthly limitations because the speculative or contemplative way of using the mind has its perfect use in beholding God through His creation as the source of all knowledge (*Convito* 4.22.13–18). Cf. Dante, *Opere Minori*, 1/2: 790–94. The *Convito* Dante relates the study of the traditional disciplines both to the knowledge of the architectonic science of ethics, which controls how and for what purposes the disciplines are studied, and to the quest for both contemplative bliss and active reform.

54. Dante, *Opere Minori*, 1/2: 469 n.15, 2. Vasoli and De Robertis relate the notion of demonstrations to Aristotle's *Topics*. Demonstrations then must be logical/mathematical proofs. Colish conflates Philosophy and Wisdom as the lady of the *Convito* (Colish, *Mirror of Language*, 171); however, Dante speaks both of

Philosophy and Wisdom, and I believe that he means to keep separate the notions of Philo-Sophia, a set of disciplines, and Wisdom or Sophia, the Logos-entity present at the creation. The *Convito*'s relating of the active and contemplative forms of knowing holds in the *Commedia* where the *Purgatorio*'s perfective effort to create a good society precedes the *Paradiso*'s contemplation of divinity and the divine creation; contemplation also suggests action because it looks at the ideal types of things (cf., for example, St. Peter's meditation on the earthly papacy in *Paradiso* 27, examining it from the perspective of the Petrine archetype).

55. The *Comedia*'s more theological presentation of the guides makes the brilliant eyes of Beatrice/beatitude reflect the double-nature of the Logos/Christ and her smile represent the persuasive power of divine love (*Purgatorio* 31.109–32, 18). Cf. Benvenuto on *Purgatorio* 31.118–20 and on *Purgatorio* 32.1–9 (Dartmouth Dante Project). Pietro, on *Purgatorio* 31.79–81, says that Beatrice's eyes symbolize the exercise of the speculative intellect in theology and that they see both the deity and the humanity of Christ in the changing griffin (Dartmouth Dante Project). For a contrasting view, see Peter Armour, *Dante's Griffin and the History of the World* (Oxford: Clarendon Press, 1984), 60.

56. Dante, *Opere Minori*, 457–58.

57. Dante, *Opere Minori*, 1/2: 256–57 n.15.

58. For Dante's fourteenth-century commentators, see Michael Caesar, *Dante: The Critical Heritage: 1314(?)–1870* (New York: Routledge, 1989). Pietro and the other commentators also make Dante's guides into various forms of grace coming down from above, a plausible move since patristic and Gnostic writers make Wisdom guides represent both the guidance of disciplinary learning that moves upward and the assistance of grace coming down from above. Both grace-based and discipline-based readings operate simultaneously during much of the *Commedia*.

59. Pietro on *Inferno* 2.51–102 (Dartmouth Dante Project). Cf. Singleton, *Dante Studies*, 122–38, for the argument that Beatrice is created as opposed to uncreated Wisdom. Dante's fourteenth- and fifteenth-century commentators down through Giovanni della Serravalle refer to mathematics and the mathematical disciplines seventy times in explaining the *Inferno* (Dartmouth Dante Project).

60. Dante Alighieri, *Epistolae*, ed. and trans. by Paget Toynbee (Oxford: Clarendon Press, 1966), 10. For a bibliography concerning the dispute about the authenticity of this letter, see Colish, *Mirror of Language*, 274. See also H. J. Kelly, "Dating the accessus section of the pseudo-Dantean *Epistle to Cangrande*," *Lectura Dantis* 2 (1987): 93–102.

61. In the first infernal realm, Virgil as Reason first leads; in the second purgatorial one, Cato leads as the representative of moral law; and in the *Paradiso*, Beatrice guides as the representative of the spiritual life and theology. Guido da Pisa on *Inferno* 2.94 (Dartmouth Dante Project).

62. Some commentators do not make Statius a guide. However, Statius is called the sage who stayed (*Purgatorio* 33.13–15) – which makes him like Virgil, the sage who left (*Purgatorio* 30.49–51); like Virgil, he gives philosophic speeches and is not bound to one circle.

63. Jordan, *Ordering Wisdom*, 146–47.

64. Dante may be having some fun here with the relationship between Statius's prodigality and the excess of his pretentious language.

65. Cf. Pietro on *Purgatorio* 8.25–27 for the serpent as suggestion; cf. Benvenuto on *Purgatorio* 8.37–39; Serravalle on *Purgatorio* 8.97–99. For the eagle-Lucia of canto 9, see Lana on *Purgatorio* 9, Nota; *L'Ottimo* on *Purgatorio* 9.52; Pietro on *Purgatorio* 9.55–57; Benvenuto on *Purgatorio* 9.13–21 (Dartmouth Dante Project).

66. Cf. Pietro on *Purgatorio* 19.19–24; the remaining commentators emphasize the lady as reason, conscience, or both (Dartmouth Dante Project).

67. Singleton remarks upon the similarity between Dante's and Boethius's siren in his comment on *Purgatorio* 31.45; see Charles Singleton, *Purgatorio, Commentary* (Princeton: Princeton UP, 1973), 763. Pietro makes explicit the parallelism between Dante's siren and Boethius's in his commentaries on *Purgatorio* 19.16–24 and *Purgatorio* 31.43–47 (Dartmouth Dante Project). The makers of love poetry come after the siren.

68. Cf. Pietro on *Purgatorio* 25.61–75 (Dartmouth Dante Project). Averroës's "possible intellect" appears to deny individual moral responsibility.

69. Pietro on *Purgatorio* 25.28–30 (Dartmouth Dante Project).

70. Francis X. Newman in "St. Augustine's Three Visions," emphasizes that the purgatory is preeminently the world of imagination and art.

71. This interpretation of the Theban waters – specifically of Langia in the *Thebiad* – as baptism does not appear until Daniello's 1568 comment on *Purgatorio* 22.88–93 (Dartmouth Dante Project). However, the notion of cleansing is apparent from the beginning.

72. Medieval commentary on the *Thebiad* makes it an emphatically ethical or moralistic poem; see David Anderson, *Before the Knight's Tale: Imitation of Classical Epic in Boccaccio's "Teseida"* (Philadelphia: U of Pennsylvania P, 1988), 242–43; cf. *Lactantii Placidi qui dicitur Commentarios in Statii Thebaida*, ed. Richard Jahnke (Leipzig: Teubner, 1898); cf. Dante's own commentary on the *Thebiad* in *Convito* 4.25.6–11. Dante, through the myth of Statius's poetic conversion, makes Statius/ethics into the poet of the images of transformed desire that mediate between the corporeal and the spiritual – the sort of image that dominates the *Purgatorio* (cf. *Purgatorio* 18.67ff.; *Paradiso* 3, 22.40ff., 21.133ff.).

73. The relationship between Lethe and penance as purification is recognized by Guido da Pisa on *Inferno* 14.130–38; Giovanni della Serravalle on *Inferno* 14.136–42; and *L'Ottimo* on *Purgatorio* 31.97–99 (Dartmouth Dante Project).

74. Pietro on *Purgatorio* 32.28–32 (Dartmouth Dante Project).

75. Modern commentary commonly says that the second age in *Purgatorio* 30.125 is youth, after adolescence; but Fulgentius's and Bernard Silvestris's Virgilian commentary makes it adolescence that follows childhood. Dante's commentators make it something similar: Benvenuto on *Purgatorio* 30.121–32 says that the second age begins in adolescence, and *Fiorentino* on *Purgatorio* 30.124–32 says that it comes after boyhood. In contrast, *L'Ottimo* on *Purgatorio* 30.124–26 says that the second age begins at 25 years. Generally, the commentators see the middle of the journey of 1.1 as coming at about 35 years, so they assume ten or more years between "Beatrice's" death and the *Commedia* experience (Dartmouth Dante Project).

76. This *Commedia* episode appears to recapitulate *La Vita Nuova*'s history: that is, Beatrice's death, Dante's following of a Lady-at-the-Window as an alternative love, and his vision of Beatrice redeemed (section 42). The commentators commonly relate the false images of the good described in *Purgatorio* 30.124–32 to Boethius's partial goods. Like Boethius abashed by Lady Philosophy, the tearful Dante cannot speak and turns his face downward (*Consolation* 1.pr.1; *Purgatorio* 30.7–21) while Beatrice plays the role of Lady Philosophy repudiating the sirens (*Purgatorio* 31.45).

77. Theology as "scientia Dei et beatorum" comes from *Summa Theologica* 1a, q.1, a.2, in *Summa Theologicae*, ed. Thomas Gilby (New York: McGraw-Hill, 1963), 1.10. That Theology comprises a peace that comes after the felicity provided by ethics is asserted in *Convito*, 2.14.17–20 (*Opere Minori*, 258–61) and the higher aspects of Wisdom are said to be sources of "beatitudine" and "felicitade" in *Convito* 3.15.2–11 (*Opere Minori*, 470–85).

78. As Beatrice appears, Dante hears the Old Testament Canticle call to the bride to come from the Lebanon of the eternal and the New Testament *Benedictus qui venis* (Matthew 23.39) that welcomes Christ to Jerusalem on Palm Sunday. Beatrice is not the church as *sponsa* but the word or Theos-Logos that the ideal church announces: cf. *L'Ottimo* on *Purgatorio* 30.11; Pietro on *Purgatorio* 30.10–12; Benvenuto on *Purgatorio* 30.10–12; Serravalle on *Purgatorio* 30.10–12 (Dartmouth Dante Project).

79. Pietro on *Inferno* 2.52–102 (Dartmouth Dante Project).

80. Pietro on *Purgatorio* 30.28–31 indicates that Beatrice's olive is Minerva's tree; cf. Benvenuto on *Purgatorio* 30.28–33 (Dartmouth Dante Project).

81. She, unlike Lady Philosophy, represents theology's capacities to represent the incarnation since, in her eyes, the commentators see the double nature of the Griffin that is the incarnate Christ, not the "demonstrativa" radiance of the *Convito*'s Wisdom. Her lips are not the *Convito* Wisdom's persuasions of rhetoric and dialectic but those of divine love and a New Testament understanding of the

scriptures. For example, Scartazzini on *Purgatorio* 31.138 says that Pietro treats the "seconda bellezza" as understanding the New Testament and the theological virtues and that Francesco da Buti, Vellutello, and Christoforo Landino name it the anagogical understanding of the Scriptures.

82. After Beatrice/theology comes into the picture with her knowledge of the incarnation, Dante draws echoes from Virgil that point to the limitations rather than the strengths of Roman belief in inversions of Virgil's "old flame" and "Give lilies with full hands" ideas. Cf. Christopher J. Ryan, "Virgil's Wisdom in the *Divine Comedy*," *Medievalia et Humanistica* 11 (1982): 11–19.

83. Pietro on *Inferno* 2.52–102 says that "[m]etaphysica de Deo creatore et gubernatore inferiorum est, et terminatur ad esse naturae" while "[t]heologia . . . est de Deo redemptore, et terminatur ad esse gloriae et gratiae." The two constitute, according to Pietro, the highest level of Boethius's Philosophy, the level where her head penetrates the skies. Cf. Pietro on *Paradiso* 8.13–15 and *Paradiso* 11.1–12; Daniello on *Paradiso* 28.40–45 points out that Beatrice, in that passage, states the essential metaphysical principle as to the relation of the creation and Creator (Dartmouth Dante Project).

84. Cf. Lana on *Paradiso* 1, Nota; Pietro on *Paradiso* 1.13–15; Benvenuto on *Paradiso* 1.7–9. Pietro on *Paradiso* 1.16–18 says that the second peak of Parnassus, sacred to Apollo, is Helicon on the mountain of divine wisdom which requires the poet to treat of matters mathematical, metaphysical, and theological (Dartmouth Dante Project).

85. Virgil exposes Dante to the mathematical disciplines by taking him to the trivium/quadrivium castle in *Inferno* 4. Dante, sometimes at the prompting of Beatrice, uses geometric figures in *Paradiso* 13.94–102; 17.13–15; 22.142–44; 23.10–12; 28.1–12; 30.1–9. The commentators are aware of the technical disciplinary context of these passages. Cf. Aquinas, *The Division and Methods of the Sciences*, 60–74; Jordan, *Ordering Wisdom*, 80–82, 120–21. The *Consolation*'s Philosophy is Metaphysics from 4.m.1 on and flies above the planets, as does the Beatrice of the *Paradiso;* cf. Pietro on *Paradiso* 4.37–48 (Dartmouth Dante Project).

86. Benvenuto on *Paradiso* 15.25–27 says that, as Aeneas descended to the infernal regions under the leadership of the sibyl, so Dante ascended to the sky under the leadership of Beatrice. Also, as Aeneas saw his father "in campo amoeno et luminoso, in quo erant animae illustres virorum sapientum et proborum," so Dante saw his ancestor, Cacciaguida, in a similar place, the planet Mars (Dartmouth Dante Project). Pietro calls Anchises the "revelatione dei" in his comment on *Inferno* 2.10–30, which is what Beatrice, as a discipline, is also (Dartmouth Dante Project).

87. *Paradiso* 1.1–12 celebrates the metaphysical light of truth glorified in

Plato's *Republic,* and in Boethius (3.m.9): Lana on *Paradiso* 1, Nota, calls light a symbol of "la virtude divina" and cites John 1 in his explanation of *Paradiso* 1.1; *L'Ottimo* on *Paradiso* 1.5–6 says that the "gloria" mentioned in that passage surpasses human intellectual and perceptual power; Pietro compares the "gloria . . . illius qui totum movet" to the power of the exemplar or Wisdom/Word in Boethius's *Consolation* 3.m.9 (Dartmouth Dante Project).

88. *Paradiso* 13.53–60 appears to make Christ the Idea, or Logos and Light related to the Father and Love as the other members of the Trinity. Cf. Lana, *Paradiso* 10, Nota; *Fiorentino* on *Paradiso* 10, Nota; Benvenuto on *Paradiso* 10, 1–6. For explanations of *Paradiso* 13.52–81 that need to be referred to *Paradiso* 10.1–6, see Pietro on *Paradiso* 13.64–81; *Fiorentino* on *Paradiso* 13, Nota; Benvenuto on *Paradiso* 13, 52–54 (Dartmouth Dante Project).

89. Benvenuto says, concerning *Paradiso* 1, 49–57, that the intellect looks to the eyes of Beatrice (i.e., to the contemplation and speculation of theology that looks to God); cf. Benvenuto on *Paradiso* 21.1–3; 22.151–54; Pietro on *Paradiso* 1.67–69, makes the passage represent the intellect's encountering the knowledge of celestial things by means of theology or metaphysics; cf. Pietro on *Paradiso* 28.1–12 (Dartmouth Dante Project).

90. Cf. Pietro on *Paradiso* 21.4–6; Benvenuto on *Paradiso* 21.1–18 and 29.25–30; and Serravalle on *Paradiso* 29.22–30 (Dartmouth Dante Project). The relationship between cosmic system and formed light is particularly obvious in *Paradiso* 30.55–120 and 33.83–146.

91. Cf. Pietro on *Paradiso* 23.10–12; Benvenuto on *Paradiso* 23.1–12 (Dartmouth Dante Project).

92. Benvenuto on *Paradiso* 1.82–84; for an elaboration of the relationship of proportionality and harmony, based on Renaissance musical theory, see Daniello on *Paradiso* 1.76–78. In contrast to Benvenuto, Pietro on *Paradiso* 1.76–78 asserts a literal belief in the music of the heavens (Dartmouth Dante Project).

93. Benvenuto and Giovanni della Serravalle relate it to an institutional or university context, though only Benvenuto claims that the scene relates to Dante's putative university study at Paris. Cf. *L'Ottimo* on *Paradiso* 24.46–48; Benvenuto on *Paradiso* 24.46–51; *Fiorentino* on *Paradiso* 24.46–48; Serravalle on *Paradiso* 24.46–51; Pietro on *Paradiso* 24.24–39; Lana on *Paradiso* 24.46–51 (Dartmouth Dante Project).

94. Cf. Benvenuto on *Paradiso* 24.133–41 (Dartmouth Dante Project).

95. Cf. Lana on *Paradiso* 26.37–39; *L'Ottimo* on *Paradiso* 26.37–43; Benvenuto on *Paradiso* 26.25–27 (Dartmouth Dante Project).

96. Pietro on *Inferno* 52–102 (Dartmouth Dante Project).

97. Cf. Benvenuto on *Paradiso* 32.85–87 (Dartmouth Dante Project) for an excellent medieval comment on the universe as book.

98. Cf. Ariès, *Centuries of Childhood,* 148. Ariès describes an argument as to whether rhetoric should be placed in the grammar schools or in higher education. The school-university sequence in the fourteenth century and after in France included Latin grammar (and probably rhetoric) in grammar school. Under Robert de Courçon's 1215 rules for the University of Paris, two university cycles were taught simultaneously: (1) the language disciplines of grammar and logic; and (2) the *cursariae* of rhetoric, the quadrivium, and ethics. For the university baccalaureate after 1366, the required subjects were possibly rhetoric and certainly logic (replacing dialectic); for the *licentia docendi,* physics and the quadrivium sciences; for the mastership of arts, Aristotle's *Ethics* and *Meteors* (i.e., work centering in moral philosophy). The higher faculties studied and taught theology, or theology and metaphysics. The late medieval sequence combines the traditional Boethian with the new Thomistic-Dantesque sequence.

99. Charles S. Singleton, "The Irreducible Dove," *Comparative Literature* 9 (1957): 129.

100. Pietro on *Paradiso* 16.73–75 (Dartmouth Dante Project).

8 PLATO REVISITED

1. For scholastic development of systems for classifying natural species, see Olson, "*The Parlement of Foules:* Aristotle's *Politics* and the Foundations of Human Society," 53–69.

2. David C. Lindberg, *The Beginnings of Western Science* (Chicago: U of Chicago P, 1992), 357–63. For a good account of medieval Aristotelian cosmology, see Edward Grant, *Planets, Stars and Orbs: The Medieval Cosmos 1200–1687* (Cambridge: Cambridge UP, 1994).

3. Johannes Kepler, *Opera Omnia,* ed. Charles Frisch (Hildesheim: Gerstenberg, 1971), 1.640.

4. Edwin Arthur Burtt, *The Metaphysical Foundation of Modern Science* (London: Routledge & Kegan Paul, 1967), 52–54. At the other end of the spectrum concerning Florentine and Platonic influence is Edward W. Strong, *Procedures and Metaphysics* (Berkeley: U of California P, 1936); Strong denies the Platonic tradition almost completely.

5. It should not be thought that scholastic philosophy encouraged much empirical fieldwork or investigation. That was done more by magicians and alchemists and awaited the Baconian revolution for its systematization.

6. Burtt's theory attributes too much to the Florentine Platonists. Their direct influence on the sixteenth- and seventeenth-century astronomers was not so great as that of the texts that they edited. For example, Novara's chief teacher, Regiomontanus, was not a member of the Florentine Platonic group but a Viennese astronomer who studied in a variety of places in Italy. Though Regiomon-

tanus believed in the ascent to God through the disciplines, especially astronomy, and published the first European treatise on trigonometry (Paul Lawrence Rose, *The Italian Renaissance of Mathematics* [Geneva: Droz, 1975], 90–142, esp. 96–97), the chief Platonist who influenced him appears to have been Bessarion of Bologna, not a Florentine Platonist.

7. Rose, *The Italian Renaissance of Mathematics*, 90–142, esp. 96–97.

8. Raymond Klibansky, *The Continuity of the Platonic Tradition in the Middle Ages* (Millwood NY: Kraus International Publications, 1982), 42–47.

9. Cf. Klibansky, *Continuity of the Platonic Tradition*, 13–37; Rose, *Italian Renaissance of Mathematics*, passim. It should also be remembered that "Platonic" figures such as Ficino often include a heavy dose of Aristotle and Thomas.

10. Hans Blumenberg and his translator, Robert Wallace, have argued that the Platonic tradition could not have been important in the Copernican revolution because Copernicus makes nothing of the notion of the Platonic Ideas and because, had Plato been the source of the revolution, it would have occurred long before. However, interest in Plato's "Ideas" is almost absent from Augustine's writings and much later Christian Platonism; Augustine's fullest discussion of the "Ideas" is to be found in question 46 of his "De Diversis Quaestionibus Octoginto Tribus," where he identifies the ideas with forms or species and with fixed reasons or laws governing things; cf. Augustine, *De Diversis Questionibus Octoginta Tribus: De Octo Ducitii Questionibus* (Turnholt: Brepols, 1975), 70–74. According to Wallace, the Platonic theory formulated by Jürgen Mettelstrass in *Die Rettung der Phänomene* requires that one assume that Augustine "transmitted Plato's mathematical rationalism, stripped of his ontological dualism by the homogenizing effect of the Christian idea of creation." Robert M. Wallace, in Hans Blumenberg, *The Genesis of the Copernican World*, trans. Robert Wallace (Cambridge: MIT Press, 1987), xvii, 687–88. In his view, this "account does not explain why the implementation of 'Christian Platonism' as natural science" in the Renaissance scientists "took place more than a thousand years after its foundations were laid by Origen, Augustine, *et al.*" However, history rarely explains why a discovery is *not* made (e.g., why the Incas made wheels for their toys and did not place them on full-sized vehicles). Thomas Kuhn's explanations of the puzzles that lead up to Copernicus (and that undermine the old view) seem to me to be compelling.

11. *The Letters of Marsilio Ficino*, trans. Language Department, London School of Economic Science (London: Shepheard-Walwyn, 1975), 1.186–91.

12. Poetry to Ficino remains essentially a civic art – prosodically organized language – a numerical science rather than a division of rhetoric, its traditional category in the middle ages. However, like traditional mathematics, number also enhances humankind's understanding of the divine, developing the soul's libera-

tion from attachment to the physical. *Letters of Ficino*, 1.42–48. The "music" and order in the mind of God are "imitated" by the music and order of the stars and planets, and the music and order of the stars and planets are imitated by the poet's music. For the civic basis of Ficino's theory, see André Chastel, *Marsile Ficin et L'Art* (Geneva: Droz, 1975), 100–106.

13. Orphic singing substitutes for astronomy as the inspired singing of the planets' songs; architecture, as a public art, replaces geometry on which it is based; and painting is the substitute for arithmetic. Marsilio Ficino, *Opera Omnia* (Basel, 1576), 1:sig. [H3[v]], sig. [Nnn8ᵛ]. Cf. E. H. Gombrich, "Botticelli's Mythologies," *JWCI* 8 (1945): 56–59. Gombrich points out that the theory of education adumbrated by Ficino reappears in Botticelli's "Pallas and the Centaur." In a related Villa Lemmi fresco, Botticelli's Venus, as the Uranian goddess of the contemplation of the divine, leads the initiate, a young bridegroom, toward the seven liberal arts: first toward three seated figures, probably arithmetic, geometry, and music, and toward astronomy, the lifted figure on the right end of the quadrivium figures. Cf. Plato, *Opera Omnia*, trans. with commentary by Marsilio Ficino (Lyons: Vincentium, 1557), sig. [H4ʳ]–[H4ᵛ]. For Plato's ideal ruler as scientist in Ficino, see Plato, *Opera Omnia*, trans. with commentary by Ficino, sig. [M5ᵛ]–[M6ʳ]).

14. For analysis relating Pico to Augustinian thought, see Charles Edward Trinkaus, *In Our Image and Likeness* (Chicago: U of Chicago P, 1970), 2.505–26.

15. Courcelle, *La Consolation de Philosophie dans la tradition littéraire*, plate 26, 2; cf. Giovanni Pico della Mirandola, *De Hominis Dignitate: Heptaplus: De Ente et Uno*, ed. Eugenio Garin (Firenze: Vallecchi Editore, 1942), 102–16.

16. Pico della Mirandola, *De Hominis Dignitate*, 118.

17. Pico della Mirandola, *De Hominis Dignitate*, 118–20.

18. Pico della Mirandola, *De Hominis Dignitate*, 122–24.

19. Pico della Mirandola, *De Hominis Dignitate*, 118, 124, 146.

20. Arthur Field, *The Origins of the Platonic Academy of Florence* (Princeton: Princeton UP, 1988), 231–32. Landino's commentary on Virgil comes in 1475 and on Dante in 1481. Cf. Trinkaus, *In Our Image and Likeness*, 2.712–21.

21. Like Ficino and the interpreters of the *Aeneid* and the *Commedia* covered in earlier chapters, Landino regards poetry as a divine art revealed to poets by the God who gives them both grace and intellectual discipline. Cristoforo Landino, *Disputationes Camaldulenses*, ed. Peter Lohe (Firenze: Sansoni, 1980), 111–19. He also treats poetry and music as arts promoting the journey to the divine; poetry, as an aspect of music, imitates the divine harmony and so exists as a segment of the mathematical disciplines that reverse the voluptuary's fall. Cristoforo Landino, *Scritti Critici e Teorici*, ed. Roberto Cardini (Rome: Bulzoni, 1974), 117, 144–45. Cf. Landino, *Disputationes Camaldulenses*, 236.

22. Ficino, *Opera Omnia*, 1: sig. Mmm4^r–sig. [Mmm4^v].

23. Landino's *Aeneid* commentary elaborately expresses Petrarch's voluptuous, active, contemplative hypothesis concerning the progress of Aeneas's journey. His interpretation of Virgil, in the *Camaldulensian Dialogues* (1475), consists, as Murrin observes, "of a series of rising curves, each broken off," beginning with Alberti's discussion of Plato's ladder. Michael Murrin, *The Allegorical Epic* (Chicago: U of Chicago P, 1969), 49–50. For some mention of the role of physics and mathematics, see Cristoforo Landino, *Questiones Camaldulenses* (Venice: after 1500, Yale University microfilm), sig. b6^v; cf. sig. a2^r–f3^r. This work is the same as the *Disputationes*. Aeneas's rising curve shows the hero working with divine aid to overcome the effects of Paris's choice of the voluptuous Helen after he leaves Paris's city of Troy behind (i.e., the early years in which the senses dominate) (Landino, *Disputationes Camaldulenses*, 120–21). As he leaves, he discovers a Venus at odds with Troy's Venus, the Venus of the "angelic mind" (cf. book 2, line 594ff.), who drives his mind toward divine beauty by moving it to find a new contemplative "empire" at Rome. Cf. Landino, *Disputationes Camaldulenses*, 123–36. In Hades, Landino's Aeneas examines the hideousness of the vices and purges his mind for the acquisition of the intellectual virtues so that he can be illuminated by these virtues and ascend to the contemplation of divine good. Landino, *Disputationes Camaldulenses*, 194–224, 253.

24. Landino, *Disputationes Camaldulenses*, 213–60.

25. Landino, *Disputationes Camaldulenses*, 254.

26. Dante, *Commedia* (1481), with Landino commentary, sig. [A1^v]–[A6^v].

27. Landino says that the seven towers of the castle in Dante's *Inferno*, canto 4 (ll.106–7) are the four cardinal and the three speculative virtues: *intelligentia, sapientia,* and *scientia* (sig. [d1^v]); these virtues appropriately lead to theology in his interpretation of *Purgatorio* 31.109–11 (sig. [mm10^r]). Dante, *Commedia*, with Landino commentary (1481). *Intelligentia* in Landino is normally defined as including the mathematical disciplines. Lombardi explains that *intelligenza* for Landino is the conjunction of things in perfect clarity, as in geometry (Dartmouth Dante Project) (from Lombardi on *Inferno* 4.106–7).

28. Landino, "Cristoforo di Cristoforo Landino, Fiorentino, sopra La Commedia di Dante Alighieri Poeta Fiorentino," *Scritti Critici e Teorici*, 156ff.

29. Cf. L. A. Birkenmajer, *Stromata Copernicana* (Cracow: Nakładem Polskiej Acadeji, 1924), 306–7. For a useful discussion of the relationships among science, magic, and religion in the period, see Brian P. Copenhaver, *Symphorien Champier and the Reception of the Occultist Tradition in Renaissance France* (New York: Mouton, 1978), 240–41.

30. For Augustine's influence on Ficino as deriving from the early Augustinian Platonist writings, see Paul Oskar Kristeller, *Renaissance Thought: the Classic, Scholastic, and Humanist Strains* (New York: Harper & Row, 1961), 85.

31. Though Copernicus (1473–1543) lives in the next generation after the flowering of the Florentine Platonists, one cannot easily determine to what extent his metaphysical assumptions coincide with those of the Florentines, since he gives one so little aside from his calculations. His earliest circulated work concerning the heavens, the *Commentariolus* (1533?), does mention the Pythagoreans but otherwise contains almost no statement about its philosophic roots; he is, of course, careful to establish the piety of his work. Nicholas Copernicus, "The Commentariolus," in *Three Copernican Treatises*, trans. Edward Rosen (New York: Dover, 1959), 59.

32. For Ficino, see Birkenmajer, *Stromata Copernicana*, 306–7; for an English translation of Rheticus's *Narratio Prima*, see *Three Copernican Treatises*, 107–96.

33. *Three Copernican Treatises*, 136–40.

34. Michael J. B. Allen, "Marsilio Ficino's Interpretation of Plato's *Timaeus* and its Myth of the Demiurge," *Supplementum Festivum: Studies in Honor of Paul Oscar Kristeller*, in *Medieval and Renaissance Texts and Studies* 49 (Binghamton NY: Medieval & Renaissance Texts & Studies, 1987): 399–439, esp. 406.

35. Gertrude Hamilton, "Ficino's Concept of Nature and the Philosophy of Light," *Annual Publications of the International Patristic, Medieval and Renaissance Conference* 7 (1982): 67–74.

36. Plato, *Opera Omnia*, trans. with commentary by Ficino, sig. $Q4^r$.

37. Plato, *Opera Omnia*, trans. with commentary by Ficino, sig. $S4^r$. For a full discussion of the complexities of Ficinian analysis of Trinitarian tendencies in the Platonists, see Michael J. B. Allen, "Marsilio Ficino on Plato, the Neoplatonists and the Christian Doctrine of the Trinity," *Renaissance Quarterly* 37 (1984): 555–84.

38. *Three Copernican Treatises*, 143. The iconology of the sun as Unmoved Mover guiding the other planets may have been suggested by the image of the king-as-sun that figured prominently in medieval and Renaissance royal iconology (Ernst Kantorowicz, *The King's Two Bodies* [Princeton: Princeton UP, 1957], 39, 101–2, 415). Cf. Augustine, *Enarrationes in Psalmos, I–L*, ed. Eligius Dekkers and John Fraipont (Turnholt: Brepols, 1956), 143; cf. Augustine, *Sermones de vetere Testamento, I–L*, ed. Cyrille Lambot (Turnholt: Brepols, 1961), 342.

39. I do not know where Rheticus got this interpretation of the meaning of Atlas's action. I find no analogy in the standard mythographies.

40. Copernicus, *Three Copernican Treatises*, 162–64.

41. *Three Copernican Treatises*, 146–47, 143–44.

42. *Three Copernican Treatises*, 163–64.

43. *Three Copernican Treatises*, 164.

44. Nicholas Copernicus, *De Revolutionibus Orbium Caelestium*, ed. Fritz Kubach (München: Oldenbourg, 1949), 2.4–5.

45. Cf. Thomas S. Kuhn, *The Copernican Revolution: Planetary Astronomy in the Development of Western Thought* (Cambridge: Harvard UP, 1957), 100–84; Pierre Duhem, *To Save the Phenomena: An Essay on the Idea of Physical Theory from Plato to Galileo*, trans. Edmund Doland and Chaninah Maschler (Chicago: U of Chicago P, 1969), 62–65.

46. The title, *De Revolutionibus*, is, according to Angus Armitage, derived from George Valla's 1501 translation of Proclus's *Hypotyposis*, which refers to Sosignes's treatise by that name; cf. Angus Armitage, *Copernicus: the Founder of Modern Astronomy* (New York: A. S. Barnes, 1957), 67.

47. Copernicus knows that he may contradict the findings of some untutored church fathers, such as Lactantius, but he says that his project began with encouragement from Bishop Paul of Fossombrone and, in its conception, has a bearing on the reformation of the ecclesiastical calendar, a work that reflects the precept in Plato's *Laws* that good astronomy allows the state properly to organize the year into festivals. Copernicus, *De Revolutionibus*, 2.6–9. Rosen says that Copernicus used the *Laws* in Ficino's translation; cf. Nicholas Copernicus, *On the Revolutions*, ed. Jerry Dobrycki, trans. and commentary by Edward Rosen (Baltimore: Johns Hopkins UP, 1978), 344; for Ficino's comment on Plato's *Laws*, see Plato, *Opera Omnia*, trans. with commentary by Ficino, sig. [Aa5^v].

48. Copernicus calls the heavens a "visibilem deum" that are "divina dispensatione dirigi" whose contemplation leads people "ad optima" (Copernicus, *De Revolutionibus*, 2.8); Ficino's translation of the *Timaeus* ends with the notion that the world (i.e., the heavens) are "visibile visibilia compraehendens animal, intelligibilis dei imago, sensibilis, maximus, interminatus, pulcherrimus, perfectissimus coelum unum hoc atque unigenitum" (Plato, *Opera Omnia*, trans. with commentary by Ficino, sig. [T3^r]). This appears to be sig. P3 (p.497), but it is actually sig. T3.

49. Cf. Copernicus, *De Revolutionibus*, 2.9. For the passage in the *Laws* on which Copernicus bases this, see Plato, *Opera Omnia*, trans. with commentary by Ficino, sig. Bb1^r–Bb2^r; for the praise of the sun as an image of God in a passage in Ficino's Plato proximate to that which Copernicus cites in this section, cf. Ficino's introduction to book 7 of the *Laws*; see Plato, *Opera Omnia*, trans. with commentary by Ficino, sig. [Aa3^v].

50. Copernicus, *De Revolutionibus*, 2.21.

51. Kuhn, *The Copernican Revolution*, 180.

52. Copernicus, *De Revolutionibus*, 2.4–6.

53. *Le Opere di Galileo Galilei*, ed. Antonio Favoro (Firenze: Barbèra, 1890), 1.34, 57, 72, 134, 167.

54. *Le Opere di Galileo*, 9.52.

55. Stillman Drake, *Galileo at Work: His Scientific Biography* (Chicago: U of Chicago P, 1978), 14.

56. Galileo Galilei, "Due Lezioni All'Accademia Fiorentina circa la Figura, Sito, e Grandezza dell'Inferno di Dante," *Le Opere di Galileo*, 9.31–57.

57. Stillman Drake, "The Evolution of the *De Motu*," *Isis* 67 (1976): 239–50.

58. Arthur Koestler, *The Watershed* (Garden City NY: Doubleday, 1960), 183–84.

59. For Galileo's conception of God, see *Le Opere di Galileo*, 1.24–26, 29–31; 3.398; 4.52; 7.129–30.

60. *Le Opere di Galileo*, 5.307–48. Cf. Stillman Drake, *Galileo* (New York: Hill & Wang, 1980), 53–72; Eileen Reeves, "Augustine and Galileo on Reading the Heavens," *JHI* 52 (1991): 563. Castelli, who had been Galileo's student, in turn, reported favorably on Galileo's work to the Grand Duchess.

61. *Le Opere di Galileo*, 5.316, 319.

62. *Le Opere di Galileo*, 5.316.

63. *Le Opere di Galileo*, 5.316–23.

64. *Le Opere di Galileo*, 5.317–19.

65. Chadwick asserts that "Porphyry's commentary on the Timaeus of Plato helped Augustine" with the problem of reconciling Genesis notions of creation from nothing and Platonic notions of creation using an original matter. See Henry Chadwick, *Augustine* (New York: Oxford UP, 1986), 88.

66. Augustine, "De Genesi ad Litteram," in *PL* 34, cols.269–70.

67. Dominic J. O'Meara, "The Neoplatonism of St. Augustine," in *Neoplatonism and Christian Thought*, ed. Dominic J. O'Meara (Albany: State U of New York P, 1982), 39–40. Cf. Henry Chadwick, *Augustine* (New York: Oxford UP, 1986), 87–90; Etienne Gilson, *The Christian Philosophy of St. Augustine* (New York: Random House, 1960), 210–16.

68. Augustine, "De Genesi ad Litteram," in *PL* 34: cols.248–50, 256, 299–301.

69. Augustine, "De Genesi ad Litteram," *PL* 34, col.262.

70. *Le Opere di Galileo*, 5.320.

71. Augustine, "Epistola CXLIII," *PL* 33: col.588.

72. Reeves, "Augustine and Galileo on Reading the Heavens," 572.

73. Chadwick, *Augustine*, 88.

74. *Le Opere di Galileo*, 5.316–19.

75. *Le Opere di Galileo*, 5.324. For a discussion of the context of the letter to the Grand Duchess Christina, see Richard J. Blackwell, *Galileo, Bellarmine, and the Bible* (Notre Dame: U of Notre Dame Press, 1991), 53–86.

76. *Le Opere di Galileo*, 5.325.

77. *Le Opere di Galileo*, 5.325–26.

78. *Le Opere di Galileo*, 5.325–26.

79. *Le Opere di Galileo*, 5.325–26. Galileo's letter to the Grand Duchess accu-

rately reflects the *De Genesi ad Litteram* and derives from it an exegetical theory that asserts that interpretations of the Bible that contradict good science cannot carry authority (*De Genesi ad Litteram*, 1.18–19, 1.21, 2.9–10, 2.18, in Augustine, "De Genesi ad Litteram," PL 34: cols.260, 262, 270–72, 280; *Le Opere di Galileo*, 5.310, 318, 327, 331, 339–41). For Augustine's general exegetical principles, see *On Christian Doctrine*, trans. D. W. Robertson Jr. (New York: Liberal Arts Press, 1958), xi and following. Galileo speaks of the scriptures as promoting the service of God and the salvation of souls (*Le Opere di Galileo*, 5.316). He follows Augustine when he argues that the plain literal sense of the scripture would attribute to God anthropomorphic qualities, ideas that require exegesis to be fully understood (Augustine, *On Christian Doctrine*, 11–12, 100–107).

80. *Le Opere di Galileo*, 5.336.

81. *Le Opere di Galileo*, 5.344.

82. *Le Opere di Galileo*, 5.346; Galileo appears to be paraphrasing *De Divinis Nominibus*, 4.5 from Ficino's edition; Dionysius the Areopagite, *Opera* (Strassburg, 1503 [Frankfurt: Unveränderter Nachdruck, 1970]), sig. E4^r–[E4^v].

83. *Le Opere di Galileo*, 5.348.

84. I have supplied heavens in the translation.

85. *Le Opere di Galileo*, 5.348.

86. The early Galileo disliked what he saw as the forced "anamorphosed" perspective of Tasso's allegories inserted in a historical narrative and rather preferred Ariosto's explicitly fantastic mode. Cf. Fernand Hallyn, "Anamorphose et Allégorie," *Revue de Littérature Comparée* 56 (1982): 319–30; Erwin Panofsky, *Galileo As A Critic of the Arts* (The Hague: Nijhoff, 1954), 13, 17–18; Dante della Terza, "Galileo, Man of Letters," *Galileo Reappraised*, ed. Carlo L. Golino (Berkeley: U of California P, 1966), 1–22. Galileo does not argue that epics should not be allegorized, but that the allegorical sections of the plot should not appear forced in relation to the remainder. Cf. his "Considerazioni al Tasso," *Le Opere di Galileo*, 9.129.

87. *Le Opere di Galileo*, 6.232. Galileo apparently does not know or believe in the allegorical interpretations of the *Iliad* and the *Orlando Furioso*, or, if he does, he may believe that the allegory posited for them is untrue.

88. *Le Opere di Galileo*, 7.28.

89. *Le Opere di Galileo*, 7.129–30.

90. Max Caspar, *Kepler*, trans. C. Doris Hellman (New York: Abelard-Schuman, 1959), 130–34, 285–86. In contrast to the supposedly rationalistic Galileo, Kepler is often treated as a strange mystical bird, but the foundations on which he builds are the same: Wisdom Theology and Platonic metaphysics, the assumption of harmony, and the fusion of physics and astronomy. For Kepler's efforts to unify physics and astronomy, see Gerald Holton, "Johannes Kepler's Universe: Its Physics and Metaphysics," *AJP* 24 (1956): 340–51.

91. Pannekoek explains the discovery as follows: "[i]f a sphere is constructed upon each of the six planetary circles, we may put between each pair of successive spheres, supposed to be exactly concentric, one of the regular solids (i.e. the five regular polyhedrons or 'Platonic figures') in such a way that its edges are situated on the exterior sphere and its planes are tangent to the exterior sphere" (explanation in parentheses mine). The five figures going from the sun outward are the eight-sided, twenty-sided, twelve-sided, four-sided, and six-sided. A. Pannekoek, *A History of Astronomy* (London: George Allen, 1961), 225. In his *Dissertatio cum nuncio Sidereo,* Kepler again develops his idea of the creation's existence in the image of God, postulating that the sun is the middle place in the fixed stars, that the earth is the middle of the planets, and that the minds of human beings as geometers reflect the image of God the geometer (Johannes Kepler, *Opera Omnia,* 2.504).

92. Caspar, *Kepler,* 63–64.

93. Johannes Kepler, *Mysterium Cosmographicum: The Secret of the Universe,* trans. A. M. Duncan (New York: Abaris, 1981), 38. The lyre was sometimes thought to be based on the heptachord in ancient Greek musical theory, a seven-note combination of two conjunct tetrachords, four-note scale fragments that share a common note – for example, in descending order AGFE-EDCB. Giorgio Valla's *De Musica* speaks of the Byzantine writer, Bryennius, and his mention of "Mercury's invention of the seven-stringed lyre" where the strings of the tetrachord imitate the four elements of fire, air, earth, and water, but where the seven strings of the heptachord also imitate the seven planets. Kepler probably is applying some such notion to the logic of divine Wisdom's music of the spheres. For further information, see Claude V. Palisca, *Humanism in Italian Renaissance Musical Thought* (New Haven: Yale UP, 1985), 63, 71. I owe this information to Professor Raymond Haggh of the University of Nebraska, who is doing an extensive study of Kepler as musical theorist.

94. Kepler, *Mysterium Cosmographicum,* 52–55.

95. Kepler, *Mysterium Cosmographicum,* 62, 92–94; cf. W. Petri, "Die betrachtende Kreator im trinitarischen Kosmos," *Kepler-Festschrift: 1971,* ed. Ekkehard Preuss (Regensburg: Naturwissenschaftlicher Verein Regensburg [Mittlebayerische Druckerei und Verlags Gesellschaft], 1971), 64–98.

96. Nicholas compares God the Father to the center of a circle, the Son to the radius, and the Holy Spirit to the circumference on the grounds that the Father is the center, the Son issues from the center, and the circumference synthesizes the center and radius. Edward J. Butterworth, "Form and Significance of the Sphere in Nicholas of Cusa's *De lido globi,*" in *Nicholas of Cusa in Search of God and Wisdom,* ed. Gerald Christianson and Thomas M. Izbacki (Leiden: E. J. Brill, 1991), 89–100. Nicolas of Cusa, *Opera* (Paris, 1514), 2: fol.95ᵛ; cf. Nicholas of Cusa, *Oeuvres*

Choisies (Paris: Aubier, 1942), 432–33. Kepler revises Nicholas's symbolism by making the Father equate with the center, the Son with the interior of the spherical surface, the equivalent of the circumference, and the Holy Ghost with the connecting space between the center and the spherical surfaces. The sun represents the Father, the sphere of the Fixed Stars stands for the Son, and the space between signifies the Holy Ghost (Kepler, *Mysterium Cosmographicum*, 92–94). Kepler mentions the *Timaeus* in this passage, and William of Conches makes Boethius 3.m.9 symbolize similar things.

97. Kepler, *Opera Omnia*, 2.131ff.

98. Kepler, *Opera Omnia*, 2.131ff.

99. Kepler, *Opera Omnia*, 2.131.

100. Kepler, *Opera Omnia*, 2.131.

101. Kepler, *Opera Omnia*, 2.128–29.

102. Kepler, *Mysterium Cosmographicum*, 92–96.

103. Kepler, *Mysterium Cosmographicum*, 122–24.

104. For an able exploration of Kepler's continued use of ideas from the *Mysterium*, see Gerald Holton, "Johannes Kepler's Universe: Its Physics and Metaphysics," *AJP* 24 (1956), 340–51, esp. 348–50.

105. Kepler, *Opera Omnia*, 2.123, 2.127ff.

106. Johannes Kepler, *Astronomia Nova*, ed. Max Caspar (München: Beck, 1937), 7–10.

107. Bruce Stephenson, *Kepler's Physical Astronomy* (New York: Springer-Verlag, 1987), 31–32, 118–21. Stephenson's *Music of the Heavens* came out too late for me to use it.

108. Stephenson, *Kepler's Physical Astronomy*, 204.

109. Johannes Kepler, *Harmonice Mundi* (Linz, 1619), sig. Aa3^r.

110. Cf. Stephenson, *Kepler's Physical Astronomy*, 203–5.

111. Kepler, *Harmonice Mundi*, sig. [Z1^v]–Z2^r.

112. For an easily understandable discussion, see Arthur Koestler, *The Watershed*, 214ff.

113. Caspar, *Kepler*, 275.

114. For a detailed explanation of this theory, see Caspar, *Kepler*, 283ff. Cf. Kepler, *Harmonice Mundi*, sig. [Cc4r], sig. Dd1r.

115. Cf. Kepler's theory of hypotheses, see his "Apologia pro Tychone contra Ursum," in N. Jardine, *The Birth of the History and Philosophy of Science* (Cambridge: Cambridge UP, 1984), 87–101.

116. Kepler, *Harmonice Mundi*, sig. P1^r–P3^r. Kepler may get the concept of the autodidact in epistemology from Plato's *Laches*, to which he contrasts Aristotle's *Metaphysics*, Book M, 1083^{a}20–1086^{a}21, M1077^{ff}. For the study of mathematics as leading to theology and God and the elevation of human ethical practice, see Kepler, *Harmonice Mundi*, sig. [A1^r].

117. Kepler, *Harmonice Mundi*, sig. O2^r–Q2^r; sig. [A4^v]–B1^r.

118. Kepler, *Harmonice Mundi*, sig. [P4^r].

119. Kepler, *Harmonice Mundi*, sig. [P4^v].

120. Kepler, *Harmonice Mundi*, sig. [P4^v]–Q2^r.

121. Kepler, *Harmonice Mundi*, sig. A1^r.

122. "O qui limine Naturæ desiderium in nobis promoves luminis Gratiæ, ut per id transferas nos in lumen Gloriæ; gratias ago tibi Creator Domine, quia delectasti me in facturâ tuâ, & in operibus manuum tuarum exultavi: Et nunc opus comsummavi professionis maeæ, tantis usus ingenii viribus, quantas mihi dedisti; manifestavi gloriam operum tuorum hominibus, istas demonstationes lecturis, quantum de illius infinitate capere potuerunt angustiæ Mentis meæ; promptus mihi fuit animus ad emendarissimè philosophandum: si quid indignum tuis consiliis prolatum à me, vermiculo, in volutabro peccatorum nato & innutrito, quod scire velis homines: id quoque inspires, ut emendem: si tuorum operum admirabili pulchritudine in temeritatem prolectus sum, aut si gloriam propriam apud homines amavi, dum progredior in opere tua gloriæ destinato; mitis & misericors condona: denique ut demonstationes istæ tuæ gloriæ & Animarum saluti çedant, nec ei ullatenus obfint, propitius efficere digneris." Kepler, *Harmonice Mundi*, sig. Hh2^r.

123. Kepler, *Harmonice Mundi*, sig. [Hh2^v]–[Hh4^v]. The *Epitome Astronomiae Copernicanae*, a kind of Copernican catechism, qualifies this great concluding statement by admitting its speculative character.

124. "Magnus Dominus noster, & magna virtus eius & Sapientiæ ejus non est numerus: laudate eum coeli, laudate eum Sol, Luna & Planetae, quocunque sensu ad percipiendum, quacunque lingua ad eloquendum Creatorem vestrum utamini: Laudate eum Harmoniae coelestes, laudate eum vos Harmoniarum detectarum arbitri: lauda & tu anima mea Dominum Creatorem tuum, quamdiu fuero: namque ex ipso & per ipsum & in ipso sunt omnia, καὶ τὰ αἰσθτὰ, καὶ τὰ νοερὰ; tam ea quae ignoramus penitus, quam ea quae scimus, minima illorum pars; quia adhuc plus ultra est. Ipsi laus, honor, & gloria in saecula saeculorum." Kepler, *Harmonice Mundi*, sig. [Hh4^v].

125. Cf. Pierre Duhem, *To Save the Phenomena: An Essay on the Idea of Physical Theory from Plato to Galileo*, trans. Edmund Doland and Chaninah Maschler (Chicago: U of Chicago P, 1969), 61–117.

126. For a summary of Lynn White's argument, see the introduction to this book.

127. I will discuss Bacon's reconfiguration of the concept of Wisdom in a later book. Thomas DaCosta Kaufmann's association of Kepler's private noetic investigations with Bacon's proposals for the creation of large collaborative scientific institutions manipulating nature for human benefit is surely misleading. See Kaufmann, *The Master of Nature* (Princeton: Princeton UP, 1993), 184–94.

128. Francis Bacon, *New Atlantis* (Cambridge: Cambridge UP, 1938), 35.

129. Bacon, *New Atlantis*, 35–45.

130. Richard Foster Jones, *The Seventeenth Century: Studies in the History of English Thought and Literature from Bacon to Pope* (Stanford: Stanford UP, 1951). Michel Foucault's notion that classical science begins with Descartes and eschews analogy is clearly incorrect; although analogy may mislead, it may also lead, as is clear in Kepler's pursuit of the *Timaean* model, the musical analogy, and the Wisdom picture of things; cf. Michel Foucault, *The Order of Things*, trans. A. Sheridan (New York: Random House, 1970), 18–48.

CONCLUSION

1. Bloom, *Closing of the American Mind*, 310.

2. Spanos, *End of Education*, 15–19.

3. Spanos, *End of Education*, 12.

4. Spanos, *End of Education*, 17–18.

5. For Thomas Kuhn's discussion of this issue, see the second edition of *The Structure of Scientific Revolutions* (Chicago: U of Chicago P, 1970), 174–210, esp. 191–98; cf. Gerald Graff, *Beyond the Culture Wars* (New York: W. W. Norton, 1992), 110–11.

6. Wendell Berry, *What Are People For* (San Francisco: North Point Press, 1990), 98–99.

7. Lynn White, *Medieval Technology and Social Change* (Oxford: Clarendon Press, 1962), 39–78; cf. David Herlihy, "Attitudes toward the Environment in Medieval Society," in *Historical Ecology*, ed. Lester J. Bilsky (London: Kennikat Press, 1980), 100–116 and bibliography, 174–77.

8. Garrett Hardin and John Baden, *Managing the Commons* (San Francisco: W. H. Freeman, 1977). For a response to this position relating primarily to non-Western peoples, see Bonnie M. McCay and James M. Acheson, eds., *The Question of the Commons* (Tucson: U of Arizona P, 1987). For a discussion of the extension of Hardin's position to medieval cultures, see Paul A. Olson, Introduction, *The Struggle for the Land* (Lincoln: U of Nebraska P, 1990), 1–38.

9. See Paul A. Olson, "*The Parlement of Foules*: Aristotle's *Politics* and the Foundations of Human Society," 53–69 (and for bibliography concerning natural law theory holding human society accountable to the natural order). Medieval natural law theory has little to do with modern legal controversy connected to contemporary natural law theory.

10. The criticisms of manipulative science that appear in Swift and Pope, especially those in book 3 of *Gulliver's Travels*, derive from the epic commentaries that play such a role in the Wisdom tradition (as I will show in a forthcoming volume).

11. For a good discussion of this issue, see John W. Bennett, *The Ecological*

Transition: Cultural Anthropology and Human Adaptation (Elmsford NY: Pergamon Press, 1976); cf. Raymond Hames, "Game Conservation or Efficient Hunting," in *The Question of the Commons;* Baird Callicott, "American Indian Land Wisdom," in *The Struggle for the Land.*

12. *Philosophical Works of Francis Bacon,* ed. John M. Robertson (New York: Libraries Press, 1970), 61, 303, 650, 840, 828–32. For Bacon, matter reflects God's divine power, and the invisible motions of matter, its beauty of form, reflect His Wisdom.

13. Bacon, *Philosophical Works,* 727. Bacon's *New Atlantis* scientists make numerous radical changes in weather, wind, and the like, and no harm derives from their activities (cf. 722–32). Cf. Jones, *The Seventeenth Century,* 10–40.

14. I am currently editing the letters of George Combe, William Ellis, and other writers related to the Utilitarian effort to create, first, the monitorial private schools for working class industrial groups and, then, the compulsory private schools related to the scientific-industrial project. For an example of significant work in this tradition that contrasts sharply with the Wisdom vision, see Jeremy Bentham, *Chrestomathia,* ed. M. J. Smith and W. H. Burston (Oxford: Clarendon Press, 1983).

15. Cf., for example, Paul A. Olson, "*Black Elk Speaks* as Epic and Ritual Attempt to Reverse History," in *Vision and Refuge in Great Plains Studies,* ed. Virginia Faulkner (Lincoln: U of Nebraska P, 1982), 3–27; J. Baird Callicott, "American Indian Land Wisdom," in *The Struggle for the Land,* 255–72.

16. Ariès, *Centuries of Childhood,* 148.

17. Jeremy Bentham, *Chrestomathia,* ed. M. J. Smith and W. H. Burston (Oxford: Clarendon Press, 1983).

18. Cf. Finn, *We Must Take Charge,* 239–49, 277–86.

19. Finn, *We Must Take Charge,* 18–19, 303–6. Interest in the canon has been central in the educational writings of William Bennett, Allan Bloom, and Dinesh D'Souza. E. D. Hirsch's concern for cultural literacy is somewhat similar.

20. Paul A. Olson, *Concepts of Career and General Education* (Washington DC: AAHE, 1977); Paul A. Olson, "The Liberal Arts and Career Education," *Monographs on Career Education* 1 (1975): 1–24. I no longer accept many of the conclusions of these pieces.

21. Petrarch, sometimes credited with some of the origins of humanistic schooling, generally emphasizes in his own writings a personal and private search outside of the schools. Bowen, *A History of Western Education,* 2.206–31; W. H. Woodward, *Vittorino da Feltre and Other Humanist Educators* (Cambridge: Cambridge UP, 1905).

22. Graff, *Beyond the Culture Wars,* 22.

23. Dinesh D'Souza, *Illiberal Education: The Politics of Race and Sex on Campus* (New York: Random House, 1992), 60–61.

24. Ariès, *Centuries of Childhood,* 146.

25. D'Souza, *Illiberal Education,* 61–63.

26. D'Souza, *Illiberal Education,* 63.

27. I. A. Richards, *Speculative Instruments* (Chicago: U of Chicago P, 1955), 107.

28. Kuhn makes clear that his position is not a conventional subjectivist or social constructivist position in his second edition; Thomas S. Kuhn, *The Structure of Scientific Revolutions* (Chicago: U of Chicago P, 1970), 174–210; cf. Graff, *Beyond the Culture Wars,* 110–11.

29. Michel Foucault, *Power/Knowledge* (New York: Pantheon Books, 1980), 131.

30. Stephen Toulmin, *On Human Understanding* (Princeton: Princeton UP, 1972).

31. Wittgenstein, *Philosophical Investigations,* I:23. Cf. John W. Cook, "Solipsism and Language," in *Ludwig Wittgenstein: Philosophy and Language* (London: Allen & Unwin, 1972), 37–72.

32. Jacques Derrida, "Living On – Border Lines," *Deconstruction and Criticism,* ed. Harold Bloom et al. (New York: Seabury Press, 1979), 81.

33. Nealon, *Double Reading,* 57.

Index